Christian History

An Enthralling Guide to the Story of Christianity, From Its Early Origins Through the Crusades and Knights Templar to Modern Times

Free limited time bonus

Stop for a moment. We have a free bonus set up for you. The problem is this: we forget 90% of everything that we read after 7 days. Crazy fact, right? Here's the solution: we've created a printable, 1-page pdf summary for this book that you're reading now. All you have to do to get your free pdf summary is to go to the following website:

https://livetolearn.lpages.co/enthrallinghistory/

Once you do, it will be intuitive. Enjoy, and thank you!

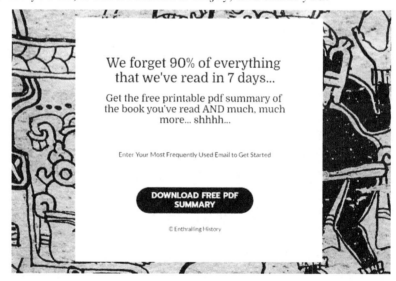

Table of Contents

Part 1: History of Christianity

An Enthralling Overview of the Most Important Events that Shaped the Christian Church

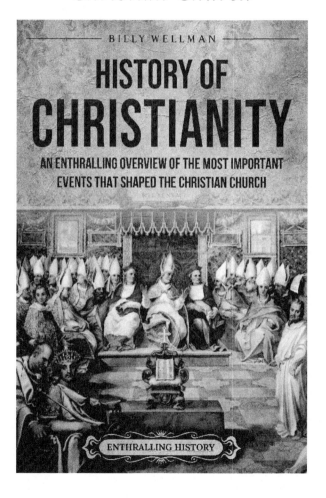

Introduction: The Universal Appeal of the Christian Faith

A lot can be said about Christianity. Even if you are not a believer, Christianity is such a common feature of human culture in general that it is virtually inescapable. The fact that Christmas is the most popular holiday in the world is perhaps the most obvious testament to this fact.

Japan's percentage of practicing Christians is estimated to be less than 2 percent. However, the celebration of Christmas has been growing there for the past few decades. The holiday is just as eagerly celebrated in Japan as it would be in more traditionally Christian nations, such as the United Kingdom or the United States. It is pretty safe to say that no other religion can claim such universal global dominance in its influence.

This book documents the history of Christianity's historic rise, as well as how the religion has continued to influence humanity throughout the centuries. This book is not an attempt to make anyone a believer in the Christian faith; rather, it is an attempt to demonstrate the irrefutable impact that Christianity has had on the world.

Explore the days of Christ, the Council of Nicaea, the Reformation, and beyond. We will examine all of the incredible twists and turns of a faith born in the obscure desert town of Bethlehem and how it influenced world history.

Section One: The Origins of Christianity (1 CE–1100 CE)

Chapter 1: One Man and a Crucifix

As one might assume, Christianity ultimately began with Jesus Christ. There are perhaps some forerunners who could be mentioned, such as John the Baptist. John's ministry was similar to Jesus' ministry in that he called for a change in the spiritual order. John has also been linked to a community of spiritual enthusiasts eager for the end of the age. The group was known as the Essenes, and they endlessly prophesied about the coming of the "sons of light." The New Testament largely depicts John the Baptist as the one who passed the torch to Jesus, who ultimately was seen as the true Messiah.

In order to get to the roots of Christianity, we have to start with Jesus Christ himself. Since Christianity is such a well-known religion, most are familiar with the story. Jesus is said to have been the product of an immaculate conception and was birthed in a stable in Bethlehem. Historians are hesitant to believe much of the biblical narrative. There are even those who are skeptical that Jesus ever existed in the first place.

But since there are many sources outside of Christianity that talk about the existence of Christ, such an argument is pretty hard to make. Jesus is mentioned, at least in passing, by Roman historians. These Roman historians had no interest in becoming Christians and presented themselves as impartial observers. Although these few references are fleeting and lacking in great detail, they are important since they clearly demonstrate that Christ was known beyond the immediate Christian fold.

However, as it pertains to Christ's life, the only detailed work that remains is the Gospels. And when it comes to the Gospels, many consider the Gospel of Mark to be both the oldest (meaning it was written closest to the time of Christ's ministry on Earth) and the most accurate. There is some mention of a so-called hypothetical "Q" source, a missing piece of contemporary text that the writers of the Gospels used, but it has never been found.

The Gospel of Mark is probably the most accurate depiction of Jesus that the world currently has, as the other canonical Gospels were largely built off of Mark. It must be noted that the Gospel of Mark does not have much of the backstory of Christ, which is provided by the other Gospels. Instead, Mark focuses primarily on Christ's ministry, his death on the cross, and his resurrection.

So, to get a better idea of Jesus' birth in the manager or the traditional Christmas story, which features wise men, a stable in Bethlehem, and a newborn king, we need to turn to the other Gospels. Critics, of course, will try to suggest that the reason the events of the Christmas story were not included in the Gospel of Mark was that they did not happen.

However, such critics would have to contend with the fact that a prominent historian and contemporary of Jesus, a Jewish-Roman chronicler by the name of Josephus, compiled two whole scrolls on the life of Herod the Great. And within these scrolls, he listed an endless stream of atrocities committed by this most dastardly of dictators. Herod was indeed great, as he rebuilt the Jewish Temple and engaged in other massive building projects across the land, but according to Josephus, he had a dark side.

Although Josephus does not mention the slaughter of the innocents, he paints a picture of a man who would not hesitate to do such a thing. Josephus even chronicles an incident in which Herod, in one of his notorious outbursts, allegedly tried to lure a large group of prominent citizens from Israel into a stadium so he could slaughter them all. Even Roman Emperor Augustus (who was Herod's boss) spoke of Herod's callous disregard for life.

In consideration of how many of Herod's own children he had killed and due to various suspicions of other atrocities, Emperor Augustus is said to have stated that he would "rather be Herod's pig than his son." In Greek, the words were more humorous since they rhymed, with Augustus saying that he would rather be Herod's *choiros* than his *huios*.

At any rate, according to the traditional Christmas narrative, after the three wise men from the East informed Herod of the portents of the star over Bethlehem, King Herod went berserk. He just could not countenance anyone being born that might outshine him, so he ruthlessly ordered all male children under two years of age to be killed. According to this account, he was so deranged that he would actually kill a bunch of innocent kids (hence the slaughter of the innocents) just to get at the newborn Christ.

This story is an incredible one, and skeptics understandably have a hard time believing such a brutal act occurred. But if we look at the examples presented by the non-Christian historian Josephus, it seems likely that King Herod was indeed capable of such a thing. So, it is clear that this one event mentioned in the Christmas story could have happened. Of course, the jury is still out as to whether or not it happened. There are many unanswered questions, such as whether Herod was even alive when Jesus was born or if this was a story that parallels Herod's murder of his own sons.

Regardless, it is in the realm of possibility that it could have, which makes it easier to consider that if one aspect might be true, who is to say that the rest of it is not? With that in mind, let us delve into the traditional Christmas narrative as presented by the Gospels. And let us start with that account of the atrocity committed by King Herod. If King Herod did indeed do such a terrible thing, this action, while certainly abominable, he would have had a fairly clear-cut reason to do so, at least in his mind.

King Herod was a Roman puppet whose power could have been squashed at any time at Rome's whim. He was only allowed to rule over his people because the Roman emperor allowed him to do so. As the Romans conquered much of the ancient world, they were clever enough to realize that it would be difficult for them to continuously rule over the vast tracts of land they had seized without local allies on the ground. As such, they began a pattern of installing friendly client kings to rule over far-flung territories. And at the time of the birth of Christ, this was very much the case with the region we know as Israel/Palestine.

Rome had given King Herod authority, but at the end of the day, he was seen as Rome's crony. In the eyes of Rome, his number one job was to keep the status quo. The Romans, who were experiencing the Pax Romana or "Roman Peace," liked to keep their dominion as orderly as possible. King Herod was tasked with making sure that his corner of the empire remained peaceful and that no revolts, uprisings, or any other form of obnoxious turmoil came to the attention of his Roman taskmasters.

If Herod failed in this duty, he could be easily dismissed (and possibly killed) by his Roman benefactors. It was, therefore, in Herod's best interest to nip any potential challenge to his (and ultimately Rome's) rule in the bud. And according to the traditional Christmas story, this was what the wily and ruthless Herod was attempting to do during the "slaughter of the innocents." The wise men prophesied to him that a king had been born in Bethlehem. Herod professed interest in seeing this king, but in reality, Herod wanted to kill the newborn king.

The wise men *wised up* to this fact. They realized Herod's true intentions (although the Gospels say an angel warned them) and managed to slip away from Herod without giving him any further information about where Jesus would be born. Infuriated, Herod decided to kill all the kids in Bethlehem who just so happened to be under the age of two in the hopes he would ensnare the newborn Jesus Christ. However, Jesus' earthly father, Joseph, was warned in a dream to gather his family and flee to Egypt.

As the Bible explains, "An angel of the Lord appeared to Joseph in a dream, and said to him, 'Rise up, take the child and his mother and escape with them to Egypt, and stay there until I tell you; for Herod is going to search for the child to do away with him'" (Matthew 2:13-15). As such, they managed to just barely escape the trap that was being set for them.

According to the Gospels, countless other families were not so lucky, and the wails of devastated mothers could be heard all over Israel. Jesus' family made their way to Egypt, where they found refuge for some time. According to the Gospels, they only returned when an angel again visited them and informed them that King Herod had perished.

The death of King Herod is yet another feature of the Christmas story that was mentioned by the historian Josephus. The Gospels tell us that he stepped out in shining garments to speak to a crowd, only to be struck down dead. The Gospels' reasoning behind his death is a bit vague. The Jewish historian Josephus goes into further detail. Herod apparently had been suffering from a wide variety of terrible illnesses and was even plagued with open, infected sores that one might expect from someone suffering from leprosy.

The issue with Herod's death is when he died. Some historians dismiss the stories of Herod the Great in the Bible because they believe he died in 4 BCE, which is before the traditionally accepted date of Jesus' birth. However, biblical scholars do believe that Herod was alive when Jesus was born and think that Jesus might have been born earlier than 1 BCE. Today, it is believed that Jesus was born anywhere between 6 and 4 BCE.

At any rate, after Christ's return to Israel proper, we are not given any other details about Christ's upbringing, save for a mention of a precocious Jesus teaching in the temple. The narrative jumps forward to the start of his earthly ministry. Jesus is believed to have been in his early thirties at the start of his ministry. He lived during a period of great tension between the people of Israel and the Roman authorities.

The Jewish leaders were trying their best to keep the status quo and prevent the wrath of Rome from coming down on them, but the situation was becoming increasingly precarious. The average citizen was crying out in agony under the yoke of Roman oppression and the perceived powerlessness of their own local leaders. There were indeed many looking for what they called the "Messiah," the one who would make all things right once again.

Rather than seeing the Messiah as a harbinger of a new faith, for most Jews, the Messiah was someone who would finally topple Roman authority and bring about a new kingdom of Jerusalem. Jesus himself often spoke of the "coming kingdom." He talked about the "Kingdom of Heaven" being at hand. The Lord's Prayer even invokes the imagery of a kingdom when it states, "Thy Kingdom come, Thy will be done, On Earth as it is in Heaven."

But Christ's conception of the coming kingdom differed from what most of his contemporaries envisioned. Christ was speaking of a "heavenly kingdom" coming down to Earth. He is speaking of heaven as a perfect place of love, justice, and peace and praying that this heavenly kingdom will be brought down to Earth so that Earth will be like heaven.

Jesus' view is much more idealistic than what most of his contemporaries' views would have been. Nevertheless, just as was the case when Jesus was born, with wise men hailing him as the newborn king, the notion that Jesus was speaking of a coming kingdom was used by his opponents to suggest that he was attempting to go against the status quo. They accused him of wanting to topple the current earthly kingdom and install himself as king.

After Jesus got on the bad side of local religious leaders who did not like his preaching, they used these accusations to have him killed. The religious establishment of the time did not take a liking to Jesus for many reasons. To the more pragmatic-minded who wished to maintain the status quo, Jesus was perceived as a great disrupter. His claims of being the Messiah and his statements about the kingdom of heaven being at hand were too disruptive for those who wanted everything to continue as normal.

Although people today tend to view Jesus as a man who inspired others, many back then disliked the attention that Jesus was bringing to the region due to his preaching and miracle. Their window of opportunity to shut down this movement arrived when one of Jesus' disciples betrayed him.

Christ's betrayer, Judas Iscariot, is a complicated figure. Judas did not betray Jesus because he was worried about him disrupting the old order. According to some scholars, Judas was becoming increasingly frustrated with Jesus because he wanted Jesus to take more action and be more disruptive. Judas misunderstood Christ's message and was hoping that he would use his power and influence to overthrow the Roman occupation of the Levant. Since Judas had witnessed Christ's miracles, one could also speculate that Judas believed that Jesus had supernatural powers and would use them to strike any Roman dead who approached.

And considering Judas' actions, it does not seem that his goal was to have Jesus crucified. It seems that he was actually trying to provoke a response from Christ. Judas wanted to be the catalyst that pushed Christ to action (or at least the action that Judas desired from him). It was only when Jesus did not strike down his opponents with fire from heaven, instead allowing himself to be taken prisoner and sent to the cross, that Judas despaired over his actions.

It did not turn out as he had planned. An entirely distraught Judas begged for the religious authorities to release Jesus. As scripture tells us, the religious authorities refused, prompting Judas to throw the thirty pieces of silver they gave him for committing the betrayal at their feet. Judas then went outside and hung himself, unable to live with the knowledge of what he had done.

Jesus was billed as an incorrigible rabble-rouser and disrupter. The religious authorities knew that anyone who was deemed subversive to

Rome could be executed. As such, they took Jesus to Pontius Pilate, the governor of the Roman province of Judaea, and charged that he was a revolutionary attempting to take down the Roman Empire. However, it seems Pilate took one look at Jesus and pegged him as more of a philosopher than a political revolutionary. He viewed Christ as a mystic and a dreamer and wished to "wash his hands" of the whole matter.

However, the biblical narrative tells us that no matter what Pilate tried to do to get Jesus released, the local leaders clamored even more vigorously that he be put to death. Finally, they threatened to go above the governor's head. Pilate could not stomach this, so he finally caved into their demands and had Jesus crucified. There are many sources that diverge at this point, but most historians believe that Jesus Christ was crucified.

The greatest divergence of all is over what happened next. For a critic, it is the most important point of contention, and for a Christian, it is the hallmark of their faith. It is said that three days after Jesus was crucified on the cross, he was physically resurrected and rose from the dead. All of the Gospels bear this out, although there are some fairly substantial differences as it pertains to certain details of how it all went down.

For example, the Gospels do not agree on who went to the tomb to discover Christ had been resurrected. Most of the accounts speak of one or two angels greeting them in the tomb and informing them of the risen Christ. Another account insists that Mary Magdalene was in the tomb weeping because she found it empty and believed the body had been taken. She then observed a man whom she thought was the gardener and asked him where the body of Jesus was. The man revealed that he was none other than Jesus Christ.

In one of the most touching scenes from the Bible, Jesus calls Mary by name, and she recognizes him. She cries out of pure joy. But according to the scripture, when she tries to hug Jesus, he warns her not to do so because he has not yet "ascended to the Father."

As the full scripture of John 20:15-17 reads, "He asked her, 'Woman, why are you crying? Who is it you are looking for?' Thinking he was the gardener, she said, "Sir, if you have carried him away, tell me where you have put him, and I will get him.' Jesus said to her, 'Mary.' She turned toward him and cried out in Aramaic, 'Rabboni!' [which means Teacher]. Jesus said, 'Do not hold on to me, for I have not yet ascended to the Father. Go instead to my brothers and tell them, "I am ascending to my

Father and your Father, to my God and your God.""

This statement is important for Christians because the traditional Christian belief is that everyone will be physically resurrected in the end, just like Christ. Believers will also be transformed into "glorified bodies." It is difficult to quantify when this glorification process happened with Christ because shortly after the empty tomb was found, all of the Gospels contend that he appeared on multiple occasions over the next forty days.

On these occasions, Jesus sat down, talked, and even ate with the disciples. And in another dramatic sequence, when his former disciple Thomas expressed doubt, saying that he would only believe if he could put his hands in the holes in Christ's wrist, Jesus appeared directly to him and allowed him to do just that. So, even though Christ warned Mary in the tomb not to touch him because he hadn't been glorified yet, by the time he ran into Thomas, the process was apparently complete since he allowed Thomas to touch his wounds.

According to scripture, after the forty-day period was up, Jesus literally ascended into heaven. During the event known as the "Ascension," the Bible speaks of Christ giving one last sermon to a large crowd before he began floating up into the air. Those down on the ground are said to have strained their eyes to watch the resurrected Christ ascend until their eyes could no longer perceive him.

While they were straining to get one last glimpse of Christ as he ascended higher and higher, they were greeted by a couple of angels on the ground who told them not to worry and that Christ would return one day. Today, many Christians take a more symbolic view of the scripture, especially the more supernatural elements like his ascension and his many miracles. However, we must remember that for the early Christians—and until fairly recently and even today—the faithful read these portrayals as literal accounts.

In other words, it was not perceived as an allegory at all. The Bible said Christ was crucified, he was physically resurrected, and he floated up into the air until he was out of sight. And this is what Christians believed. For them, there was no symbolism. There was Jesus, there was the cross, there was a physical resurrection, and then a risen Christ—end of story.

Chapter 2: The Bible: Meet the Authors

There are some Christian faithful who might take umbrage at even mentioning the "authors" of the Bible. It might seem sacrilegious to them to attempt to dissect and name those who wrote certain verses since they consider it all to be "divinely inspired" or, as it is often said, the literal "Word of God." But those who know the Bible have to admit that it was indeed written by actual people.

One could certainly argue that these authors were tools of God and that they were directed to write what was in God's will, but the authors existed and wrote the passages all the same (although historians now contend that the books may have been written or supplemented by followers of a certain disciple).

It is fairly well known among biblical scholars that Moses was most likely the author of the first five books of the Bible. In Judaism, the first five Mosaic books are called the Torah. This collection includes two of the most powerful books of the Old Testament: Genesis and Exodus.

Exodus deals with how the "children of Israel" were led out of bondage in Egypt. Moses is the central character in this story, as he has the lead role. Most of it is considered to be firsthand accounts, likely all witnessed by Moses himself. For Genesis, Moses had to cast his mind back in time to the beginning of creation.

It is perhaps the notion that Moses was writing the creation story long after it happened that might bother some Christians. Many Jews and

Christians believe God dictated the biblical accounts to Moses. But if one wants to stay firmly on the ground or does not believe in Christianity or Judaism, there is a simple explanation for the first five books of the Bible: Moses was not writing eyewitness accounts but was chronicling stories that already existed.

Prior to Moses writing anything down, there was an oral history of what was said to have happened. Whether you believe this oral history passed down all the way from Adam and Eve is up to you.

Many ancient cultures had oral histories that were passed down from generation to generation. This situation changed for the Hebrew people when Moses came along, collected the narratives, and decided to write them all down. Most people believe this is how the Book of Genesis came about, although there are some who contend Moses did not write down anything (there is no firm proof one way or the other). No author was listed, and no author will likely ever be found because society back then didn't consider that important. However, most biblical scholars believe Moses wrote it and that he simply chronicled oral testimonies that had been passed down long before he was even born.

Such a thing becomes easily understandable when one considers the fact that the New Testament accounts of the risen Christ were likely written several years, if not decades, after the fact. Thus, the first accounts of what happened must have been orally transmitted. In other words, one person told another of the astonishing things to which they had borne witness.

The Gospels of Mark, Matthew, Luke, and John are all believed to have been written long after the events they described. There are some who believe that the Book of Mark, which is believed to be the text written closest to the events it describes, may have been written from a previous, older source that has been lost. This could very well be the case, but as of this writing, we do not know this for sure.

So, it is generally accepted that the Gospels were all written at least twenty years after the events they described. We don't know the exact process, but it could be that the authors went around speaking with witnesses who were still alive. It would be like someone in 2023 speaking with survivors of the terrorist attack in New York that took place on September 11th, 2001. The year 2023 is fairly far removed from the year 2001, but it is not that far removed.

And if someone gathered up enough 9/11 survivors with good memories, it is likely that they would have a fairly large amount of source material to use for their book. The same could be said for the authors of the Gospels. And when we say authors of the Gospels, we have to keep in mind that there have long been arguments that the appellations given to these works were primarily pseudonyms. Matthew, Mark, and even Luke have been called into question.

The only book that most scholars consider to be written by the named author is the Gospel of John. But having said that, there is still plenty of room for debate on this issue.

First, let us take a look at the oldest written Gospel, the one that is closest on the timeline to the actual events: the Gospel of Mark. The Gospel of Mark is believed to have been written around 50 CE (so roughly twenty years after the fact).

It has long been believed that Mark was actually an early church figure named John Mark, who was St. Peter's interpreter. He interpreted Peter's words in the early years of the church as the Gospels (or at least the oral transmission of them) were being spread. Since Peter is widely believed to have been illiterate, it is believed that John Mark might have served as a scribe for Peter as well. He has sometimes even been credited as being the one who penned Peter's words in the epistles of 1st and 2nd Peter.

If the Book of Mark was indeed written by a person with such a close relationship to the Apostle Peter, it would greatly bolster the veracity of the accounts. It could be assumed that much of what was written in the Gospel of Mark came straight from the mouth of a chief eyewitness: Apostle Peter. This lends great veracity to the New Testament since this would be about as close of a reference as one could hope to get as it pertained to writing the Gospel since Jesus was unavailable.

Even if it was written down many years later, with John Mark interviewing an elder Peter who was nearing the end of his life, it would still serve as an excellent primary text. Time may have altered some recollections, such as how many angels were in the tomb, but whatever words Mark took from Peter likely was a fairly accurate portrayal of the main events of Christ's ministry. The notion that Mark used eyewitness testimony may even be alluded to in the next oldest Gospel: the Gospel of Luke.

Luke 1:2 mentions a certain "minister" who gathered up the testimonies of eyewitnesses and other ministers. It is believed that the

Gospel of Luke was written roughly ten years after the Gospel of Mark, dating back to around 60 CE, although some believe it took until 80 or 90 since this Gospel was likely a combination of several authors. Luke was largely written as a companion piece to the other book attributed to Luke, the Book of Acts. The Book of Acts is a dynamic work and continues the biblical narrative directly after Christ's ascension.

The Book of Acts describes the early church's struggles and how early church leaders came together. Peter and James played a key role in the Jerusalem church and faced much persecution. Some of this persecution came from the future Apostle Paul. Prior to Paul's conversion to Christianity, he was a zealous Pharisee (a member of a strict Jewish sect) and known as "Saul of Tarsus." The Book of Acts describes how Saul was determined to crush the Christian sect since he sincerely believed they were all a bunch of heretics.

Saul arrested Christians and even oversaw their execution. Such a thing was vividly portrayed in the account of how Stephen was stoned to death after preaching the gospel. Saul was a witness to this killing, and he would come to liken himself to a murderer in his epistles. However, Saul was converted after a mysterious instance occurred to him while traveling the road to Damascus.

The Book of Acts tells us that Christ appeared to Saul and asked him a simple question. "Saul, Saul, why do you persecute me?" Jesus was standing in as the persecuted church, but Saul initially had no idea who he was dealing with and asked the figure, "Who are you?" It was then that Jesus is said to have answered, "I am Jesus, whom you are persecuting."

Saul was then said to have been struck with blindness due to an intense blast of light. He would be healed by one of the Christians at a local church in Damascus, which he had been traveling to in the first place, although his intentions were not good. After his healing, Saul became fully dedicated to the cause of Christianity. It is not known for sure what happened out there on the road to Damascus, but by all accounts, the transformation was incredible.

Ready to embrace a complete change of character, Saul insisted he be called Paul. He went from being one of the most zealous persecutors of the faith to one of the most zealous promoters of the faith. In fact, Paul would give his life for the cause. Although it is not specifically mentioned in the scripture, it is widely believed that he perished in the Neronian persecution of the church, which occurred in 67 CE.

Nero instigated the persecution after a terrible fire burned Rome. Nero blamed the Christians, no doubt citing the fact that many apocalyptic Christian preachers were known for their fire and brimstone sermons about the impending end of the age. So, the idea went that some renegade Christians might have attempted to kickstart the apocalypse by setting Rome on fire!

To this day, no one really knows what happened, but Nero's efforts to scapegoat the Christians ultimately backfired, and he would be blamed. Nero would go down in history as the guy who "fiddled while Rome burned," although this likely never occurred. Even so, before it was all said and done, many Christians, including Apostles Paul and Peter, would be killed in this Roman crackdown on Christians.

Since this event is widely known to have occurred around 67 CE, it is believed that the Book of Acts (which does not specifically mention Paul's or Peter's death) was written a few years prior to this. So, Mark is believed to have been written in the 50s, Luke in the 60s, and the Book of Acts a short time later.

But what about the Book of Matthew? Early church leaders actually thought the Book of Matthew was written first, which explains why it is placed as the first book of the New Testament. Early church fathers thought the Book of Matthew was written around 40 CE. If so, it would have been a fairly fresh account since it would have been compiled just a few years after the events it describes. But this goes against the general consensus of biblical scholars today.

Today, it is widely believed that the Gospel of Matthew must have been written around 80 CE, if not later. Matthew had long been thought to have been compiled by the tax collector Matthew, who was mentioned in the Gospel. In the Book of Matthew, we get a full account of the tax collector whom Jesus—to the chagrin of many of his other followers—had befriended.

Interestingly, Jesus calling a tax collector to the ministry is mentioned in Mark and Luke, except in these two Gospels, he is not referred to as Matthew but rather "Levi." There is a wide range of plausible explanations for this. First of all, Levi is a traditional tribal group within Israel. Also, Levi could have been this person's Hebrew name, with Matthew being his Hellenized Greek name. There is also the chance that Jesus renamed Levi the tax collector as Matthew when he joined the ministry.

There is a precedence for this. Such a thing would have been similar to Jesus declaring that Simon Bar-Jonah (Apostle Peter) was "Petros" or the "rock" on which he would build his church. The Greek word for rock is *petros*, which would ultimately be rendered in subsequent translations as "Peter."

At any rate, if we entertain the notion that Matthew or Levi, the tax collector and a contemporary of Christ, wrote down this particular Gospel, it would be a very important account since it would have been written by someone who was there on the ground when much of it happened.

However, most scholars today date the Book of Matthew to around 80 CE. Matthew would have been an elderly man at the time this account was written. People simply did not live as long as they do now, which casts doubt on the theory that Matthew wrote the account. While it is true that the average person may have perished at fifty rather than seventy or eighty, there were always a few outliers. Such instances may have been rare, but they did occur. So, it would not be out of the realm of reason that Matthew just so happened to be among those rare few.

After all, it is widely believed that the author of the Book of John, John the Revelator, lived to a fairly old age. Speaking of John, the Gospel of John perhaps has the most widely agreed-upon precepts. Both the early church and modern scholars believe that the book is likely the last of the Gospels to have been written.

It is evident that the church believed as much due to the simple fact that the Book of John was placed last. Modern-day scholars and historians have plenty of reasons for believing that the Book of John was the last and final Gospel to be included. The Gospel itself has some clues to its finality.

As John 21:24-25 relates, "This is the disciple who is testifying to these things and has written them, and we know that his testimony is true; but there are also many other things that Jesus did; if all of them were written down, I suppose that the world itself would not contain the books that would be written."

Yes, lending credence to the notion that John had the last word as it pertains to the Gospels, this statement sounds almost like someone was making a "case closed" definitive argument. John is acknowledging here that there are many things that Jesus might have done that were not included in the testimony simply due to the fact that they were too numerous to tell.

But the question remains, who is the author? Was it really the Apostle John? Or was it someone else?

As early as 180 CE, an early church father by the name of Irenaeus, a known authority on matters of scripture, declared that this particular Gospel was written by the Apostle John. According to Irenaeus, "John, the disciple of the Lord, who also had leaned upon His breast, did himself publish a Gospel during his residence at Ephesus in Asia."

If we do assume that John was the writer, it must be acknowledged that the Gospel of John has some striking differences compared to the previous Gospels. The Gospel of John is much more oriented toward the Greek concept of the divine. After all, the Greek philosopher Plato spoke of there being a supreme all-powerful force of good known as the "Logos."

Plato believed that it was from the Logos that all things originated, and yet the Logos—this ultimate force—was still connected to all of the creations that had emanated from it. But what does all this have to do with the Gospel of John? Plenty! The Book of John starts off by stating, "In the beginning was the Word." Well, actually, in the original Greek, John wrote, "In the beginning was the Logos."

And that makes all the difference in the world. John was intentionally invoking the Greek concept of the Logos and associating it with Jesus. Here is the full passage, with "Logos" replacing "Word." "In the beginning was the Logos, and the Logos was with God, and the Logos was God. Through him all things were made; without him nothing was made that has been made. The Logos became flesh and made his dwelling among us. We have seen his glory, the glory of the one and only Son, who came from the Father, full of grace and truth."

These complicated concepts find their way into scripture in an almost subliminal fashion, but the Greek-speaking world most certainly would have picked up on the mention of "Logos." John was saying that Jesus was the Logos and that the Logos had been made flesh to "dwell" on Earth. The Greeks thought that the "divine mind" of the Logos periodically sent out its divine thoughts in what was known as "emanations," which manifested into actual beings.

Interestingly enough, these Platonist notions are quite similar to beliefs in Hinduism. Many misunderstand the Hindu faith as being polytheistic, but this is not the case. While it is true that Hindus have a wide variety of god-like figures, Hindus, like the Greeks, believe that everything ultimately came from one eternal god. Whether it's Lord Vishnu, a human being, a tree, or your cat Fluffy, everything ultimately emanates from one divine source. The Hindus called this divine source the "Brahman," whereas the Greeks called it the "Logos."

The fact that a Gospel writer would try to reconcile Greek philosophy with Christian theology was not a unique phenomenon in the 1ˢᵗ century. There was quite a bit of cross-pollination between the two. This was also the case with Christianity's predecessor Judaism, as it was seen in the efforts of intellectuals like the Jewish thinker Philo.

Philo did something quite similar to what John did, except he actually stated that Moses was the Logos. One could argue that Philo's assertion is a bit harder to comprehend since we have scenes of Moses standing before the burning bush as a manifestation of the eternal God, who insists that he is "I AM." In other words, he is the original, all-encompassing reality. He is the Logos.

Did Philo think that the burning bush and Moses were both manifestations of the Logos at the same time and that their dialogue was merely an illusion of two beings who were one and the same but being made to appear separate? It would be similar to how many Christians have notions that God the Father, God the Son, and the Holy Spirit are three parts of the same person. Yes, this sort of theological discourse can get rather complicated.

At any rate, the Gospel of John has the same main narrative as the other Gospels, but it does not go into as much detail. It seems that some of these extra details that were omitted were instead replaced with much more lengthy discourses on philosophical or spiritual beliefs. And then, after it's all said and done, the author seems to have acknowledged this omission. In fact, the author basically apologizes for it by rationalizing that there just was not enough room to include everything. (All the world could not hold it!)

As for the other authors of the Christian scriptures, we would be quite remiss if we did not mention Apostle Paul. To this day, it's still frequently argued over whether or not Paul even realized that his epistles would be included in the actual Christian canon. It must be remembered that epistles were simply letters. Paul's writings were letters that he had penned to local churches or believers in which he expounded upon his beliefs and issued words of encouragement.

Paul was a prolific and profound writer, although the authorship of some of his letters is disputed. Despite this, much of his tremendous insight, although ostensibly directed at just one particular church, such as the "Church of the Corinthians," the "Church of the Galatians," or the "Church of the Romans," were so eloquent and rich that they can quite easily be applied to all believers in general. People today still draw great inspiration from Paul's works.

But having said that, we cannot forget that Paul was writing letters to specific churches and specific people. The fact that he ended up in the Bible at all would be akin to someone writing a book on business management and then finding some really good e-mails Steve Jobs wrote to Steve Wozniak and just slapping them in the book.

That is not to take away from how moving and inspirational Paul's words are, but the fact that he wrote letters rather than Gospels makes it unclear whether he ever intended for his writing to be included in the canon.

Having said that, Paul's writings have often caused a bit of dissension in the church. There have always been those who absolutely swore by them, but there have also been those who warned against them.

Even Apostle Peter seemed somewhat conflicted. Peter simultaneously praised Paul but also issued a kind of cryptic warning about his teachings. In one of Peter's epistles, we find Peter saying, "And count the patience of our Lord as salvation, just as our beloved brother Paul also wrote to you according to the wisdom given him, as he does in all his letters when he speaks in them of these matters. There are some things in them that are hard to understand, which the ignorant and unstable twist to their own destruction, as they do the other scriptures" (2nd Peter 3:15-16).

Peter does not say that Paul is wrong, but he warns that he speaks about complex theological beliefs that many who are "ignorant" get mixed up and misunderstand what he is talking about. Interestingly enough, later Christian writers of the 2nd century would blame Paul for inspiring the Christian Gnostics.

The Gnostics denied the physical resurrection and further insisted that all physical reality was evil and that the end goal was to be released and become a spirit. And the Gnostics indeed favored Paul, counting him as a fellow Gnostic and seeing him as a great inspiration. This was apparently because they enjoyed the fact that Paul seemed to castigate the flesh just like they wished to do. Paul stated, "Flesh and blood will not inherit the kingdom of God."

This statement, which was written in one of Paul's epistles, seems to endorse the later Gnostic view that flesh and blood are inherently evil. But while seeming to bolster the Gnostics, the troubling verse is completely at odds with all other aspects of the Christian faith. The cornerstone of Christianity is the physical resurrection of Jesus. And during the ascension, people apparently stood and watched as Christ floated up into the skies.

Furthermore, original Christian doctrine attests that all (believers and non-believers) will be physically resurrected in the end. Some would be resurrected to bliss, while others would be resurrected to face judgment. So, one really has to wonder where did Apostle Paul get the idea that "flesh and blood will not inherit the kingdom of God?"

According to the rest of the Bible, when New Jerusalem comes to Earth and the physically resurrected Jesus returns, the saints will also be physically resurrected. All of the erstwhile believers will take part in a very real kingdom of God. It will be just like the Lord's Prayer: "on Earth as it is in Heaven."

Considering all of this, it is quite clear that whatever Paul's intentions were, his words in this particular passage—as Peter warned might happen— cause plenty of confusion, even today. Despite this one random statement about flesh and blood not inheriting the kingdom of God, Paul himself seems to have thoroughly believed in the physical resurrection.

Paul clarified this belief in a profound way in his famous letter to the Church of Corinth by stating, "If there is no resurrection of the dead, then not even Christ has been raised. And if Christ has not been raised, our preaching is useless, and so is your faith. More than that, we are then found to be false witnesses about God, for we have testified about God that he raised Christ from the dead. But he did not raise him if in fact the dead are not raised" (1ˢᵗ Corinthians 15:13-15).

If these words to the Corinthians came after his declaration that "flesh and blood do not inherit the kingdom of God," one would think he was doing a bit of damage control. Perhaps some of the "ignorant" new believers that Peter spoke of took his words and ran with them. Maybe they went around shouting from the roofs, "Paul said flesh and blood do not inherit the kingdom of God; therefore, there is no resurrection!"

But this was not the case at all since these words, which seemingly clarify the physical resurrection, come from the same exact epistle in which Paul crafted the words "flesh and blood do not inherit the kingdom of God." In fact, Paul made this clarification *before* he uttered those infamous words. Paul had been doing everything he could to insist that the physical resurrection of the dead was indeed what Christians should be looking forward to.

Paul then goes on to state, "For if the dead are not raised, then Christ has not been raised either. And if Christ has not been raised, your faith is futile; you are still in your sins. Then those also who have fallen asleep in Christ are lost. If we have hoped in Christ only in this life, we are of all people most to be pitied. But Christ has indeed been raised from the dead, the first fruits of those who have fallen asleep. For since death came through a man, the resurrection of the dead comes also through a man. For as in Adam all die, so in Christ all will be made alive" (1ˢᵗ Corinthians 16:16-22).

Yet as Paul continues his long, complex theological musings, toward the end of this very same epistle, he makes the statement, "I declare to you, brothers and sisters, that flesh and blood cannot inherit the kingdom of God, nor does the perishable inherit the imperishable" (1ˢᵗ Corinthians 15:50).

So, did Paul speak in riddles? As Peter warned, it could just be that some of his sayings are hard to understand at times. If Paul was just using "flesh and blood" as a euphemism for "sinfulness," his words make sense. There are many to this day who might equate "sin" with "fleshly" behavior. Thus, it is possible Paul saying "flesh and blood" or "sinful behavior" will not allow one access to the kingdom of God.

Such a statement would have lined up with previous teachings without any problems. But if this was simply Paul's shorthand at work, only those who knew him well enough to understand his lingo would have fully grasped what he meant. Thus, it is important to consider his audience. He was speaking directly to the congregation at Corinth. Paul had received word they were engaging in inappropriate behavior, so he was correcting them. This could very well be why he warned them to cease and desist their "fleshly" works since it would do nothing to promote their growth as Christians.

Moving on from Paul as a biblical author, the only other acknowledged authors who remain are two brothers of Jesus—James and Jude. Now when we say the word "brothers," we have to be careful because the mention of Jesus having flesh and blood relations often causes some contention among Christians. Through the Christian lens, Jesus was born of his mother, Mary, through the agency of God, making him the "son of God."

Even if you believe in the immaculate conception, there is no denying that Mary and her husband, Joseph, had children together after Jesus was born. So, even if you believe that Jesus was the son of God and Mary, her subsequent children would be Jesus' half-siblings. Thus, the New Testament authors James and Jude were the half-brothers of Jesus, depending on your view of the immaculate conception.

When one thinks about it, it really is quite remarkable that Jesus' two brothers—especially James—did not write more than they did. James has two epistles attributed to him, and the words of Jude are nothing more than a footnote right before the epic final book of the Bible: the Book of Revelation. James' briefness is especially surprising since, after the resurrection, he became a major leader of the Jerusalem church.

James has an interesting backstory. It is said that he initially did not believe his brother's claims. The incontrovertible proof of the resurrected Christ appearing to James made him change his mind. From that point on, James apparently became a zealous promoter of the faith and would lead the Church of Jerusalem for many years. James was ultimately martyred for his faith, but two epistles, 1st and 2nd James, are attributed to him.

Jude's contribution was very minimal but provides us with one of the most interesting passages in the Bible. Jude actually references the once-lost Book of Enoch, speaking of how the fallen angels had come to Earth and interbred with human women, creating half-angel, half-human creatures called the Nephilim.

Jude alludes states, "And the angels who did not keep their positions of authority but abandoned their proper dwelling—these he has kept in darkness, bound with everlasting chains for judgment on the great day" (Jude 1: 6). Jude also strangely warns against "slandering celestial beings." He goes on to state, "In the very same way, on the strength of their dreams these ungodly people pollute their own bodies, reject authority and heap abuse on celestial beings. But even the archangel Michael, when he was disputing with the devil about the body of Moses, did not himself dare to condemn him for slander but said, 'The Lord rebuke you!' Yet these people slander whatever they do not understand, and the very things they do understand by instinct—as irrational animals do—will destroy them" (Jude 1: 8-10).

It is interesting to note the sense of familiarity with which Jude refers to "celestial beings," considering that the Gospels speak of how angels repeatedly visited both of his parents during the Christmas story. Could he be speaking from some of his own personal experiences with these celestial beings? If you believe the family was visited by angels during the Christmas story, it is not much of a leap to imagine that these visitations might have continued as Jesus, James, and Jude grew up under Mary and Joseph's roof.

At any rate, even though the Book of Enoch was not included in the official canon, Jude goes on to reference it once again as a means of describing how he viewed the current state of the church. Jude declares, "Enoch, the seventh from Adam, prophesied about them: 'See, the Lord is coming with thousands upon thousands of his holy ones to judge everyone, and to convict all of them of all the ungodly acts they have committed in their ungodliness, and of all their defiant words ungodly sinners have spoken against him.' These people are grumblers and faultfinders; they follow their own evil desires; they boast about themselves and flatter others for their own advantage" (Jude 1: 14-16).

Jude's message is most certainly an intense one. He again alludes to the celestial host, stating that "the Lord is coming with thousands upon thousands of his holy ones to judge everyone." He then ends his missive with an exclamation by enjoining believers to "be merciful to those who doubt; save others by snatching them from the fire; to others show mercy, mixed with fear—hating even the clothing stained by corrupted flesh."

This seems like a final closing statement. And if the Book of Revelation was not included in the Bible, one could almost envision these being the definitive words of the scripture before closing the book. Interestingly enough, there were some who wanted to take out the Book of Revelation. Martin Luther famously wished to remove it from the Protestant canon.

However, Luther had his own reasons, as he felt that the Book of Revelation's mention of casting "Hades" (a temporary place) into the "Lake of Fire" (an apparently eternal final destination) sounded as if it bolstered the Catholic concept of the temporary holding place of purgatory, which he was against at the time.

Speaking of the Book of Revelation, it is believed that the same author of the Gospel of John was the author of this prophetic work. When John was sent into exile by the Romans to the island of Patmos, he had several revelatory experiences. John apparently wrote down what he saw, rendering a long narrative of prophetic imagery. There is quite a bit of argument to this day over how much of the Book of Revelation is literal and how much is symbolic.

There are some who would like to take a completely literal stance, but this is rather hard to fathom since at the beginning of the Book of Revelation, the angel who begins John's presentation of revelatory imagery uses the symbolism of "seven lampstands," which the angel itself insists represents the "seven churches" that were present in Asia Minor. Since the angel said as much during the revelation itself, it seems pretty clear that at least some parts of the Book of Revelation were meant to be symbolic. But even so, the question remains, where do you draw the line?

What's symbolic? And what's not? Continuing in this vein, perhaps one of the more perplexing issues is when John bore witness to the "Battle of Armageddon." He apparently saw armies wielding swords and fighting on horseback. This would have been common fare in John's age, but in the modern world, we view Armageddon as being fought by tanks and jet fighters.

For portions of this scripture, symbolism is usually invoked. For example, when John is presented with imagery of "locusts" that bring death to a large portion of humanity, some have theorized that John was actually being shown modern-day Apache attack helicopters, which, to an untrained eye, do resemble locusts. And if John, who had no idea what a helicopter was, saw this great contraption, he likely would have identified it as some great beast he was familiar with, like a locust.

At any rate, John's prophecies have long been argued over in a wide variety of ways. Many argue whether or not these prophecies had already occurred, if all of them were yet to come, or if he had any prophecies in the first place.

At any rate, these were the authors of the scripture, and their influence on Christianity continues to this day.

Chapter 3: Christianity Takes Shape

Although Christianity was founded by Christ, it was built by Christ's followers. And the core of this religious zeal for the purportedly resurrected Jesus can be traced back to the group of people who claimed to have seen him resurrected, from his first alleged appearances at the tomb to his further appearances in homes, on roadsides, and speaking before vast multitudes. According to the scripture, Christ's resurrection set a fire in his followers and caused them to "turn the world upside down" for him.

Whether you believe the resurrection happened or not, one has to concede that early Christians believed in it. And such an event is a good explanation as to why the first Christians became so galvanized to preach the gospel. We see this at work in the attitudes of Christ's closest disciples. Immediately after the crucifixion, they were a depressed and paranoid lot. They stayed indoors and kept their heads low in fear that with Jesus gone, they might be next. The best terms to describe their state of mind might be defeated, dispirited, hunted, and hounded.

Yet, according to the scripture, on that third day, the resurrected Christ appeared before them. Everything changed. Their sadness turned to joy, and their fear turned into certainty that the cause they believed in was right and just. They were so sure of themselves that they barged right into the middle of the temple to declare Christ had been resurrected from the dead, even though they knew they could be arrested and put to death just for saying as much.

Acts 4:7-13 has a very powerful account of this, depicting Peter fearlessly standing up to the temple authorities. It reads, "Then Peter, filled with the Holy Spirit, said to them: 'Rulers and elders of the people! If we are being called to account today for an act of kindness shown to a man who was lame and are being asked how he was healed, then know this, you and all people of Israel: It is by the name of Jesus Christ of Nazareth, whom you crucified but whom God raised from the dead, that this man stands before you healed. Jesus is the stone you builders rejected, which has become the cornerstone. Salvation is found in no one else, for there is no other name under heaven given to mankind by which we must be saved.'"

Bold words like this could have brought about immediate death. When Peter spoke them, he was said to have miraculously healed a lame man by praying in the name of Jesus. And when questioned about it, rather than denying Christ, as Peter had done prior to the resurrection, he boldly proclaimed his belief in Christ. He stood up to those in charge and declared that he would never stop proclaiming Christ and basically dared them to do their worst.

One has to ask, why would he be willing to die for a lie? It is hard enough for many people to die for the truth, let alone something someone has made up. The fact that these men and women were willing to die rather than renounce Christ is a strong testament to the fact that—if anything else—they truly believed what they were saying. We can argue that they were delusional, but whatever was going on, they sincerely seemed to believe in the resurrection of Jesus Christ.

At any rate, the purported resurrection served as the catalyst that sent the early church into action. Christ's followers would preach openly in the streets of Jerusalem and then make their way much farther afield. By the 2nd century, Christianity had spread, to some degree, to virtually all of the Roman Empire.

During this period, Christians were periodically tolerated and persecuted by various Roman regimes and Roman citizens. Much of this persecution was often based on simple misunderstandings as to what Christianity was all about. For example, Christians were secretive about their gatherings and often met in graveyards. The Christians likely met there because they could meet there in peace without being bothered.

But for anyone who was not a Christian and happened to see a congregation gathering in a graveyard themselves, it would have been quite a strange sight to behold. Christians were also accused of cannibalism due to a misunderstanding of Communion. This perhaps sounds like nonsense to us today, but consider the words attributed to Christ for the ceremony: "This is my blood, this is my body." For those who did not know the symbolism or what it all meant, it is easy to see why they thought Christians were talking about drinking blood and eating people.

Because of all of these misunderstandings, Christian apologists became prominent. To be clear, a Christian apologist was not someone apologizing for their faith. On the contrary, an apologist was someone who clarified and defended their faith. The word "apologist" comes from the Greek word *apologia*, which literally means "defense." One of the most famous Christian apologists was Justin Martyr, who lived during the 2nd century and wrote long treatises defending Christian beliefs in terms that are fairly familiar to Christian ideology in the modern age.

And by the 4th century, a large chunk of the Roman empire was Christian. In 313 CE, Roman Emperor Constantine issued his famous Edict of Milan, in which he declared Christianity a lawful, tolerated religion. The church, which had once been so persecuted, would become the main religion of the Roman Empire. And shortly after this, what we know today as the Catholic (universal) Church was formed.

However, the Catholic Church claims that its roots go all the way back to Apostle Peter when he became the first bishop of Rome (making him the first pope) shortly before he was martyred. Catholics can point to a long history of stewardship, at least as it pertains to the role of the bishop of Rome (also known as the pope). Pope Linus, a man who was said to have been personally picked by Peter himself to be his successor, took on the mantle after Peter. Linus was also mentioned in one of the letters to Timothy (2nd Timothy 4:21, to be exact). And the line of popes has continued to this very day.

At any rate, after the Christian-friendly Roman Emperor Constantine decided that Christianity should be tolerated, he became determined to use it as a binding, unifying force. But to do this, there had to be a set standard, a universal doctrine that all Christians must abide by. Constantine's sheer ambition to achieve this goal led to one of the most consequential events in Christian history: the Council of Nicaea. Held in

325 CE in the eastern Mediterranean city of Nicaea, church leaders came together to formulate the universal church doctrine that would be known as the Nicene Creed.

This creed was the official professed statement of what Christians proclaimed to believe. It cut through nearly three centuries of confusion, during which time Christians vigorously debated among themselves about everything from Communion to the nature of Christ's divinity.

Those gathered at the Council of Nicaea proclaimed:

"I believe in one God, the Father almighty, maker of Heaven and Earth, of all things visible and invisible. I believe in one Lord Jesus Christ, the Only Begotten Son of God, born of the Father before all ages. God from God, Light from Light, true God from true God, begotten, not made, consubstantial with the Father; through him all things were made. For us men and for our salvation he came down from Heaven, and by the Holy Spirit was incarnate of the Virgin Mary, and became man. For our sake he was crucified under Pontius Pilate, he suffered death and was buried, and rose again on the third day in accordance with the Scriptures. He ascended into Heaven and is seated at the right hand of the Father. He will come again in glory to judge the living and the dead, and his kingdom will have no end. I believe in the Holy Spirit, the Lord, the giver of life, who proceeds from the Father and the Son, who with the Father and the Son is adored and glorified, who has spoken through the prophets. I believe in one, holy Catholic and Apostolic Church. I confess one baptism for the forgiveness of sins, and I look forward to the resurrection of the dead and the life of the world to come. Amen."

Even in this creed, you once again see the word "Catholic" or "universal" being stressed. Constantine's project was a big one, as he wished to unite all Christians in his realm under one banner. Considering the divergence of views that existed prior to the Council of Nicaea, it really is rather incredible that the council was as successful as it was in uniting the factions.

It is said that church leaders from far and wide traveled to Nicaea and vigorously debated their views on scripture before they came up with this universal creed. Just imagine all of these elder statesmen of the church, some still bearing the visible scars of previous persecutions, gathering to hammer these things out together.

Once this "universal" or "Catholic" church was established, it was up to church leaders and subsequent Roman rulers to make sure that it did not fall apart. The institutions that were established were fairly strong.

The Roman Catholic Church has indeed stood the test of time. The Catholic Church survived the fall of the Western Roman Empire, safeguarding not only Christianity but also Roman civic customs and bureaucracy. If one really thinks about it, the structure of the Catholic Church is largely parallel with the structure of the old Roman government.

The pope is essentially an emperor, and his multitude of cardinals in the Vatican serve basically the same role as senators did in the Roman Senate. The Church of Rome was so strong that even after barbarian armies poured into the "Eternal City," the barbarians chose to submit to the pope and become Catholic themselves instead of toppling the institution!

Some of these newcomers had already become Christians prior to Rome's fall. Roman emperors had long recruited warriors from surrounding regions, and many were introduced to the Christian faith while fighting for Rome in this capacity. There were many incentives for them to do so; for instance, it would be in their best interest to better identify with their Roman taskmasters. This early contingent of converts would better aid the conversion of later subsequent waves of pagans.

Shortly after Rome fell in 476 CE, one of the warlords, a Frankish king named Clovis, was convinced to drop his pagan beliefs and become a Christian. Demonstrating how widespread Christianity had become, his own wife, Clotilde, was already a Christian before Clovis changed religions. Clovis had his own problems. He faced constant warfare with the various tribes that had descended upon the western half of the Roman Empire, so he was being pressed in on all sides. Allegedly in the midst of a fierce battle, in which he feared all was lost, he called upon the Christian God for help.

In many ways, it was a repeat of the miraculous sign that former Roman Emperor Constantine the Great was said to have experienced. Constantine was in the middle of a pitched battle when he supposedly saw a flaming cross in the sky. He took this as a sign to trust in Christ, so he rallied his troops and emerged victorious. In a similar way, Clovis saw what he interpreted as a supernatural victory, although it is not known for sure what he saw.

After this, he apparently submitted to Christianity and to the pope in Rome. Not only that, but he also directed all of his followers to do the same. This would be a continuing trend in western Europe, which allowed the Catholic Church to thrive, despite the fact that the Western Roman Empire was in ruins.

In the meantime, the Eastern Roman Empire, which would become known as the Byzantine Empire, continued to thrive. Constantine founded the Eastern Roman capital of Constantinople on the old site of the Greek city of Byzantium in Asia Minor (modern-day Turkey). The Eastern Roman Empire would continue for quite some time, with its own emperor ruling from Constantinople.

Although the West and the East were politically separated, their tenuous connection through the Catholic Church would remain for the next few centuries. Even so, many differences began to surface. These differences were both of a political and theological nature. For one thing, the Eastern Roman emperors in Constantinople thoroughly expected the pope in Rome to recognize them as the legitimate Roman emperor.

This became an odder and odder prospect. The Byzantines had waged a losing war against the Ostrogoths in Italy, yet any real imperial hold of Rome was fleeting at best. Yet the Byzantine emperor still wanted the pope to recognize him as sovereign, even though the Eastern emperor was not fulfilling his role as the protector of Rome or the pope. Such a relationship was bound to come to ruin.

Despite any claims to the contrary, the popes were increasingly dependent upon friendly kings in the West for military aid rather than the Eastern Roman emperor. For instance, in 754, the Lombards attempted an all-out invasion of Italy. The pope turned to a Frankish (as in French) king in the West for aid.

The so-called "Apostle of Germany," Saint Boniface, had been friendly with King Pepin of the Franks, and this friendship paid off when King Pepin was persuaded to stop the Lombard advance in its tracks. Not only that, but his armies also gifted the sitting pope, Pope Stephen II, with large tracts of land they had seized in central Italy, which would become known as the Papal States. Ever since the fall of Rome, the popes had long learned to become Machiavellian strategists of the greatest sort, balancing one power on top of another just to keep their heads above water.

But now, the popes turned to the Franks of western Europe. In 799, Pope Leo III was nearly beaten to death in the street. This rather under-protected pope came to the pragmatic realization that his relationship with the Franks should be made binding. So, in 800, Pope Leo III infuriated the Byzantines by crowning King Charlemagne of the Franks as the "Holy Roman Emperor."

Charlemagne would go on to found what would later be known as the "Holy Roman Empire," which consisted of modern-day Germany, most of France, and northern Italy. And until Napoleon toppled it, the Holy Roman Empire would have a long line of emperors who descended from Charlemagne.

At any rate, back in 800 CE, when the pope crowned Charlemagne emperor and made him the temporal "defender of the faith," the Eastern Roman emperor was furious. This was perhaps the first major fissure between Western and Eastern relations, although theological differences were already present. After this sundering of the political relationship between East and West, the theological differences began to fester. These differences would only grow worse until a "Great Schism" ensued.

Chapter 4: The Great Schism (1054 CE)

It occurred seemingly without warning one sunny day in 1054. The pope's personal legate, Cardinal Humbert, was in Constantinople paying a visit to the great Greek monastery, the Hagia Sophia. He was not there to pay respects, though; rather, he was there to inflame sentiments. Upon entering the church, he walked right up to the altar and deposited an official bull of excommunication squarely on it. As the cardinal and his fellow colleagues from Rome filed out of the church, they were followed by a local priest, who, realizing what had happened, began to plead with them to reconsider.

However, the papal legate was entirely unmoved, and the excommunication stood. But as sudden as all this seemed, the tremors beneath this theological earthquake between the Christian East and the Christian West had been going on for quite some time. Some have since tried to argue that the Great Schism of 1054 was similar to a medieval reformation. But it must be said that what happened in 1054 was much more political than it was spiritual.

Even though some fairly minor doctrinal differences were highlighted, the key dispute was over sovereignty and who should have it. The dispute involved four figures vying for various forms of power—the pope of Rome, the Holy Roman emperor, the patriarch of Constantinople, and the Byzantine emperor. Ever since the Latin pope decided to crown the Frankish king, Charlemagne, as emperor, great animosity had been building over the exact order of temporal and spiritual power.

For the Byzantines, the fact that the pope would turn to the West and hail a Western ruler as emperor smacked of betrayal. The Byzantines viewed Charlemagne as an unworthy usurper of the imperial title and the pope's decision to crown him as a terrible error. In the minds of the Byzantines, this act was schismatic.

Fast forward to the 11th century, and the political discord created all those years prior provided the perfect backdrop for exacerbating certain theological tensions. The East, for example, had taken umbrage to the fact that the West had added the phrase "and the Son" to the Nicene Creed. The traditional creed was modified to state that the "Holy Spirit" came not only from the "Father" but also the "Son."

This modification was minor yet major at the same time. Not all Greeks necessarily disagreed with the notion, but it was viewed as an unauthorized adaptation. The real point of contention was the authorization to edit the creed. The East was sick and tired of the West trying to call all the shots. And when it was learned that Greeks in Byzantine enclaves in Italy were being forced to abide by the Latin creed, the patriarch of Constantinople, Michael Cerularius, took action by insisting that Latin Catholics in Constantinople be forced to use the Greek version.

The Latin Catholics refused, and the Greek patriarch retaliated by shutting their churches down. All of this led to the pope sending his legates, who were led by Cardinal Humbert, to Constantinople in 1054 to see if some compromise could be made. The attempt at reconciliation did not go well, so Cardinal Humbert, who claimed to have authority given to him by the pope, dropped the bombshell: the infamous bull of excommunication.

Not to be outdone and true to form, the patriarch then turned around and excommunicated Pope Leo IX. However, the pope had already perished, doing so in April. Word traveled slowly in those days, and unbeknownst to both parties, Pope Leo had passed away while Cardinal Humbert was busy excommunicating the Greek patriarch in his name. If Leo had died, did Humbert have the authority to excommunicate the patriarch? Technically, he did not, but the damage had already been done. The West and the East now viewed each other as heretics.

This was a shocking move, but it would take some time for the direct split of the two main branches of the church to be felt. So, what caused this breach? On the surface, it appears that these two religious leaders were quarreling over minor issues, such as the use of unleavened bread in the Eucharist. And while these issues were important to them, they likely would not have caused a major fallout in the church. Most historians believe the larger issue was about who was calling the shots.

The Western popes wanted to maintain papal supremacy, meaning they wanted to be the top religious leader in charge. But the patriarch of faraway Constantinople disagreed.

The Great Schism would continue to grow and be exacerbated further by political problems. As the Christian West grew stronger politically and militarily, the old Christian East grew weaker. Constantinople was being increasingly threatened by the Turkic tribes of Anatolia (modern-day Turkey).

The Turks had adopted Islam several centuries before, and their warlord leaders had made it, more or less, their goal to topple what remained of the Byzantine Empire. They were quite good at chipping away at this ancient institution, and this threat to the empire's continued stability led the Byzantine emperor to plead with the pope for aid.

Yes, it is indeed ironic that one of the roots of the Great Schism was the fact that the pope had decided to turn away from Constantinople in 800 CE in favor of strong Western rulers, such as Charlemagne. This was done out of the pragmatic reality that the Eastern emperor was no longer able to defend the faith when push came to shove.

Yet, by the end of the 11th century, the Byzantine emperor was not only failing to physically defend the pope, but he was also pleading for the pope to defend him! And his request did not fall on deaf ears. Due to the Byzantine emperor's pleas and reports of Christian pilgrims being harassed in the Holy Land, Pope Urban II launched his famous call for a crusade in that fateful year of 1095.

The Great Schism was in recent memory, so it is likely Urban was hoping to reconcile the church and heal the division. And the subsequent military aid mustered by the West led to the East reconsidering its drift from Rome. Until the fall of Constantinople in 1453, many efforts were made to patch things up. There were even a few declarations that a reunion of the East and West would happen. The most famous of these was, no doubt, the Council of Florence.

This ecumenical council took place between 1431 and 1449. Under great pressure and threat of being overrun by the Ottoman Turks, the

Eastern Church grudgingly agreed to the terms of the Council of Florence, with only one Byzantine bishop, Mark of Ephesus, protesting the decision. Mark, who would later be hailed as a saint in the Orthodox Church, wrote a stinging rebuke of the whole exchange.

In 1440, he penned a letter that rejected everything for which the Council of Florence stood. The letter began with the following:

"From Mark, Bishop of the Metropolis of Ephesus—Rejoice in Christ!

To those who have ensnared us in an evil captivity—desiring to lead us away into the Babylon of Latin rites and dogmas—could not, of course, completely accomplish this, seeing immediately that there was little chance of it. In fact, that it was simply impossible."

Mark of Ephesus then went on to note that even after all of the pressure and prodding, the Latin Catholics could only manage a botched compromise of sorts that "stopped somewhere in the middle." Mark rails against the clumsy way that compromises between the Greek and Latin rites were made and deems both approaches to be absolutely worthless. He likened it to resembling the mismatched "centaur" of ancient myth. The centaur was not quite human but not quite animal, and Mark railed against the compromise as being a "false union" that was not quite Latin yet not quite Greek either.

He then went on to state, "But one should examine in what manner they have united with them; for everything that is united to something different is naturally united by means of some middle point between them. And thus they imagined to unite with them by means of some judgment concerning the Holy Spirit, together with expressing the opinion that He has existence also from the Son. But everything else between them is divergent, and there is among them neither any middle point nor anything in common."

Mark highlighted the folly of making compromises over which side of the debate was right. In his mind, either the Latins were right and the Greeks were wrong, or the Greeks were right and the Latins were wrong! For him, compromising over such crucial aspects of religious doctrine to claim that the East and the West were united, resolving the Great Schism in the process, was utterly absurd.

Mark of Ephesus summed up his thoughts by stating, "If, then, the Latins do not at all depart from the correct Faith, we have evidently cut them off unjustly. But if they have thoroughly departed [from the Faith]—and that in connection with the theology of the Holy Spirit, blasphemy against whom is the greatest of all perils—then it is clear that they are heretics, and we have cut them off as heretics."

Obviously, St. Mark of Ephesus took a hardline view of the Orthodox brethren of old, saying that it was the Catholics of the Latin West who were the heretics and not the Greek Christians of the Orthodox East! Sentiments like this, of course, had led to the infamous excommunications in 1054. With both theological barrels firing, Mark of Ephesus then entirely unloads on his theological opponents, declaring:

"If the Latin dogma is true that the Holy Spirit proceeds also from the Son, then ours is false that states that the Holy Spirit proceeds from the Father—and this is precisely the reason for which we separated from them. And if ours is true, then without a doubt, theirs is false. What kind of middle ground can there be between two such judgments? There can be none, unless it were some kind of judgment suitable to both the one and the other, like a boot that fits both feet. And will this unite us?"

For Mark of Ephesus, the notion that such incompatible views could be united together was patently absurd, about as absurd as the centaurs described in ancient Greek myths. Yet, on the official level, the union went forward. The East came to terms with the Latin version of the Nicene Creed and the nature of papal authority. In return, the Byzantine emperor hoped the pope would call another crusade that might prevent his kingdom from being destroyed.

Ultimately, however, the promised military aid from the West came too little, too late. There was only a half-hearted attempt in 1444, with the pope rallying some twenty-five thousand troops to march on the Ottomans in the Balkans in what was known as the Crusade of Varna.

But unlike the crusaders of old, who pushed the opponents of Eastern Christendom back from Constantinople's gates and descended upon the Holy Land itself, this contingent of would-be crusaders was not enough to stop the Ottoman juggernaut and was soundly defeated.

The light of the Byzantine Empire was finally snuffed out by the surging Ottoman Empire in 1453. Under Ottoman occupation, the succeeding bishops of the Eastern Orthodox Church thoroughly renounced the Council of Florence and for all that it stood. The Turkish authorities saw the division of Western and Eastern Christendom as advantageous, but there was also simmering resentment over the terms of the council, as was so vociferously expressed by Mark of Ephesus. So, despite all efforts to the contrary, the Great Schism would remain intact.

Section Two: Reform and Resistance (1100–1800 CE)

Chapter 5: Medieval Christianity (1100–1380 CE)

The medieval period is sometimes known as the Dark Ages. This name is supposed to signify a perceived loss of some of the knowledge that had been gained during the high-water mark of antiquity. But to say that the medieval age was all dark and dreary without any hope of enlightenment would be misleading. If anything else, the Christians of the medieval period still had their faith, and for them, their faith meant everything. And their faith was not something in the abstract but a very tangible aspect of their lives.

This was demonstrated on November 27th, 1095, when Pope Urban II stood before the masses and declared that Christians needed to "take up the cross" to defend Christian interests in the East. Among the reasons given for this call to arms was to aid the Byzantine Empire, which was being hammered by Islamic forces, and to protect Christian pilgrims who had recently suffered harassment at the holy sites.

But in the minds of many medieval Christians, there was a much larger goal in mind, one that would correct what they perceived as a major wrong: the wresting of the Holy Land from the Muslim forces. Jerusalem had fallen to Islamic forces in the 7th century. At the tail end of the 11th century, Christians were rallying to take it back. Many who heard Urban II speak came to one conclusion: God wills it!

The zealous crowds chanted this phrase over and over, and this way of thinking would lead European Christians from far and wide to converge in the Middle East to take back what they believed to be theirs. Although later historians would try to cast the crusaders as nothing more than colonizers, there was more to it than that. The religiously minded people felt they were fighting for God. And a call to defend the faith could rouse folks from all walks of life to come running to join the cause.

This was perhaps best demonstrated in the so-called "People's Crusade," which was led by a lay minister and mystic called Peter the Hermit. Although the People's Crusade was not considered an official crusade as much as a mad mob of zealots, this massive wave of Christians actually reached the Levant before the First Crusade (the one that had been officially sanctioned by the pope). And the peasants of the People's Crusade met absolutely disastrous results!

This unorganized mob (and that's really what the people amounted to) was not at all trained in warfare. Nevertheless, they traipsed across Europe, causing havoc wherever they went until they somehow found themselves in Constantinople. The Greek emperor quickly washed his hands of the motley crew and allowed them to exit out his back door to the Bosporus. They made their way through Anatolia until they were utterly annihilated by the Turks who intercepted them.

Again, this was not a professional army. Just imagine a bunch of villagers armed with pitchforks, sticks, and shovels, and you get the idea. As the Turks faced this bizarre group, with scimitars cleaving through wooden staffs, they must have thought the world had gone mad. "Who were these people? And why were they here?" were likely some of the questions that came to mind.

As hard as it is for us to fathom today, these zealous medieval Christians were there because of their strong and uncompromising faith in God. It is a faith we might find utterly alien and irrational today, but this kind of unrelenting faith was very present in the Middle Ages.

At any rate, after Peter the Hermit's mob was decimated, the first official contingent of crusaders—official as in armed knights and soldiers led by kings, princes, and barons—made their way to Constantinople. Arriving at Constantinople's gates in 1097, this group was seen by the Byzantine emperor as a *real* army, so he did what he could to actively coordinate with and accommodate them.

A joint group of crusaders and Byzantines recovered the recently lost Byzantine city of Nicaea. While retaking this ancient Christian city, where the Nicene Creed was agreed upon all those years ago, the Byzantines effectively aided the crusaders, using their navy to blockade the nearby Lake Ascania so that the occupiers would be hemmed in without any hope of further aid.

The crusaders and Byzantines then hammered the Muslims from all sides until their opponents admitted defeat. Byzantine flags were soon unfurled at Nicaea once again, and the Byzantine emperor had the Latin crusaders to thank for the recovery of his lost city. At this point, the relations between the crusaders and the Byzantines were quite good, perhaps even at their highest mark, as the Byzantines were thankful for the support. They helped to lead the crusaders to their next target—Antioch.

The city of Antioch, located in the far northwestern corner of what is termed the Levant, is another ancient focal point of Christianity. Apostle Paul often used Antioch as his home base when carrying out missions farther afield in Greece and Asia Minor. In October 1097, the crusaders began their siege of Antioch. This would prove to be a long and protracted affair, with the crusaders having to hunker down for the winter. They could not take the city until the following year, in the summer of 1098.

With the conquest of Antioch, the crusaders began a pattern of refusing to honor previous pledges to return lost lands to the Byzantine Empire. Antioch had belonged to the Byzantines prior to it being taken from them by the Turks. Yet the crusaders decided to keep Antioch for themselves, beginning what would be a trend, as they would forge their own "Crusader Kingdom" in the Middle East. Antioch would form part of the larger Principality of Antioch.

The Christians marched from Antioch and reached their ultimate goal of Jerusalem in 1099. Upon their arrival, the crusaders initially could do very little, thanks to the city's immense walls. The local governor was no doubt hoping he could wait out the Christian invaders and hold on long enough for reinforcements to arrive. However, the resources within were finite and running low.

Likely due to the dwindling supplies, the governor decided to boot out all of the Christians from the city. Although the governor could be commended for not slaughtering the Christians outright, it is likely that he realized that dumping a large population of civilians on the crusaders would serve as a great distraction and further deplete the resources of his antagonists.

After all, the Christian crusaders had a duty to protect Christian civilians. But within this group of hangers-on, the crusaders found a real diamond in the rough. Among this rabble was a man known as Blessed Gerard. He was a caretaker of a local hospital and claimed to have inside knowledge as to how the crusaders could overcome the mighty walls of Jerusalem.

Gerard pointed out the most vulnerable parts of the walls and then proceeded to direct the crusaders on how best to break through them. This led to a siege tower being constructed. It was placed at one of the gates, and the crusaders were able to pour over the walls. A bloody battle ensued, with crusaders and Muslims fighting for every inch of the city. Ultimately, the crusaders prevailed, and Jerusalem—or what was left of it—was theirs to claim.

In the end, the bloodshed that occurred to obtain this prize was shocking, even to medieval sensibilities. Nevertheless, it was the foundation of what would become the Crusader States.

Now that the crusaders controlled the Holy Land, they had to figure out what to do with it. The first pressing problem was the fact that the cities and other outposts they controlled were severely understaffed. The population of Jerusalem, for example, saw a majority of its previous residents be either exalted or slaughtered. The city was a small fraction of what it had once been. There was such a shortage of personnel that many portions of the city walls went unguarded. And the situation outside of the city walls was even worse.

Christians who wished to travel to other holy sites quickly found out they were taking their lives into their own hands by doing so. The ever-present danger of being waylaid by bandits and other aggressors led to the establishment of permanent military orders to safeguard the civilian population.

The most famous of these orders would be the Knights Templar and the Knights Hospitaller. Initially tasked with safeguarding pilgrims, the various monastic orders of knights essentially became the "special forces" of the medieval period. These brave knights would give their lives for a cause that they (rightly or wrongly) believed to be bigger than their own life.

The Crusader States reached their high point in the 12th century. However, Jerusalem was lost in 1187, when the mighty Islamic commander Saladin managed to seize the capital of the Crusader States.

From this point forward, the Crusader States went into decline.

The crusaders attempted to rally during the Third Crusade, which was launched in 1189. This effort was largely led by a king from England known as Richard the Lionheart. Richard would make remarkable progress and restore lost ground, but he would fall short of reclaiming Jerusalem.

The crusaders' fortunes would then go on to ebb and flow until 1291. That year, the last crusader toehold in the Holy Land—Acre—was overrun. And yes, a group of Templars, Hospitallers, and their auxiliaries defended this final outpost to the bloody, bitter end.

But on May 18th, 1291, Acre was flooded by its enemies. The city's defenders were eventually corned in the Templar House, where they positioned themselves for their final stand. Among them was a large segment of the civilian population. Many others had fled the city before it was too late, but there were still plenty of civilians who remained. They sought the safety of the Templars, Hospitallers, and other knights, all of whom swore to protect them.

The sultan grew weary of the standoff and offered to allow the civilians safe passage as long as they laid down their arms. The knights knew the battle had been lost and decided this would at least allow them to fulfill their pledge to protect the innocent. But accounts say that as soon as their antagonists entered the compound, they began to mercilessly harass the women and children.

Furious and disgusted, the knights picked their swords back up and drove their enemies from their midst, leading to a renewed standoff. This final standoff only ended when the sultan's engineers attempted to blow holes in the walls of the Templar House to gain access. The explosives were too powerful and severely damaged the foundation.

It has been said that immediately after the walls were breached and the enemy forces came pouring in, the whole structure collapsed, killing all inside. In one fell swoop, the crusaders, those under their charge, and a large portion of their opponents were all killed. It was an entirely dramatic way for the Crusades to end.

But as important as the Crusades were to medieval Christianity, they were not the only story of this age. The Western Schism, which took place in 1378, was also of great importance. This schism is not to be confused with the Great Schism of 1054, which separated the Eastern Church from the Western Church. On the contrary, the Western Schism was only within the Catholic Church. A series of popes claimed to be the sovereign of the Roman Catholic Church.

The roots of this rupture stemmed back to 1309 when Pope Clement V decided to move his papal court from Rome to the French city of Avignon because of political instability in the region at the time. However, it would set a precedent, and over the next several decades, a succession of popes would set up shop in Avignon instead of the "Eternal City."

In 1378, Pope Gregory XI decided to establish himself in Rome, just like the popes of old. This fact was resented by the clergy that had grown powerful in Avignon, and bitter backbiting between French and Roman cliques began to unfold. This set the stage for much controversy, especially when Pope Gregory XI abruptly perished that year. Gregory's immediate successor, Pope Urban VI, hailed from the Italian city of Naples.

The French clergy grew increasingly resentful and decided not to recognize the results of the papal election that brought Pope Urban VI to power. They convened in Avignon, where they held an election of their own and brought Pope Clement VII to power. He would preside over the court of Avignon, France. Of course, the Roman Catholic Church could not have two popes, so this presented an obvious dilemma for the church.

Incredibly enough, this situation persisted for about forty years, with one pope being elected in Avignon and another in Rome. Both would claim legitimacy and have their own set of cardinals in their own papal courts. And both sides would seek recognition from the various heads of state around Europe. An attempt was made to address this tumultuous situation in 1409 with the Council of Pisa.

This council determined that the only way to get things back to normal would be to cast off both current claimants and declare the popes in both Avignon and Rome as illegitimate. Then they could start anew. And that is precisely what they did. The church declared that the two popes were fake while nominating a third. However, doing such a thing was easier said than done since the popes in Avignon and Rome refused to step down.

In reality, all the Council of Pisa seemed to accomplish was additional confusion, as three popes now vied for power. The popes that were not recognized by the other factions involved would be labeled as "anti-popes," and the chaos and confusion would continue for some time.

The situation was not cleared up until 1414 when the Council of Constance was held. The pope who had been appointed at the Council of Pisa—Alexander V—had abruptly perished and was replaced by Pope John XXIII. By the time the Council of Constance was held in 1414, Pope John XXIII had fallen out of favor. He was under great pressure and distress and actually tried to escape from his handlers in 1415. However, he was ultimately rounded up, arrested, and officially removed from office. One anti-pope down; two more to go.

The next pope to be taken out was Gregory XII of Rome. The Roman pontiff saw the writing on the wall and decided it was in his best interest to step down. He issued his official resignation later that year. Benedict XIII, the pope in Avignon, tried to stick it out but was forcibly removed in July of 1417, although he continued his papacy in the Kingdom of Aragon (the only place that recognized him). Once all of the "popes" had been subdued, a new official election was held. Martin V was hailed as the one and only pope of the Roman Catholic Church.

After all of this drama came to a close, it seems the Catholic Church learned many things as it pertained to papal elections. It no doubt learned that the more one questions the results, the more trouble it creates in the long run. At any rate, throughout the subsequent centuries, most papal successions were smooth affairs. Even if there were problems, they were nowhere near the controversy that the Western Schism and its anti-popes had brought about.

Interestingly enough, the Council of Constance, which was instrumental in bringing this madness to an end, also sowed the seeds of future tumult for the Catholic Church and Christianity. During this ecumenical council, the excommunication of a great spiritual thinker by the name of Jan Hus took place.

Hus had views that did not correspond with the official doctrine of the Catholic Church. Unlike today, where folks are usually free to "agree to disagree," in the medieval period, if you lived under the dominion of the Catholic Church, any deviation from the faith could not only brand you a heretic but also lead to your death. Hus was executed for what were deemed to be contrary beliefs in regard to the sale of indulgences (the practice of donating money to the church so that certain perceived moral failings or shortcomings could be "indulged").

As we will see in the next chapter, this same criticism would form a cornerstone of Martin Luther's rebellion against the Catholic Church.

Along with criticizing indulgences, Hus also took issue with many other practices of the clergy and insisted that the average Christian should have a more direct relationship with God without the need for intermediaries. Hus paid the ultimate price for his divergence of thought and was burned at the stake.

But Hus's followers, the so-called "Hussites," attempted to carry on his teachings. This would lead to the Hussite Wars, in which the Catholic Church attempted to forcibly squash the movement. More importantly, however, Jan Hus and his followers would set an example and forge a template for what would eventually become a full-fledged reformation of the Christian Church.

Chapter 6: The Protestant Reformation

As it pertains to the Protestant Reformation, the most immediate event that probably comes to mind is the action of Martin Luther nailing his *Ninety-five Theses* to the door of a church in Wittenberg. For many, this one incident seems to crystalize the call to arms to break away from the Catholic Church. But in reality, Martin Luther could hardly have foreseen how profound the fallout from his religious questioning would be.

Because yes, at the end of the day, that was all that Martin Luther was trying to do: he was simply nailing questions, arguments, and suggestions to the door of the cathedral, if that event even happened, as there is no firm evidence to suggest that it did. But regardless, the imagery has stuck, and it makes for some fun comparisons to the modern day, as Luther was like a blogger posting his thoughts for others to see. And the actions of influencers can have larger consequences than they think. When Luther posted his *Ninety-five Theses* to the door of the cathedral, he was not trying to break away from the Catholic Church; he was simply trying to reform it.

The *Ninety-five Theses* he nailed on the door were ninety-five arguments he wished to raise with the Catholic Church, which he believed was in need of some serious reform. At the top of Martin Luther's list was the notion that the church needed to end the sale of indulgences. Indulgences were a Catholic practice for centuries. Sinners were promised that their sins would be somehow nullified or "indulged" if they donated money to the church.

Catholics believed that the pope had the power to lessen one's time in purgatory. If one were to simply donate money to the church, the pope could indulge them or their loved ones and lessen the time that they might spend in the limbo realm of purgatory. Whether or not one believed in Catholic doctrine, the practice had become troublesome enough for many. While some of the money went to supporting charities and hospitals, most of the money went to decorating churches that were already lavish enough or into the pockets of church officials.

As mentioned in the previous chapter, the sale of indulgences had already been questioned by Jan Hus and his Hussites. Luther certainly was not the first to openly wonder whether or not this practice was being done appropriately.

There is, of course, nothing wrong with churches raising money. It makes sense that churches would accept donations since it helps keep them running and allows them to support charities. Churches of all denominations today still raise money on a regular basis. They take money from church members through the collection plate. Mega-churches might even host telethons on TV to accept funds from anyone willing to support their ministry.

The sale of indulgences was frequently used to build and maintain churches. It was not really the fact that churches accepted donations that angered Luther; it was more the way in which they solicited those donations. The priests were so systematic about it and flaunted the notion that people could practically buy their way out of purgatory, which thoroughly bothered the German monk Martin Luther.

And so, this ambitious and thoughtful theologian wanted to do something about it. Luther simply wanted to spark a discussion about current church practices and what could be done to change them. And he certainly sparked a debate. The very next day, Luther was asked to rescind the majority of his arguments.

Interestingly enough, Luther had supposedly nailed his arguments to the church door on October 31st, 1517. The following day, November 1st, was (and still is) a Catholic holiday known as All Saints' Day. October 31st was known as All Saints' Eve and, in some quarters, All Hallows' Eve. Today, of course, we know October 31st by another name: Halloween.

Martin Luther chose October 31st because it was the day before All Saints' Day. He knew that plenty of people would be passing through the doors of the church on that day and be able to read the notes he posted on the door. Luther was simply a savvy marketer, posting his ideas on what was akin to a bulletin board when he knew a bunch of people would be passing by.

Along with railing against indulgences, Luther's key points were about the nature of papal authority. He also argued that one was saved by faith alone with no need whatsoever for good works. Luther argued that indulgences were wrong since all one has to do to be saved was believe in Jesus Christ; a peasant did not have to pay a priest money just to have an easier afterlife. Most Christians today would probably agree with this watered-down version of Luther's thoughts.

But he was also speaking in many generalities as it pertained to the Catholic Church. Catholics did not believe that faith was insufficient; they just believed it was a continuing process. It was believed that some may not have gotten completely right with God in this life, and God was gracious enough to give them an opportunity in the afterlife by purging the process of purgatory. Just as in the Book of Maccabees, which Catholics often quoted and has the living righteous praying for the backslidden dead, Catholic belief hinged on both faith and penance in this life, as well as potential penance in the next.

Martin Luther would end up going to the other extreme, as he wished to excise the whole notion that one should do any works at all. In his later arguments, he even went as far as to suggest that the New Testament Book of James should be removed from the Bible because he took umbrage with the fact that James proclaimed, "Faith without works is dead." Martin Luther later snubbed James by calling it nothing more than an "epistle of straw."

Considering the Catholic point of view in all of this, it is pretty understandable why they looked at Luther with such contempt. The Catholics must have been thinking, "Who was this guy who thought he knew better than everyone else? Even better than Apostle James?"

In Luther's initial arguments, he refrained from criticizing the pope outright. He leveled his primary blame on his subordinates. Luther even stated that he was certain that the pontiff would fix the issues he brought up if he knew about them. The pope would soon learn all about Martin Luther, and there would be consequences for Luther's actions.

Regardless of whether you agree with his theological criticisms or not, one must hand it to Luther for his boldness. In Martin Luther's day, it was not common to openly criticize the church in this manner. Others had lost their lives for less stinging criticism. However, Luther had an ace up his sleeve. He was in good with the local German ruler, the Elector of Saxony, Frederick the Wise.

A little bit of background is required to understand this figure. As mentioned previously in this book, for several centuries, a conglomeration of central and western European states known as the Holy Roman Empire existed. Although Martin Luther was German, spoke German, and wrote German, the nation-state of Germany did not yet exist. It would not exist until 1871.

Back during the Reformation, Germany was a large chunk of the Holy Roman Empire. The interesting thing about the Holy Roman Empire is that it had developed a system of electing its emperors. Scattered throughout the Holy Roman Empire were electors who made up a college, which had the final say in who would become the Holy Roman emperor.

If you are from the United States, the notion of electors serving an integral part of an election likely sounds familiar to you. This is no coincidence. The Founding Fathers of the United States scoured the globe for inspiration when they crafted the framework of how the US should function.

At any rate, in the Holy Roman Empire, these electors wielded formidable power, and no one wanted to get on their bad side. Fortunately for Martin Luther, he was on the good side of the elector of Saxony. So, as much as the pope might have wanted to burn Luther as a heretic, he dared not do so lest he anger this crucial component of the Holy Roman Empire. And Frederick's importance only grew when the sitting head of the Holy Roman Empire, Maximilian I, passed away in January 1519.

Maximilian's grandson was the leading claimant to be the next Holy Roman emperor. But again, even though he was favored, the position was not a straightforward hereditary role. Charles V still had to make sure he received enough backing from all of the electors to ensure his seat on the throne. For this reason, both Charles V and the pope were unwilling to risk alienating Luther's benefactor, the elector of Saxony.

And this was the real reason behind Luther's success. He had a powerful political backer that ensured he would be able to continue to speak his mind. And when Luther was assailed by a prominent Catholic theologian by the name of John Eck, he decided to strike back. He entered into an angry literary exchange with Eck, in which both trounced each other and each other's views.

At one point, Luther even referred to Eck as being nothing more than "an irritated prostitute." All of these angry words culminated in a face-to-face debate in Leipzig in June 1519. During this debate, Luther argued against the infallibility of the pope or any human being and instead urged Christians to depend upon the infallible word of God.

Luther's argument sounds great on the surface. He was basically saying not to worry about the pope's interpretation of things but to open up a Bible and draw your own conclusions (at least, that is, those who were able to read). It was this line of thinking that would create an explosion of countless Protestant denominations, as just about everyone had their own interpretation of just about everything, from how to perform a baptism and Communion to what it actually meant to be saved.

These differences in opinion would ultimately spark bloody persecution and all-out wars, not just between Catholics and Protestants but also between various Protestant denominations that would battle it out to see whose interpretation was "best." This religious persecution led the Pilgrims to pile into the *Mayflower* and head to North America. They were not persecuted by Catholics but by other Protestants.

So, as noble as Luther's efforts might have been, he was truly opening Pandora's box by inviting people other than the pope and trained clergy to interpret the scripture. The Council of Nicaea had been held centuries before to create a universal interpretation of the scripture and a universal creed, yet Martin blew all of that to bits when he gave freedom to himself and his fellow Protestants to interpret the scripture in any way they saw fit.

As had been the case in the 1st and 2nd centuries, matters that had been deemed long settled by the church were now suddenly open for debate. Even Martin Luther, in his later years, would get into heated arguments with other Protestants over just what the scriptures meant. So, playing devil's advocate for the Catholic Church, one can certainly understand why the Catholics might blame Martin Luther for being the source of all of this chaos and confusion.

At any rate, Eck predictably insisted that the pope, as the head of the church, be trusted as the supreme director of the faith. Luther dissented, bringing up the Great Schism of 1054. He pointed out that the Greeks of the Orthodox East had been happy for centuries, and they did not listen to the pope. Luther was still being subtle in his dissent at this point, but in his private writings, he was already referring to the pope as the greatest enemy of Christianity.

After the debate ended, the backlash against Luther was palpable. Many universities began to burn his works and castigated the bold monk for his statements. The ax finally fell in 1520 when the pope sent a papal bull that found forty errors in Luther's beliefs. He gave Luther sixty days to personally appear in Rome to answer for them. If Luther refused to do so, he would be promptly excommunicated.

Despite all of his previous hubris, this was a grim and desperate moment for Martin Luther. He really only had three choices, and all of them would have dramatic consequences. He could choose to go to Rome and throw himself at the pope's feet while begging for forgiveness and promising to correct the "error" of his ways. Even if he decided to do such a thing, there was no guarantee that his image would be fully rehabilitated. If Luther were anything less than penitent and submissive, the outcome likely would not have been good.

Needless to say, if he showed up in Rome and shook his finger in the pope's face and declared the pope to be the anti-Christ, he likely would not have fared too well either. Ultimately, Luther took the third option: he did not go to Rome at all.

This option, of course, meant that after the sixty days were up, he would be officially excommunicated from the church. By deciding to ignore the summons, Luther knew there would be no turning back. He was deemed an enemy of the Catholic Church. Luther was not one to do anything halfway. He decided that if he was the pope's opponent that he would make sure he was the best opponent the pontiff ever had.

As soon as the sixty days had passed, rather than grieve, Luther celebrated. He and his supporters even started a bonfire, tossing the papal bull and other Catholic books into the flames. The pope pushed back more vigorously on January 3rd, 1521, by officially declaring the excommunication of Luther and all who followed him.

In the meantime, the Holy Roman Empire had successfully elected Charles V, who was a staunch Catholic. Charles V convened the famous Diet of Worms and ordered the renegade monk, Martin Luther, to attend. Luther was still being guaranteed protection by the elector of Saxony, so other than another round of condemnations by Catholic theologians, there was really nothing more that anyone could do to him.

The Diet of Worms was held on April 17th, 1521.

The meeting was held with great fanfare, and people gathered from miles around. Initially, Luther was shaken up a bit by the high-profile members of the diet. He ended up asking for more time to consider how to answer questions presented to him. Luther was given another day to think everything over, and he returned on the 18th, visibly more relaxed and ready to play ball.

Although Luther admitted that he had perhaps gone a bit too far with some of his rhetoric, especially as it pertained to personally attacking other religious leaders, he stood by the key tenants of his beliefs. Luther managed to get on the bad side of Holy Roman Emperor Charles V. But Charles was cautious enough not to upset the elector of Saxony, so he held his punches.

Charles V did not go as far as to order any harm done to Martin Luther, but he did officially declare his own personal belief that Martin Luther was a heretic. Although no official call was made to seize Luther, the fact that he had been disparaged by such important figures put his personal safety into question, as any would-be Catholic vigilante might decide to take him out.

As such, Luther knew that he had to tread very carefully. He decided to hide in the friendly confines of Wartburg Castle and even temporarily changed his identity to Junker Jörg or, as it would be rendered in English, Knight George.

In the meantime, Luther's supporters at Wittenberg continued the reform that Martin Luther had begun. Other leaders of the Reformation would emerge elsewhere, such as in Switzerland with the rise of Ulrich Zwingli in 1522. Zwingli's initial form of protest might seem almost comical, but it drove home a point. He simply told his followers to eat some "sausage." The Catholic Church had a tradition of not eating meat just before the advent of Easter (this period is also known as Lent). Zwingli wanted to poke holes in all manner of Catholic traditions, so he began with this one. One can almost imagine him shouting aloud, "The pope does not want us to eat meat before Easter, so let's have some sausages!"

It sounds patently absurd, but this is essentially how Zwingli's major movement toward reform first gained steam. And Zwingli was deadly serious about his beliefs. He was serious enough to fight for them. This Protestant reformer ended up perishing at the head of a literal army in

1531. If Catholics feared that all hell would break loose if folks just haphazardly interpreted the scripture any way they chose, this would have been a perfect moment for them to have pointed the finger and declared, "I told you so!"

The Anabaptists of Switzerland also squabbled and came to blows over the proper means of baptism. They argued against the Catholic practice of baptizing babies and were willing to die for this belief. Many of them did. The city of Zurich began cracking down on the Anabaptists, and in their persecution, many were rounded up and forcibly drowned out of anger over the practice of baptism.

Many Anabaptists would flee to the United States, where they founded communities. Their descendants still carry out their traditions in Mennonite and Amish communities.

These were some of the initial main reformers of the Protestant Reformation, but more reforms would soon follow, especially in France and England.

Chapter 7: Religious Reform in France and England

France's reformation may have come a little later than that of Germany, Switzerland, and other regions, but it was just as powerful. The French Reformation was led by a firebrand French preacher by the name of John Calvin. Calvin was a little younger than Luther at the time of his rise to prominence, and it is perhaps his youthful exuberance that explains his willingness to push things much further than Martin Luther ever dared to do.

Martin Luther had carefully pried open the door for change, and radicals like Calvin were the ones who charged right through the open doorway. John Calvin began his life in the French town of Picardy, just north of Paris. His family was a prominent one, so they were sure to give their son a good education. They sent him off to the University of Paris, where he initially set out to study law. Calvin switched gears after his dad passed away, deciding to study Hebrew and Greek instead.

He developed his skills in the two main languages of the Bible, which would allow him to better understand the intricate interpretations of the scripture. After the Reformation erupted, Calvin began to apply this knowledge to his own interpretations of religion. By the 1530s, Calvin had become fully devoted to the cause of religious reform. However, as a leader of religious dissent, things became a bit too difficult for him in Paris, with the king of France deciding to push back against religious reform. This prompted Calvin to run off to Basel, Switzerland.

Switzerland, which had been the launching pad for Zwingli, was already a powerful bastion for reformers. Calvin sought refuge here, heading to the Protestant town of Strasbourg before setting up shop in Geneva. In Geneva, in 1536, Calvin published his famous work, *Institutes of the Christian Religion.*

Here, Calvin set forth his beliefs. Chief among them was the idea that the true knowledge of God could only be gained from one's own interpretation of the Bible. According to Calvin, one could not find God through reason and logic but instead needed a personal connection to the word of God. Furthermore, unlike Martin Luther, who at times wished to excise various books of the Bible that did not line up with his own viewpoints, Calvin insisted that all of the scripture was sacred and that none of it should be omitted.

He also put a much heavier emphasis on the Old Testament than other reformers. But the most famous belief Calvin developed was his notion that everything was preordained. He believed that God, being omniscient, must know in advance who would gain salvation and who would turn their back on their creator. This theory of everyone being predestined for either salvation or damnation would become known as "predestination," and it became a key Calvinist belief.

In many ways, Calvin's idea of predestination makes sense. If God is an omniscient, all-powerful being outside of space and time, it makes sense that he would know how everything would play out. It would be like one of us sitting in front of a cartoon strip and being able to clearly see the beginning and the end of it.

For some, this creates a problem because they feel it negates free will. But really, it just depends on your interpretation. A Calvinist does not believe that we are all pre-programmed robots that God set in motion. We still have free will, and it is still us making choices. But God is literally outside of space, time, and all human experience, so Calvinists believe he already knows what we are all going to do.

If one were to dig even deeper, one could find scripture to bolster this argument. The New Testament champions the idea that God knew that Adam and Eve would choose to rebel against him ahead of time, stating that Christ was the "Lamb slain from the foundation of the world" (Revelation 13:8).

At any rate, when this notion that God knew from the very beginning who would do what was presented to the masses, this teaching caused quite a bit of consternation and chaos. And it wasn't just people outside of the Calvinist fold. Suddenly, Calvinists became utterly consumed with trying to figure out which side of the predestination scales they might be on. They went on frantic, neurotic quests to figure out whether or not they were destined to be saved or doomed to be damned. This worry and fear caused so much consternation in the Calvinist movement that steps had to be made to encourage all Calvinist believers to stop worrying over their predestination and simply do all they could to live a good Christian life.

Yes, what should have been the goal of all Christians in the first place had to be painstakingly reintroduced to the Calvinists so they could once again sleep peacefully at night. It makes one appreciate the biblical admonition to "lean not to your own understanding" (Proverbs 3:5). It seems that every time a great thinker of the Reformation introduced a bold new understanding of scripture, the Protestant masses erupted in chaos, as they were confused or worried about how that belief impacted them.

After some of the confusion of predestination died down, Calvin was able to establish a strong church hierarchy in Geneva, complete with pastors, teachers, elders, and deacons. These were the "fourfold ministry" that Calvin believed to have been revealed by the scripture. To Calvin's credit, Geneva soon became what has been termed a model Christian commonwealth. The success of Geneva would serve as an inspiration to others, including the growing Protestant movement in England.

England was a different beast when it came to public sentiment and the attitudes of the royals. England had some upswelling of Protestantism, but by and large, the majority of the English were still Catholic. And more importantly, their king, Henry VIII, was a very staunch Catholic. In fact, King Henry had been dubbed the "Defender of the Faith" by the pope. He earned this title by publishing writing that railed against Martin Luther and condemned the Reformation.

Henry had no problem at all with Catholic belief until the pope's authority crimped his style as it pertained to his personal life. You see, Henry desperately wanted a son, as he wanted a male heir to succeed him on the throne. His first wife, Catherine of Aragon, seemed unable to give him one. So, Henry wished for an annulment. As Catholic tradition dictated, he had to look to the pope for permission.

Granting such an annulment would have been no easy thing for the pope since Henry's wife was Holy Roman Emperor Charles V's aunt! The pope knew that if he granted the annulment, he would have to deal with Charles V's wrath. However, the pope did not wish to anger either monarch. He tried to play out the clock, not giving a direct answer either way. But as the pope dithered, it became clearer to Henry that he would not get what he wanted. So, King Henry began to turn his back on the pope.

The first real break occurred in 1534 when King Henry issued an edict known as the Act of Supremacy, which sought to negate the pope's authority. Henry declared himself the supreme head of the Church of England. In other words, Henry had officially broken away from the Catholic Church. And as Henry began to turn away from the papacy, English reformers, such as Thomas Cromwell and Thomas Cranmer, began to come to prominence as they advocated for change. However, for the most part, the Church of England was very similar to the Catholic Church.

Henry had his own problems to deal with, though. He married another woman, Anne Boleyn (the two actually married in 1533, the same year Thomas Cranmer annulled his marriage to Catherine of Aragon). His new wife proved just as unable to give him the son he so desperately craved. Infuriated, Henry put away his wife and had her beheaded on trumped-up charges of sedition. Henry then married a woman named Jane Seymour, who succeeded where others had failed, giving birth to a boy named Edward. To Henry's great grief, his beloved Jane perished shortly afterward.

Even so, the widowed Henry did not take long to remarry, wedding Anne of Cleves next. This marriage would be incredibly brief. After just a few months, Henry backed out of it, using his newfound powers over the church and state to render this latest marriage null and void.

Henry then went on to marry a lady named Catherine Howard. She would be accused of adultery and lost her head. And finally, Henry married Catherine Parr, who would stay by Henry's side until he died.

King Henry was aghast at some of the reforms taking place in his own backyard, and the old "defender of the faith" decided to take a stand against the multiple interpretations of scripture that were being made.

He issued another edict, the Act for the Advancement of True Religion. This act apparently took up the old biblical injunction to "lean to your own understanding," as it stated that there should be limits on who had access to scripture so that folks would not run around developing a multiplicity of ideas.

Just like the Catholic Church, Henry wished to make sure his subjects stuck to the same doctrine and interpretation rather than drawing their own conclusions. The fact that King Henry had broken from the pope yet still sought to take similar measures of control that the Catholic Church had sworn by for centuries led many Protestant reformers to understandably grumble that the reforms were not going far enough.

But after King Henry's passing in 1547, the reformers would have their chance to reshape religion in England. The country would ultimately become largely Protestant-leaning as a result, especially under Queen Elizabeth I.

Section Three: Key Christian Themes

Chapter 8: Catholic Saints

The Catholic Church has long been known for its adoration of saints. It is a source of great pride for those who adhere to the Catholic faith while also often being a source of derision for those who do not. Catholics are sometimes derided by Protestants for praying to dead saints, but Catholics take pride in their belief that the venerable spirits of the saints who have left this mortal coil can still be a source of good in this world today.

The first great saint of the Catholic Church—at least of those outside of the official biblical canon—is no doubt the theological giant Saint Augustine of Hippo. Saint Augustine lived during a pivotal time, during the 5th century when the traditional Roman Empire was in decline. Rome was being threatened on all sides, and at one point, it was even sacked.

Augustine wrote his epic work *On the City of God Against the Pagans* to explain why such things might happen. At first glance at the title of his treatise, one might think that Augustine was promoting Rome as the city of God. But this was not the case. Augustine was instead urging Catholics to lift their eyes away from Rome and look toward the eternal "City of God," which had not yet been experienced by humanity.

Augustine was pivotal in fashioning much of what the Catholic Church would crystalize as its official doctrine. Interestingly enough, Augustine had something for the later Calvinists who believed in predestination and those who abhorred them because it seemed to erase the concept of free will. As it turns out, all the way back in the 5th century, Augustine wrote that "God orders all things while preserving human freedom."

Yes, Augustine believed in the omniscience of God's knowledge and the agency of human freedom to fulfill what God essentially already knows. Saint Augustine had views on original sin, grace, and the nature of evil, which would be highly influential on the Roman Catholic Church. Augustine also had some intriguing views about the nature of God and the state of time and space.

Augustine was one of the first to suggest that God was literally outside of space and time. He explained eternity to be a timeless state outside of the human timeframe as we know it. Augustine was obviously a deep thinker, and his mind frequently plumbed the depths of the greatest mysteries of existence.

But at the end of the day, Augustine knew that certain questions could not be answered, but he still could not help but wonder. He never lost his sense of wonder or his sense of humor when considering the nature of creation. On one occasion, he made what was perhaps one of the greatest wisecracks of any great Catholic theologian.

He was musing about people who might ask what God was doing before creation. Yes, what was the creator of the universe up to before the universe was created? The idea seems hopelessly unanswerable and even absurd. *What was God doing?* Can we picture the creator just kicking back, taking it easy?

Augustine had a great answer to this question. When he was asked what God was doing before creation, he suggested, "Preparing hell for those who pry too deep!" as if there was a special compartment of purgatory for folks who were too inquisitive for their own good. All joking aside, Augustine was as inquisitive as anyone, and he relished pondering mysteries on a regular basis.

Another Catholic saint who was highly influential was Thomas Aquinas. Thomas Aquinas was steeped in his Catholic faith and had been gifted with a powerful sense of logic and deductive reasoning. Aquinas was a follower of the ancient Greek philosopher Aristotle and sought to apply the wisdom of such ancient thinkers to his day and age.

His penchant for ancient philosophers occasionally got him in trouble with his religious peers, but by and large, the genius of his synthesis has come to be recognized. The interesting thing about Aquinas was that he believed many aspects of life could be figured out through reason. However, he did acknowledge that logic and reason were insufficient to realize the most profound mysteries of life, such as the nature of God and the origin of the universe.

Aquinas believed that for the most unfathomable of questions, logic fell short and that only faith and divine revelation could suffice. In pondering the greatest of mysteries, Aquinas also listed five positive statements about the nature of God. Aquinas stated that "God is simple, without composition of parts, such as body and soul, or matter and form. God is perfect, lacking nothing. God is infinite, and not limited in the ways that created beings are physically, intellectually, and emotionally limited. God is immutable, incapable of change in respect of essence and character. God is one, such that God's essence is the same as God's existence."

Aquinas also argued over what he saw as five rational proofs for the existence of God. One of his most famous was the notion that there was an "unmoved mover." "Everything that is moved is moved by a mover, therefore there is an unmoved mover from whom all motion proceeds, which is God." Aquinas saw the universe in motion and rationally deduced that something must have caused it to go into motion. In his mind, it made sense that the mover would be the still, unchangeable, unmovable God.

Another great figure of the Catholic Church was Saint Francis of Assisi. Saint Francis hailed from a wealthy family and began life as a seeker of material comfort. However, he would reach a crossroads as a young man, as he would have visions of God telling him to "rebuild the church."

Francis gave up his material wealth and began to live a life of monkish modesty. He initially took the commands he heard of rebuilding the church as literal ones. At one point, Francis was begging on the street for stones and other building materials to help repair a dilapidated local church. Francis would start his own order of monks and came to realize that he was meant to rebuild not just a building but also the entire framework of the Roman Catholic Church.

There are many interesting anecdotal tales of Francis's gentleness and kindness. He is especially known for his love for animals. Francis was said to have been able to literally commune with nature. He stood in the wilderness preaching to birds and other woodland creatures.

There is also an interesting tale about when a wolf attacked local villagers. The villagers wanted to hunt down and kill the beast, but Francis supposedly went right up to the wolf and soothed the animal with just a few words. Thereafter, the wolf was as tame as a dog and a favorite pet of the village.

Whereas theological giants like Augustine and Aquinas are known for their treatises, Aquinas is remembered and relished as a man who was a living example of what a good Christian should be. Through his own personal actions, he demonstrated the great depth of God's love.

Chapter 9: Religious Expansion and Global Outreach

The expedition that led to the European discovery of the Americas in 1492 had religion as one of its catalysts. Spain had long been waging a bloody Reconquista to reclaim territories that had previously been seized by Islamic armies. In 1492, the very last Muslim enclave of Grenada had been conquered by the Spaniards, bringing the Reconquista to a close.

The Reconquista was immediately followed by one of the darkest periods in Christian history: the Inquisition. There would be several versions of the Inquisition, with the main ones taking place in Spain, Rome, and Portugal. Spain would largely be ground zero for religious intolerance of the worst kind.

Just prior to the close of the Reconquista, Spain had been a multicultural/multireligious melting pot of Jews, Christians, and Muslims. However, once the Christian powers retook the Iberian Peninsula, they were determined to make sure that Christianity was the unquestioned religion of the land. Jews, subsequently known as "conversos," were forced to convert, as were the Muslims, who were known as "moriscos."

But ultimately, these forced conversions were not good enough for the Christian authorities, who suspected that many of these conversions were false. So, in 1492, an inquisition—or inquiry—was made into who was a Christian and who was not. In the first wave of the Spanish Inquisition, which was kickstarted in 1492, Jews and conversos were mercilessly targeted, leading to torture, death, and a massive expulsion.

Spanish monarchs Ferdinand and Isabella, who were responsible for starting the Spanish Inquisition, financed Christopher Columbus to set sail to find a westward passage to Asia (as you might already know, money and new resources were also major catalysts for discovering the Americas). However, Columbus and his crew were not looking to find the Americas; they inadvertently stumbled upon the Caribbean islands. Columbus would go to his deathbed thinking he had sailed to India, but the enormity of the discovery would soon be realized and exploited.

There were those looking for monetary gain in the New World, but there were also those who were avidly seeking converts. Missions soon popped up all over the New World, and the Catholic doctrine, as well as the languages of Spanish and Portuguese, were being vigorously taught to the inhabitants. New World settlements began in the Caribbean and then moved to Mexico, Central America, and South America.

Everywhere the Europeans went, they brought the cross, the sword, and diseases. One of the most dramatic instances of forced conversion happened during the toppling of the Aztec Empire in Mexico. The Aztecs had a religious system in place that the Spanish conquistadors viewed as appalling. And to be fair, Aztec religious practices would be appalling to modern sensibilities as well.

Unless you are a fan of human sacrifice, you likely would not have enjoyed what the Aztec priests did. The Aztecs had a long-held tradition of a priest standing on top of one of their majestic temples and ripping out the still-beating heart of a sacrificial victim. The blood of this poor victim would stream down the grand steps of the temple for all to see.

What was the reason for all of this? The Aztecs believed that if they did not engage in daily human sacrifice, the sun would cease to rise and set, and the world would come to an end. More specifically, they believed that a hungry sun god by the name of Huitzilopochtli needed fresh blood and human hearts to ensure that the sun could travel across the skies unhindered.

It is unclear how and when they convinced themselves of such a thing. We also are not sure how often these sacrifices took place.

The Aztecs were a mighty force in the region, and at the time of the Spanish conquest, they had brought just about every neighboring tribe under their dominion. It has been theorized that as the power of the Aztecs grew, the human sacrifices took on not only a religious meaning but also a political or psychological one.

At any rate, by the time the Spanish arrived on the scene, the Aztecs were apparently sacrificing folks in great vigor, although it is possible the Spanish saw one or two ceremonies and assumed that the Aztecs did it daily. When the Christians saw such a thing in practice, it was quite easy for them to peg the Aztecs as a bunch of heretics of the worst sort. So, it is really no surprise when these religious zealots from Iberia engineered the downfall of the Aztecs and instituted a colonial Catholic government in its place.

But the conquest of the conquistadors is perhaps not as dramatic as it is sometimes presented. The key to their success was toppling the leadership of those they conquered. The Aztec imperial line had been extinguished. Additionally, the Aztec leaders had been quite ruthless to the common people over which they ruled. The average citizen's life was not easy. As such, it was fairly easy for the Spanish to convince the population, especially those from rival tribes, that the abolition of this government they did not like (and did not want to be sacrificed for) was in their best interest.

If the Aztec government had been popular with the average citizen, one could imagine a prolonged guerilla war and a much greater struggle. But this was not the case. After the downfall of the Aztec government, some of the local indigenous people flocked to the Spaniards' religion, Christianity. Perhaps helping them in their decision to leave their old faith was the pure and simple fact that the world didn't end.

After the Spaniards ended the practice of human sacrifice, it became quite clear to the indigenous people that the sun continued to rise and set. It was also clear that the Aztec leaders had either lied to them or were incredibly deluded. Considering as much, it is no wonder that the new religion of Christianity might have seemed appealing to them.

But to say that all indigenous people immediately gravitated toward Christianity would be false. There were plenty of locals who resented the religion that had been foisted upon them. There were also some instances of violent rebellions against religious enforcers. The most common form of rebellion was much more subtle and involved fusing indigenous beliefs with Christianity.

This fusion of cultures was probably best demonstrated in the vision of the Virgin of Guadalupe. Around 1531, in Mexico City, the Virgin Mary was supposedly seen by some of the local populace. Rather than scoffing at such a thing, the local Catholic authorities were impressed. They believed in the absolute sincerity of those who told them of the vision, and it became an established miracle of the Catholic Church. At the forefront of much of the religious undertaking in the New World was the Jesuits. The Jesuits were founded by the visionary and mystic Saint Ignatius of Loyola and were determined to establish missions throughout the New World, which would serve as focal points of the faith. The Iberian cousins of the Spaniards, the Portuguese, also made great efforts to convert the natives.

The Portuguese not only founded Brazil in South America but also several outposts in Africa and Asia. The Portuguese famously sailed all the way to India in 1498, stating that they were in search of "spices and Christians." It might seem a rather odd statement to make, but many Europeans had heard rumors of Christian communities existing in the Far East, and these Portuguese explorers wished to find them.

And they did find a small isolated community of Christians that supposedly dated all the way back to the efforts of Apostle Thomas, who allegedly traveled to the Far East. The Portuguese went on to establish an outpost in India called Goa. This would become a trading outpost and a forward base for the spreading of Catholicism.

The Jesuits would play a major role in the outpost of Goa as well, as Jesuit mission leader Francis Xavier would arrive on the scene in the early 1500s. Francis worked with a group of locals known as the Paravas, who lived in fishing communities on the coast. This group had seen massive conversions and showed an interest early on. Xavier worked to increase their understanding of the Catholic faith, teaching them the proper use of sacraments and the Nicene Creed. Xavier's efforts were quite successful, and he carried on his work in Sri Lanka and eventually Japan.

The missionary efforts of Catholics were indeed aggressive during this period, but the Protestants would not go unchallenged. However, their approach would be markedly different. The Protestant missionary outreach often worked seemingly in reverse of the Catholic one.

While the Catholic missionaries usually had the official backing of the Vatican and their national governments, the Protestants were more likely to be fleeing from their governments. Some of the first North American colonies were founded in an attempt to set up religious societies free from the control of the English Crown. Some would even refer to these outposts as "shining cities on a hill" in reference to Christ's words in the New Testament that likened Christians to much the same thing—a light for all the world to see and pattern themselves after.

A group of religious diehards known as the Puritans, named for their notions of keeping their faith and religious practices pure and true to form, made their way to North America in large numbers in the 1630s. They sought religious freedom and came in massive numbers; some historians have dubbed it the "swarming of the Puritans."

Since they were far away from England and its control, they were able to set up their own version of society, which they called the "Holy Commonwealth." The first governor of this commonwealth—John Winthrop—was the one who made the famous notion of America being a "shining city on a hill." Winthrop would go down in history as stating, "We must consider that we shall be as a city upon a hill, the eyes of all the people are upon us."

These religious pilgrims knew that everyone was watching their little project and that it was up to them to make sure that it was successful. The Puritans lived and breathed the scripture, and they likened themselves to the "Children of Israel," a reference to the Old Testament of the Bible, with whom God had made a covenant. The Puritans felt that they had been given a special charter by the Almighty to establish themselves in a new land.

Of course, we must remember that this land was already inhabited. But unlike the brutal conquest of the conquistadors, these religious pilgrims would not initially take their lands through violence. There were certainly conflicts in this early stage of colonization, but it was not on the scale of what was being done in Mexico and Central and South America. These religious pilgrims were not hellbent on conquering people. That was not why they came to North America.

The widescale oppression of Native Americans in North America would not occur until an official government structure was established and standing armies were brought over, which would slowly push the Native Americans westward. And the next wave of religious pilgrims from England—the Quakers—were even more pacificist than the Puritans.

In the late 1600s, led by William Penn, this group of religious freedom seekers would end up founding Pennsylvania. It is well known that William Penn had excellent relations with neighboring Native American tribes. In line with Quaker beliefs, Penn believed that all human beings had a spark of God within them, something the Quakers called the "inner light of God."

In that sense, everyone was naturally united as brothers and sisters of creation. And it is no coincidence that Penn named the capital of what would become Pennsylvania "Philadelphia." This was a reference to the older Greek city of the same name, but the meaning of the name also reflects Penn's values. The Greek translation of "Philadelphia" is "city of brotherly love."

After Penn passed away in 1718, relations began to break down, and a long, sad history of bloodshed and oppression would erupt. The interesting thing about William Penn and the Quakers is that they displayed a surprising degree of religious tolerance. Although they were quite serious about their own personal beliefs, they did not believe in forcing them on others. The Quakers felt that if one were to accept religious truths, one had to accept them of their own accord; they could not be forced down people's throats.

So, unlike the Puritans, who were hellbent on "purifying" the religious beliefs of others, the Quakers invited all manner of religious denominations to live in their communities. The Quaker faithful had been persecuted back in England (and they were persecuted to an extent in the New World), so they knew how important religious tolerance was.

One of the persecuted denominations of Europe who found refuge in Pennsylvania was the German-speaking Anabaptists. These people would later become known as the Pennsylvania Dutch.

France, in the meantime, would remain staunchly Catholic, although, by the 1700s, there was an increasingly popular movement known as Deism. The Deists believed that there must be some sort of higher power, but they believed that the evidence for this supreme being was available to all simply by looking at nature itself. Even before any knowledge of the "big bang theory," Deists were convinced that the universe could not have just popped into existence from nothing and that there must be a creating agent behind it. It is simple but profound logic. We exist; therefore, there must have been something that made us exist.

However, the Deists did not believe in what they termed "manmade religion." The Deists sought to tear down what they viewed as artificial, manmade constructs when considering this omniscient deity. The Deists sought to broaden the horizons of conventional faith. It has often been said that the movement toward Deism could have been a direct consequence of previous missionary outreaches to far-flung parts of the globe.

As Christian missionaries sought to "enlighten" various peoples of other religions, some of these missionaries came away from the exchange as the ones receiving enlightenment. In other words, the religious and mystical ideas of other religions began to convince some Christians that there were real kernels of wisdom available in other faiths. And if other faiths could be so wise, was that not proof that the creator had shown himself in countless ways to countless people all over the world? Those were the sort of questions that a Deist would ask.

Rather than believing in the New Testament scripture that states the path to heaven (enlightenment) is a narrow one, the Deists began to believe that enlightenment was essentially on top of a mountain. And there were several winding roads that might lead one to the top. French writer Voltaire was a famous proponent of Deism, and after the French Revolution, many French intellectuals became Deists. The notorious general-turned-dictator Napoleon Bonaparte was known for his Deist beliefs.

Back in North America in the 18th century, a religious revival was occurring under John Wesley and his Methodists. The Methodists, just like the Puritans and the Quakers, did not name their own movement. Just like their predecessors, their names began as derisive epithets that were given to them by their opponents. Those who did not appreciate the efforts of Wesley and his followers sarcastically called them "Methodists" because Wesley had prescribed methods for prayer, fasting, praise, and everything in between.

And just like many other derided faiths, the Methodists took what was meant as an insult and wore it as a badge of honor. Yes, they would come to be proud of their peculiar methodology and sought to spread their Methodist notions far and wide. Major progress was made in 1784 when Wesley appointed a man by the name of Thomas Coke as bishop.

Around the same time, the passionate evangelism of Henry Alline was gaining notice in the northern reaches of Canada. Alline spoke from the heart, and his evangelical fervor would become known as evangelicalism.

Evangelicalism was opposed to what was viewed as the cold logic and reasoning of previous movements, such as the Calvinists and Puritans. This movement was more about personal experiences and one's connection to God rather than methodical reasoning. Alline's evangelicals would soon spread farther south, and the so-called "evangelical movement" would become one of the main threads in the tapestry of

American Christianity. It has been argued that the American Revolution kicked off just as the evangelical movement first gained steam. It has been suggested that evangelical calls for freedom of expression were another factor in stimulating the cause for making a final break with England.

All of these religious movements in North America began with religious freedom in mind, and they would be in prime position after the American Revolution came to an official close in 1783. All would be prepped and primed for further religious growth as the new century of the 1800s dawned.

Section Four: Modern Christianity (1800–Present Day)

Chapter 10: The Many Faces of Christianity and the Separation of Church and State

Although at various times, Christian authority figures have attempted to suppress new strands of interpretation, there has always been a multiplicity of faces of the Christian faith. This potential for multiple interpretations has always been a source of strength and a source of conflict in the Christian Church.

During the 1st and 2nd centuries, religious views were extremely diverse. This diversity often led to confusion. If just about every sect had a different view of the divinity of Christ, what was one to believe? The desire for the uniformity of the faith and a so-called "universal" or "Catholic" church led Emperor Constantine to call for the Council of Nicaea, in which a standard and uniform doctrine was encapsulated within the Nicene Creed.

The creed was the glue that held Christian beliefs together for centuries, with only one great crack occurring in 1054 when the Eastern Church and Western Church split. The Western Church would hold the faith together quite well until a German monk by the name of Martin Luther called for reform. His teachings on reform and, most importantly, justification by faith alone sent shockwaves through the Catholic Church.

The Reformation led to new splinter groups of Christian belief. Initially, the Protestants predominantly hailed from the far northern reaches of Europe. It is interesting to note that the oldest bastions of Catholicism in southern Europe, such as Spain, Portugal, France, and Italy, would remain Catholic while those countries that had more recently converted to Christianity in the far north (just think of the Norse Vikings of Scandinavia) were the quickest to switch from Catholicism to Protestantism.

Many faces of Christianity developed, and these faces would soon find themselves taking up shop in the New World and farther afield, with Christian expansion reaching a global level. Although Mexico, Central America, and South America would be the "beneficiaries" of a massive conversion program to Catholicism, North America remained an interesting experiment in the diversity of religion. North America would not have one predominant Christian religion; rather, it would be home to a multitude of Christian faiths.

The sheer diversity of religious beliefs in North America led the Founding Fathers of what would become the United States to make freedom of religion an important tenant of the Constitution. The idea that the government should not infringe upon one's own personal beliefs would lead the United States down the road of what would become known as the separation of church and state.

Thomas Jefferson, a Founding Father who wrote the Declaration of Independence, viewed the long history of conflicts over rather trivial religious differences. He famously stated that the religious beliefs of the individual "neither picks my pocket nor breaks my leg." In other words, as long as religion stayed in the private sector and state law stayed out of religion, then the government could just focus on being an able and just administrator. And as long as no one infringed on the rights of someone else and followed the laws of the nation, one should be allowed to have their own personal beliefs.

This strain of thought emerged in the US Constitution's First Amendment, which, along with ensuring free speech and several other freedoms, also insisted on the freedom of religion. Unlike many of America's European predecessors, there would be no established national religion in the United States. Still, for a country steeped in Christianity, it was not always easy to find that sweet spot of neutrality.

In an effort to find more neutral footing, many of the Founding Fathers looked toward ancient Greece and Rome for inspiration. It is for this reason that so many aspects of the US capital reflect the civic symbols of antiquity, as they were largely a means of moving away from the polarizing aspects of religion. These symbols, of course, predate Christianity and can be viewed as being neutral or even ambiguous.

Just think of the back of a US dollar bill. There are no crosses or other religious symbols but vague symbolism, such as pyramids, obelisks, and eagles. And contrary to popular belief, the phrase "In God We Trust" was added to US currency recently. The phrase was approved under the Eisenhower administration and did not appear on paper money until 1957.

Much of the inspiration for putting this phrase on money back then was said to have been out of a surge of religious fervor during the height of the Cold War. It was a dark and scary period, as people feared that a nuclear holocaust could be unleashed at any moment. As is usually the case in such dark times, religion was a great source of comfort.

Although most Americans approve or do not care about the statement, there have been any dissenters. People state that the placement of such a motto on government currency is a clear violation of the separation of church and state. Interestingly enough, in official defense of the phrase, the notion of "ceremonial deism" has been invoked. This involves the argument that vague references to a higher deity are allowed as long as all distinct religious affiliations have been removed. Thus, one can speak of God as long as they are not too specific as to the nature of the deity that has been invoked. Every American is free to create their own interpretation and view the invoked deity through their own theological lens.

At any rate, the separation of church and state was championed by Thomas Jefferson, who would go on to be elected America's third president. He would serve from 1801 to 1809 and helped ensure that the trend for the separation of church and state, which he had long envisioned, would continue.

Chapter 11: Christian Conformists and Conspiracies of the 19th Century

The 19th century was most certainly a century of change, as advancements in science, technology, and cultural understanding were made and shaped the latest strains of religious thought. After all, the 19th century was the century that saw the rise of Charles Darwin and the subsequent atheistic beliefs that would follow. Atheists sought to describe the advent of the universe as the product of natural evolution with no intelligent designer behind it, although it must be noted that Darwin never saw himself as an atheist.

The changes in mainstream thought in the 19th century continue to have ramifications on religious discourse to this very day. Even though not everyone believed in evolution back then (and even today), the 19th century promoted a strong brand of Christian secularism. Christianity was viewed in more symbolic and general terms than it had been in the past.

To be sure, there were still plenty of literalists out there, but in the 19th century, secularization first received widespread popularity. After the end of the Napoleonic Wars in 1815, much of the Christian West changed. Protestant lands in the European north and in North America began to lead the way for even more religious reforms.

In that same fateful year of 1815, the first evangelical bishop was appointed in North America. Evangelicals of this period began to turn away from theological debates and religious doctrine and focused more on ways to improve society. In contrast to Martin Luther's dislike of the emphasis on "works," this new strain of evangelicals had come to agree with Apostle James's words all those years ago when he emphatically stated that "faith without works is dead."

Evangelical Christians of the 19th century led the charge in the establishment of charitable works, such as orphanages, schools, aid for the poor, and treatment for the sick. These efforts would be crystalized by the formation of the Peace Society in 1828, which championed many of these causes. It seems that there was a decision to move away from theological debates and instead lead by example.

Even more imperative, many came to believe that it was incumbent upon Christians to make Earth just a little bit more like heaven. Christians needed to work to establish the kingdom of heaven on Earth in the present so that it would be ready and waiting for Christ when he returned. These were some pretty lofty goals for the 19th-century church, but many were eager to see them fulfilled.

Some were more militant than others, with some even creating their own "army." This was the case with British evangelical William Booth, who founded the Salvation Army. The Salvation Army was a charitable organization dedicated to the uplifting of the poor and the betterment of society. Taking on the trappings of a literal military host, to this day, the bell ringers of the Salvation Army ask for donations on street corners and can sometimes be seen decked out in military-style uniforms.

At this point, North America, in particular, had a peculiar problem. Although good works were being carried out, even the most obtuse of evangelical Christians could not fail to recognize the terrible bad works that were afoot in the Western world in the form of slavery. If Christ was going to come, they reasoned he most certainly would not return to a country practicing slavery.

Soon enough, evangelicals led the cause to abolish slavery once and for all. British evangelicals succeeded in this goal before their American counterparts. Britain had abolished slavery throughout its empire (including in Canada) by the 1830s. It would take America another thirty years to do the same thing. The interesting thing about the evangelical movement and the desire to abolish slavery is that sentiments were divided in America.

In Britain, the evangelicals presented a united front in standing up to slavery. But over in America, the Northern evangelicals and the Southern evangelicals were split over the issue. While the North churned out an endless stream of Christian abolitionists, Southerners, who were deeply wedded to the slave culture, were much more hesitant to get involved. Even after the Civil War came to a close in 1865 and slavery was abolished, a palpable split would remain between Northern and Southern Christians.

Charles Darwin's work *On the Origin of Species* had been published in 1859, enticing many Christians to give up on Christianity altogether. For the first time, many considered an alternative explanation for their reason for being. Some began to speculate that life was just the product of a natural evolutionary process from an otherwise eternal universe.

At any rate, both non-Christians and even some Christians were captivated by Charles Darwin's research. However, a rather dangerous philosophical belief (at least in regards to religion) arose from his scientific explanations. Rather than depending upon a benevolent God, Darwin described all of life as a product of the environment and that the success of one organism over another was the result of "survival of the fittest."

According to Darwin, one's environment and conditions for living are what shape and hone any given organism, and it was merely the game of survival that makes species what they are. This mindset led to something called social Darwinism. And the notion of social Darwinism would create some very dangerous ideas. With God taken out of the equation, some would take Darwin's observations of "survival of the fittest" and work them into an extreme ideology that asserted only the fittest should be allowed to survive.

Of course, these ideas are quite contrary to the old Christian ideals of charity and caring for the sick and poor. The social Darwinists, like some puffed-up lions prowling the savannah, would take it upon themselves to pounce on the afflicted, and rather than help them, they actively worked on finishing them off. It sounds like the plot of some disturbing dystopian novel in which folks of the future fling wheelchair-bound patients off cliffs simply because they were not "fit" enough.

The ugly side of humanity surfaced as a direct result of Darwin's theories. It must be noted that there is no proof that Darwin himself supported social Darwinism. For the most part, Darwin applied his theories strictly to the biological level. Others, most notably fellow biologist and philosopher Herbert Spencer, took the leap and applied it to social constructs on a massive scale.

Nevertheless, Charles Darwin's findings inspired many to turn away from the Christian faith. Further scientific and even archaeological discoveries also delivered blows to the religion. The discovery of dinosaur bones and the development of carbon dating suggested that Earth had existed for billions of years (rather than the ten thousand or so years conceived by many theologians), which would confuse and dismay many believers.

It suddenly seemed as if there was a whole epoch of history for which the Bible did not account. Nevertheless, as Apostle John said in the Gospel of John, if everything Christ did (let alone everything God did before the creation of humanity) had been recorded in the scripture, the Bible would have to be much bigger to contain all of the information.

Having said that, most Christians today accept that Earth is indeed billions of years old and acknowledge the existence of dinosaurs. These Christians tend to look at the scripture as something that was compiled as a need-to-know basis for humanity. Human beings did not need to know about dinosaurs, so the Bible did not mention it. Others view the stories in the Bible as stories and not truths; for instance, they don't believe Adam and Eve were necessarily the first humans. Instead, they believe the stories impart important truths to apply to their lives. In the case of Adam and Eve, God will grant good and wondrous things if one only believes and follows his instructions.

In this sense, Christians have come to put a laser focus on God's plan of salvation and how it directly reflects on them. They accept that there are many things that we do not know and might never know. Yet, at the same time, they believe we do not need to know everything. As many mainline Christians today might tell you, all you need to know is Jesus!

One last interesting note about the whole debate between Christians and dinosaurs is the arguments that some theologians have made suggesting that the Bible is not wrong. It is just the age-old interpretation of the creation story that is at odds with what the scripture is actually telling us. Contrary to popular interpretation, the Book of Genesis does not start off with God creating Earth from scratch.

If one pays close attention, the arrival of humans in Genesis seems to start somewhere in the middle of the creation story rather than at the very beginning. Yes, the narrative does start off with the words "In the beginning," but by the time the narrative shifts to the creation of human beings, distinct clues are dropped that indicate Earth (as in prehistoric times) already existed before humanity came on the scene.

In the first verse of Genesis, scripture tells us very simply that, "In the beginning, God created the heavens and the Earth" (Genesis 1:1). This is in reference to the very beginning, as in the big bang beginning. But in the second verse, one can sense that the narrative has jumped forward in time because it goes on to say, "Now the Earth was formless and empty, darkness was over the surface of the deep, and the Spirit of God was hovering over the waters" (Genesis 1:2).

It seems like there is a gap in time between the initial creation of the heavens (the universe) and Earth. Those who point out this apparent gap in the biblical timeline have become proponents of the aptly named "gap theory." This theory insists that Genesis is adequately relating to how the material universe, including Earth, was created. They saw there was a gap between the initial creation and the later establishment of humans.

That gap very well could have spanned billions of years, during which time dinosaurs and other prehistoric creatures roamed Earth. Most scientists believe that the great extinction event that killed the dinosaurs was likely from a comet or asteroid that smashed into the planet. This asteroid would have sent up huge clouds of dust and blocked out the sun. And just as the Bible puts it, there would have been "darkness over the surface of the deep."

So, gap theory proponents suggest there was a tremendous gap between the first verse of Genesis, which established creation, and the second verse, which mentions that Earth was shrouded in darkness. If prehistoric life had previously been annihilated in an extinction-level event, then the creation that God began in the second verse was not the first creation of life on Earth but rather the recreation of life, which included the advent of humanity.

It is an interesting theory since the subsequent verses of Genesis talk about what one would expect to transpire in a world recovering from asteroid bombardment. Earth was shrouded in darkness, and God said, "Let there be light." The clouds finally parted, and life began to form once again on Earth.

If we were to ask our gap theory proponents why God did not mention the four billion years of history that occurred between Genesis 1 and 2, they would most likely say we do not need to know about it.

At any rate, whether you believe in the accuracy of the Bible or adhere to an Abrahamic faith or not, it is fun to see just how flexible the scripture and faith can be. Time and time again, from Friedrich Nietzsche to Charles Darwin, there have been those who have speculated that Christianity might soon be relegated to the dustbin as an obsolete relic of the past.

Yet, time and time again, we are surprised by just how adaptable the Christian faith is. If major world religions are gauged on their theological ability to adapt, Christianity almost always seems to come out on top, astonishing everyone with its incredible resilience and adaptability. Part of this can be attributed to the fervent love and devotion Christians have for their faith.

In addition to the discovery of dinosaurs and the advent of carbon dating, there was quite a fervor when the *Epic of Gilgamesh* was discovered buried in the dust of ancient Mesopotamia (modern-day Iraq). The *Epic of Gilgamesh* has a flood story that seems to predate Moses's description of the flood yet is strikingly similar in both detail and scope.

Many have since wondered if this was the source of Moses's account. But even if the stories are similar, it could very well be that both accounts are different versions of the same event. It does not necessarily mean the flood did not happen. Moses was just given a different variation of the same account, which would make sense since he would have written about it long after the flood had occurred (if he wrote it down at all, as modern scholars believe the early books of the Old Testament were written long after his death).

Such a thing is not so surprising when one considers the fact that the father of the Hebrew people—Abraham—originally hailed from Mesopotamia before he was led to the promised land of Israel. Abraham predated Moses's compiling of Genesis, and he was likely aware of a flood story, although, during his life, it might have been passed down as an oral legend.

Rabbinic scholar Robert Wexler believes this to be the case. In a commentary dating back to 2001, he went on the record to state, "The most likely assumption we can make is that both Genesis and Gilgamesh drew their material from a common tradition about the flood that existed in Mesopotamia. These stories then diverged in the retelling."

At any rate, there were plenty of happenings in the 19th century that caused some Christians to begin to doubt their faith. Others found new and intriguing ways to continue to support their beliefs.

Chapter 12: Christianity since the 20th Century and Beyond

At the outset of the 20th century, Christian believers all over the world were hopeful that the new century would bring forth a golden age of renewed faith in Christianity. Despite the fact that the 19th century began a lasting trend of secularism, many were upbeat at the prospect of bringing "the light of Christianity" to all corners of the globe.

Many preachers spread the message that Christianity had reached its "final phase" and that, as soon as the gospel reached the whole world, Christ's return would be imminent. And for those who leaned more toward a social gospel of uplifting the everyday lives of their fellow humans, it was believed that Western Christianity, coupled with notions of democracy and a proactive progressive civilization, would naturally promote peaceful and justice-loving societies all over the world.

From our vantage point, well over one hundred years later, it is easy for us to scoff at such notions. Even with the most cursory examinations of a history book, we know that the 20th century was one of the most violent and disastrous centuries humanity has ever known. Rather than the light of Christianity bringing universal love and brotherhood and peace descending like a dove, the people living in the 20th century suffered two devastating world wars, international terrorism, and the advent of world-destroying nuclear weapons.

But as 1899 rolled over to the year 1900, Christians had no idea what lay in store, and many were quite hopeful that technological progress, coupled with renewed Christian evangelism, would bring about peace and prosperity. This was the general view among Protestants, and the Catholic view was very similar.

In 1905, Pope Pius X famously declared, "The civilization of the world is Christian ... The more completely Christian it is, the more true, more lasting and more productive of genuine fruit it is." Pope Pius insisted that society was on a wayward trend for the better but that the Catholic Church needed to take a more proactive stance for a "more completely Christian" transformation. Both Protestants and Catholics were hedging their bets that the 20th century would indeed be a Christian one.

The First World War would shatter much of those assumptions, as strategic alliances led practically the entire planet to war. World War One was triggered by a Serbian nationalist who assassinated a visiting archduke from Austria. Austria-Hungary was understandably incensed at this turn of events and issued a series of draconian demands.

The Serbs had no intention of meeting all of the demands, some of which were absurd. Austria used this rejection as an excuse to declare war on Serbia. Russia, which was allied with Serbia, then declared war on Austria-Hungary. Austria's ally Germany declared war on Russia. Britain and France then declared war on Germany. And the next thing anyone knew, just about all of the major world powers had declared war on each other over an incident that should have been an isolated event, although other factors were certainly at play.

Young men all over the world paid the price. They were sent to the trenches to be gassed and riddled with machine gun bullets. Many wondered not only what the point of the war was but also what was the point of life and their faith in God. Such questions tend to arise when change comes so rapidly and drastically. Chaos does seem to either drive people away from their faith or drive them closer to it.

Some instances of the revival of the Christian faith can be traced to the onset of World War One. Considering how easily the world had descended into an apocalyptic situation, it is understandable why previous Christian notions of universal peace under Christ were shattered. Perhaps most peculiar is the fact that mainstream Christians even had such a mindset in the first place.

The Christian New Testament was written in the tumultuous time of the 1st century when Jesus and his early disciples lived under the oppression of Roman occupation. The views of the early Christians were that before things got better, they would get a whole lot worse. And although it was agreed that peace would triumph in the end, much of their ideas of the future had more to do with Armageddon than peaceful coexistence among the nations.

Perhaps the disappointments of the breakdown of international peace and order shifted the Christian mindset back toward this old Christian worldview. And in many ways, it has been stuck there ever since. You are indeed more likely to hear Christians today speaking that the end is near and that they are "ready for the Rapture."

The world wars shattered the notion that Christianity would be the glue that would hold the international world order together, and there was a great return to the apocalyptic outlook. Immediately after World War One, many "old world" orders were destroyed. Both the Austro-Hungarian Empire and the Ottoman Empire fell apart. The loss of the Austro-Hungarian Empire redrew the borders of Europe. Perhaps even more importantly, the loss of the Ottoman juggernaut dramatically refashioned the geographical areas of the Middle East and North Africa.

The destruction of the Ottoman Empire would create the British mandate over Palestine. Palestine, or, as it is otherwise known, "Eretz Israel" or the "Land of Israel," is the land talked about in the Bible. Western Christians did not have control over the Holy Land since the Crusades. And now they were back.

Prior to this event, it was popular for Christians to believe that God's covenant had shifted to the Christian Church. In the Old Testament of the Bible, God is said to have a covenant with the land of Israel, but something happened in the interim, with Israel becoming largely irrelevant. After the British successfully seized this land from the Ottomans, the development of the modern nation-state of Israel began. The Christians' view began to shift, and prophecy prognosticators began to again look toward the land of Israel as being pivotal to God's plan.

In the meantime, Europe was severely shaken by World War Two. The conflict was a terrible one, but one group whose suffering is often overlooked is the German Church. Early on, German nationalists attempted to co-opt German Christians by promoting a blend of Christianity that was linked to the German state. Many fell for this redressing of the church, but by the mid-1930s, when extreme reforms called for radical changes in Christian ideology, such as dropping the Old

Testament and even the epistles of Apostle Paul, German Christians finally (albeit much too late) tried to take action.

Religious dissidents in Germany formed what was known as the Confessing Church, which sought to uphold the word of God as sovereign no matter what Hitler or his cronies told anyone. These efforts were crystalized in the 1934 Barmen Declaration, which officially condemned what the German state was doing and sought to reaffirm the traditional beliefs of the church. The declaration declared, in part, "We reject the false doctrine [that nationalism can dictate to the churches] as though the Church were permitted to abandon the form of its message and order to its own pleasure or to changes in prevailing ideological and political convictions."

By then, the German state was firmly in the hands of the extremists, and it did not take much to send any dissidents to the concentration camps. In a short period of time, well over seven hundred German pastors who protested what was happening in their country were seized. One of the loudest German voices to stand against what the government was doing was Christian theologian Dietrich Bonhoeffer.

Although Bonhoeffer faced a fate worse than death, he refused to stand down. He was ultimately rounded up and liquidated by the German authorities. Those who were not arrested were repeatedly threatened with imprisonment and far worse until they meekly put their heads down, caved to the pressure, and kept their mouths shut. As much as we might want to condemn these Germans for not standing up to their government, there are likely plenty of people today who might cave to the demands of a totalitarian regime. It can be hard to put yourself in someone else's shoes. This is not to excuse the German Church's choice to back down in the face of aggression, but it does explain why most Christians ended up acquiescing so easily.

And speaking of totalitarian regimes, in the Soviet Union, Christianity faced a surprising turn of events. Since the days of Karl Marx, the communists derided religion as nothing more than the opiate of the masses, the carrot that was strung above the heads of the poor and weary so that they would keep moving forward and keep punching in their time clock until the day they died.

The communists taught the people that religion was a delusion and was used to keep people in line with the promise of a false reward at the end of their lives. As such, it should not be surprising to learn that when communists took over Russia in 1917, they began persecuting the Russian Church. What is surprising to learn is that during the darkest days of World War Two, totalitarian dictator Joseph Stalin decided to reopen the church!

As the Russians were being beaten back by the Germans, it was feared that a march on Moscow was imminent. Stalin was crafty enough to realize that the Russians needed a powerful symbol, a unifying force to hold them all together. Stalin, who had at one time considered becoming a priest, knew the only thing that could unite Russians was religion.

Stalin not only reopened churches but also actively encouraged the people's belief in Christianity as a means of holding his people and ultimately the Soviet Union together. His bid seemed to work well enough, as the average Russian seemed to view the protection of their homeland and way of life as something more akin to a holy war and a fight for their survival.

On the heels of World War Two, Christian theologians latched on to what they perceived to be a portent of biblical proportions. After the war came to a close, the United States and the United Nations facilitated Israel becoming a nation again in 1948. At this point, one can clearly mark the shift in Christian beliefs regarding the "end times." Apocalyptic prophecies were once again given a Middle Eastern background, with Christians beginning to foresee an imminent "end times" showdown in Israel.

It was proclaimed that enemy nations would march on Israel right before the Rapture. Israel's destruction would only be prevented by the return of Christ himself. The fact that Israel wasn't even considered in end-times prophecies for hundreds of years is rather telling. It demonstrates just how elastic some of the interpretations of scripture and apocalyptic prophecies can be.

As it pertains to the Catholic Church, the Vatican seemed to come out stronger after the war. This is surprising, considering the still lingering controversy over how the Catholic Church interacted with Italy's fascist government of Benito Mussolini. The church has been criticized for its perceived cooperation, but in truth, the church made more efforts than perhaps any other institution behind the walls of fascism to actually do something about what was happening in the country.

The church worked to actively save many from the horrors of the Holocaust. Even so, many might have predicted that the Catholic Church might splinter or become irrelevant after the war, with the pope being viewed as a compromised political tool of despots. But in reality, the Catholic Church became stronger and managed to retake its traditional role as an international arbiter.

The Vatican regained its status as a nation-state, and the pope was again the potentate. He just so happened to have the support of over a billion faithful Catholics all over the world. Then there came the watershed moment of "Vatican II." This ecumenical council kicked off in September 1962, with subsequent meetings taking place all the way until the year 1965. The council called for the Catholic Church to take on a much more active role in world affairs, among other things.

And considering the efforts of popes like John Paul II (who is credited with being instrumental in bringing communism to an end) and the present (at least as of this writing) Pope Francis, the Catholic Church has largely followed this pattern of positioning itself as an arbiter for world dialogue and change. One of the most pivotal results of Vatican II was the voiced determination to end the long-standing antagonism that had developed between Catholics and Protestants.

Since the Reformation, the two branches of Christianity have often been at each other's throats. However, Vatican II decided it was time to cease competing with the Protestants and try and cooperate with them as much as would be feasible.

In the United States, some mainline Protestants and Catholics would embrace something that would become known as the Social Gospel. This movement was similar to what had occurred previously in the 19th century, as Christianity was again used in the social uplifting of humanity. But unlike its predecessor, this new variant had a much more urgent call to action. It was closely intertwined with popular social movements, such as the civil rights movement and the feminist movement.

The Social Gospel stressed that the time to act to make the world a better place was now and urged folks to step out of the churches and into the streets to take a more active role in shaping the society in which they lived. Those who adhered to the Social Gospel would often stand in sharp contrast with the more conservative brand of evangelical Christianity, which, in the West, was being led by the likes of Billy Graham and other similar firebrand preachers.

Billy Graham was not as likely to preach on immediate social change as he was to warn people that the end was near. Billy Graham came up with a very resonant message: the end times were fast approaching. He often galvanized the masses to convert through the powerful imagery that he conveyed.

Of course, Billy Graham was not the first preacher to convey that an apocalypse was nigh. But considering the advent of nuclear weapons and the fact that, by the early 1960s, the United States and Russia had amassed enough nuclear armaments to blow up the whole planet with the push of a button, Billy Graham's message became palpable. It seemed as if an uncontrollable and unrelenting Armageddon really was about to blow up in everyone's faces.

The idea of a nuclear Armageddon was quite influential on Christian thought. It really cannot be overemphasized how powerful these world events were in shaping the notion among Christians that the end was near. Such things could have been suggested in the past, but the threat seemed much more realistic during the Cold War. Even today, when the brink of nuclear war occasionally raises its head, there will inevitably be many preachers who speak up to declare that the long prophesized "end of days" is about to commence.

As an indication of how powerful this "end times" imagery is, Christian theologian Hal Lindsey wrote a book about how he thought the end would play out called *The Late Great Planet Earth*. The book came out in 1970 and was an immediate bestseller. Rather than losing relevance, the book is still popular to this day, and Hal Lindsey himself still claims it to be an accurate portrayal of what might happen. The only difference is the level of "imminence" of the end.

Preaching of the end times has not really abated much; however, the goalposts keep shifting. In truth, the Christian Church has been looking for the end to come since Jesus first preached that the "kingdom of heaven is at hand" in the 1st century. The early church was waiting for the end times two thousand years ago, and Christians are still waiting today. Although the Bible itself suggests that the end will come, it does not set dates.

When asked about when the final trumpet might sound, Jesus declared, "Only the Father knows." As Matthew 24:36 tells us, "But nobody knows when that day or hour will come, not the heavenly angels and not the Son. Only the Father knows."

The scripture also states that, to God, "a day is like a thousand years, and a thousand years are like a day" (2nd Peter 3:8), leading some modern-day preachers to quip that two thousand years is nothing in the grand scheme of things. Evangelist Jesse Duplantis is fond of brushing off any notion that the Second Coming is taking too long by stating that, from God's perspective, only a weekend has passed since the resurrection. For him and many other preachers, there is no delay—God is still right on schedule.

Another great shift in Christianity in the 20th century that cannot be overlooked is Pentecostalism. The Pentecostal faith champions a direct, personal connection to God, which is often demonstrated by means of expressive religious experiences, such as lifting hands, falling down, and speaking in what has been termed "tongues."

Pentecostals believe that when they are filled with the Holy Spirit and make a direct connection to the divine, these experiences occur. Pentecostalism began as a fringe movement in the early 20th century but has since become one of the most popular and growing brands of Christianity. To gauge just how popular Pentecostalism has become, all one has to do is flip on Christian television.

Christian TV, by and large, is dominated by promoters of the Pentecostal faith. Billy Graham may have been a firebrand Baptist who braved the airwaves, but today, almost every TV evangelist you see is likely of the Pentecostal faith. Pentecostal beliefs are also rapidly spreading all over Latin America.

Practitioners of the Catholic faith are now finding stiff competition among Pentecostal believers in Latin America. In Brazil, for example, it is said that over 16 percent of the population is Pentecostal. As these Christian movements continue to grow, we can be sure that the future will provide even more enrichment and development of the Christian faith.

Conclusion: The Reason for the Season and the Reason We Keep Believing

It is fairly safe to say, now that some two thousand years have gone by, that the Christian faith has stood the test of time. Although its practitioners have adapted some of their practices and views over the centuries, the faith itself is still going strong. Christianity not only has the most adherents by sheer numbers but is also one of the few religions that actually gets celebrated by those who do not even believe in it.

If one would like to see evidence of the global dominance of Christianity, all one has to do is consider the celebration of Christmas. Almost two hundred countries today celebrate Christmas.

Although one might be tempted to discount the significance of such a thing and suggest that it is just the influence of Western commercialism at work, such a notion does not adequately explain the pure joy with which Christmas is approached and celebrated. And whether we realize it or not, the themes of Christ and Christianity have permeated even the most supposedly secular renderings of the holiday.

Just take, for example, the tale of "Frosty the Snowman." This is a perfectly secular tale with no religious connotations whatsoever, right? It speaks of a snowman who was "magically" brought to life (the immaculate conception) one day. The snowman gained a following because of his kindness and pureness of heart (he was a jolly, happy soul). In the 1969 animated movie, the snowman perished in a heroic act of self-sacrifice.

A girl was freezing to death in the cold, so Frosty took her to a warm greenhouse even though he knew he would melt. He died so others could live. The girl is then found crying her eyes out (just like Mary Magdalene crying in Christ's tomb), only for the benevolent, fatherly figure of Santa to show up and bring Frosty the Snowman back to life (the resurrection). The kids rejoice but are sad to see Frosty fly off with Santa to the North Pole (the ascension). But even so, Frosty "waved good-bye, saying, 'Don't you cry—I'll be back again someday!'"

Now, perhaps this silly analogy might provoke some laughs. But in all seriousness, one cannot help but be astonished by how the themes of Christ and Christianity seem almost inescapable as it pertains to Christmas, even when we try to suppress or avoid them. Perhaps they are just so ingrained in our hearts and souls that even when a secular writer is tasked with writing a Christmas tale about a snowman, they somehow can't help subconsciously giving that frosty fellow some rather Christ-like attributes!

And there has to be a reason for that. The reason for the season has always been Jesus Christ and the followers of the Christian faith, who have long kept Christian beliefs front and center in the consciousness of humanity as a whole.

Part 2: Early Christianity

An Enthralling Overview of Jesus, the Twelve Apostles, the Conversion of Constantine, and Other Events in Christian History

Introduction

A savior, a prophet, a good man—despite varying opinions about what role Jesus filled, history agrees on his existence and the impact his words had on the world. What he taught revolutionized the Jewish world of his time. Why? What was so profound about his existence and teachings that thousands of people changed their lives and the way they worshiped?

It is important to understand the Jewish position, thinking, and culture of the time. They were waiting for someone who would save them, but from what? And did Jesus fulfill their expectations? The historical context surrounding the years before and not long after Jesus was born help us gain insight into why Jesus was such an important figure and how the political and social climate affected the birth of Christianity.

This journey through early Christianity will start about one hundred years before Jesus was born and discuss some of the most notable aspects of his life and his teachings. It will continue through what we know about Jesus' life and the message he spoke. We will take a look at the impact Jesus had on the men who became his first disciples and how his message began to spread. Jesus' story as a man on Earth ends with his execution at the relatively young age of thirty-three. Despite the short time he was part of history, it was not the end of his legacy—it was just the beginning.

His teachings carried on through close friends like the apostles John and Peter and through evangelizers and writers like Luke, Paul, and Timothy, among many others. Their backgrounds, whom they wrote to, whom they spoke with, and why give insight into what was happening culturally and religiously during this time of great change.

Eventually, the Jewish world experienced great political upheaval and the catastrophic loss of their center of worship through the iron-like army of the Roman Empire. The budding Christian congregations were also affected by turmoil brought on by imperial rule. What was life like for early Christians? How did they become organized amidst such a chaotic political backdrop? How could they survive intense persecution and stay intact as one united entity?

Through the gospels and epistles, it is evident that Christianity was not just for men. They were not the only ones moved by Christian teachings, nor were they the only ones who faced the fire of persecution. Numerous women in the early Christian congregation are mentioned by name and noted for their faith and good deeds. What was the early Christian view of women, especially in comparison to the Jewish viewpoint? Who were some of the important women whose names are engraved in early Christian history?

This walk through early Christian history will give a glimpse not only of the first Christian congregations and their teachings but also the stories of eyewitness and those who experienced its birth and progression. It will also tell how things slowly began to evolve as the political scene changed.

Early Christianity left its mark on religion, worship, art, and culture. As a bonus, this book explores some early Christian artwork and their meanings and what we can learn about life and Christianity through the creativity of those who lived it.

Chapter 1: Origins and Background

The Jewish people had been in eager anticipation. The time they had been waiting for more than one thousand years—the appearance of the prophesied Messiah—was near at hand. Most were familiar with the words of the earlier prophets and understood the general timeline of events as laid out in prophetic writings. What did they know just before the birth of Jesus that led them to believe he would soon be born?

The Jews had not been left to guess who the Messiah would be through vague or confusing information. Although they did not know what his name would be, the Jewish writings[1] had hundreds of prophecies containing details that would help them identify the Messiah once he came. What were some of these?

Even those who did not believe Jesus was the one they were waiting for recognized certain facts about the Messiah, namely that he would have a royal lineage. He would be a descendant of King David of the tribe of Judah. The Hebrew prophecies were specific about the place he would

---

[1] Most are included among the books of the Hebrew Scriptures (also known as the Old Testament). Books that contain prophecies about Jesus span multiple authors and periods and were written on scrolls during this period and prior. According to Alfred Edersheim in his book, *The Life and Times of Jesus the Messiah, the Hebrew writings contain more than 400 prophecies about the coming Messiah. In fact, the entirety of the Hebrew Scriptures is in some way connected to the Messiah and is a virtual pathway toward his existence.*

be born—Bethlehem Ephrathah.[2] However, how would the Jews know *when* to expect this Messiah?

Prophets held in high regard by the Jewish people, like Daniel, provided a timeline of when the Messiah would appear. Daniel 9:25 (Rotherham) states: "From the going forth of the word to restore and rebuild Jerusalem" until the Messiah (literally meaning Anointed One) there would be sixty-nine weeks.[3] That "word" or royal decree was given by Persian King Artaxerxes Longimanus in 455 BCE when he allowed the exiled Jews to return and rebuild Jerusalem. What happened sixty-nine weeks after that decree? Nothing of significance.

However, the Encyclopedia Judaica states the understanding of the term "weeks" would actually be weeks of years (one "week" equaling seven years) a calculation method that was not uncommon for the Jews. By that calculation, seven times sixty-nine, the Jews arrived at 483 *years* from 455 BCE. Since there was no year zero, 483 years would bring the arrival of the Messiah to 29 AD. Did anything notable happen during that year? Yes, it was the year Jesus was baptized and began his ministry.

Though it doesn't appear the Jews knew the exact day, month, or year the one they were waiting for would come, they had a general idea and expected his arrival not long after the first quarter of the century. Right after Jesus' birth, Luke 2:38 says that the prophetess Anna told the event to "all the ones waiting for deliverance of Jerusalem."[4]

Why were the Jews, including historian Flavius Josephus, so eagerly waiting for deliverance, and from whom? The historical context gives us a clear view of the situation leading to the beginning of the first century.

Relationships with Greece and Rome

The mighty Alexander the Great was dead, and four of his generals had split his empire. Two generals, Antigonus and Ptolemy, split Judea down the middle. Although they did not have the same power as the man who came before them, they continued his quest to spread Hellenism

---

[2] During that time, two cities carried the name Bethlehem. One was in Zebulun. However, Micah 5:2 specifies that the Messiah would be born in the small town of Bethlehem Ephrathah in Judea, the same city King David was born in. Though there has been debate about Jesus' birthplace due to his being called a Nazarene, the designation was given because he was *raised* in the town of Nazareth.

[3] The Encyclopedia Judaica notes that there would be seventy weeks, but the "anointed prince" would be cut off, or killed, near the end of the seventieth week.

[4] The city of Jerusalem housed the temple and was the spiritual center of worship for the Jewish people, making it a place of high value and significance.

throughout the empire, which eventually knocked on the door of the Jews in Judea.

At least in the beginning, the Jews resented the Greeks and found pagan Greek culture abhorrent. In particular, the Greeks' large pantheon of colorful gods was vastly at odds with the Jewish belief in one Almighty God. The Greeks wore clothing that the Jews would have considered immodest, not to mention the nude wrestling and prevalence of homosexuality—violations of scriptural law. To have these influences thrust on them would make it more difficult to maintain the purity of their worship—a fundamental element of who they were.

But as Greek culture spread its fingers into Jerusalem and the surrounding area, Jews had a choice to make. Many chose the traditional route and kept themselves separate from pagan influences. Other Jews saw that the only way to get ahead and achieve elite status was to have a "when in Vegas" (or, in this case, Greece) philosophy—they learned Greek, gave their kids a Greek education, and became Hellenized to some extent. A schism formed between the two lines of thought, and in Jerusalem, a stir began over how much Hellenization was acceptable.

Many of the nobles and priests in Jerusalem favored adopting Greek culture more fully. In 175 BC, the High Priest Jason had a Greek-style gymnasium (a Greek center for education) and other Greek buildings built in the city.[5] He even paid the Seleucid ruler Antiochus Epiphanes (Antiochus IV) to officially label Jerusalem a Greek city. This was more than just advancement on his part; it was a power move. Establishing a gymnasium would tempt any prominent families who were against Hellenization. If they wanted to be educated and have their kids educated, it would have to be through a Greek educational system.

Antiochus IV also dangled Greek citizenship in front of the Jews— anyone who wanted the distinction and benefits of Greek citizenship must have a Greek education. For boys, that did not mean just academic learning but Greek military training.

Problems really began to heat up in 167 AD when a Jew named Menelaus tried to overthrow High Priest Jason and *buy* his way into the high priest position. Since Antiochus IV had the final say in appointing the high priest, the position could go to the highest bidder. Short on

---

[5] At this time, Jerusalem and the Jewish population did not have a political ruler, but the high priest was considered their spiritual and quasi-political leader.

funds, Menelaus looted gold from the temple in Jerusalem to get enough money to pay his way to being the high priest—an outrageous act that was viewed as stealing from God himself.[6]

Fighting broke out among Jewish factions and rioting ensued. The chaos became so great that Antiochus sent in the military—Syrian forces under Greek command marched into the city.

Radical changes began to take place. The temple was turned into Greco-Syrian barracks. This was another severe affront to faithful Jews, yet it was only the beginning. Circumcision, which was to be strictly observed according to the Mosaic Law, was banned. In fact, observance or even reading of the Torah, the first five books of the Bible containing Jewish laws, was now forbidden. Copies were searched out and burned.

Many Jews were compelled to hide their circumcision to appear more Greek. Others joined in pagan celebrations, adorning themselves with ivy and marching in a procession celebrating the Greek god of wine and debauchery, Dionysus. Some accounts say that a pig, an animal considered unclean under Mosaic Law, was sacrificed on the temple altar. As an additional insult, Antiochus IV had the most holy area of the temple turned into a center for pagan worship, a chamber rededicated to the Greek Zeus.

Until this time, the Greeks had left the Jews to follow their own laws uninhibited. The Jews had governed themselves and maintained and preserved their religious beliefs. But Antiochus IV did not like that the Jews felt accountable only to God and not a human ruler. He made more efforts to limit and or outright forbid Jewish religious practices, including the observance of the Sabbath and other sacred festivals. Many Jews felt that pagan Hellenistic ways were being forced onto them. They were also unable to govern themselves according to their laws and beliefs, and perhaps worst of all, the temple, their center of worship, was being grossly desecrated.

Some Jews believed this was all a pleasant mixing of cultures, perhaps thinking they were modernizing their culture. But to Jews faithful to their laws and beliefs, this was apostasy. Ultimately, these differences were the fuel for what became known as the Maccabean Revolt, launched by priest Mattathias and his sons.

---

[6] The temple in Jerusalem was the most important structure to the Jewish people, a representation of God's presence.

When Greek officers accompanied by a Jewish priest came to the village where Mattathias lived, they tried to enforce a royal mandate that everyone make an offering to the gods. Although promised that this one act would earn him friendship with the king, Mattathias remained steadfast in his refusal to worship other gods. The Jewish people only worshipped one God, Yahweh.[7]

When another Jewish man complied and made the offering, a serious sin under Jewish law, Mattathias killed the man and one of the king's officers. Jews, Syrians, and Greeks now had a grievance with him—he had committed murder, which was against secular *and* Jewish law. So, he fled to the mountains with his sons. However, this was just the beginning of the uprising for Mattathias and his sons. It was the event that touched off the Maccabean Revolt.[8]

Mattathias and his sons did not remain alone in the hills—many followed them. From their location in the mountains, Mattathias and his sons gathered an army and began a campaign of guerilla warfare against the much more powerful Greco-Syrian army and Jews who had compromised their faith. It was as much a civil war among the Jews as it was a battle against the Greeks and the enforcement of Greek laws and pagan customs.

After a series of battles and the death of Mattathias in 166 BCE, the Jews, now under the command of Judas Maccabaeus, finally recaptured Jerusalem in December 164 BCE. Later that month, they rededicated the temple and cleansed it of all traces of pagan Greek worship, much to the celebration of the people.

A brief peace negotiated with the Syrian Greeks following the death of Antiochus IV gave both sides a break from the fighting—but it didn't last long. This time, the Jews turned to Rome for help, laying the groundwork for a situation akin to letting in the tiger to get rid of the wolf.

However, for the next 100 years, the Jews regained control of Judea and ruled themselves. That was, until the fierce Roman General Pompey marched into Jerusalem in 63 BCE. By this time, the Roman Empire was

---

[7] From the original Hebrew letters YHWH, the Latinized translation of which is Jehovah.

[8] The family name was actually Hasmoneus. The moniker Maccabaeus or Maccabee was an honorary title later given to Mattathias' son Judah when he took leadership of the revolt after his father's death. He was perhaps given this title after scoring some decisive victories. The Maccabee name was later extended to include the entire family. Translations from Hebrew give possible meanings as "the hammer" or "the extinguisher."

on the rise, steadily conquering territories. However, Judea was still under Jewish leadership in Jerusalem. That leadership was fractured, with two factions headed by two brothers, Hyrcanus and Aristobulus, fighting a bloody war for control.

After accusations by Aristobulus against Pompey's Syrian representative, Pompey brought his troops down to Jerusalem to see what was happening. This gave Rome a dangerous foothold in the city. When he arrived, Pompey chose to side with Hyrcanus. After the Romans built a siege dam near the north wall, the incessant beat of battering rams and deluge of heavy stones from catapults finally broke through the walls, and the Roman army entered Jerusalem.

Like the Greeks before them, the Romans entered the temple and walked into the Holy of Holies—a place only the high priest could enter during certain times of the year. Though many Jews were killed by the Romans, many killed themselves rather than see the desecration of their temple again. Pompey set up Hyrcanus as the high priest and sole political leader of the nation. That was, until Julius Caesar appointed a regent, Antipater, to rule alongside Hyrcanus. After Hyrcanus became a prisoner of war in 40 BC, Antipater's son Herod (later known as Herod the Great) was set on the throne as the sole ruler of Judea.

That's not to say Rome gave up control of the area. Herod was put on the throne as a semi-independent vassal king of the Roman Empire. This began the Roman occupation that the Jews were oppressed by into the first century. Though Rome did not have a daily presence among the Jews, their domineering power could be felt in everyday life. For the most part, however, Rome allowed the Jews to live according to their customs and even made exceptions for them regarding certain mandates like military conscription.

Brilliant and ambitious, not to mention brutal, Herod wouldn't put up with any opposition from Jewish rebels discontented with him or Rome. However, he struck a good balance between keeping Rome happy and protecting the Jewish way of life. He even rebuilt the temple into an architectural marvel, making it somewhat of a tourist attraction for Jews and Gentiles alike. However, tensions with Rome and among the Jews continued to simmer.

Once Rome started appointing procurators over Judea around the start of the first century, things quickly slid downhill. Typically low-status officials in Rome, the procurators easily fell into corruption. The people often never saw the benefits of money designated for public projects. Instead, it was embezzled by officials who continued to grow richer. One of the most grievous cases was when Pontius Pilate needed to build a new aqueduct for the city's water supply. He stole money from the temple treasury to fund it, touching off a protest that ended in a Jewish slaughter.

Some Jewish zealots who believed in returning control of the land back to Jewish hands went further than protests. A rebel simply known as "The Egyptian" gathered 30,000 men in a failed attempt to take on the Roman army garrison in Jerusalem and install himself as ruler. Rome often swiftly came down on dissenters, whether minor protests or armed rebellions, with excessive and brutal force.

Roman taxes were a particularly prickly subject because the Jews were already suffering under an economic system that caused many small businesses and landowners to lose their livelihoods. More and more Jews went into poverty and debt. So, when procurators forced people to pay double the tax amount set by Rome so that they could keep the extra for themselves, the Jews were enraged.

While initially Rome had no issues with Jewish religious customs, contempt and intolerance of their practices crept in with the installation of procurators. The Roman historian Tacitus wrote that a certain Jewish ritual was "preposterous and morbid." Disrespect for long-held Jewish beliefs and customs made for an unfriendly atmosphere.

But it wasn't just the Romans who treated the Jews with contempt—so did their own religious leader. Calling the common people *am ha'aretz, an insulting Hebrew term meaning "people of the land or dirt," the upper religious classes of the Pharisees and Sadducees began enslaving their own people with oppressive and rigid religious observances.*

So, it was against this backdrop of more than 200 years of fighting, foreign domination, and religious oppression that the Jews were desperately looking for the promised *savior. The Jewish Encyclopedia* says, "They yearned for the promised deliverer of the house of David, who would free them from the yoke of the hated foreign usurper, would put an end to the impious Roman rule, and would establish His own reign of peace." The Jewish people believed salvation from their oppressor would be from God, but through a political entity that would restore their kingdom when he came. However, little did they realize that their expectations for the Messiah were not exactly in line with Jesus' broader purpose.

By the time Jesus came onto the scene, the Jewish province of Judea, ruled by Herod, was under the umbrella of the Roman Empire.

Chapter 2: The Gospels

Good news! This is the very meaning of the word "gospel." The four gospel accounts of Matthew, Mark, Luke, and John contain information about the life of Jesus and talk about the "good news" that he preached during his three-and-a-half-year ministry. Though none of the accounts are a comprehensive biography of Jesus' life, they tell certain details about his birth and childhood that would be especially important to the Jewish people in expectation of the fulfillment of prophecies regarding the Messiah. Not much is told about his childhood, teenage years, or young adulthood. Instead, the Gospels focus on Jesus' ministry and his teachings, telling of his purpose and laying the foundation for the first Christian congregations.

A Synopsis of the Gospels

Some might think that the Gospels are all the same, and to some extent, they are.[9] This is mainly because they or the eyewitnesses who related events to them, were seeing and hearing the same things. Yet the books are not the same because the people who wrote them were different—their backgrounds, education, occupations, relationships, and perspectives all varied. That affected how their Gospels were written and the details included. The details a physician might view as important to write down might not be the same as those a fisherman would zero in on. Although some of the stories overlap, they create a picture of the life of Jesus. This is the account they tell.

---

[9] The Gospels of Matthew, Mark, and Luke are often referred to as synoptic, or "like view," because of the similarities between the writings.

In 3 BCE Nazareth, a young, unmarried, virgin woman named Mary was engaged to a Jewish carpenter named Joseph. Though she was a very faithful Jewish woman, she was still surprised to be visited at her home by an angel named Gabriel, appearing as a man. He announced he had good news to tell her. But Mary was not the first person Gabriel appeared to with stunning news.

A few months earlier, he had appeared to an older Jewish priest named Zechariah, a man whose wife was a relative of Mary's. Shockingly, he told Zechariah that his wife, Elizabeth, would have a son. Zechariah was in disbelief—his wife was too old to have children! Not long after, Elizabeth became pregnant. She gave birth to a son named John, who became known as John the Baptizer (or Baptist).

That same angel told Mary something she found just as astonishing: that, although she was a virgin, she would give birth to a son. Stunned, she asked how that was possible. Gabriel told her it would be with the help of God's holy spirit, and the child would be God's son.[10] Mary was somewhat skeptical, but to prove that what he said was possible, he told her about the unlikely pregnancy of her relative, Elizabeth.

Shortly after the angel left Mary, she visited Elizabeth and found that her older relative was pregnant as Gabriel said. When Elizabeth found out about Mary's pregnancy, she exclaimed that the younger woman was truly blessed. But Mary knew that when she went home and it became obvious she was pregnant, not everyone would feel the same way. In fact, she could be in real trouble.

Mary had valid feelings of worry—how would she explain her pregnancy to her family, let alone her fiancé? Not only that, but according to Jewish law, a married or engaged woman who willingly had a sexual relationship with another man would be given a death sentence.

It had been three months since she had seen Joseph, and she had a lot to tell him. She confided to him what happened; unsurprisingly, he found it hard to believe. He went away very grieved, wondering what he should do. He knew Mary was a good woman and loved her, but he couldn't see

---

[10] The Bible uses the Hebrew word *ru'ach* and the Greek word *pneu'ma* for spirit, both of which mean "breath" or "wind," symbolic of life energy or life force. Second-century Christian Justin Martyr explained the Holy Spirit (*pneu'ma hagion*) as the "influence or mode of operation of the Deity." Simply put, he was saying it was the energy or force God used to do things (like creating). Therefore, some Bible translations also use the term "God's active force" when referring to the Holy Spirit.

any other way she could be pregnant except by another man. Still, he didn't want Mary to die in disgrace. So, he considered secretly divorcing her.[11]

When he went to sleep one night, an angel appeared to him in a dream and confirmed what Mary had told him. Following the angel's instructions, he went ahead and married Mary. A few months later, while Mary was heavily pregnant, a census decreed by Roman emperor Augustus Caesar required Joseph and Mary to return to Bethlehem, the city of Joseph's birth, to participate in the registry.[12] When they got to Bethlehem, it was so crowded with travelers that the couple had nowhere to stay except a stable. It was there in the hay, surrounded by stable animals, that Mary gave birth to a son, Jesus. She wrapped him in some pieces of cloth and laid him in a manger, or trough, used for animal feed.

In the fields outside the city that night, some Jewish shepherds were suddenly surrounded by a bright light.[13] An angel appeared before them and told them there was good news: the savior they were waiting for had been born. The angel also told them where to find him—a stable in Bethlehem. Before they could leave, other angels appeared and sang with joy, "Glory in the heights above to God, and upon earth peace among men of goodwill."

The shepherds wasted no time rushing to Bethlehem to find Jesus. When they did, they told Mary and others in Bethlehem about the angel and what was said to them.

To complete Jewish rituals surrounding the birth of a baby, Joseph and Mary stayed in Bethlehem for over a month. In the meantime, foreign

---

[11] Mary and Joseph were only engaged at the time, but in ancient Jewish culture, an engagement was binding and would need a divorce to break it off.

[12] Census registrations were common in ancient history. There were several recorded during the reign of Augustus Caesar. According to fourth-century historian Orosius, this census, recorded by Luke as taking place in 2 BCE, may have been the event where all the nations under the Roman Empire swore an oath of loyalty to Caesar to unite them as one society.

[13] Though tradition holds that Jesus was born on December 25th, the Gospels do not say when he was born. In that region, December is typically a cold, rainy (and sometimes snowy) month, so shepherds would not have been outdoors with their flocks. It is also unlikely that Joseph, Mary, and others would have traveled for a census in that weather or that Caesar would have required a winter journey of people already on the verge of rebellion. The Catholic Encyclopedia says that "the celebration of Christmas is of Roman origin and dates from around 330 AD ... It had been customary for Roman pagans to gather at Vatican Hill to worship deities of the east, the choice of December 25..." Some details in the Gospels point to Jesus being born around late September or early October, yet there is no record or evidence of early first-century Christians celebrating the birth of Christ.

astrologers saw a strange sight in the night sky—a new star that had never appeared before.[14] It led them to Jerusalem, where they visited King Herod the Great. They told him they had followed a strange new star to Jerusalem and were going to Bethlehem to see "the one born king of the Jews" and pay their respects. Herod, who tolerated no rivalry for his position, was disconcerted by this "king of the Jews" report. Pretending that he, too, wanted to pay his respects, Herod told the astrologers to report back once they found him.

The astrologers left and again followed the star right to the house where Joseph and Mary were staying and brought their gifts. When they were about to return to tell Herod, they were given a divine warning in a dream not to do so because Herod actually wanted to kill the child. They decided to avoid Herod altogether by going home another way.

Angered that he hadn't been told where Jesus was, Herod took drastic and unthinkable action—he gave an order to kill all baby boys two years old and younger in and around Bethlehem.[15] To save Jesus' life, an angel appeared to Joseph and told them they must flee to Egypt as quickly as possible. The three escaped just in time. After Herod the Great died, an angel again appeared to Joseph and told him it was safe to return home. They returned to Judea and settled in Nazareth, avoiding the sphere of Herod's unpopular son, Archelaus, who was now the ruler of the province. There, Jesus grew up as a carpenter's son.[16][17]

---

[14] The original Greek word used here is magi (plural form), which most people use and recognize. Magi (singular magos) is sometimes translated as sorcerer, conjurer, or in this instance, astrologer. Given the men's knowledge of the stars, astrologer appears to be a logical translation. Though traditionally it is said there were three magi, none of the Gospels state the exact number that visited Herod or Mary and Jesus. The book of Matthew says they came from the east, likely Persia/Babylon.

[15] There are no contemporary secular records of Herod's massacre of the babies, but there is historical context for the event. Herod went down in history for being ruthless and brutal. Bent on keeping his throne and tolerating no hint of rivalry, he had forty-five men murdered for supporting a potential rival. He even had his closest friends and family members executed, including three of his sons, his beloved second wife, her brother, her grandfather, and many others. In the eyes of historians, this makes it highly plausible that Herod would murder a group of young children in an attempt to wipe out a "king of the Jews" who might have been born and could become a potential threat to his rulership. Also, Roman writer Macrobius (ca 400 AD) wrote in his book *Saturnalia* that he had heard about the incident.

[16] Based on Josephus' history and chronology, Herod died around 4 or 5 AD. With the threat removed, Joseph and Mary could safely return to Judea with their young son.

[17] Some Bible scholars believe that Jesus' parable of the minas recorded in Luke 19 might have been inspired by Archelaus.

The Gospels don't detail Jesus' life growing up, except for one incident when he was twelve. Luke details a time when the family was traveling back home from Passover celebrations in Jerusalem with a large group of family and friends. Believing that Jesus was among the group, Joseph and Mary did not realize he was not with them until the next day. Returning to Jerusalem to look for him, they found him at the temple with the Jewish religious leaders, asking questions and listening to them speak.

Mary, quite frazzled and distressed, asked her son why he would do this to her. He replied, "Did you not know I would be in the house of my Father?"

From there, it is seventeen years before Jesus' story picks up again. Matthew and Luke record Jesus' early years, giving context to his life (and, in Matthew, proof that Jesus was fulfilling prophecies about the Messiah). However, Mark and John start their accounts before and during Jesus' ministry—something they wanted to highlight. Within Christendom, there is often much focus on Jesus' birth and death, but all four Gospels emphasize Jesus' ministry and purpose.

All four gospel writers also spend time detailing the ministry of John the Baptizer, whose work was to prepare the Jewish people to accept the Messiah.

In the spring of 29 AD, the region around the Jordan River was abuzz with talk of a man who wore a camel hair shirt and leather girdle. He lived in the wilderness, eating honey and locusts. He was also a relative of Jesus (the son of Mary's cousin Elizabeth). But it was his message that stirred people the most. He told the Jewish people, "Repent, for the kingdom of the heavens has drawn near." He began baptizing people as a symbol of their repentance.

Six months into John's ministry, Jesus, now thirty, went to see him. John baptized his relative in the Jordan River to set an example for the disciples that would follow. John the Baptizer put Jesus under the water, and when Jesus came up, Matthew, Luke, and John (an eyewitness to the event) all say that God's holy spirit appeared in the form of a dove. A voice was heard from heaven saying, "You are my Son, the beloved; I have approved you."

This was a pivotal moment in Jesus' life because it touched off his ministry and, according to some gospel teachings, was when he officially became the Messiah.

Matthew, Mark, and Luke record that right afterward, Jesus was tempted three times by Satan (the devil) in the wilderness. In his last audacious attempt, Satan offered Jesus the power and prestige of ruling the world's governments if Jesus would just agree to bow down in one act of worship. Jesus denied all three of Satan's attempts and firmly told him, "Go away!"

Not long after, some of John the Baptizer's disciples believed that he was the Messiah. The first of these were Andrew and his brother, Peter. A few days later, they, along with Jesus and other new disciples John, Philip, Nathanael, and possibly James, went to a wedding celebration in Cana. When John wrote about this, it wasn't a diary of a social gathering but a recounting of Jesus' first miracle—turning large jars of water into very good wine.

Not long after that, in the spring of 30 AD, Jesus and some of his disciples went to celebrate the Passover in Jerusalem. When they got to the temple, what Jesus saw filled him with righteous indignation. Merchants were exploiting people by overcharging for sacrificial animals and exchanging foreign money.

He braided together some rope into a whip and used it to chase the crooked merchants away, overturning their tables in disgust. He told them, "Get these (things) away from here; do not make my Father's house a market."

Later, when Jesus was traveling to Galilee, he went to get water from Jacob's well near Sychar (modern day Nablus). There, he met a Samaritan woman. Asking her for water led to a poignant conversation where he revealed he knew her tainted social background and the bias against her for it. During this conversation, the unnamed woman became the first person Jesus outright told that he was the Messiah.[18] She went off and told others in the city. Word got around, motivating many to become followers of Jesus.

As he traveled, Jesus performed various miracles. He said they served a purpose besides just helping those who needed it. When an official in the court of Herod Antipas found out that Jesus was in Capernaum, he

---

[18] This is historically and culturally significant for a few reasons. First, during this time, women were treated like second-class citizens, even in Jewish society. Jewish men would never be seen in public talking to women who weren't relatives. Secondly, Jews and Samaritans generally hated each other and had very deep-seated prejudices. This was an example of Jesus' respect for women and lack of prejudice based on gender or race.

rushed to meet him. He asked Jesus to help his son, who was sick and about to die. Jesus told the man that he would perform miracles because "unless you people see signs and wonders, you will never believe." He informed the official that his son was, in fact, now alive and well. When the official returned home, his servants told him his son was healed in the hour Jesus said.

It was not the only healing recorded by the Gospel writers. They also record him healing many who were sick or had disabilities, including a completely paralyzed man, lepers, a blind man, people with chronic illnesses, and the apostle Peter's mother-in-law.[19] He even expelled demons from those afflicted by possession. On one Sabbath day, he healed a man with a withered hand, something that shocked and angered the Pharisees, who interpreted this as forbidden "work" on the Sabbath day[20]. This attracted their attention negatively, and from then on, they were on the lookout for ways to discredit or even kill him.

Even though many flocked to Jesus because of his miracles and sermons, some took offense at the truths he spoke. In one instance, he referenced a prior historical situation and applied it to the selfishness and faithlessness of the Jewish people as a whole. This made the crowd in the synagogue violently angry, and they pushed Jesus out of the city and to the top of a mountain. At the top, they tried to throw him over a ledge headfirst. However, Luke says that Jesus escaped the harrowing incident by walking right out of the crowd.

Later, after Jesus chose twelve apostles, the thirteen men were sitting on the Mount of Olives.[21] They were tired and trying to rest, but people from miles away had gathered to see Jesus. A large crowd formed on the hillside, hoping to get healed or hear him speak. Although exhausted, Jesus did not want to disappoint those who had come. All those in the crowd who came to be healed, he healed. Against this backdrop, Jesus

---

[19] Leprosy was a terrible disease that could leave a person severely disfigured or even lead to death. It was very contagious, and according to Jewish law, no one was to touch a leper. Someone with leprosy was not to go near other people without calling out to warn them. So, it is notable that the Gospels mention incidents of Jesus touching lepers to heal them, even though he healed others without using touch. The Gospels say this was purposeful, as Jesus felt pity for them and recognized their emotional need for human contact.

[20] Pharisees were highly educated Jewish religious leaders who often added to and enforced Jewish law.

[21] The Greek word for apostle means "someone sent by another" or "a messenger." Even though the term is sometimes loosely applied to many or all of Jesus' disciples, in this context it is the twelve disciples specially selected as representatives.

gave one of the most famous speeches in history—the Sermon on the Mount.

The sermon, which Matthew records in lengthy detail throughout three chapters, hits on many subjects. Throughout, Jesus talked about how to gain happiness, control anger, the benefits of spiritual thinking and living, the trap of materialism, and how to deal with being offended. He condemned hypocrisy and emphasized the importance of showing love to others. He also taught the dangers of being overly critical towards others, gave an example of how to pray, highlighted the reasons for trusting in God, and told his disciples that their actions, not just empty words, would prove who they really were. Perhaps the most well-known of his points is what many now call "The Golden Rule" in Matthew 7:12: "All things, therefore, that you want men to do to you, you must likewise do to them."[22]

Matthew, Mark, and Luke record the crowd's reaction to the sermon—the people were "astounded" by his words. This is mentioned several times in the Gospels. Jesus often used thought-provoking questions and easy-to-understand stories and illustrations in his teaching method. He became renowned for his talent as a teacher.

Later, Jesus and some of his disciples found themselves in a frightening situation. One night, they took a wooden boat and crossed the Sea of Galilee.[23] In the dark, a sudden and fierce storm whipped up across the waters.[24] While the storm raged, Jesus slept peacefully on a pillow at the stern of the boat. Even though the disciples were experienced fishermen and had undoubtedly weathered storms before, they had trouble controlling the boat and started to fear for their lives. They woke Jesus and desperately asked him, "Don't you care that we are about to die?!"

Jesus got up calmly and called out to the storm, "Peace! Be still!" The storm immediately died down. The disciples were so amazed by the miracle that they fearfully asked each other, "Who is this that even the wind and the sea obey him?"

---

[22] This verse is often quoted as "Do unto others as you would have them do to you."

[23] Sometimes referred to as the "Sea of Galilee Boat" or the "Jesus Boat," these common ancient fishing vessels were typically around twenty-seven feet long, 7.5 feet wide, and 4.3 feet high.

[24] Though often mild, the Sea of Galilee is occasionally battered by sudden and intense storms with dramatic waves (up to ten feet, as recorded in 1992) that could swamp a smaller boat.

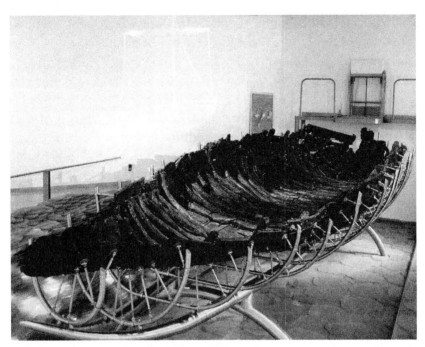

Sea of Galilee boat.
Travellers & Tinkers, CC BY-SA 4.0 <https://creativecommons.org/licenses/by-sa/4.0>, via Wikimedia Commons; https://commons.wikimedia.org/wiki/File:JesusBoat.jpg

The incident with the storm did not deter Jesus or the others from getting back in a boat and going onto the Sea of Galilee again. But this time, all four Gospel writers recorded a different type of miracle. To get a break from the crowds, Jesus and his disciples crossed the water to go to a more isolated location. However, the crowds followed, and Jesus felt bad that they had traveled a long way to get healed and hear him speak and were now hungry. It was late in the day and nearly impossible to get food for the almost 10,000 people there. This is the scenario behind one of Jesus' most well-known miracles—feeding thousands with just five loaves of bread and two small fish. He and his disciples broke up the food and distributed it. No one went hungry, and in fact, there were twelve baskets of leftovers.

Between the healing, the food, the sermons, and other miracles, many Jewish people were convinced that Jesus was the savior they had been hoping for and tried to make him their king. He refused, time and again emphasizing that God's heavenly kingdom was the only solution to their problems. But it was not the answer they expected. The people were confused. Many stopped following him because they believed he was sent to be their ruler and rescue them from oppression right then. Many questioned whether he was really the Messiah of prophecy.

The religious leaders—the Pharisees, in particular—didn't like Jesus, especially because, on more than one occasion, he condemned their oppression and contempt for the common people. He butted heads with them many times, and they decided they needed to get rid of him. They looked for reasons to have him arrested, but Jesus slipped through their fingers every time. On one occasion, they even tried to grab him and stone him to death for blasphemy, but he again escaped their grasp.

Jesus went north to escape the mob, but it was then he received devastating news: his good friend Lazarus had fallen sick and died. However, there was a bit of an issue. Going to see Lazarus' family would mean going back to Judea where the people wanted to kill him. But his disciples were on board with going, and together they headed toward the village of Bethany, where Lazarus' sisters Martha and Mary lived.

When he got there and saw the sisters crying, he was overcome with empathetic grief and cried with them. Lazarus' body was in a cave with a large boulder covering the entrance. Everyone went to the tomb to mourn. Jesus told some men to move the boulder, but Martha objected, and for good reason. She said, "He has been here four days; his body must smell by now!"

Jesus reassured her it would be okay. He prayed out loud in front of everyone and called into the tomb, "Lazarus, come out!" To everyone's astonishment, Lazarus, bound in his funeral cloth, walked out of the cave. They unwrapped him so he could be reunited with family and friends.

When word of the resurrection got out, more high-ranking religious leaders plotted his death. Jesus again eluded them for the time being.

In early spring, he went up to Jerusalem just before Passover. It was then that he foretold something truly disturbing to the Jews—the future destruction of their beloved holy city.[25] This did nothing to quell the murderous rage of the Jewish religious leaders, but they had to tread carefully because many people believed he was a prophet. So, instead of an all-out violent encounter, they tried to trick him with a question about taxes, hoping he would say something they could claim was seditious. Jesus didn't fall for it, and their plan failed again. However, despite

---

[25] The destruction he was alluding to happened thirty-seven years later when the Romans, under General Titus, besieged and destroyed the city.

escaping time and again, Jesus knew his death was approaching and made reference to it before sharing some of his final teachings.

On the day of Nisan 12, Jesus was lying low because he knew there was a plot brewing against him. Meanwhile, the religious leaders who wanted to kill him were practically handed the tool to do it: one of Jesus' apostles, Judas Iscariot, agreed to betray Jesus to them for thirty pieces of silver (the typical price for a slave)

While the other disciples prepared for the Passover, it seems Jesus was already suspicious of Judas and didn't give him any details that might allow him to interrupt their Passover celebration.

During the Passover meal, Jesus told his disciples this would be his last meal with them. He then got a towel and washed their feet to set an example of love and hospitality.[26] Afterward, he made a shocking announcement: "One of you will betray me." The apostles were stunned by the revelation. Yet Jesus did not outright say who it was. Instead, he told Judas to leave and do what he needed to do. When Judas left, Jesus told his apostles that he was instituting a new commemoration for his followers instead of the Passover.

After a heart-to-heart talk with the men, he warned them that things would not be easy going forward. In fact, they could expect sometimes violent opposition and persecution. With that in mind, he reminded them of their need for strong faith and careful obedience to what he had taught them. Jesus reassured them that God's holy spirit would be given to them to help them once he was gone. He prayed with and for them before they got up to leave around midnight.

When they left, the men went to the Garden of Gethsemane for a while. There, a mob including soldiers, the high priest, and others approached Jesus, carrying weapons and torches. The man leading the crowd? Judas Iscariot. He approached Jesus and kissed his cheek. It was not a sign of affection but a predetermined signal to identify Jesus to the men who would arrest him.

Peter, in a characteristically impulsive moment, took a sword and cut off the ear of the high priest's servant. Healing it, Jesus told Peter to put the sword away because "all those that take up the sword will perish by the sword." Afterward, Jesus was taken into custody, and all but one of his

---

[26] An ancient Middle Eastern tradition usually performed by a host because travelers got dust on their feet while walking on unpaved roads with sandals.

disciples ran from the garden.

Jesus was eventually subjected to a trial in front of Pontius Pilate, the prefect of Judea, who found him innocent of any crimes. Yet the Jewish religious leaders incited the people to hatred. They demanded that he be sentenced to death, even after Pilate gave the crowd a choice to release Jesus or a murderer named Barabbas.

Feeling like he had no choice but to give in to the wishes of the crowd or risk his own position, Pilate symbolically washed his hands of the matter and had Jesus whipped with a scourge.[27] Afterward, the soldiers spit on him, slapped him, mocked him, and shoved a crown made of thorns onto his head. His dignity in the face of the abuse impressed Pilate, who then presented a beaten Jesus to the crowd to evoke pity. However, the crowd was determined.

On Nisan 14, after an agonizing day, Jesus and others slated for execution carried the large wooden stakes that they were to be hung on.[28] Jesus, thoroughly exhausted, collapsed. The Romans grabbed a man from the crowd, Simon of Cyrene, and compelled him to carry the stake for Jesus. The grim procession finally stopped at a location fittingly called Golgotha or "Skull Place."

Jesus and two criminals with him had their hands and feet nailed to the poles, which were then placed upright in the ground. Jesus' mother, Mary, was among those in the crowd watching the execution. Understandably, Mary would have felt as if her own body were being pierced with a sword.

At the moment Jesus died, a huge earthquake shook the area around Jerusalem, even damaging the temple. The Roman army officers and people in the crowd became afraid. The army officer in charge was moved to exclaim, "Certainly this was God's son!"

---

[27] A small whip of several strips of leather intertwined with iron or animal bone, constructed to tear the flesh on contact.

[28] Although traditionally many English Bibles use the word cross, the original Greek word used was *stauros*. According to the Imperial Bible Dictionary, the word meant an "upright pole...on which anything might be hung." The Roman usage of the word *crux* (translated as "cross" in English) also originally indicated an "upright pole." The Catholic Encyclopedia says, "Certain it is, at any rate, that the cross originally consisted of a simple vertical pole, sharpened at its upper end." Sticking to that, some Bible translations use the word "stake" or "tree" instead of "cross." Some Bible writers also used the Greek word *xylon*, meaning a piece of timber or tree, instead of *stauros*. Because of this, certain Bible translations, like the Jerusalem Bible, use the word "tree" in this context.

A member of the Sanhedrin (the Jewish high court) against the execution of Jesus was present when he died. He asked for the body and had it taken to be entombed. Two days later, several female disciples went to the tomb to properly treat the body with spices. They were shocked by what they found.

The large, heavy stone covering the entrance to the tomb had been moved, and the cave was empty. Jesus' body was missing. They ran off to tell Peter and some of the other disciples while Mary Magdalene stayed behind. Crying, she was approached by a caretaker who asked what is wrong. It took her a moment, but she suddenly recognized the man speaking to her—it was Jesus!

In the following days and weeks, hundreds of other disciples also saw and spoke to the resurrected Jesus. Some, like Thomas, had a hard time believing at first. But Jesus gave evidence through miracles that he was who he said he was.

Luke recounts both in the gospel he wrote and in the book of Acts that, after spending time with the apostles and disciples, giving them some last instructions and assurances, Jesus ascended to heaven in front of the apostles with no public fanfare.

Taken as a whole, the four books make a more complete account of Jesus' life and ministry. But what do we know about the men who wrote the Gospels and their original writings?

Matthew

Matthew was loathed by his own people because of his profession; some even considered what he did traitorous. He was a tax collector. To his fellow Jews, tax collectors were nothing more than an irritating thorn, a constant reminder that the Romans were their imperial overlords. Tax collectors were often viewed as sinners, largely because many of them dishonestly demanded more money than required to skim some for themselves. Most Jews considered tax collectors low class and avoided any voluntary association with them.

Matthew wrote his take on events through the lens of his profession. As a tax collector, it is no surprise that he mentions details relating to money and numbers. Likely treated to insults and contempt by his fellow countrymen, he emphasized Jesus' kindness, as reflected in the words he chose to record in Matthew 11:28-30: "Come to me all you who are toiling and loaded down, and I will refresh you...I am mild-tempered and lowly in heart and you will find refreshment for yourselves." Though his fellow Jews despised him for his profession, Matthew found a refreshing difference in how Jesus treated him and others. He enjoyed a close friendship with Jesus and became one of his first apostles. Matthew wrote numerous times regarding mercy, a quality he probably valued very highly.

Matthew wrote the book that bears his name in Palestine, his writings covering the years 2 BC to 33 AD. Although the exact year it was completed is not firmly known, later manuscripts date it to 41 AD. Nowhere in the book does Matthew mention himself as the writer, yet the unanimous belief that he penned it has been unwavering since the second century AD. Early Christians such as Papias, who was a contemporary or very nearly a contemporary of the apostle, attest to Matthew's authorship.

Looking into the language he wrote his original work in, the main objective of his writing, who he was primarily writing to, and the historical context make even more sense of the contents. Fourth-century Greek historian of Christianity Eusebius and fourth/fifth-century Christian scholar Jerome both repeatedly say that Matthew wrote the original manuscript "in his native tongue," Hebrew (later translated into Greek for non-Jews) Jerome backed this up by confirming that there was a Hebrew language copy in a library collection in Caesarea during his day. Since Matthew was in Palestine and his target audience was primarily Jews, it is logical that he would write in their language.

Right from the start, Matthew gets to the heart of his matter—proving to the Jewish people that Jesus is the promised Messiah they have been waiting for. He starts by tracing Jesus' lineage to Abraham, knowing its legal and prophetic importance would not be lost on faithful Jews. His very first words outline Jesus' lineage through Mary, tracing him back to King David of the Israelite tribe of Judah.[29] He then gives a detailed account of the events surrounding Jesus' birth and childhood, presenting unique details not found anywhere else.

Matthew's logical way of thinking is seen in the order in which he writes events. The Gospel is not written chronologically as if it were a journal. Although he writes chronologically where it makes sense or is necessary, he groups Jesus' sermons and parables in topical order, emphasizing key teachings. He writes with the detailed precision one would expect from a man who served in a job that required precision and

---

[29] According to Jewish prophecies in the Old Testament/Hebrew Scriptures, the Messiah would come through the line of Judah.

accuracy.

Mark

On the night Jesus was arrested, a certain young man was among his disciples, having apparently rushed out to the Garden of Gethsemane wearing nothing but an outer coat. He had either heard that Jesus and the apostles had gone to the garden and rushed out to follow or heard about the arrest in progress. All the rest with Jesus that night scattered and fled when the soldiers took him, but one stayed behind. Following Jesus nearby, he was soon spotted. When he was recognized as someone associated with Jesus, the soldiers and chief priests attempted to capture him, too. They grabbed onto his outer garment, but he managed to escape by wriggling out of his clothing running away completely naked.

John Mark (Roman Marcus, his surname), the writer of the Gospel of Mark, is the only one who mentions this young man, likely a firsthand account of his own harrowing escape. Mark was not an apostle, and he implies that he was still young around the time of Jesus' arrest. Mark packs a lot of action into his account of Jesus, some of it as an eyewitness but much of it as a recorder of the apostle Peter's eyewitness account. Second-century Christian scholars like Origen, Papias, and Tertullian attest that Mark wrote his gospel "in accordance with Peter's instructions" and confirmed that Mark was Peter's interpreter. Mark traveled with Peter and had a close relationship with the older apostle. Peter even referred to John Mark as "my son."

Even though Mark's telling of events closely mirrors Matthew's, some unique details and perspectives reflect Peter's influence—for example, when he writes about the terrible storm that rose up on the Sea of Galilee. In his telling, Mark takes the time to mention seemingly insignificant details, such as the fact that Jesus was sleeping on the stern of the boat and using a pillow. These are things that a fisherman such as Peter might take note of.

The storm on the sea of Galilee is just one example of the fast-moving style and content included in Mark, another reflection of the emotional, impulsive, and very observant Peter. But in the details, we can also see that, although Mark was only an earwitness to some of the things he wrote, he was meticulous about accuracy. Eusebius said that "he gave attention, to leave out nothing of what he had heard and to make no false statements in them."

The shortest of the Gospels, Mark doesn't start at the beginning of Jesus' life but instead picks up at the beginning of Jesus' ministry and covers events over the years 29-33 AD. Mark wrote his account around 60-65 AD. He was in Rome at the time, and his target audience was Romans, apparent by the way he explains Jewish customs, culture, and other things that would not be familiar to non-Jews.

However, the gospel account is not where Mark's story ends. He reappears in the book of Acts alongside Paul, in one case as the subject of the older man's most heated incident on record.

Luke

Although Luke is referred to as an evangelist, that was not his first profession. The highly educated man was not an apostle, either. He was a physician, a fact that is reflected in his expansive vocabulary and detailed writing about those who suffered physical ailments—something he would naturally take notice of.

Luke also starts at the beginning of Jesus' story and covers the same years as Matthew—3 BC to 33 AD. He begins in chronological order, but after Jesus begins his ministry, Luke sometimes strays from linear writing and tells certain events and teachings by topic instead. For instance, while Matthew puts Jesus' family tree first, Luke doesn't list it until the third chapter, talking about it in terms of how Jesus' lineage through Joseph was recognized by the Jews at the time of his baptism.

Luke, not an eyewitness to the events he wrote about, interviewed many who were present to compile his writing. Even though his book comes third among the Gospels, Luke wrote it in 56-58 AD, between the time Matthew and Mark wrote theirs. Whereas they wrote to specific groups of people, Luke wrote for anyone who wanted to listen.

Like Mark, Luke's story doesn't end with his Gospel. He also traveled on missionary tours with Paul and is generally accepted as the writer of the action-packed account of the apostles and other first-century Christians in the book of Acts.[30]

John

Filled with fiery zeal and at one time asking if they could call down fire from heaven in vengeance, John and his brother James were labeled

---

[30] Luke is confirmed as the author as far back as second-century writers Irenaeus and Clement of Alexandria and according to the Muratorian Fragment, which is believed to have been written around 170 AD.

"Sons of Thunder" by Jesus.[31] It is interesting to see through John's writings how this dynamic apostle matured and accepted Jesus' teachings, later writing extensively about love.

Likely Jesus' cousin through Mary's sister Salome, John is said to be the apostle with the closest friendship with Jesus. In fact, while Jesus was on the stake dying, he entrusted his mother, likely by then a widow, to John's care.

A fisherman, he and Peter were disparaged as "plain illiterate men" by religious leaders who heard them preach. However, John proved them so very wrong. Far from illiterate, he wrote four books of the Bible besides the Gospel that bears his name.

When he wrote his gospel near the city of Ephesus in 98 AD, John was the last living apostle. He gives the most intimate picture of Jesus and who he was—and the most unique. Only 10 percent of what he covers is mentioned by the other Gospel writers.

In John 20:31, the apostle tells why he wrote his Gospel, saying these things were "written down so that you may believe that Jesus is the Christ, the Son of God" and so that readers "may have life by means of his name."

The accuracy of the four Gospels, Matthew, Mark, Luke, and John, has been confirmed by the writers themselves, those who knew them, and other early Christians who came later. However, there are books that touch on Jesus' life that did not make it into the Bible canon. What were they, and why were they left out?

Apocryphal Books

The four included in the Bible are considered the only divinely-inspired Gospels. However, after these were written, "gospels" of a more fanciful nature began to turn up in writings and oral stories – about thirty of which are known. These have been called "apocryphal," an interesting term from the Greek language that translates as "to hide away." What was alleged to be hidden?

Some claimed to have a greater insider knowledge of Jesus and his teachings—things no one else knew about. For instance, the "Infancy Gospel of Thomas" talks about Jesus' life as a child, portraying him as more of a supernatural Dennis the Menace than the future Messiah. In

---

[31] Jesus quickly corrected the overzealous men and told them that would not be a proper response to the situation.

this work, Jesus used his miraculous powers for mischief and vengeance. Instead of using his power to heal and resurrect the dead, the gospel claims that, as a child, he used it to maim and kill.

In the Gospel of Mary, the title character is the woman most loved by Jesus, who is given special teachings and understandings that she later shares with the apostles and disciples.[32] At one point, she is said to have confronted the apostle Peter over leadership and authority in the congregation.

Other apocryphal books, such as the Gospel of Judas and the Gospel of Peter, attempt to turn villains into heroes and vice versa. Judas' betrayal of Jesus is portrayed as nothing short of heroic, as the book claims he knew the real Jesus better than anyone. In one instance, it tells of a time when Jesus mocked his apostles over a lack of knowledge. In the Gospel of Peter, the writer exonerates Pontius Pilate from any responsibility over Jesus' death.

Many apocryphal books contain writings that experts consider more legend than fact and contradict what is written in the Bible Gospels. For instance, The Birth of Mary presents the idea that although Jesus' mother Mary married Joseph, she remained a virgin for the rest of her life.[33]

So, what are the differences between the Gospels included in the Bible and those that weren't? The biblical Gospels were written by those who knew Jesus or his apostles and were firsthand accounts from their own viewpoints or those who witnessed events. The non-canonical accounts were written by people who never personally knew Jesus or his apostles and often make bold claims that they reveal hidden truths about Jesus. Much of what is written in these is considered to be dubious or outright historical fiction.

Bible scholars have found no real evidence to question the authenticity of the inspired Gospels. But in contrast, Irenaeus, a professed Christian writer of the late second century, wrote that these apocryphal books were the works of apostates that "they themselves have forged, to bewilder the minds of foolish men."

After the biblical Gospels about Jesus ended, what then? After his death, what happened to Jesus' apostles and the work he started?

---

[32] There are questions among scholars about which biblical Mary this refers to, but many believe it to be Mary Magdalene. Most scholars consider this to be a Gnostic text.

[33] The Gospels mention other sons of Mary, Jesus' brothers.

Chapter 3: The Apostles' Missions

With Judas' betrayal of Jesus and subsequent suicide, there was a spot left to fill among the apostles. However, that spot was not filled by Paul but by Matthias. In fact, Paul was not an original apostle (though he is often labeled as one), and he would not show up on the scene until later.

The apostles spear-headed and joined in the ministry work, performing miracles and spreading the "good news" in the temple and "from house to house." However, persecution of what was viewed as a new sect was just beginning to rear its violent head.

One of the fiercest persecutors of Jesus' disciples was a Pharisee named Saul. However, on his way to persecute Jesus' disciples in Damascus, Syria, he had a life-changing experience.

Seeing an extraordinarily bright light flash from the sky, Saul was rendered blind. A voice from heaven asked him, "Why are you persecuting me?" The voice then instructed him what to do next. This voice is identified in the book of Acts as none other than Jesus, now returned to heaven. To his own benefit, Saul decided to follow the instructions, leading to him being healed by a man named Ananias. When Saul regained his sight, he still went to Damascus, but this time, to preach about Jesus instead of persecute.

Things did not go well in Damascus, and Saul fled to Jerusalem. But once there, his reception by the disciples in the city was less than warm—Saul's reputation had preceded him. The disciples had a hard time believing that Saul had made such a drastic and complete turnaround and worried he was there to set a trap for them. However, a kind disciple named Barnabas jumped to Saul's defense and explained to the apostles and others how such an immense change had occurred for Saul.[34]

When word got back to Jerusalem that preaching to the Greeks in the Syrian city of Antioch had good results, Barnabas took Saul to Antioch. There, they found a "considerable crowd," and their work helped continue "adding to the Lord."

This was a very key year in the history of Christianity. The disciples in Antioch assembled over the next year, listening to the teachings that Jesus had left behind. Before Barnabas and Saul left them, by "divine providence," the disciples became known as Christians for the first time.

Sometime after this, Saul and Barnabas set out on their first missionary tour, and it was likely about this time that Saul decided to be known by his Roman name—Paul.

The ministry and missionary tours of the apostles were pretty action-packed, but none more than those of Paul. Shipwrecks, mobs, riots, beatings, stoning, imprisonment, and more plagued his ministry, but that hardly stopped the brave and highly zealous evangelizer.

Paul and Barnabas traveled through numerous cities and countries that roughly encompassed the area from modern-day Italy to Turkey and as far south as Syria and Judea. Despite their initial success in Antioch, things were not all smooth sailing for the evangelizers. They dealt with mixed reactions to their message, ranging from faith to murderous hatred.

Many times, they were forced to make a getaway for their own safety. One of the cities Paul and Barnabas fled to was Lystra, another Roman colony with many buildings and structures carved into the volcanic tuff rock the city was built upon. Their visit started with a miracle but quickly descended into chaos. Paul healed a man who had been crippled his whole life. When the man jumped up and started walking, the people believed it to be the work of their deities. They were convinced that Paul and Barnabas were gods who took the form of men, calling them Hermes and Zeus.

Wanting to show gratitude, the people insisted on sacrificing bulls to Paul and Barnabas despite the apostles' protests. It took some doing, but the evangelizers eventually stopped what would have been an

---

[34] A prominent first-century Christian whose first name was Joseph. The apostles gave him the surname Barnabas, which meant "son of comfort." Like Paul, he was later styled as an apostle even though he was not one of the original twelve.

inappropriate sacrifice to them. But the trouble in Lystra was just beginning.

Sometime later, Jews from Antioch and Iconium came down to Lystra to stir up the city against Paul and Barnabas. It worked. The crowds dragged Paul out of the city and stoned him, leaving only after they believed he was dead.[35] However, when other disciples found out and went to see whether Paul was still alive, they found he had survived. He got up and went with them back into the city. The next day, Paul and Barnabas left for Derbe. Despite the persecution, their ministry succeeded—they had made "quite a few disciples" (Acts 14:21) in the cities they visited.

Boldly, they returned to Antioch, Lystra, and Iconium to check on the new disciples and appoint elders (mature, stable men who could oversee each group) in the congregations they helped establish.

Paul, Silas, and Timothy also got mixed reviews when they reached Thessalonica, a sophisticated center of culture and trade along the *Via Egnatia*. After they spent three Sabbaths in the city synagogue reasoning with the people using scriptures, many Jews became believers. As word got around the city, many Greeks (used here by Luke to include all non-Jews) became believers, as well as quite a few prominent women of Thessalonica.

But then, as in other cities, some of the Jews became outraged by Paul and his companions. Intent on making trouble, they gathered criminals from the streets and started a riot in the city, marching over to the house where Paul and Silas were staying as guests. The crowd shouted that Paul, Silas, and other Christians were "stirring up trouble" throughout the whole world. Essentially accusing the men of sedition, the crowd claimed they opposed Caesar and supported this Jesus as king—a very dangerous claim that made the city rulers sit up and take notice. Paul and Silas were again forced to flee the city. From there, they went to Beroea (Berea), a city that may have had a very sizeable Jewish population.

Though the Beroeans (Bereans) eagerly listened to what Paul had to teach, they did not just take his word for it. Instead, they checked what he was saying against the scriptures to make sure what he was saying was true. For this, Luke called them "noble-minded." Through teaching and

---

[35] Stoning was an ancient punishment in which large stones were thrown at an offender until they died.

research, many in the city became believers, including many notable men and women of the city. But soon, Paul's Thessalonican troubles followed him to Beroea.

The Jews who had stirred up the people of Thessalonica followed Paul to Beroea to continue to stir up the people against Paul and the others. Things deteriorated again, and Paul, Silas, and Timothy were forced to leave Beroea. Paul was secreted away to Athens, and he waited for Timothy and Silas to join him there.

Paul, not one to stay idle, went about preaching while he waited for the others to reach Athens. His interactions there were quite different from those in other cities. Athens was an epicenter of religion, philosophy, and enlightened learning. Paul took the time to observe what was happening around the city and tailored his speech to the people.

However, the Epicurean and Stoic philosophers who heard him labeled Paul an ignorant "chatterer" who spouted nonsense.[36] [37] Others were bewildered that he talked about a god unknown to them.[38] However, because the city was generally tolerant of new thinking and ideas, people were curious about what Paul had to say. They took him to the Areopagus, a hill that served as the site of the Athenian court system. There, he gave a clever and thought-provoking speech starting with the typical Greek opening line "Men of Athens." Although he knew what he would tell them was vastly at odds with their beliefs, he took the time to commend them for being spiritually minded.

Even though Paul carefully tailored his speech to his Greek audience, not everyone present was won over by his words. When he introduced certain teachings to the people, such as the resurrection, some scoffed in derision while others believed. Yet, many did believe. Among them were prominent Athenians, including a judge on the Areopagus council. The speech was so noteworthy and compelling that a plaque commemorating it remains at the Areopagus to this day.

---

[36] Epicureans, followers of the philosopher Epicurious, believed that pleasures and fine things were life's ultimate goal, but with moderation to avoid bad consequences.

[37] Followers of Stoic philosophies held radical ethical views and believed that a person could get rid of negative emotions like fear and envy through moral and intellectual perfectionism.

[38] Though the Roman Empire was tolerant of the wide variety of religions found within it, it was against Greek and Roman law to introduce new gods, especially if they were not in line with the existing religion of a city or region.

Next, Paul traveled to Corinth, a relatively large, wealthy port city and center of trade with a notorious reputation for moral decadence. Here, Silas and Timothy finally met up with him. Though they again experienced some stiff and abusive opposition from a Jewish contingent, many in the city became believers. Despite this, Paul stayed for a year and a half, long enough to help establish a congregation—the same congregation to which Paul would later write two letters.

Their preaching seemed to succeed quickly in Philippi, a city along the Via Egnatia that had been settled by many Roman military veterans and whose people were proud of their Roman citizenship.[39]

Not all experiences involved large crowds. Some individuals and their families responded directly to the message from the apostles. One of these was in Philippi. There, they met a woman named Lydia, who was seemingly unmarried or widowed. A merchant from Thyatira, she sold clothing made from the famed purple dye of her hometown. Lydia responded favorably to the message and showed extraordinary hospitality to the preachers. Soon, she and her entire household were baptized.

One unexpected response came after a rather surprising incident.

Paul and Silas had been arrested. Deep in the lower parts of a damp prison, the men were painfully held fast in stocks. But during the night, an earthquake shook the jail, opening the cell doors and freeing all the prisoners, including Paul and Silas, from their bonds. The jailer came and saw the cell doors open and immediately assumed all the prisoners had escaped. Despondent, he was about to kill himself with his sword when Paul called out for him to stop, letting him know none had fled.[40]

The jailer, relieved and grateful, now gladly accepted Paul's message, and he and his entire family were baptized "without delay."

Though Paul and his companions were often troubled by groups of people, certain individuals caused some intense trouble. One of these was a sorcerer who went head-to-head with Paul and Barnabas.

The men had set out on their first mission to Cyprus, an island under the rule of the Roman Senate and Barnabas' native country. While there, they preached to a Roman proconsul named Sergius Paulus, who was

---

[39] It is possible there was no synagogue there, and some scholars believe it may be because of the strong military character of the city that Jews were not allowed to gather for worship.

[40] Ancient jailers bore a lot of responsibility for their prisoners. If any escaped, the sentence of the escapee would be imposed on the jailer. So, thinking a whole prison of inmates had escaped, the jailer naturally feared the heavy, unpleasant penalties that would be imposed on him.

interested in what they had to say. But the proconsul's companion, Bar-Jesus (also known as Elymas which means "sorcerer) tried to disrupt them and dissuade Sergius Paulus from believing the men. Paul did not put up with it for long. Mincing no words, he told Bar-Jesus that he was "full of every sort of fraud and every sort of villainy" before calling him a "son of the Devil" and an "enemy of everything righteous." With that, he miraculously rendered the sorcerer temporarily blind, letting him know it was from the hand of God. For his part, the proconsul was astounded by what he saw and the things Paul taught and became a believer.

Another incident in which Paul cured a demon-possessed girl soon landed him in trouble. Paul and Silas were dragged to the city magistrates by an angry mob, had their clothes torn off, and were flogged before being thrown in jail.

Sometimes, Paul and the other apostles had to overcome problems from within their ranks. After spending some time in Antioch and Jerusalem, Paul and Barnabas were ready for their second missionary tour in late 49 or early 50 AD. This mission was to check on and encourage disciples in the congregations that had formed. However, they experienced a rough start: an argument over whom they should take with them on the mission. Barnabas wanted to take John Mark.[41] In fact, Barnabas was "determined" that he come with them. Paul, however, objected on the basis that John Mark had (for some undisclosed reason) left in middle of their first mission.

"A sharp burst of anger" ensued over the matter, and the two men parted ways. Barnabas took John Mark and went on a mission to Cyprus, while Paul took Silas to visit the congregations in Syria and Cilicia.[42] This mission would take Paul back to Lystra and Derbe.

While in that area, Paul met a young man named Timothy. Paul was told many good things about Timothy and wanted him to accompany them. Timothy would become a good, loyal friend and lifelong traveling companion to Paul and would play an important part in the ministry and strengthening of the congregations.

---

[41] Acts says "John, the one surnamed Mark"—the Gospel writer and a cousin of Barnabas.

[42] Silas was member of the Christian congregation in Jerusalem, likely also called by his Roman name Silvanus. Possibly the same Silvanus who later acted as Peter's secretary, helping him write the books of the Bible named after him. Silas and Timothy also helped Paul write both letters to the Thessalonians.

Paul, Silas, and Timothy set off for Asia, but the account in Acts says that, along the way, they were blocked "by the spirit of Jesus" and redirected. So, instead, they traveled through Galatia (modern-day southern Poland and western Ukraine). Attempting to travel through Bithynia (northwestern Turkey), they were again blocked and redirected. This time, they traveled to the city of Troas in the district of Mysia (another northwest district of ancient Turkey). Once there, Paul had a divinely inspired vision in which he was instructed to preach in Macedonia (an area that today encompasses Greece, southwestern Bulgaria, and the Republic of North Macedonia).

Despite his busy preaching schedule, Paul kept in touch with what was happening in congregations he had previously established or visited. When things got tough for some, he wrote to encourage and comfort them.

While in Corinth on his second missionary tour, he wrote to the congregation in Thessalonica. Even after Paul fled from the mob violence the Jews had incited, the Christians that remained in the city continued to suffer persecution, loss, and other heavy pressures. Paul's concern moved him to write his first letter to encourage, support, and give some gentle reminders about how Christians should act.

But, sometimes, the congregations got off course, and he needed to write stronger letters of counsel to help them correct matters. Sometime after his first letter, Paul heard that some in Thessalonica were teaching inaccurate things about Jesus and had strayed from the original truths they were taught. He attempted to correct them in his second letter. He also saw that some had not followed his reminders in the first letter, so he again admonished them to behave decently as a follower of Jesus should.

Although Paul and his companions focused heavily on their ministry, they also traveled to encourage and support those who had already become Christians in various cities. That is how Paul kicked off his third missionary tour: traveling around Galatia and Phrygia to strengthen those who were already disciples. Meanwhile, Apollos was sent back to Corinth.

Sometimes, that support came in the form of corrective teaching. A prime example of this was in Ephesus. Accompanied by Timothy and Erastus, Paul spoke in the synagogue for three months. Even though Paul used reasoning and persuasive speeches, not all accepted what he was teaching. In fact, some got up and railed against the beliefs of the

Christian way.[43]

Other times, as with Thessalonica, Paul's support came in the form of letters to congregations experiencing issues. For instance, during this third missionary tour, Paul was disturbed by the reports he was getting about the congregation in Corinth. He corrected them regarding unity, immorality, and rejecting false teachings. He had also apparently received questions from the congregation, which he took the time to reply to. He wrote them two letters, now known as the Bible books of First and Second Corinthians.

Paul spent the next two years preaching in this area of Asia, but much of the action happened in Ephesus. There, Paul, accompanied by Timothy and Erastus, performed many miracles, including casting demons out of those possessed. In one incident, a demon-possessed man heartily beat up seven sons of a priest. That event put a solid fear of the wicked spirits into the people Paul was preaching to. After that, many took their books on magical arts and burned them in a huge fire, even though they were worth a lot of money. The book of Acts says after this, the Word of God spread even more, and people changed their lives according to what they had learned.

That was not the end of the action in Ephesus. A great riot was stirred up, instigated by an angry silversmith. Ephesus was famed for its grand temple to the goddess Artemis (one of the seven wonders of the ancient world). Because of this, there were many silversmiths in the city—a whole guild of them—who made and sold shrines and other religious items connected to the worship of Artemis. Paul, Gaius, Aristarchus, and other Christians began teaching that the gods the city worshipped did not exist and were no more than manmade idols. Many people in Ephesus became Christians due to this, but this denouncement did not go over well with everyone. These teachings were bad for business as far as the silversmiths were concerned. Demetrius, a silversmith, also worried that aside from business, the Christian teachings would also dim the magnificence of their city, temple, and gods.

Demetrius gave an angry speech, whipping the city into a frenzy. As a result, a riot ensued, and the confused mob rushed into the city's theater arena, taking Gaius and Aristarchus with them. Paul tried to follow but was stopped by fellow Christians and some concerned city officials.

---

[43] The first-century Christians called their newfound beliefs "The Way." For them, it was not just a new religion but a newly adopted way of thinking and life.

Inside the arena, the people loudly yelled about various things, most not even knowing why they were there. Finally, a Jewish man named Alexander was pushed forward to calm the crowds. Alexander had a real challenge on his hands. On seeing that he was a Jew, the crowds chanted, "Great is Artemis of the Ephesians!" for two hours, not letting him get a word out.

A city official finally stepped in to help. He declared that Paul and the others had broken no laws, but the crowd was in imminent danger of being charged with sedition. He told them that if they had a problem, it should go through the proper legal channels—not an angry mob scene. His words hit their mark, and the crowd dispersed.

After this, Paul, Timothy, Aristarchus, Sopater, and several others decided to travel back to Macedonia through Greece, stopping at several places. After a few months and a side trip to Syria to avoid a plot by the Jews, Paul knew his ministry was coming to an end. He told the others that the Holy Spirit was leading him towards Jerusalem, where he would face imprisonment. Along the way, he said tearful goodbyes to many in the congregations he had helped form and strengthen. He did not go alone. At least Luke accompanied him to Jerusalem, where he *was* arrested and began a different phase of his life and ministry.

The rest of the apostles and missionaries continued their work in preaching and with the congregations. But the Christians had reached a new phase. Their foundations were being solidified, and Christians were spreading the word wherever they were.

Chapter 4: The First Church

Though the apostles and other Christians preached with wildly varying results, until 36 AD, their focus was on persuading the Jewish population that Jesus was the Messiah and had instituted a new way.[44] The Jews were the first priority, so the apostles started in the city with perhaps the greatest concentration of Jewish people—Jerusalem. It's no surprise, then, that this is where the first Christian congregation was also established. But who was going to lead it?

There is no indication in the scriptures that one particular man was the congregation's leader, but the apostles John, James, and Peter were mentioned as pillars, with the dynamic Peter characteristically taking the lead as spokesman on many occasions.[45] They were not alone to shoulder the responsibility of the growing Christian discipleship. Others besides the twelve apostles, referred to as "older men" or elders, helped oversee the congregation in Jerusalem.

However, there were many Jewish people and communities outside of Jerusalem and Judea. The Diaspora, or dispersed Jews, had settled far and wide, hence the need for a preaching campaign. Though the Judeo-Christians were preaching to people of the same background, it is evident from Acts that they did not always receive a warm welcome.

---

[44] After that, the message was opened up to Gentiles, or non-Jewish people.

[45] This was the apostle James. After his death, Jesus' half-brother James replaced him in the governing body.

Though they had long awaited the Messiah, not all Jews accepted the teachings of Jesus, and many were even hostile towards them. As we saw from the previous account of Paul's travels, the Christians had some success in speaking to the common Jewish people, yet some were vehemently opposed to the spread of these new teachings. The Jewish religious leaders had the apostles arrested and brought before the Jewish high court on several occasions and the apostles were imprisoned multiple times for their message.[46]

Yet, there was a lot of positive response as well, particularly from the Greek-speaking Jewish communities.

Many Jews had migrated and settled throughout the Mediterranean region, living in cities surrounded by Hellenistic culture and Greek-speaking neighbors. It was inevitable that Greek culture and ideas would seep into Jewish communities. Still, these migrants continued to practice their Jewish religion and traveled to Jerusalem for the annual Jewish festivals.

Greek Influences

Even though the Roman Empire reigned supreme at the time, Greek culture was still a hot trend (even for the Romans). The early Christians weren't totally immune to its influence and, in some ways, adapted their message to a Greek-obsessed Mediterranean world.

The apostle Paul had a real knack for this. Highly educated, he was familiar with many Greek philosophical concepts, such as those of the Stoics and Epicureans. Paul found common ground even among people with completely opposite outlooks. He cited poets like Aratus and Cleanthes to support his points and used understood concepts and terms to explain his message.

Paul also referenced Greek life in his teachings, using well-known cultural icons like the "temple of the unknown god" and athletic games such as foot races to help make his points come to life in a way people would understand. Some Greek words, such as *karpos*, meaning fruit or fruitage, were used metaphorically by the Christians to explain concepts or paint a picture that could be easily understood and embraced.

It wasn't just Greek life that colored the writings of the first-century Christians. Many books now in the Bible were either written or translated

---

[46] Though, on more than one occasion, they were miraculously freed from prison.

into Greek to reach a wider audience.[47] They borrowed Greek terms, Greek sentence structures and style, and ancient Greek pop culture. But one thing the first-century Christians adamantly rejected was philosophical or pagan Greek religious beliefs. Many Greek teachings clashed hard with Christian values, so Christians were admonished not to mix Greek-inspired beliefs with what they were taught. In fact, in several letters Paul wrote to the congregations, he highlighted the need to avoid the influence of these sorts of Greek teachings—quite a feat in a world dominated by them.

On the other hand, Judaism had mixed itself with Greek culture and thinking to some extent, thanks in part to prominent Jews like the first-century writer Philo. Philo was a fan of certain concepts taught by the Greek philosopher Plato, although he was not entirely sold on what the famed thinker had to say. Still, Plato influenced him to accept the teaching on the immortality of the soul—something not taught or accepted by the apostles and most first-century Christians, nor most Jews for that matter. Philo was not a Christian or a convert, but his ideas influenced some professed Christians, including other Christian writers who accepted his concept. In part, this concept may have found its way into the thinking of some Christians through Jewish converts to Christianity.

The immortality of the soul was not the only Greek concept to make its way into some Jewish and Christian circles. Philo's take on the Greek word *logos* (meaning reason, or the word), along with the influences of Plato, Aristotle, and the Stoics, also formed the basis for a teaching that became popular in Christendom later on—the Trinity.[48]

The shadows of Hellenization could also be discerned in the works of later writers such as Clement, Origen, and Eusebius. Subsequent generations of Christian writers, including Gregory of Nazianzus (dubbed the "Christian Demosthenes") and Gregory of Nyssa (who also had a

---

[47] As the Greek language dominated society, Hebrew was pushed into the background, even among Jews. The meaning and understanding of important scriptures written in Hebrew would be lost to vast swaths of the population unless it could be translated into Greek. Through the last three centuries BCE, Jewish scholars meticulously translated Hebrew scripture into Greek. The result? What is today known as the Greek Septuagint version of the Hebrew scriptures. *The translation into Greek was an epic game-changer. Without this translation into Greek, the context of the Christian message could not have been understood on such a large scale. People of diverse backgrounds and cultures could now understand the important history and concepts that led to Christianity.*

[48] The word "trinity" is not found in the Bible writings.

trendy moniker—"the Father of Mysticism") turned out poetry and other artistic works that were said to rival those of the Greeks.[49]

Though Greek teachings, religion, and philosophy were all but non-existent in the original Christian congregations, the language and culture influenced first-century Christian writings. However, Greek philosophy slowly began to permeate the works and teachings of later Christian writers, as will be seen later on.

---

[49] Demosthenes was a Greek statesman, orator, and prolific speech writer.

Chapter 5: Early Christian Communities

As the number of Christians grew, so did the need for responsible men to get things organized and operating. Some of these responsible men, mature Christians, joined the apostles to comprise a central "governing body" that oversaw the expansion of the Christian congregations. They also gave instructions, clarified doctrinal teachings, and made decisions based on scriptures and Jesus' teachings. This governing body helped appoint elders in other congregations and appointed overseers to help with special projects like relief collection and food distribution to Christians in famine-plagued areas. [50] The elders also had assistants who helped them with non-spiritual tasks within the congregation. These men were called *diakonos*, a broad term for minister (some translate it as deacon).

For the most part, early Christians were on board with this structure, though some had to be counseled for being too prominence-oriented. Yet, there was no real "ladder" to climb. Being given oversight meant more responsibility, which most shouldered admirably. None were paid; it was voluntary self-sacrifice to work for the good of the congregation, done out of love and passion for the work. Leaders were regular men with secular jobs and families to care for. Christians saw this way of doing things as God's arrangement guided by the Holy Spirit.

---

[50] Men who were responsible for the care of the congregation.

One of the greatest tasks of the governing body was organizing the preaching work. This was a massive undertaking. Jesus' apostles and disciples were initially tasked with preaching to Jewish people "of all nations." This would be difficult for their small numbers. Jews were spread throughout the Roman Empire and spoke many different languages. However, the current disciples only spoke a few of these. How could they possibly get this job done?

Acts 2:1-4 tells of a miracle among a gathered group of disciples that made this widespread preaching possible: "Suddenly there was a noise from heaven, just like that of a rushing, stiff breeze, and it filled the whole house where they were sitting. And tongues as if of fire became visible to them and were distributed, and one came to rest on each one of them, and they all became filled with holy spirit and started to speak in different languages, just as the spirit enabled them to speak."

Given the miraculous ability to speak in foreign languages, the disciples could now preach to Jews from other nations. Jews from all over the Roman Empire and beyond were gathered in Jerusalem for a religious festival at the time, and the disciples preached to them in their native languages.

The people were stunned, but the reception was mixed. Some were "perplexed" as to how it was possible they were being spoken to in their own language, and others thought that the disciples were drunk. Peter, however, quickly cleared things up. In a speech to the crowd, he told them that the disciples were not drunk at all; the Holy Spirit had given them this miraculous ability. From then on, word about Jesus and all he had done spread ever faster.

But it wasn't until 36 CE that the job of preaching broadened considerably. It all started with a Gentile (non-Jewish person) named Cornelius. A wealthy man of status, Cornelius was a Roman centurion (a military commander in charge of 100 soldiers) in the city of Caesarea. Despite his elite status, Cornelius often used his wealth to help the needy. Although he wasn't a Jew or a convert, Acts describes him and his family as devout and God-fearing.

One afternoon, Cornelius was praying when an angel approached him in a vision. The angel told him that God had seen his good works and sincerely devout nature and taken special note of it. He was directed to summon the apostle Peter, who was in another city thirty miles away. The next day, Peter got the memo in the form of his own perplexing vision.

Just as he walked downstairs, trying to figure out what the vision could possibly mean, the men from Cornelius came knocking at his door. Peter went with him, and long story short, Cornelius and his entire household were baptized. They became some of the first non-Jewish Christian proselytes, and under divine guidance given to Peter, the door to Christianity was now open to everyone, no matter their religion or background. With that, Christianity took off on a whole new level.

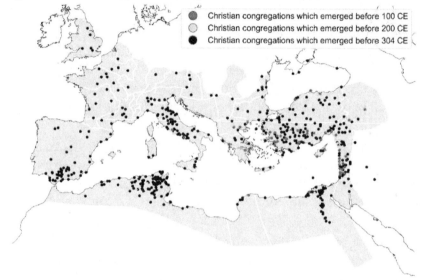

Distribution of Christian congregations in the first three centuries.

Jan Fousek, Vojtěch Kaše, Adam Mertel, Eva Výtvarová, Aleš Chalupa. Citation: Fousek J, Kaše V, Mertel A, Výtvarová E, Chalupa A (2018) Spatial constraints on the diffusion of religious innovations: The case of early Christianity in the Roman Empire. PLoS ONE 13(12): e0208744. *https://doi.org/10.1371/journal.pone.0208744, CC BY-SA 4.0 <https://creativecommons.org/licenses/by-sa/4.0>, via Wikimedia Commons; https://commons.wikimedia.org/wiki/File:Distribution_of_the_documented_presence_of_Christia n_congregations_in_the_first_three_centuries.tif*

For Jewish and Gentile converts alike, Christianity was not simply about changing their religion; it was an entirely new way of life—a whole different culture. The foundation of that culture was love. Not romantic love (Greek *eros*) but love based on principle and true family-like affection (Greek *agape* and *philia*). That *philia*—brotherly love—inspired Christians to call one another brother and sister.

That love was to be without prejudice—race, background, class, social status, and occupation didn't matter. That's not to say that some Christians didn't have their hurdles to overcome regarding ingrained prejudices—even the apostle Peter struggled for a while. But Paul preached that God welcomed all who wanted to learn about him without bias and that those in the congregations should do the same. So, the early congregations had a wide range of ethnic and social diversity—from free men to slaves, from the uneducated to the highly educated, from lower class to nobles. They were tentmakers, fishermen, soldiers, weavers, merchants, nobles, prominent citizens, officials in the emperor's court, senators, and people from all backgrounds. Yet, they were not split apart by their differences. Love bound them together.

Jesus said this type of love would identify them as his true disciples, and it became a hallmark of their culture. It affected everything they did and said, even when life and death were on the line. Second-century Christian author Tertullian wrote that non-Christians noticed this love that Christians had among themselves and observed that "they are even ready to die for one another."

Christians didn't limit their love to just one another. They worked at being good neighbors to everyone. Their love was about more than just not harming others or doing immoral things. It was an active and proactive type of caring. They were encouraged to be forces for good in their communities.

They worked and lived modestly to provide for themselves and their families and have a little extra in case others were in need. Arrangements were made to care for widows, orphans, and others who needed help within the congregation. In some cases, those who had the means sold property and possessions and pooled their resources, giving what they had to the apostles arranging the distribution. This arrangement was very effective—so much so that Acts 4:34 says that "there was no one among them in need."

Christians didn't just help those in their immediate area but were part of an interconnected network that stretched as far as there were congregations. The first recorded example of Christian relief work took place during the reign of Roman Emperor Claudius. There was a famine in Judea, and most of the poor had no resources to acquire food. Christians in Antioch took stock of what they could give and, with the help of Paul and Barnabas, arranged for relief contributions to be sent to Judea.

Interestingly, all the funds collected were given voluntarily and distributed by volunteers. No one gave because they were embarrassed or forced into it, took a cut of the money, or were paid for their efforts in distributing (some of which took considerable time, effort, and travel). It was all done out of love and care for each other. Everything that was collected went directly toward caring for those who needed it.

Not long after that, near the beginning of Roman Emperor Nero's reign in 55 CE, many Christians in Judea were still struggling with poverty. Paul headed up a massive collection effort by the congregations in Galatia, Achaia, and Macedonia. In 56 CE, they took everything they collected. Paul, accompanied by several Christian men for safety's sake, personally delivered the contributions to those in Judea.

Aside from helping one another, Christians were law-abiding citizens. They viewed the governmental authorities—yes, even the much-hated Romans—as allowed by God to be in their positions. Law and order brought a measure of peace and stability to their society, and they did their part to cooperate, as it benefited all. They did not want to take those benefits without giving back.

Christians quietly paid their taxes, even though for many of the Jews, the taxes were a real sore point and the catalyst for violent clashes over the years. They also willingly performed whatever civic duties the government asked of them, applying the principle Jesus spoke of in Matthew 5:41: "If someone under authority impresses you into service for a mile, go with him two miles."

There were, however, limits to their compliance. Although Christians obeyed governmental authorities, they obeyed God first and foremost. So, if they were commanded or compelled to do something that went against God's laws and principles or their trained consciences, that is where their compliance with human laws ended. For example, there were many instances when the apostles and disciples were imprisoned and commanded to stop preaching. Their response? "We must obey God as ruler rather than men." They would not allow anything the authorities commanded to jeopardize their relationship with God.

The lives of first-century Christians revolved around spiritual matters. There are many examples in the Bible and the testimony of writers like Tertullian, who spoke about the Christians meeting together to discuss, teach, and listen to the holy writings. When some of the Hebrew-speaking Christians slacked off in this area, Paul reminded them not to "forsake the gathering of themselves together." This was for their benefit and to encourage others they met with. This made the congregational arrangement beneficial to all who participated.

They also made preaching and Christian teaching a focus in their lives. Both men and women went from house to house in an organized fashion, the most efficient way to ensure everyone heard the message. They also tried to reach those in the markets and other public places.

Despite the good works and love among the Christians, they were still imperfect people. They experienced real problems like anyone else. Paul and the other apostles had to give counsel on numerous occasions, warning that some congregations needed to get their act together. The Christians were to maintain high moral conduct, but not everyone did so. Some were mixed up in dishonest behavior and immorality; others became apostates promoting sects, drunkards, extortioners, and slanders. In one case, a man was sleeping with his father's wife. Many turned around when corrected, but a few were unrepentant, and these weren't allowed to stick around and influence others. They were removed from the congregation so as not to contaminate its moral cleanness.

Flaws and all, the early Christians strived to maintain the right balance between being good family members, citizens, congregation members, and, most of all, good in God's eyes. But they were still refining themselves to get it right according to what Jesus taught.

Chapter 6: Removal of Jewish Characteristics

While it's true that Jesus and some of the apostles laid down some scathing words on the Jewish Pharisees, his purpose was not to create animosity between his followers and the Jews. However, many of the Jewish religious leaders were offended by the continued proselytizing and conversion of Jews to Christianity. Aside from that, one of the biggest points of contention between Jews and Christians was the identity of the long-awaited Messiah.

Even though there was continuity between Jewish beliefs and the teachings of Christians, the gap between them was obvious. Both groups believed in one Almighty God, believed the Hebrew Scriptures were sacred and divinely inspired, highly regarded the prophets and faithful men of ancient times, and rejected pagan beliefs. The Gospels can't be read without bumping into copious quotes and citations from the Hebrew Scriptures. These Jewish teachings and beliefs comprised a body of information that pointed to the Messiah. But just who that was and what his purpose was—well, that is where their paths diverged.

Christians taught that the old Jewish belief system was replaced by the new way that Jesus had started. His death had started a new covenant in which the Jewish people were no longer solely God's chosen people, but God's acceptance of their worship was contingent on their acceptance of Jesus as the Messiah. "Out with the old and in with the new" did not sit well with everyone. This proved to be true even among Jews-turned-

Christians.

Perhaps one of the most hotly debated topics of the day was circumcision. Jewish law required all males to be circumcised eight days after being born. And if a man were a convert to Judaism, the requirement of circumcision still stood, even though it would be far more memorable as an adult. Many Jewish Christians felt that the requirement also applied to Gentile men who converted to Christianity. They argued that they would need to be circumcised to be approved by God.

Paul and Barnabas strongly argued with those in the congregations in Syria, Antioch, and Cilicia against the Christian need for circumcision. Since they couldn't agree on such a sensitive topic, the matter was brought to the central governing body in Jerusalem to sort out.

Peter was the first to speak in favor of not adding the burden of circumcision to Christians. James, speaking next, backed him up. The decision from the whole governing body was a unanimous vote to not impose circumcision on *anyone*—probably to the great relief of many. This decision was just one area in which the Christians were leaving their former Jewish customs behind.

Under Jewish law, certain animals (such as pigs) were considered unclean to eat and were never found on the dinner table of a law-abiding Jewish person. But one day, Peter had a vision, and pork, among other formerly forbidden foods, was now allowed on the menu. In this vision, recorded in Acts 10:11-15, Peter saw a large sheet come down from heaven, and all sorts of four-footed animals, birds, and reptiles were on it. A voice from heaven told Peter to eat. Peter was horrified—he would never dare eat an unclean animal. Three times, the voice assured him it was okay to eat, giving divine permission to have whatever meat they saw fit. However, it is nearly certain that many Jewish Christians had the same repulsed reaction as Peter. Later, Paul told the Corinthians that if they were guests in someone's house, to "eat whatever is put before you."[51]

Another avenue where Christianity diverged from Jewish custom was in the socializing between Jews and Gentiles. The two groups previously did not mix socially, let alone eat together. According to Jewish religious leaders, any Jew who even *entered* the house of a non-Jew was considered

---

[51] Here, Paul was primarily talking about meats offered to pagan gods and then sold in the market. Some Christians objected to eating these because they had been used in pagan rites. However, he would not have told the congregation to eat whatever they were served if there were divine restrictions on certain meats.

ceremonially unclean. Peter, after converting Cornelius to Christianity, set a precedent for eating meals with Gentile Christians and apparently did so for the next thirteen years—that was until he landed in Syrian Antioch. Many Jewish Christians had been slow to shed their previous ways of thinking and doing, and this was one thing they strictly adhered to.

When Peter found out some Jewish Christians were coming in from Jerusalem, he suddenly abandoned mealtime with Gentile Christians, pretending it never happened out of fear of being ostracized by the visitors. The other Jewish Christians followed suit, with even Barnabas jumping in on the charade. Paul, however, caught wind of what was happening and gently but firmly corrected them. All Christians should be unified regardless of background.

What Peter and the others had done was not just a matter of meal habits. By adopting that attitude, they would be all but voiding the decision made by the governing body in Jerusalem. When they made their decision on circumcision, the governing body had concluded their words by saying, "For the holy spirit_and we ourselves have favored adding no further burden to you except these necessary things: to keep abstaining from things sacrificed to idols, from blood, from what is strangled, and from sexual immorality." Effectively, they declared the Mosaic Law no longer binding for Christians—everyone only needed to follow the new way.

In general, the Christians were not slowly separating themselves from their Jewish roots in a bid to cause division. Their whole goal was to help the Jewish people understand Jesus' teachings. And, for the most part, they tried to do it with love.

A good example is a well-known second-century dialogue between Justin Martyr, a Christian, and the Jewish Trypho. Rather than being confrontational, Justin appealed to his Jewish companion by first assuring him that he had the utmost respect for the Jewish people. Justin used persuasive words tempered with a brotherly tone to convince Trypho that Jesus is the Messiah. Though in the end they agreed to disagree, they parted as friends.

Certainly not all interactions between Jews and Christians went that well, but it helps show the complex and varied dynamic between the groups. However, it wasn't long before it was just the Jewish beliefs that Christians departed from - many began to depart from the original teachings of Christianity itself.

Chapter 7: One Religion, Many Versions

The apostles John and Paul called it correctly (under divine inspiration). By the end of the first century, deviation from the original teachings of Jesus and the apostles had begun. The mixing of philosophies and other religious ideas, old and new, gave birth to many new offshoots that operated under the banner of Christianity.

One of these movements, Gnosticism, got a foothold in the first century but had started to become popular by the second century AD. Partly mystical, partly Stoic philosophy, among other things, Gnosticism is believed by some scholars to have been started by a magician named Simon, who is referenced in the book of Acts.[52]

The idea of being aware of deeply hidden mystical things, such as the special knowledge embedded in Bible numbers, appealed to some. The concepts behind Gnosticism were nothing new, even for the first century. Gnostics took little bits from here and there—a dash of Judaism, a smattering of ideas from ancient cultures like Babylon and Egypt, a few concepts from eastern religions, and later, a sprinkling of Christianity.[53]

According to Gnosticism, the God of the Jews and Christians was not the almighty Creator but a lesser god who ruled one of 345 heavens. They

---

[52] Unlike the sleight-of-hand magicians of today, Simon practiced magical arts connected to the occult.

[53] Some of the eastern religious concepts included were things like balances of good and evil—yin and yang

believed that the creation of the universe was a big, reckless mistake by a more supreme deity named Sophia (or Wisdom). With the help of a semi-divine "craftsman", Sophia inadvertently created a world (earth) that was simply a copy of another existing realm. The malevolent craftsman, Demiurge (corresponding the Christian and Jewish Almighty God Yahweh) had an obvious bias for the Jewish people and set himself up in this world as the only existing god, angering other, higher deities. If that wasn't enough to cause the first church fathers to declare Gnosticism a heresy, there was more. Demiurge, an angry, jealous sort, causes all kinds of problems on earth because of his favoritism. In a bid to save humans from all this trouble, the gods of the other 364 heavens sent Jesus Christ to Earth as a rescuer. A later Gnostic philosopher, Basilides, declared that Jesus did not actually die. His death was a delusion or vision.

Though these beliefs were deemed heresy, not everyone agreed. Some, like the Gnostic teacher Valentinus, believed the movement meshed well with Christian teachings. Instead of contradicting Christian teachings, some Gnostic teachers put a spin on the original teachings, infusing them with a Stoic flavor at times. They traded the ideas of sin and repentance for the concepts of sin and faith as consequences of merely existing. Instead of salvation being open to anyone, it was only available to those with special mystical knowledge. Instead of freedom through Jesus' sacrifice, it was attained by denying oneself any bodily desires.

Inconsistent and difficult to comprehend, Gnosticism was largely rejected by early Christians as an aberration encased in a thinly veiled layer of Christianity.

Possibly cropping up as the Temple of Jerusalem was destroyed by the Romans in 70 AD, the Ebionites sprang from a splinter group of Jewish Christians. With no archaeological evidence to support their existence, they might have forever stayed in obscurity if it weren't for the accounts of their critics. Justin Martyr and Irenaeus mention them, but the most complete account was written by Epiphanius in the fourth century, even though what he says about them only provides a general description. The Ebionites were among eighty sects that Epiphanius denounced as heretical.

The heretic label was fastened to the Ebionites due to their mixing of Judaism and Christianity. Though it may seem similar, the Ebionites should not be mistaken for Jewish Christians. There was a big difference. Jewish Christians were Jewish by birth and converted to Christianity, fully adopting the Christian faith and accepting that they were no longer under Jewish law. The Ebionites, however, were Jewish Christians who adopted the fundamentals of Christian teachings but "stubbornly clung" to Jewish law, holding it as an obligation, even though Christians were no longer under the Mosaic (Jewish) law. [54] They maintained that since Jesus was a Jew who used the Mosaic Law in his teachings, it was the right way to live.

Like the Jews and Christians, they believed in one Almighty God, but unlike Jews or Christians, they believed in Jesus with a certain twist. They reportedly only embraced Matthew's Gospel except for the virgin birth part.[55] They believed that Jesus was a true prophet and the awaited Messiah but did not have a divine origin. As far as they were concerned, he was a regular human and the natural son of both Mary *and* Joseph. The only reason he could claim Messiah status was that he strictly followed Jewish law—a lofty example that they strived to imitate. Sure, he was a great example, and one had to listen to his teachings to find the Kingdom of God, but many Ebionites did not believe his sacrifice covered their sins.

Still, the Ebionites didn't hold onto *all* Jewish practices. They deemed the long-standing practice of animal sacrifices no longer necessary or required due to the distinctly Christian belief that Jesus' death was a final sacrifice covering their sins. Part of their resistance to completely moving away from Jewish law might have been fueled by the opening of Christianity to the Gentiles and their "anything goes" diet. The Ebionites preferred to strictly adhere to Jewish dietary guidelines and the no-fraternizing-with-Gentiles rule of the past. The Christian congregation was now a melting pot of cultures, and they could not accept that.

It wasn't just the Gentiles the Ebionites took issue with. They also had a big problem with the Apostle Paul, who had been a Jewish Pharisee before he saw the literal light of the Lord on the road and converted. Regarding him as an apostate, the Ebionites completely rejected his writings. Unlike them, Paul taught the end of Jewish law and practiced it, too—one of the things that led the Ebionites to conclude he was not as faithful to the teachings of Jesus as they were. Per Epiphanius, the hot gossip among the Ebionites was that Paul was not born a Jew but was a Greek convert who scandalously adopted Judaism solely to marry the

---

[54] As per the words of Irenaeus

[55] They later also found Matthew's Gospel unsatisfactory and reworked it, naming their book the Gospel of Ebionites. There is no surviving text of this work.

daughter of the high priest. But the word was that she rejected him, leading to his apostasy.

Speaking of apostasy, the irony here was that, as the first few centuries wore on, the Ebionites held more faithfully to the original Christian teachings than most who professed to be fully Christian. They rejected ideas that had crept into Christian teachings, such as the Trinity, but kept the teachings about God's Kingdom and its future role, Jesus having a pre-human existence in heaven, and the governing body of Jerusalem taking the lead among early Christians as opposed to just Peter.

The Ebionites, however, were not the only Judeo-Christian sect. Closely linked to these were the Nazarenes. Some Christian writers of the first few centuries differentiated between the two groups. Some mistook them for Jews. Jerome, on the other hand, believed the Ebionites and Nazarenes were one and the same. But with no surviving information from the time, there is no concrete way to know why he believed this.

In the book of Acts, non-Christians referred to Christianity as the "sect of the Nazarenes," perhaps due to Jesus being from Nazareth. It's possible that non-Christians confused facts and used an inaccurate label or lumped all those who believed in Jesus into one group.

The Nazarenes seemed to have a lot in common with Ebionites in that they, too, held onto the Jewish customs and law. Another thing they held in common was their distaste for Paul (ironic, since he is accused of being the ringleader of the "sect of the Nazarenes" in Acts 24:5), likely due to his preaching that Jewish law was now obsolete. And this is where the Nazarenes diverged from the Ebionites. The Ebionites believed that *everyone* needed to adhere to Jewish law, while the Nazarenes believed that it was only necessary for those born Jews.

Whichever beliefs they leaned toward, the Nazarenes were not the same Nazarenes referenced in Paul's day. It seems that the later Nazarenes faded into obscurity by the fifth century, the last time they are mentioned in writing. But they weren't the last of the Judeo-Christian sects mentioned.

The enigmatic Elkesaites emerged in the early second century.[56] Who were they? It is almost hard to say as they seemed to have an identity crisis regarding what they believed. Though the Elkesaites adopted some

---

[56] Alternately spelled Elcesaites. There are varying opinions about how they got their name—a town called Elksai, a mysterious founder named Elxai, or the name of the chief holy book of the sect.

Christian beliefs or versions of them, their doctrines held a distinct Gnostic edge. Yet they were closely associated with the highly disciplined Jewish Essene sect. They also picked and borrowed from some Eastern pagan religions, mixing naturalism, astronomy, and magic and using the stars to pick auspicious dates for important events like baptism.

Like other Judeo-Christian sects, Elkesaites were staunchly obligated to Jewish laws such as observing the Sabbath, facing Jerusalem when praying, and, in particular, the very divisive matter of circumcision. But they cast aside one of the main tenets of Jewish law: animal sacrifices. They may not have fully agreed with the other sects on certain matters, but one thing they all embraced was a rejection of Paul and his writings.

Although later more "Christianized," the Elkesaites were less committal than full-fledged Christians, their views on Jesus bordering on ambiguous. They did support the virgin birth of Jesus. However, some thought he was just an angel, while others adopted a reincarnation view of the Christ—a continuous cycle of him dying and being reborn to earth, a cycle that started with Adam. Like early Christians, they celebrated what is commonly called the Lord's Supper, originally a commemoration of Jesus.[57] death. Like early Christians, the Elkesaites were big proponents of marriage. However, they believed it was okay to leave their faith when persecution got a bit too fiery.

So, how did Gnosticism come into the mix? A great example is the Elkesaites' main holy book, writings that were not part of the Torah or the Bible. The book of Elxai (Elchasai), a strong influence among the sect, was reported by Origen to have fallen straight from heaven. (Other accounts say it was given by an angel). In true Gnostic fashion, the book's contents could only be revealed to a person who was sworn to secrecy never to reveal its words.

But how did some of the early Church Fathers feel about the book? Epiphanius said the book was for people who were "neither Jews nor Christians nor pagans" but for those who stood firmly in the middle ground of these three religious ideologies. As the Catholic Encyclopedia puts it, the Elkesaite creed was a "wild medley of heathen superstitions" mixed with Christianity and Judaism, making the Elkesaites one of the hardest groups to define. They seemed to defy any one category of religion.

---

[57] Also referred to as the Last Supper and the Lord's Evening Meal.

Although few contemporary texts discuss these groups, there is abundant evidence that, by the second century, Christian or pseudo-Christian beliefs had found their way into other religious groups or were mixed with other teachings. What the apostle John had written came true: after the apostles died, the original Christian teachings became diluted.

Chapter 8: The First Church Fathers

Who were the men who took the lead in the early Christian congregations, and what were their stories? Important to the history of Christianity and fascinating for their faith and monumental deeds, here are the stories of some of the men who left their mark on Christianity in the first few centuries.

Of course, we must start with some of the apostles, men who helped form the original governing body of Jerusalem and made some of the most important decisions in the history of Christianity.

Not much is known about Peter's personal life other than that he was a married fisherman who sometimes acted a bit rash. Nonetheless, he was known to be bold, courageous, and fiercely loyal by nature. He was one of those considered "unlettered and ordinary"[58] by the Pharisees. Yet when Jesus called Peter to be his follower, Peter dropped everything without hesitation. His life became anything but ordinary.

Outgoing with a big, colorful personality, Peter was, unsurprisingly, the spokesman for the apostles. Jesus also gave him the important metaphorical "keys of the kingdom." What did they unlock? Returning to Peter's vision of the animals coming down from heaven, we see that it was not just about getting to eat tasty meats. It had a second meaning.

---

[58] This did not mean he could not read and write; rather, he had no formal education from a rabbinical school and held no position of status within the Jewish ranks.

Previously, the Jews viewed the Gentiles as "unclean," but in the vision, Peter was told to "stop calling unclean what God has called clean."

Those keys, as they were called, opened the message to three distinct groups: the Jews and Jewish converts, the Samaritans, and the Gentiles.[59] Jesus had told Peter in John 21:15-17 that when he was no longer with them, Peter should "feed his little sheep," meaning he was to play a major role in caring for the disciples spiritually. The main way Peter did this was through preaching and organizing the preaching work done by other disciples. With Peter taking the lead, everyone would have the opportunity to hear what Jesus had preached and decide whether to be baptized into the Christian way.

Peter shouldered a huge responsibility, but how did he feel about his role among fellow Christians? Interestingly, nowhere does Peter make decisions for anyone or claim a spot as the head of the Christian congregations. Instead, he referred to himself as an "older man" or "elder" and an apostle, working with the other elders and apostles appointed. Despite his sometimes-brash beginnings, Peter's later humility was highlighted when he stopped Cornelius from kneeling, prostrating himself, or rendering any form of worship to him.

Aside from preaching and making important decisions, Peter had been given the power to perform miracles. He is mentioned as healing two men on two separate occasions and was also the first apostle to perform a resurrection when he raised a woman named Tabitha from the dead.

Not everyone was a fan of Peter. He particularly raised the ire of Judean ruler Herod Agrippa I. Wanting nothing more than to see Peter dead, he passed a death sentence down on the apostle. No doubt Jesus' words from years ago telling Peter he would die a martyr's death were ringing in his ears. However, this was not the time. Just hours before he was set to be executed, Peter escaped from his guards and out of Herod's grasp with the help of an angel.

However, death and martyrdom would still find Peter. Although the Bible does not specify how he died, in the most common version of his death, Emperor Nero catches up with him during the persecution of Christians in Rome.[60] The historian Eusebius wrote that Peter, bound and

---

[59] Samaritans were half-Jewish people who had adopted some Jewish customs and beliefs, such as high regard for the first five books of the Hebrew Scriptures. However, they were not considered part of the Jewish nation.

[60] There are numerous versions of how Peter died, as many as fifteen different stories.

led away, died the same way Jesus did—hung on a stake. But according to Eusebius, there was a twist: Peter asked to be hung upside down because he felt unworthy to die in the same manner as his master. There is no evidence of which version is accurate, if any.

Undoubtedly a pillar of the early congregation, Peter wasn't the only one shouldering responsibility for the young fledgling Christian group. Many other responsible men were doing their share. One of these was Jesus' half-brother, James.

Growing up with Jesus, James did not see his brother as the Messiah. He may have even been among Jesus' relatives and townsmen who thought he had lost his mind when he started his ministry. It wasn't until after his brother's death that James changed his thinking.

A resurrected Jesus made a personal appearance to James. While the Bible doesn't describe the exchange or how James reacted, it apparently convinced James that his brother was indeed the Messiah. He became a believer and may have had a hand in convincing his other brothers, who also became believers.

In fact, James was so thoroughly convinced of Jesus' identity that he became a prominent leader in Jerusalem. Dubbed an apostle (in the broad sense of the word) James was named as one of those who "seemed to be pillars"—an indication of his great support to the early Christians and their work. James was among those making important decisions, one of the most noteworthy of which was weighing in on the circumcision debate. Besides Peter, his is the only other recorded speech on the matter.

Interestingly, the books of Galatians and Acts note that Peter and Paul reported important events to James, and he was even among the elders who gave Paul advice when rumors about him started to escalate. But it wasn't just to Paul that he gave advice. One of his greatest contributions to Christianity came in the form of a letter known by his name. In the book of James, he gives advice on the importance of drawing close to God, endurance, patience, love, faith, and self-examination. He also warns about letting fleshly desires get the better of a Christian, the bad kind of pride, going back on your word, the pitfalls of riches and corruption, keeping the tongue under control, the dubiousness of faith without actions to back it up, and favoritism.

But none of the prominence, responsibilities, or even the fact that he was the physical brother of Jesus (a fact he doesn't mention) caused him to be haughty or arrogant—absolutely the opposite. Tradition has it that he was called "James the Just," a testament to the type of person he was.

Although the Bible doesn't say how he died, Josephus fills in the story. While Judea was between governors after the death of Festus in 62 AD, the Jewish high priest Ananias and the Sanhedrin jumped on the opportunity to mete out punishment to James and other Christians. The harshest penalty for allegedly breaking Jewish law was handed down—death by stoning.

James and Peter weren't the only ones who died for their Christian faith. There were many—some who were named in history, and some who died unknown to modern Christendom. As the original apostles and those labeled apostles in the first century died, some of their contemporaries wrote works that were not included in the Bible canon. These men are often referred to as "Apostolic Fathers"—men who either knew one of the twelve apostles personally or were separated from them by one degree, having been taught by disciples who learned directly from the apostles[61]. Some consider what they wrote the most historically valuable writings outside of the Christian Greek Scriptures/New Testament.

As the ship the man was forced onto made its way to sea, the other men aboard began to fasten a rope around him. At the end of that rope was tied an anchor, an object that would forever symbolize the man tied to it. Who was he, and how did he come into this predicament? More importantly, is his story true?

Not much is historically known about the life of Clement of Rome. Tertullian and Irenaeus list him as a contemporary of the apostles, and he may have even been an eyewitness to their preaching. Some scholars wonder if he was the Clement mentioned by Paul in his letter to the Philippian congregation. However, it's unlikely, as traditionally he was not presented as a big fan of Paul.

But Clement is believed to have written his own letter, the *First Letter of Clement*, to the Corinthian Christians to help sort out a controversy over leadership there.[62] After setting them straight about trying to depose their leaders, he reminded doubters that even though Jesus had not

---

[61] The Apostolic Fathers lived between the first and second centuries. Men known as "Church Fathers" lived between the second and fifth centuries.

[62] His only surviving work

returned when they expected, they needed to have faith that he would come at a future time. The letter is an insight into the state of the Corinthians found nowhere else.

Several other pieces of highly regarded literature, such as the *Second Letter of Clement,* are attributed to him. However, there is some debate over how much was written by his own hand. He is also historically credited with distributing the Apostolic Constitution, a draft previously said to have been written by the apostles. (It is now believed to have been written around 380 AD, almost two hundred years after the last of the original apostles died, and could not have been around in Clement's lifetime).

Even though Clement is believed to have been a leader in the Roman congregation at the end of the first century, it seems he was a popular figure far and wide.[63] That didn't change much after his death. Though none of his writings are included in the Bible, third and fourth-century Christians regarded his works so highly that they viewed them as scripture.

As alluded to previously, tradition has it that Clement's death was positively legendary. After Clement had converted hundreds of notable people, an angry Emperor Trajan banished him far from Rome—all the way to the Crimea. Clement was undeterred and continued his ministry there, performing miracles and converting hundreds more to Christianity. Word of Clement's doings got back to Trajan, and he ordered Clement's death. Under the emperor's command, Clement was put on a boat that set out on the Black Sea. Away from land, an anchor was tied to his body, and he was thrown overboard, dying a martyr's death.

As sensational as the story is, it is also almost certainly untrue. Early biographers Eusebius and Jerome never mentioned any of this. Most sources say he died a more low-key death of natural causes while in exile. Though Clement was sainted by the Catholic Church and identified throughout history with an anchor symbol, the Catholic Encyclopedia notes that the first time the story appeared was hundreds of years after his death.

---

[63] He is sometimes called a bishop of Rome, and some refer to him as the third pope. However, the early Christians didn't have a distinct clergy class. Each early Christian congregation was led by a group of older men or elders, not just one man. It wasn't until later that the hierarchal system of bishops and popes was used.

He wasn't the only famous Clement of early Christendom's history. Around the same time lived Clement of Alexandria, a theologian and philosopher who boasted Origen as one of his students. Not much is known about his personal life except that he was born to pagan parents, was probably married, and converted to Christianity. But why did he leave the religious beliefs of his birth, especially when he seemed to have extensive knowledge of Greek mythology and other mystical faiths?

Early in his life, Clement was turned off to pagan beliefs due to what he considered the shocking lack of morals within the religion, particularly among the Greek gods. This sent him on a journey to find beliefs he could agree with—wandering through Asia Minor, Palestine, Greece, and Egypt, searching for answers.

It was in Alexandria that Clement finally found his mentor in Christian studies, Pantaenus. Clement took up the battle against Gnostic teachings and, like his mentor, based his thinking and teachings on both the Bible and philosophy. Although philosophy had been creeping its way into Christian beliefs, Clement was the most influenced by Greek thinking via the works of Plato and the Stoics. He is said to have solidified the marriage of Christian religious beliefs with Greek philosophical concepts, effectively "Hellenizing" Christianity.

Considered the most educated and knowledgeable of the Church Fathers of his time, the scholarly Clement proposed there were three steps to reaching the peak of knowledge: science, philosophy, and Christian teachings. His thoughts on politics and economics and efforts to corral contemporary Christians into aligning their lives with gospel teachings are a big part of his legacy.

Clement of Alexandria wore many hats, so to speak: defender of Christianity (also known as an Apologist) controversial debater (polemicist) discourse writer, and missionary to intellectuals and the Greeks. When Pantaenus quit as head of his religious school, Clement took over until fleeing town to avoid the persecution brought on by Roman Emperor Severus. The school was taken over by his most gifted student, Origen.

Clement never returned to Alexandria, dying in Palestine in the early third century. Some Christian sects later declared Clement a saint, but his martyrdom was revoked in the fifteenth century due to his sometimes-heretical writings and teachings.

"How can I blaspheme my King who has saved me?" The eighty-six-year-old man who uttered these words had lived a life that backed them up. Likely the last surviving link to the apostles, Polycarp had learned much from the beloved apostle John and others who knew Jesus.

Born in Smyrna, Turkey, Polycarp grew up to become a cherished overseer in the congregation there. Materially poor, the Smyrna congregation was at one time complimented for being spiritually rich. Polycarp assisted the congregation amidst a climate of hostility and hatred against them, pagan practices around them, and heated pressure to worship Roman gods.

Polycarp's notable kindness, generosity, self-sacrificing spirit, and love for the scriptures made him a beloved figure. So, when he wrote a letter of counsel to the Philippian congregation (*Epistle of Polycarp to the Philippians*), they undoubtedly paid attention to his words. Quoting numerous New Testament scriptures, many of them the words of Paul, Polycarp warned them about the love of money and other practices that were not approved by God, urged them to be zealous in doing good, reminded wives to love their husbands, and encouraged congregation elders to treat those under their care with compassion and mercy.

That didn't mean Polycarp didn't have enemies, including powerful Roman authorities. Near the end of his life, Polycarp escaped the enemies who wanted him captured, but only for a while. When the police and horsemen were led to his farm cottage hideout, he did not resist arrest but asked to pray before being taken away. It was said that his faith and demeanor caused the arresting officers to regret what they had to do.

When he said the words stated earlier, he was standing in the middle of an arena facing the Roman governor Statius Quadratus, surrounded by a hostile mob calling for his life. His offense? Refusing to worship their gods and discouraging others from doing so, as well. Ironically, they called him godless for sticking to his Christian beliefs. The governor approached Polycarp with an ultimatum: recognize the "genius" of Caesar and announce "away with atheists" or pay with his life. Looking around at the pagan crowd, he said the words with conviction, albeit with a different meaning than what Caesar had in mind. The governor, however, was not satisfied. Pressing the elderly man further, he urged him to take an oath to renounce his faith. The older man remained steadfast in his determination, uttering his famous words.

After Polycarp's continued refusal to meet the governor's demands, preparations were made for his execution. The crowds gathered firewood, and although it was the Sabbath, hostile Jews in the stadium were very eager to help. Wood was piled up at the stake, and death by fire was set to take place. Alleged eyewitness accounts say that before he died, Polycarp tried to prevent any kind of worship or reverence to his body after death. Yet those who claimed his remains considered his bones "more precious than jewels or gold."

A living legacy that Polycarp left behind was his student and fellow Smyrnaean, Irenaeus. Although not much is known about Irenaeus' personal life beyond his Christian upbringing on the Aegean coast, he left a powerful testimony to the accuracy of the four Gospels.

During Irenaeus' lifetime, the New and Old Testament were developed. Not everyone agreed with which books should be in the canon, mainly because many works claimed they should be included as scripture. But only a few generations removed from Jesus and the apostles, Irenaeus put unshakable faith in the accuracy and divine nature of the Gospels, asserting that all four were indeed written by the men bearing their names. For this, he attested that they belonged in the biblical canon.

But it wasn't just the Gospels that he found essential to faith. Irenaeus emphasized the importance of many of Paul's teachings (namely his letters), especially regarding salvation. More than that, he believed in the validity of the Hebrew Scriptures/Old Testament and promoted the importance of the two parts of the Bible.

The Gnostics, on the other hand, did not put stock in the Hebrew Scriptures. Irenaeus' most well-known work, *Against Heresies,* was a targeted tearing down of Gnostic thinking. He did not buy into their idea of special knowledge. Instead, he steadfastly proclaimed salvation through real knowledge of the Christ. He used the scriptures to expose their false doctrines and show that what they taught had no merit according to the biblical canon.

At some point, Irenaeus moved to Lyons (in modern-day France). He narrowly escaped intense persecution and probable death when Emperor Marcus Aurelius sanctioned the mass killing of Christians in his city. Thanks to a letter he wrote and was personally delivering to Rome, Irenaeus was out of town when things went awry. However, many in Lyons did not escape the persecution. So, when he returned, he was given a leadership position in the congregation there. Though undoubtedly busy with these duties, he never stopped combating the Gnostics and other heretical groups, continuing to write *Proof of Apostolic Preaching* and other works.

There is no evidence regarding the reality of Irenaeus' death, only legend. In the sixth century, Gregory of Tours talked about his death during persecution, alongside many other converts. Perhaps because of this, he went down in history as a martyr, but the real truth of his death remains as mysterious as his personal life.

Irenaeus' death was not the end of his legacy, though. He heavily influenced the next generation, which included famous names like Tertullian and Hippolytus.

Hippolytus, a leader of the congregation in Rome around 199-217 AD, was a very busy writer—partly because he had a lot to write about. Disgusted by heretical and pagan teachings creeping into Christian doctrine, he wrote a large body of work called *Refutation of All Heresies*—a compilation of ten books. He wrote about the Christ, the Antichrist, the prophecies of Daniel, and church law. His *Apostolic Traditions* gives an insightful look into what rites were used in Rome during his time. But the most famous part of that larger body of work, *Philosophumena (https://www.britannica.com/topic/Philosophoumena)*, challenged the Trinity teachings.

Despite his close connection with Rome, Hippolytus' attitude toward the church was already souring over his disagreement about Trinity teachings. It soured even further when he was passed up for leadership in favor of Calixtus. His disagreement with the Roman leader was taken to new heights when he was scandalized by Calixtus' decision to pardon grave sins such as adultery. His high moral sense offended, Hippolytus split from Rome and became the leader of a breakaway group. A schism broke wide open in Rome, two leaders opposing one another. This move had him labeled in history as the first "antipope."

Hippolytus' death was also the stuff of legends. Roman poet Prudentius drew a parallel between the second-century Hippolytus and the mythological Hippolytus, son of the Greek Theseus, who died being dragged by wild horses.[64] Prudentius claims that the historical Hippolytus suffered the same gruesome death as a martyr. Although it is more likely

---

[64] Hippolytus in Greek means "loose horse."

he died from being forced to do hard labor in a mine, Hippolytus is still associated with horses in modern times.

The other person highly influenced by Irenaeus was Tertullian, a prolific historian of Christianity in his era. He was also one of the most well-known and biting Christian writers in history. His witty yet withering commentary and his often-paradoxical statements had people saying he was "incapable of being dull."

The highly educated son of a Roman centurion, Tertullian was one of the best lawyers in Rome. When he became a Christian in 193 AD, he devoted himself to a whole new type of defense—defending his spiritual beliefs. No one knows the circumstances of his conversion, but apparently Christians dying for their faith attracted his attention. However, it was not long before he became disenchanted with the version of Christianity he saw around him. The poor spiritual condition he witnessed had him leaving behind his original congregation and fleeing to Montanism—a sect that was highly devoted to prophecy and strict, no-frills lifestyles.

Many of Tertullian's logical arguments, observations, and thoughts are still quoted today, one of which is "Those who flee live to fight another day." Though considered genius-level brilliant, Tertullian also made some head-scratchingly odd statements, such as: "God is great when he is small," "The Son of God died: it is *immediately* credible—because it is silly," and "[Jesus] was buried, and rose again; the fact is certain —because it is impossible."

No one was safe from Tertullian's blistering pen. In one instance, he called a woman "the doorway of the devil." Of those who mixed secular beliefs with Christianity, he asked, "What has Athens to do with Jerusalem?" To Christians who attended pagan entertainment, he said, "How monstrous it is to go from God's church to the devil's—from the sky to the stye." And regarding self-centered people, he said, "He who lives only to benefit himself confers on the world a benefit when he dies." He did not leave out the pagans, mocking them and their ritual sacrifices.

It was against the backdrop of Christians being vilified through superstitious and irrational reasoning that Tertullian came to their defense with his famous *Apology*. In this literary work, he notes with flair and wryness, "[Opposers] consider that the Christians are the cause of every public calamity and every misfortune of the people... If the Nile does not rise to the fields, if the weather will not change, if there is an earthquake, a famine, a plague—straightway the cry is heard: 'Toss the Christians to the lion!'" He tried to show that Christians were good, law-abiding citizens, and when they were executed for their faith, it was a loss to the world. He also pointed out that, although Christians were often considered traitors against the state, when several attempted government coups went down, the Christians were nowhere to be found among the treasonous.

But Tertullian's writings had a point beyond just a scathing take on what was happening at the time. His intention was to defend church doctrine, but in the end, he at times corrupted it. Though he condemned Christians for adopting Greek concepts and philosophy, the "doctrines of men and demons," he used them when it suited.

During his time, the relationship between God and Jesus had become confused, especially among previously polytheistic Greeks who did not grasp the concept of a single Almighty God and Jesus as the Messiah. When theologian Praxeas offered an explanation, Tertullian jumped to counteract Praxeas' teaching[65] with his essay *Against Praxeas*. Considering Praxeas a corruptor from the devil, Tertullian used the scriptures to reason that God and Jesus were separate beings. Yet later, in true Tertullian paradoxical style, he presented the idea that God, Jesus, and the Holy Spirit were three distinct beings existing as one divinity that "could not be divided." This theory, considered by some to be one of his biggest contributions to Christendom, laid the framework for the Trinity doctrine later debated by the fourth-century Council of Nicaea.

Unlike some of his fellow theologians, Tertullian lived to old age, dying in 225 AD. The details of his death appear to be lost to history, but much of his work has lived on for almost 1,800 years.

Famous moralist writers like Jerome and Justin Martyr preached the value of living an ethical life, but after their deaths, one man took things to a new level. Born in mid-300s Turkey, Basil the Great was one of ten children in a large, wealthy, religious family. One might think that with a moniker like "great" he stood out at home, but there was competition over who was the most pious in the family. Both his parents, his grandmother, two of his sisters, and two of his brothers were all declared saints by the church.

---

[65] His teaching was known as Modalism, which basically taught that God was different versions of himself at different times– the Father as creator, the savior as Jesus, and the Holy Spirit after Jesus' ascension to heaven.

Basil's life wasn't always one of strict piety—he spent time as a teacher and lawyer. But after meeting a monk, Eustathius of Sebaste, things took a dramatic turn for Basil. Realizing he needed to be fully devoted to God, he wrote that he had "wasted much time on follies and spent nearly all of (his) youth in vain labors." After the encounter, he felt his eyes were opened, proclaiming, "Suddenly, I awoke as out of a deep sleep. I beheld the wonderful light of the Gospel truth, and I recognized the nothingness of the wisdom of the princes of this world."

Deciding to adopt a life of extreme piety, Basil apprenticed himself to famous hermit monks. But unlike them, he did not completely give up secular life. He opened a school in Caesarea and once again practiced law. Even so, he still was devoted to his austere life. He didn't just write about prayer and monastic community life but helped set its guidelines.[66][67] He also formed and lived in a monastic community that included some of his family members. For that, Basil was dubbed one of the fathers of communal monasticism. However, the extreme austerity of monastic life didn't sit well with Basil, so he got to work reforming the rules of monastery life. Instead of making stricter rules, Basil moderated them, loosening up the austerity and campaigning for a more balanced approach.

Basil was considered a reformer. Well-known for helping the poor, he also wrote a sermon about caring for others' physical needs as if they were your own. He wrote more than just sermons, though. His large body of work covers work-life balance, material wealth, doctrine, morality, prayer, and observations on nature, to name a few.

But perhaps Basil's most famous contribution was his support of the Trinity doctrine as outlined in the Nicene Creed. At that time, doctrine around the Trinity was under fierce debate. However, his heavy influence in religious and political spheres carried a lot of weight for his side of the issue. Even so, the debate raged on for years. (The Nicene Creed was modified several times over the centuries.) But Basil did not live to see the end result. Ironically, his excessively ascetic lifestyle hastened his demise, along with liver disease.

---

[66] Relating to monks, nuns, and those who took religious vows. At first, many lived as hermits, but later, they formed communities and built monasteries.

[67] His liturgy, *The Diving Liturgy of Saint Basil the Great*, is still used in Eastern Catholic and Orthodox churches on feast days.

Many, many men shifted, reshaped, and remolded Christianity after the death of the apostles and into the first three centuries. Space will not allow us to mention all, but the collective influence of these men is seen throughout modern-day Christendom.

However, it was not just men who were devout in their faith or left their mark on history. Many women of the Bible and the first few centuries have also left their stories. Who were these women, and how did they make it into history?

Chapter 9: Women of Christianity

"Greetings, you highly favored one." How those words from an unknown man must have startled the ordinary, unmarried Jewish girl.[68] But this is how the angel Gabriel greeted Mary, perhaps the most well-recognized woman in Christian history. Gabriel was about to deliver the most shocking news—news that changed the life of Mary, her fiancé Joseph, and the world. It would also give her the most unique distinction in history.

The Gospels, however, don't give many details about Mary, particularly during Jesus' ministry. Despite being traditionally referred to as the Virgin Mary, Jesus' mother lived a fairly normal life after his birth. It was customary for Jewish couples to have large families, and Mary and Joseph were no exception. All four Gospels and the book of Acts either allude to this (calling Jesus Mary's firstborn) or directly discuss Mary's other children. Mark mentions four sons by name and also references their sisters. Mary must have spent much of her life as a busy wife and mother. She remained in Nazareth during Jesus' lifetime, probably unable to travel with her son as he and his disciples spread the divine message.

Sadly, though, she likely spent many years of her life without her husband. The last time Joseph is mentioned is fairly early in Jesus' life—when he is just twelve. Though the Gospels never mention what became of Joseph, it is presumed Mary became a widow at some point during Jesus' life. When she helps out at the wedding in Cana, Joseph is

---

[68] Historians speculate she was around 15 or 16 years old at the time, but there are no historical records confirming her age.

nowhere to be seen. Just before Jesus dies, he tells his apostle and close friend John to make sure his mother is taken care of. [69] Would he have needed to do that if Joseph were alive? Unlikely.

Mary was not sheltered from loss and hardship, losing her husband and then watching her firstborn son die an agonizingly cruel death as an alleged criminal. It's hard to imagine the depth of that type of grief. But after Jesus died, not much is known about what happened to Mary.

Though she had obviously been a very faithful Jewess, it is apparent that Mary listened to and accepted her son's message. She is mentioned in Acts as gathering for worship with the apostles in Jerusalem around Pentecost in 33 CE along with her sons, who also became believers after the death of their brother. In context, it seems she was on the ground floor of the first Christian congregation right as it was forming. However, this is the last time we see Mary mentioned in the scriptures.

Details of how she spent her last years and how and when she died are not in any Bible accounts, and there are very few historical records that say what happened. Apocryphal accounts like that of Hippolytus of Thebes in the seventh/eighth century say she didn't live very long after Jesus' death, with varying reports putting her death somewhere between 41-48 AD. Where she died is also a big question mark. Some scholars believe she died in Jerusalem, while other church traditions hold that she moved to Ephesus in Turkey and died there in her home.

As important as Mary's role was in early Christianity, she was not the only Mary in Jesus' life. Mary Magdalene stood next to Jesus' mother at his crucifixion, lending support to her dear friends during such a tragic time. Though a faithful believer in Jesus and a close friend of the family, Mary has often gone down in history for a more infamous reason—her alleged former profession as a prostitute. But was she?

Luke 7 tells about a woman, a "sinner" (thought to be a prostitute) who found out where Jesus was dining one day and went into the home to see him. Moved by his compassion and mercy, she rubbed very expensive perfumed oil on his feet. Crying, her tears fell onto his feet and mixed with the oil. In a very caring gesture, she used her own hair to wipe away the tears and excess oil. Nothing in the Bible indicates who that woman is for certain, but Origen and other early Christian writers did not identify

---

[69] Before his death, Jesus' brothers had not yet accepted his teachings. Jesus likely wanted to entrust his mother to someone who shared her faith in him as the Messiah and would care for her spiritually.

her as Mary Magdalene. Centuries after Mary Magdalene died, a prominent clergyman claimed she was the sinner of this account. She was, however, known among the disciples for a different reason—one that involved demons.

Luke mentions that she had been afflicted by not one or two but *seven* demons. Jesus had been the one to release her from their possession and a life of tortured misery. It is not surprising, then, that she showed her faith and appreciation for what he did by supporting him and the disciples as they traveled and preached.

Mary did have a distinct privilege mentioned by the apostle John. He relates that while Mary was weeping at Jesus' empty tomb, she was approached by two angels who asked why she was crying. After telling them that she was grieved because Jesus' body had disappeared, she turned around to see another man standing behind her. Thinking he was the gardener, she asked if he knew where Jesus' body would be. The stranger called her name, and the voice was familiar. The light of realization struck her —the man was not a gardener but Jesus himself. Mary Magdalene was the first person the resurrected Jesus appeared to after his death—even before the apostles. During their brief interaction, Mary, who literally clung to Jesus for fear he would be raised up to heaven right then and there, was tasked with telling the apostles and disciples that he had risen. For this, some churches have dubbed her an "apostle to the apostles."

Many rumors have swirled around Mary Magdalene over the centuries, some of which have landed her in infamy. One apocryphal book claims there was tension between Mary and the apostles, particularly Peter, due to jealousy over a vision. But perhaps one of the most controversial claims is that she was secretly married to Jesus. As fascinating as a secret romance might be, there is no evidence to support it. Mary Magdalene accompanied and supported Jesus and the disciples during their ministry, but she wasn't the only one. Several other women are mentioned for their supporting roles. Some of them married, but none are mentioned as his wife, including Mary.

But that's not the only rumor surrounding Mary's love life, nor was Jesus the only man she has been linked to in legend. Medieval legend places her as the apostle John's wife, possibly based on some church traditions that say she accompanied him to Ephesus, where she later died. The French might argue that. Their tradition has it that she went on a preaching mission to Provence in southern France and died there after living thirty years in a mountain cave.

But there was yet another Mary that was close to Jesus. Tears streaming down her face, in her grieved state she fell at Jesus' feet and declared, "Lord, if you had been here, my brother would not have died." A few days earlier, she and her sister Martha had sent word to Jesus that their brother Lazarus, his close friend, was very ill. Yet Jesus did not reach them for a few days, and by that time, the sisters were mourning the death of their beloved brother. Their grief was so potent that Jesus himself began to cry with them. Yet, just minutes later, Mary and Martha had their brother Lazarus returned to them through a miracle.

It was obvious by Mary and Martha's statements during this incident that they had tremendous faith in Jesus. But it was more than just that. Mary and her siblings were close friends with Jesus, often hosting him in their home. One of those visits was recorded in the Bible, giving a glimpse into the personalities of both sisters.

Martha was very hospitable and concerned for the needs of her guests in the tradition of good hostesses of her culture. With no one helping, she ran around the house making food and preparing everything for her guests. She stopped, annoyed, when she saw her sister sitting at Jesus' feet, listening to him. Frustrated, she complained to Jesus about her sister's lack of help. Jesus, however, reassured her that she didn't have to frantically prepare a lot of dishes and that Mary had made the wiser choice in listening to him teach.

The "sinner" or prostitute was not the only one mentioned as putting perfumed oil on Jesus. On a separate occasion, this Mary did, as well. She took a very expensive perfumed nard, one that cost about a year's salary, and poured it on Jesus' head and feet. This shows that her family was probably somewhat well off and that they valued Jesus and things with spiritual meaning more than material possessions. What's more, they had a life rich with good friends and tight family bonds.

The history of women in Christianity is not just limited to the Gospels. Priscilla worked hard. As refugees from the persecution of Emperor Claudius around 40 AD Rome, she and her husband Aquila fled to Corinth.[70] While there, the apostle Paul called them his "fellow workers in

---

[70] The imperial order forced Jews to leave Rome. Though they had converted to Christianity, as natural-born Jews, the order still applied.

Christ." But they were more than that to him. At times, they all worked together, making tents to support themselves and their ministry.

When Paul went to Ephesus, Priscilla and Aquila went with him. There, Priscilla showed she had rock-solid faith. Both she and Aquila are noted as helping to correct and explain "the way of God" to a well-versed man named Apollos.

Priscilla showed that courage was not just a trait of her husband and that being a Christian (especially one associated with a controversial figure like Paul) was risky business. In his letter to the Romans, Paul mentions that they both "risked their necks" for his sake. Did they save his life in some way? There are no details given about what might have occurred, but it was something big enough that congregations in different countries were grateful to them for it. Despite the risks they took, they could not save Paul in the end. However, they maintained a friendship with him until his death, a friendship he cherished.

Priscilla is mentioned six times in the Bible, always mentioned together with Aquila. Likely, they had a strong bond as they worked and worshipped together. Tradition has it that they both died together as martyrs, though that might be a romanticized notion of what happened. Early historians only mention Aquila as being executed for his faith, while Priscilla's ultimate fate is left a mystery of history.

Many women are mentioned in the Gospels, the book of Acts, and the epistles—more Marys, the Samaritan woman at the well, Joanna, Susanna, Lydia, Tabitha, and others. A whole book could be written on the women who were on the ground floor of Christianity, but some of the most epic stories of martyrdom involve later Christian women.

Catherine of Alexandria is one venerated and sainted by certain churches. According to legendary accounts, the noble and intelligent Catherine went head-to-head with Emperor Maximinus over his violent persecution of Christians. She didn't stop there. Catherine also pointed out how bad it was to worship the false gods the Romans cherished. Unable to combat her cleverness on his own, the emperor called in scholars and philosophers to debate with the young woman. However, they, too, were stumped by her witty and intelligent reasoning. So compelling was her speech that several of those who came to debate her were converted to Christianity on the spot. Those instant conversions led to their instant deaths.

As for Catherine, the enraged emperor had her whipped and thrown into prison. His empress, Valeria, was curious about Catherine and visited her in prison. She and her entourage of 200 were also immediately swayed by Catherine and got baptized. However, being part of the emperor's household did not save them from the sword, and they, too, were killed for their faith.

Having enough of her, Maximinus ordered that Catherine be executed on a spiked wheel—a terrible instrument of torture. But when she was brought to the wheel and touched it, the device crumbled to dust. In a rage, the emperor had her beheaded, and she died a martyr.

As fascinating as the story is, it was not part of the early Christian canon. Nothing was written about her before the ninth century, and many scholars doubt she was an actual person. If she was, her story is believed to be far more fiction than fact. However, there is a chance her story is based on a real person. Some scholars believe her story echoes that of the maiden Dorothea of Alexandria; others think she was based on the Greek philosopher Hypatia. In the 300s, Eusebius also wrote about a young woman called to the emperor to be his mistress. Upon refusing him, she had all her wealth stripped and was banished. But Eusebius never mentioned a name, so it remains uncertain whether she was the basis for Catherine's tale.

Saint Catherine of Alexandria, 1598-99.
Caravaggio, CC0, via Wikimedia Commons;
https://commons.wikimedia.org/wiki/File:Caravaggio_-_Saint_Catherine_of_Alexandria_(post-restoration_image).jpg

Catherine's story is not the only one of its kind to have made it into the halls of Christian history. Barbara (known as the Great Martyr in some churches) and Agnes of Rome were also young virgins who were said to face horrifying deaths unless they renounced their faith.

The "princess in the tower" legend of the beautiful Barbara is said to have started in fourth-century Nicomedia, Turkey. Her pagan father, a wealthy and prominent man, had extreme paternal jealousy over his beloved daughter. Worried about her virginity, he kept her imprisoned in a tower so that her beauty might not tempt her or any man to violate her chastity. Although she was kept from the outside world, her father lavished her with luxuries so that she lacked nothing materially.

Sitting in her gilded prison, she contemplated the gospel teachings that had reached her via her tutor. The more she learned and meditated on the beauty of the natural world outside her window, the more she was convinced that what she had been taught was true.

This, however, did not go over well with her father. On his return from a trip abroad, Barbara broke the news to him: she had become a Christian. Enraged, he demanded that she renounce her faith.

When she refused, the persecution mounted quickly. Her father began heaping abuses on her in the hope that he could pressure her into recanting—all to no avail. Barbara remained firm in her stance, even as she faced torture and death.

Seeing that he was getting nowhere, Barbara's father turned her over to the governor, her only crime being her faith. Despite being subjected to extreme physical torments, Barbara was said to have some help from above. Torch fire could not come near her skin without being miraculously extinguished, and angels healed her wounds every night.

After enduring cruel tortures, Barbara was handed her death sentence: beheading. Even worse, the sentence was to be carried out by her own father, who would rather she die than be a Christian.

Statue of Barbara.

There are several versions of the story, one involving betrayal by a shepherd who was turned into a marble statue for his treachery. In another version, when her father grabs her hair and raises his sword to strike the fatal blow, Barbara's long hair bursts into flames. Her father survives the spontaneous hair combustion but cannot escape punishment for killing his daughter. He is struck by lightning and consumed by flames on his way home.

No version of her story is found before the seventh century, but she began to be worshipped as a saint a few centuries later, invoked as protection against lightning. Despite being venerated by some in modern times, Catherine's absence in authentic early Christian writings raises serious doubts about whether she existed, and some churches have removed her from their list of saints. Still, her story has made her a popular figure in many churches today.

Then there is Agnes, another beauty and perhaps the youngest of the legendary women. A tender twelve years old in 304 AD, when legend has it she was martyred, Agnes became a symbol of purity and chastity. During her short life, Christianity was declared a cult by the Roman Empire, and as was the case for others, being found out meant death—even if one was very young.

In one version, the noble-born Agnes learned about the Gospels from her nursemaid despite her pagan-believing parents. Not short on rich, young suitors, Agnes caught the particular attention of the governor's son. Despite showering her with precious jewels, he could not win her over as she declared that she was "already the spouse of a Lover much more noble and powerful than [him]."

Not taking the rejection well, the young man turned around and told his father that Agnes was a Christian. Brought in for questioning, she freely admitted it was true. She was then sent to the temple of Vesta, the Roman virgin goddess. Ordered to become a Vestal Virgin of the temple or at least offer a sacrifice, Agnes refused any pagan worship whatsoever. Since, by Roman law, virgins could not be executed, the judge ordered her to a more humiliating fate. Agnes was punished by being stripped naked and brought to a brothel. At the brothel, she had many gawkers, all of whom were so awed by her pure presence that they refused to touch her—except for one rather bold Roman youth. He dared try to violate her and, for his efforts, was struck blind by divine sources.

However, her end was the same as many of her fellow believers. In some versions, she is executed during a wave of persecution by Emperor Diocletian. In another more shocking version, she is declared a witch and set to be burned at the stake. Naked, she is tied up in front of onlookers. To protect her modesty, her hair miraculously grows long and flowing to cover her body. When the wood refuses to ignite, an officer goes in for the fatal blow, brutally stabbing or beheading her. The gruesome death of one so young is shocking even to the blood-lusting pagan Romans, and supposedly, this leads to some sympathy for the Christians.

Since the fourth century, many customs, traditions, and shrines have been dedicated to Agnes. Her tale has changed over the centuries. In some cases, the details of her life are limited to her age and the fact that she was executed. However, in the mid-fourth century, in the version told by Pope Damascus I, Agnes immediately outs herself as a Christian when the imperial edict against Christians is made. Describing her as courageous and modest, the account says she used her long hair to cover her body at the time of her death.

Her legendary modesty and chastity got her honored as a saint and a patron for virgins, young girls, engaged couples, and victims of sexual assault. She is honored by both Catholic and Orthodox churches down to today.

Whether these stories are the stuff of legends or authenticated, it is no myth that women suffered persecution for their faith along with their Christian brothers. Yet what motivated the Roman Empire to run down and execute people of a love and peace-based faith?

Agnes before her martyrdom. Painting by Jusepe de Ribera, 1641.
https://www.wikiart.org/en/jusepe-de-ribera/st-agnes-in-prison-1641

Chapter 10: Persecutions

Pagan worship, war and patriotism, violent and sensational entertainment—these were the things that enveloped the lives of many Romans. These were encouraged, if not almost mandatory, across the Roman Empire. The Romans did not particularly care what religion anyone practiced. In fact, they rarely persecuted anyone for their religion. They didn't care as long as everyone went along with the cultural crowd, so to speak—performing military service and sacrificing to the gods, including the emperor. Just one pinch of incense was all it took to stay alive, but the Christians refused to compromise their beliefs. This made them stand out as different and put a target on their backs.

It wasn't just their refusal to worship the ancestors, emperor, and gods of the empire that made Christians different. They actively spoke out against pagan beliefs and taught something that starkly contrasted with what the Romans held dear. Christians stood on their own in these areas and in their general behavior, favoring peace and love. They refused military service and condemned the depravity of Roman entertainment in the colosseums and amphitheaters.

In general, the persecution of Christians was nothing new. John the Baptist suffered beheading for confronting Herod, and Jesus said it was just the beginning. Paul also knew a thing or two about persecution. While the persecution of Christians in Roman territories was never empire-wide, some of the pockets of persecution that occurred were intense and terrifying. Starting in 64 AD, Nero ramped up the brutality to new levels, and its impacts on Christians were profound.

Nero

After the city of Rome burned that year, turmoil and unrest plagued the empire even more. [71] Many simplify the explanation for Nero's persecution of Christians, boiling it down to him needing a scapegoat for the disastrous fire. But in reality, it was more complex than that.

There was plenty of unrest in Nero's kingdom, and in his eyes, Christians presented another threat to the established order. Roman society had its hierarchies, but here came the Christians preaching that God was not partial based on status or background, and neither were they. They recognized the authority of God above all, rejecting the idea of Roman gods and the divinity of the emperor. Christians promoted the idea that all humans were equal in God's eyes—not an appealing idea to someone who held himself above the rest.

Although Christians were generally peaceful and law-abiding, to an already suspicious ruler, the ideology and swift growth of the movement could have raised the alarm regarding another potential rebellion on his hands. Especially troubling to Nero was that some of the newly baptized Christians were in positions of authority and/or had considerable influence among their communities. In his opinion, this increased the threat.

According to the historian Tacitus, Christians faced mass executions for what Nero and Roman society labeled "hating the human race." As such, they deserved horrific deaths that, in many cases, became a matter of sport.

Nero's reaction to this perceived threat was absolutely brutal and humiliatingly public. He staged spectacles where blood-lusting crowds gathered to watch Christians covered in animal skins and chased by vicious dogs or torn to shreds by fierce animals. Others were crucified in the common way Romans executed criminals, while others faced an even worse fate. Tied to stakes and covered in tar, they were set on fire and used to light the roads at night. Nero himself used these human torches as ghastly nightlights to line his spectacular gardens.

Nero's torture of the Christians was so appalling that it garnered sympathy from ordinary citizens who saw what was happening. But public outrage wasn't going to change Nero's mind, and the people were told that the Christians' capital punishment was for the ultimate good of the

---

[71] Historian Tacitus wrote that Nero started the fire, but some modern scholars dispute that claim.

empire. Yes, this was only the beginning of the 250 years of uncertainty and persecution faced by those who professed to be Christians.

Domitian

As appalling as Nero's tortures were, it was his successor, Domitian, who was dubbed the "beast from hell who sat in its den, licking blood." Reveling in his own sense of unwavering divinity, he styled himself "God the Lord," "Lord of the Earth," and "Thou Alone" while pressing those around him to hail him as "Glory," "Holy," and "Invincible." Obviously, Christians would strongly disagree with his hearty sense of self, which was a problem for him.

Early Christian writers/historians Eusebius, Tertullian, and Melito all wrote about Domitian's slanders, accusations, persecutions, and cruelty against Christians. Irenaeus reported that he had the apostle John exiled to the island of Patmos. Other stories tell of Domitian's cousin and Roman consul Titus Flavius Clemens and his wife converting to Christianity and shortly thereafter being exiled and executed at Domitian's command.

But none of these stories came out during or remotely near the time they happened. Not until at least 300 years later did these stories begin to crop up. Among those circulating these stories, not one was a pagan author. With little evidence to go on, some modern archeologists have labeled Domitian's persecutions as fake news. There is plenty of evidence that he persecuted Jews—of that there is no doubt—but did he have it in for the Christians? At the time, Christians were not widely recognized as separate from the Jews, so could Domitian's persecutions of the Jews have enveloped some Christians as well?

The persecution of Christians under Emperor Domitian is up for debate, and there is a lot of speculation. Given what is known about several other Roman emperors and their feelings about Christians, it is not out of the realm of possibility or probability. However, there is definitive evidence of how his successor viewed the Christian movement.

Trajan

Though his predecessors appeared to lump the Christians in with the Jews, Trajan saw them through a different lens—one that made them a separate entity. He wasn't as antagonistic towards the Christians as Nero. He didn't bother to actively hunt them down and punish them, and he acknowledged they didn't commit any crimes. But the exchange between Governor Pliny the Younger and the emperor gives a clear view of

Christianity under Trajan.

Pliny was stumped as to what to do. Several Christians had been dragged to court to be judged by the governor. Yet, he was not sure what the exact charges against them were; neither did he get a clear answer from those who charged them. As far as he could tell, they seemed harmless. None of them had committed a crime. Could he legally execute them just to get the matter over and done with? It seemed the best course. After all, they stubbornly and defiantly refused to recant their faith, which he had labeled a "contagion." Not only that, but the number of sacrifices in the city and the merchants who sold them were being affected: Christianity was not good for the pagan sacrifice business. Yes, execution was the safest route, but he just needed to check to ensure he did the right thing. So, Pliny wrote to the emperor for advice.

The emperor took a non-committal stance on the matter. He assured Pliny that he had done the right thing, but the emperor wasn't looking to actively pursue Christians. But if Pliny did find them in court, he was free to convict and punish any who refused to repent of their Christian ways. But some "Christians" who had come to Pliny's court were now former, having given up the faith. That in itself was no crime. As long as they had put their Christian days behind them and proved it through sacrificial incense to the gods, they were free to go about their lives. Pliny and Trajan were not the only ones to adopt a moderate stance regarding Christians. Trajan's successor, Marcus Aurelius, followed suit—at least at first.

Trajan.
https://commons.wikimedia.org/wiki/File:Traianus_Glyptothek_Munich_336.jpg

Marcus Aurelius

Marcus Aurelius' moderate stance was more an official one than a true reflection of his feelings. While Marcus Aurelius is considered one of the more benevolent and liberal emperors, not everyone around him was as open-minded. Trusted anti-Christian advisors got in his ear and convinced him that the peace-loving Christians were, in fact, quite a force of dangerous revolutionaries. And, to top that off, they were "grossly immoral" in their refusal to worship the gods. He became convinced that they were a danger to Roman society.

The greatest danger was perhaps not from the emperor himself but from the anti-Christian propaganda he encouraged and allowed to circulate. The result reported by later writers was one filled with horrifying tortures and gruesome deaths in a reign of terror. Among the victims of this wave of persecution were Irenaeus and Justin Martyr.

Yet, this extreme violence seems to be at odds with the emperor's character. Many modern scholars question the sensational reports of those who were not alive during this period. It also contradicts Tertullian's take on Aurelius, whom he called "our protector and patron." Tertullian also referenced letters from the emperor in which he claimed Christians in his army saved the troops from certain death through prayer. For that, Marcus Aurelius dissuaded others from exacting the death penalty on them, although he didn't change the punishment for practicing Christians.

So, the truth about persecution under Marcus Aurelius, though not totally understood, seems to lie somewhere in the middle. It is obvious by the death of two well-known Christian writers that terrible persecutions were heaped on the Christians during that time, but these were perhaps not directly sanctioned by Aurelius. A similar story unfolded during the reign of Severus.

Severus

Severus didn't have any particular grudge against the Christians. In fact, the nursemaid who took care of his son was a professed Christian. Still, this did not stop him from issuing an empire-wide law forbidding anyone from converting to Christianity (or Judaism, for that matter). That edict kicked off another wave of ferocious persecution that not even the skilled pen of Tertullian could combat. This time, the bulk of the action took place in North Africa.

During this time, Clement of Alexandria and Origen's father died. It was also when the martyr Perpetua penned her dramatic final memoir detailing her time in prison. Only twenty-two, she anxiously pined away for her baby, who was still breastfeeding. Eventually, she and her infant were reunited in her jail cell. Her pregnant servant/friend Felicitas was imprisoned along with her, giving birth in her dark cell at eight months pregnant. Perpetua details the indignities heaped on Felicitas while they awaited execution, along with some vivid dreams she had regarding what would happen. Her narrative ends the night before they are sent to the arena, but her story is picked up by another narrator, who continues their story. He tells how those about to go into the arena were forced to wear the robes and tunics of priests and priestesses of the gods, yet to the end Perpetua refused to compromise even in this last detail. For her faith, she and Felicitas were stripped naked, put in nets, and dragged into the arena. The crowd was put off by this, and the two were brought back and given simple tunics before returning to the arena floor. They and others were accosted by angry animals and, though injured, did not die. The bloodlust of the audience calling to be satiated, the survivors were brought back into the arena, where soldiers finished them with swords.

There is little doubt that Perpetua was a historical person. No matter how much of her story is true or embellished, it gives readers a glimpse into what professed Christians endured during this time.

However, with the end of Severus' life came the end of persecution—at least for the time being. Christians enjoyed fifty more years of peace before their troubles renewed.[72]

Decius

When persecution returned in 249 AD during the reign of Decius, it returned in a big way. With invading barbarian hordes and other troubles weakening the empire, Decius wanted to solve the problem by reinforcing the traditional worship of the gods. An edict commanding everyone in the empire to offer incense to the gods was an obvious problem for the Christians, and their refusal irritated Decius. After having prominent clergyman Fabian of Rome executed, Decius said he would take a "rival to the throne rather than another bishop of Rome." From this imperial aggravation stemmed the first empire-wide persecution of Christians, and

---

[72] Though there was a brief period of turmoil during the three-year reign of Maximinus.

it was intense. It also set a precedent for the emperors who followed.[73]

Valerian

When Emperor Valerian first took the throne of Rome, he was unbothered by the Christians and let them be for the most part. But as war, civil unrest, and plagues began to spiral out of control across the empire, Valerian needed a scapegoat. Taking a page out of Nero's playbook, he pinned Rome's problems on the Christians. Added to this was the manipulative persuasion of one of his anti-Christian generals, making the year 257 AD a turning point in his attitude. From then on, Valerian not only enforced Decius' policies but increased their intensity.

As under Decius, Rome's "religious tolerance" showed in the fact that the emperors didn't care that Christians practiced their faith so long as they also observed Roman forms of worship. In his new edicts, Valerian demanded that all Christian clergy members sacrifice to the gods or face an agonizing death. Valerian followed through on his word.

Numerous clergymen across the empire, including prominent men like Sixtus and Cyprian, were executed. Barbarity reigned in many cases, such as that of Saturninus of Toulouse. After being subjected to horrific indignities, he at last had his feet bound and tied to the tail of an angry bull. The animal was let loose to rampage down the temple steps with the unfortunate clergymen bouncing and dragging behind until his head was crushed.

In Utica, 300 Christians were gathered and placed around a burning kiln. After refusing an order to sacrifice to Jupiter, all 300 were sacrificed in the kiln. This burning alive was by no means an isolated incident. As far away as Spain, prominent clergymen were set on fire.

Others, including devout women, had tigers and other fierce animals unleashed on them. Some endured unimaginable ordeals—first scourged with whips before being strung up on the gallows. Yet, they were not allowed to die. After they were taken down, their skin was burned with chemical lime before they were roasted over flames and then finally beheaded.

Those of the higher class who escaped gruesome deaths had their property stripped from them by the state. The more unfortunate Christian servants of the imperial household were shackled and sent off to slave away in Roman mines.

---

[73] Until this point, persecutions were in localized pockets instead of empire-wide.

Towards the end of his reign, Valerian was captured by the Persians during a war and suffered a fate similar to the one he imposed on Christians. When his son Gallienus took over, he had a far more sympathetic outlook on the Christians, reversing his father's policies and even restoring confiscated property. Things remained relatively safe for the Christians for several more emperors until Diocletian took the reins of Rome.

Diocletian

Despite the fact that his wife was a Christian, Diocletian went all-out in resurrecting the persecution against Christians. He wasn't just satisfied to have Christians sacrifice to the gods; he was going for complete extermination of the entire religion. This fiercest onslaught began what became known as The Great Persecution.

Diocletian had tolerated Christianity for many years, but like other rulers before him, he was looking for a way to stabilize the tumultuous empire. So, he turned to creating uniformity by enforcing Roman religious rites. And again, Christian refusal was taken as a disruption to the peace and morality of the empire.

Once more, an anti-Christian advisor helped an emperor become more inflamed against the Christians. All Christian worship was utterly forbidden by imperial decree. This included the destruction of places of worship and Christian literature and the arrest of any Christian who didn't wholeheartedly perform an act of worship to the Roman gods. Not even the imperial household escaped the Christian purge, with the empress and their daughter also being swept up in the persecution.

In some regions, Christians fought back against the imperial order. Incensed by the violation of civil rights, a professed Christian named Nicomedia publicly destroyed a copy of the edict, earning him death by being burned alive.

In Phrygia, a small village inhabited entirely by Christians was burned to ash. Yet other persecutors took the time to refine their brutal punishments. Eusebius, alive at the time this was happening, wrote that Christians not executed or forced into the mines suffered perhaps even worse physical cruelty, having their eyes pulled from their sockets or feet hacked off from their legs.

However, not everyone was on board with this indiscriminate slaughter. Prominent community leaders like judges and other officials risked their lives to protect Christian family and friends. This stood in defiance of apostates and traitors who turned Christians over to authorities.

Galerius

After Diocletian abdicated the throne in 304 AD, his successor and son-in-law Galerius took up the torch of persecution. Though Diocletian had given the original orders, it was Galerius who earned the credit for instigating the persecution behind the scenes. Now in full command, he continued the ruthless campaign.

That campaign came to a screeching halt in 311 AD when Galerius became deathly ill. Inflicted with a gruesome and painful disease (possibly gangrene or intestinal cancer), Galerius quickly changed his tune. Fearing that his sickness was divine retribution from the fed-up Christian god, he was eager to appease. Galerius was willing to issue orders that undid his former edicts against the Christians—on one condition. The Christians needed to collectively pray for the emperor's health to be restored. Two years after falling ill, Galerius issued empire-wide edicts of full tolerance towards Christians. This time, Christians experienced lasting peace (for the most part) until the end of Roman power.

Yet the Roman emperors were not the only powerful rulers who affected the history of the Christian religion. What was life like under the declared Christian emperor Constantine the Great?

Chapter 11: Constantine's Contribution

In 311 AD, imperial letters were sent to all governors of the Roman Empire. Emperor Constantine and his co-emperor of the eastern provinces, Licinius, issued edicts reversing all previous restrictions against Christians. Far be it from him to interfere with anyone who wanted to "give their mind to the cult of Christianity" or any other cult, for that matter. In reality, Christians who had their property confiscated would not get everything back. But who was the real man behind this apparently benevolent order, and how exactly did he embrace Christianity?

As a young man, Constantine witnessed the violent and intrigue-filled imperial court of Emperor Diocletian. The execution of rivals and finger-pointing was an early education. When Diocletian murdered his way to the top, his first order of business was to divide the empire into what he called the Tetrarchy. There would now be two emperors (Augusti). One would rule the Eastern provinces and the other the Western. These would be helped out by their vice-emperors (caesares). This way, it would be far easier to manage borders and enemy attacks across the vast empire.

In the West, Augustus Maximian set up court in Milan, with Constantine's father, Constantius I Chlorus as his second in command. Constantine, however, stayed with Diocletian and served as a bodyguard before becoming an officer in the military.

An intelligent, energetic, and natural-born leader, Constantine made a habit of chatting up his troops, smartly gaining a rapport with his men and earning their loyalty. The young general was ambitious and driven to succeed at any cost—even that of someone else's life.

Besides being an outstanding general, Constantine excelled as an organizer and administrator. Throughout his life, he worked hard to learn as much as possible. He was also religious to the point of being superstitious and very emotional. Because he wanted to be popular, he was easily deceived and taken advantage of. He suffered from fits of anger brought about by a highly suspicious and jealous mind, occasionally resorting to murder.

When Constantine's father became one of the new Augusti in 305 AD, he was expected to make his son Caesar. Instead, Constantine was passed over in favor of more nepotistic choices that would make his co-Augustus Galerius happy. However, the men serving under Constantine were offended by this snub of their commander. They believed he should have rightfully been promoted.

When Constantius died the following year, the roller coaster of Constantine's promotions and demotions began in earnest. Constantine's troops saw an opportunity and tried to grasp it for their leader, declaring him the new Augustus. Galerius, however, put the brakes on Constantine's elevation to grand status, instead promoting Severus to Augustus and placing Constantine as his Caesar. Even though he had his troops behind him, Constantine did not believe he could fight Galerius and Severus on this, so he accepted the Caesar-ship and bided his time.

Retired Augustus Maximian and his son Maxentius were also not keen on Constantine's missed promotion, so they took it upon themselves to declare him Augustus. Severus and Galerius went to war with them over it, with disastrous consequences. Severus and Galerius' armies were defeated, and although Severus surrendered, he was executed. Struck with fear, Galerius turned and retreated.

A few years later, Galerius his nerve and again demoted Constantine to Caesar while promoting Licinius to Augustus. But Constantine wasn't having it this time. He refused the title change and resolutely went about as Augustus. Now there were three Augusti and only two parts of the empire, so Galerius had to make room for Licinius as ruler of the Illyrian provinces.

Just a few years after making Constantine ruler, Maximian lost favor with him. Shamed after being defeated in battle, Maximian took his own life. Maxentius stewed, viewing Constantine as the cause of his father's death. After his victory, Constantine ended the Tetrarchy and again put the kingdom under one allegedly rightful ruler—himself. Maxentius begged to differ. He had a much stronger hereditary claim to the throne. Eventually fighting broke out, culminating in the history-making Battle of the Milvian Bridge.

Safely secured behind the heavily fortified walls of Rome, Maxentius was feeling lucky. Thinking the omens were in his favor, he made an overconfident and ultimately catastrophic mistake in judgment. Leaving the city, he led his troops to confront Constantine head-on. However, there was one little problem—Maxentius had destroyed all the bridges across the Tiber River going to Rome, including the Milvian Bridge. Now needing to cross to meet up with Constantine's troops, Maxentius had his men make a pontoon bridge, placing their boats side by side across its width.

The armies clashed fiercely, and one of Maxentius' flanks was pushed back onto the makeshift boat bridge. The weight of the soldiers strained the boats until, overladen, they sank into the Tiber and took the men down with them. Maxentius was among the drowned, and his head was taken by Constantine's troops and proudly paraded in victory.

So, what does this obviously political fight have to do with Christianity? Eusebius and Constantine tell of a sensational event right before the battle—perhaps the turning point for the superstitious Constantine.

According to Constantine (and later written down by Eusebius), the noon sun was high in the sky the day before the battle. Looking up, he saw a "cross-shaped trophy" sitting over the sun. On the cross were etched the words "By this conquer." Constantine and his accompanying body of soldiers stood in amazement.

That night, he kept thinking about what the sign could mean when, finally, he was overtaken by sleep. Constantine claimed he was told in a dream to paint the mark of the Christ, an X, on the shields of his men. This mark was said to protect his men from enemy attack. It also inspired Constantine to create a jewel-encrusted gold lance (the man loved his jewels) on which hung a silk banner embroidered with a wreath bearing Christ's name.[74]

---

[74] This banner, called a labarum, was always taken by Constantine on military exploits from that time forward and eventually became the symbol of the Byzantine Empire.

Yet it wasn't enough. Outside the gates of Rome, Constantine had the Sibylline Books brought to him so he could check what the oracles had to say. It was there he found the words he wanted to see: "On this day the enemy of the Romans will perish." Confident in all sorts of divine backing, he marched out to victory.

It is generally said that these incidents sparked Constantine's conversion to Christianity (though he was not baptized until right before his death). But did the man whose favorite gods were Mars and Apollo truly convert to Christianity, and what were his motives for doing so?

Constantine's conversion by Peter Paul Reubens.
https://commons.wikimedia.org/wiki/File:Constantine%27s_conversion.jpg

Like any good superstitious soldier, Constantine likely believed in covering his bases. In his mind, if he wanted to win politically and militarily, all the gods, regardless of religion, should be appeased to increase his chances of success. To mistakenly offend a god by leaving them out would be to risk divine retribution. For him, Christianity was less about Jesus' ransom sacrifice and more of a magic talisman for his victories.

Similarly, "conversion" didn't seem like a big deal to Constantine. He already worshipped the sun, so it was a small leap for him to worship the

Son. In fact, he was the one who introduced Christmas, an event that melded sun worship with Son worship.

So, in 313 AD, Constantine made it official: not his conversion but the decriminalization of Christianity. The Edict of Milan allowed every citizen of the empire freedom of worship. Though Rome was usually tolerant of other religions, it was a radical move for the empire—a step that would take it from Christian persecutor to Christian patron.

But the perpetual pesky problem of a fractured empire plagued Constantine's reign. Like others before him, he sought religious unity as a way to hold the empire together. However, he couldn't just toss out hundreds of years of native pagan culture without consequence. After all, he had just granted religious freedom to Christians with an edict that technically allowed everyone else to worship as they pleased. So, how was he going to work this sticky problem out? By meshing together pagan and Christian beliefs, he hoped that the various peoples of the empire would unite in happy brotherhood. However, Christianity itself had become divided.

Two sects, the Donatists and Arians, were the main players at this time. The Donatists had a very strict view of holiness and were not keen on Roman emperors interfering in their godly affairs. They didn't approve of the way things were being run from the church in Rome either, causing a break from the main branch at the time. Saying that all other branches of Christianity were not worthy or holy enough did not win them any popularity among other professed Christians. An uproar ensued, and violent attacks were made on Donatist churches in North Africa.

The Arians, for their part, maintained the first-century beliefs about the divinity of Jesus. They refused to accept the now more common teachings that Jesus had supreme status as part of the Trinity. Rather, they held that he was created as an individual subject to God rather than equal to him. Although this teaching was original to Christianity, times had changed, and the idea created quite a stir. This became the main sticking point during the famed Council of Nicaea in 325. In the two years before that, Constantine had sent letters to the church, trying to get them more united. When that didn't work, he convened the council to have them work it out face-to-face.

Although not baptized, Constantine took part in the debate. Making his entrance into the council, Constantine was arrayed in all the splendor of his gold and purple attire, his jewels radiating their glow as he walked down the aisle in his imperial pomp. In Constantine's opening statement, it is apparent how much the internal strife among Christendom plagued him. In part, he stated: "For, in my judgment, internal strife within the Church of God is far more evil and dangerous than any kind of war or conflict, and these our differences appear to me more grievous than any outward trouble." He indicated he didn't think the matter was worthy of the debate it was causing and that it primarily arose from academically inclined clergymen having too much time on their hands. He encouraged those present to come to one conclusion on who Jesus was in relation to God.

Tired and in disagreement with the Arians, Constantine sided with the rest of Christendom on the matter. All but two of the clergymen gathered voted to accept Jesus as equal to God, and they wrote down a formal statement of belief (the Nicaean Creed) to seal it in writing. The council condemned the sect's leader, Arius, as dangerous and heretical. Arius was then excommunicated, and the emperor shipped him into exile (though he returned to good graces a few years later).

Within Christendom, the events in Nicaea are considered the pinnacle of Constantine's religious transformation. Yet another transformation would take place several years later. In 330 AD, Constantine moved the empire's capital to a little town on the Bosporus strait known as Augusta Antonina. Previous Emperor Septimius Severus had razed it, but Constantine came along to raise it back up and turn it into the "Queen of Cities." He renamed it Constantinople, and its gleaming wealth created the backdrop for a new epicenter of Christian intellectualism and culture.

Though he continued to phase Christianity into the empire, the emperor was still not baptized. What was the hang-up? He was certainly making changes to the Roman system—passing laws that tightened up morals and tried to prevent abuses, especially of a sexual nature.[75] There is ample evidence that he was strong in his convictions regarding his faith. He set himself up as a patron of Christians—commissioning new Bibles for congregations in Constantinople, favoring them with money for houses of worship (such as the original Hagia Sophia), doling out high-ranking positions, and exempting the clergy from taxes. If that weren't enough, he styled himself the head of the church and promoted unity

---

[75] But sometimes these were savagely enforced. In some cases, moral crimes could lead to being burned alive or the offender having molten lead poured down their throat.

within Christendom.

Though he certainly may have had some genuine conviction about what he learned, adopting Christianity wasn't without its perks for the emperor. Eusebius wrote in the emperor's biography that he "derived the source of imperial authority from above" and was "strong in the power of the sacred title." If he could claim divine backing for his imperial authority, well, that would put him in an advantageous position. After all, he believed his rise to power and success were linked to divine support.

The problem was, as he was helping Christians and attempting to bring the empire in line with Christian morality, his personal life left much to be desired. Temperamental, paranoid, megalomaniacal, cruel, violent, and prone to murder even within his own family, Constantine hadn't quite refined his Christian character, and he seemed to know it.

As emperor, he had blood on his hands from wars and other unsavory acts he may have considered necessary. But in his thinking (perhaps a common way of thinking at the time), as long as he wasn't baptized, he couldn't be condemned for any of those sins. His plan seemed to be to repent and be absolved of all prior sins at just the right moment, when he was at death's door and could commit no more transgressions. He was essentially aiming to go to his grave "sin-free." Eusebius' writings hint that perhaps the clergy were reluctant to allow his baptism for the ethical and moral reasons already stated. Either way, Constantine's baptism into Christianity didn't occur until seventeen days before his death, as he lay sick and in mortal peril. But to the very end, Constantine was a man who wanted to cover all his bases. The day before he died, he also offered a sacrifice to Zeus.[76]

When Constantine died in 337, Rome was still a mix of pagan and Christian worshippers. But as his legacy, he had legalized Christianity and made it an officially recognized religion of the state, meaning Christians could now freely meet for worship without fear. But even though Constantine helped usher in a historically significant change and made Christianity a state religion, it would not become *the* state religion for another forty-three years. And in that time, many more branches would sprout.

---

[76] He still held the title Pontifex Maximus (or supreme priest) of the pagan Roman religion.

Chapter 12: State Religion and Heresies

After Constantine, most emperors either embraced or, at the very least, tolerated Christianity, as it seemed good for the business of the empire. However, a hiccup in the path of Christianity becoming the official state religion came during the reign of Emperor Julian, starting in 361 AD. While much of the empire was changing from paganism to Christianity, Julian ran the opposite way. Having been taught Christian teachings, in part by Eusebius himself, Julian later preferred the classic Greek and Roman philosophies and deities, earning him the nickname Julian the Apostate. He didn't exactly re-criminalize Christianity; in fact, he was fine with the Donatists, who were busy fighting against corruption in the Roman church. He welcomed them back from the exile imposed on them by the previous emperor.[77] Still, he did make it a point to ban certain church rites and to harass Christians so they could not protest the empire's reintroduction to paganism.

In the grand scheme of things, Julian's bid to return to the paganist and philosophy-filled days didn't last long, and it hardly stemmed the tide of Christianity. Neither did it put the kingdom back together as one united empire as he had hoped.

---

[77] This came back to bite later emperors when the Donatists threw their support behind a rebellion of farmers who were angry over taxation.

In 380 AD, Emperor Theodosius I threw the full imperial weight of the state behind Christianity. After suffering a bout of illness, the newly baptized emperor issued the Edict of Thessalonica. This edict made Christianity the official religion of the empire. However, by this time, Christianity was far from one religion, and numerous sects were constantly contending for supremacy and squabbling over doctrine. The first council in Nicaea hadn't been enough to unify their beliefs. The debate between Nicene and Arian ideas of the Trinity continued to rage.[78]

Theodosius sought to end the controversy once and for all and, as many before him, sought to unify the empire through unified doctrine. The Archbishop of Constantinople, Gregory Nazianzus, was on the same page as the emperor. They called all of Western Christendom together for the First Council of Constantinople (the second ecumenical council). The council spent three months hammering out the details of the Trinity doctrine that had not been dealt with at Nicaea. Some argued for the divinity of the Holy Spirit, while others were not keen on the idea. Accusations flew, condemnations were made, and bishop titles were snatched away.

In all, seven canons were established, though only four were doctrinal. The other three dealt with procedures regarding the Bishop of Constantinople and what to do with certain heretics in the church.

The council also established the doctrine under the Nicene Creed, specifically the Trinity teaching, which they tweaked, to be the official dogma of the church (set in stone with the new Nicene-Constantinopolitan Creed). Turning a deaf ear to continued Arian protest, the church declared the following: (1) Jesus is God, (2) Jesus died and was resurrected, (3) others will also be resurrected from the dead, (4) the Holy Spirit was part of the Trinity godhead, and (5) the establishment of one universal church.[79]

Any other contrary teachings were declared heresy, and these involved quite a few sects with varying takes on how the Trinity worked.[80] For example, Collyridianism declared that Mary and not the Holy Spirit was

---

[78] The Nicene Creed touted the divinity of Jesus as part of the Trinity, whereas Arians believed Jesus was created and so did not have supreme status as God or part of the Trinity.

[79] The term "catholic" means universal, so the term Catholic Church correlates to the declared universal church.

[80] Heresy is any teaching considered false, wrong, or contrary to what was accepted by the mainstream church.

the third party of the Trinity and that marriage between God and Mary produced Jesus.

Those who disagreed with the Nicene Creed could die for it at the end of a sword. Just a few years later, Priscillian, Bishop of Avila, earned this fate, making him the first Christian "heretic" to be killed by other Christians.

Nicene Christianity became rooted as the state religion, while most other Christian sects faced new difficulties. Now, their persecution was being backed by the emperor *and* the church. Declared heretics and "foolish madmen" for not accepting the newly outlined beliefs, the other sects were stripped of legal status, and their property was taken by the state.

Politically speaking, Theodosius officially accepting the Nicene Trinity doctrine was a risky move. With the emperor involved in church appointments, Constantinople, a decidedly Arian city, would be tricky to keep in order. It was bad enough that different Nicene-supporting sects in Alexandria and Antioch were locked in heated opposition over the bishopric of Constantinople, keeping the city fraught with bubbling tensions. The emperor was in a religious-political minefield when it came to making appointments: inevitably, someone would be unhappy.

Even outside the empire, politics tinged religion when it came to "barbarian" tribes. Many wished to be Roman, coveting the perks of citizenship in the empire. But increasingly, they would be required to give up their old religious system and convert to Christianity if they wanted to become part of the empire.

Christianity continued its spread around the empire and beyond its borders, expanding in North Africa, the Middle East, and farther east. It became a spidery network of splintered factions and sects, many with slightly varying beliefs. Many disagreed with the main church of Rome, appointing their own leaders and formulating their own brand of Christianity.

However, while the main churches debated doctrinal issues, some tired of the arguing, politicking, and divisiveness. These left for a life of solitude, hoping to find their way back to true spirituality.

Chapter 13: Monasticism and Asceticism

Being appointed to a church position by the emperor was a big deal, and heads began to swell with pride and arrogance. Many who saw this pattern of privilege and corruption were disgusted, longing to return to a simpler, purer form of spirituality. By getting rid of material things, living an extremely frugal life, and rejecting all physical or worldly pleasures, those who chose a life of asceticism wanted fewer distractions to concentrate on spiritual matters and cultivate virtue. They worked to keep fleshly desires in check and cultivate a good name in the heavens. That meant no marriage, kids, possessions, eating food for pleasure, baths or hygienic practices, and no creature comforts. It was an exercise in extreme self-discipline designed to tame the human will and hone deep spiritual power.

Why did so many adopt such an austere, no-frills lifestyle? Reasons varied. As many spiritually-minded people saw the church taking a path towards material possessions, power, privilege, and moral corruptness, they ran in the opposite direction, looking to purify their souls and their spirituality. They wanted to leave behind the secular world and the main church in a bid for their salvation.

Some moved into isolated locations to get away from persecution and the traitors who would hand them over. But once the empire declared Christianity legal, there was no more martyrdom. Most rejoiced in that, but not all. Some had seen martyrdom as the ultimate sacrifice they could make, so now they were at a loss as to how to make the greatest sacrifice possible. So, instead of death, they essentially martyred their desires by living a life of austerity and solitude. Taking a page from the ascetics of the East, many Christians began their own monastic movement in the West.[81]

The idea of monasticism was nothing new by this point. Scriptural examples like John the Baptist, who lived in the desert eating locusts and honey, mixed with Judaism and Greco-Roman philosophy, had long formed the basis for the culture. But by the time the third and fourth centuries rolled around, monastic life looked far different and took a more prominent role as professed Christians put a new spin on it.

With such a simple lifestyle, what did ascetics do with their time? More moderate ascetics centered their lives around prayer, meditation, worship, and the basics of survival. Some begged for their basic needs while others performed manual labor, were teachers and counselors in their communities, or received visitors to impart encouragement and spiritual wisdom. Some were more extreme in their self-denial, chaining themselves to rocks and eating grass like beasts of the field. Others, like Simeon Stylites, spent decades seated on a pillar out in the open, praying. All were linked to sin, redemption, and a higher relationship with God.

Paul of Thebes, also known as Paul the Hermit, set the stage during this era. After his parents died at age sixteen, he got word that his brother-in-law was planning to betray him and turn him over to persecutors. Fleeing, he ran for safety into the desert of Thebes, Egypt. There, he survived by eating dates and drinking from a small desert oasis near his mountain home. He spent the next ninety-one years in constant prayer all day long. He set a precedent for the man that would follow him, one of the most noted models of ascetic life: Anthony the Great.[82]

Known by some as the Father of All Monks, Anthony was not the first to live a bare-bones lifestyle, but he did ignite the movement in the West. After his wealthy parents died when he was twenty years old, Anthony took the scripture in Matthew 19:21 about "selling all you have and giving to the poor" very literally and entered a life of voluntary poverty under

---

[81] Those involved in monastic life were known as monks and nuns, having taken religious vows that often involved giving up worldly pleasure and material things (asceticism) and living in communal buildings like monasteries and convents.

[82] Also known as Anthony of Egypt, Anthony of the Desert, and Anthony the Hermit, among other nicknames.

the discipleship of another hermit. A minimalist in the diet department, Anthony lived on just bread, water, and salt, with a few fasts sprinkled in throughout the week.

According to his biographer, Athanasius, Anthony had some pretty legendary experiences fighting phantasmic women and wild beast-shaped demons (who, at one point, nearly beat him to death) while living around tombs on the outskirts of his village. When he finally decided he was tired of dealing with people, he moved to a desert mountain (Mount Colzim) near the Nile River to enjoy complete solitude.

The Torment of Saint Anthony by Michaelangelo.
https://commons.wikimedia.org/wiki/File:Michelangelo_Buonarroti_-_The_Torment_of_Saint_Anthony_-_Google_Art_Project.jpg

Anthony took up residence in an abandoned Roman fort and would not set foot outside his dwelling space for the next twenty years. How did he manage to get food? The community wasn't about to let him starve, so they threw food over the wall to him. Sometimes, the faithful would make pilgrimages to see him, but he was all about solitude and refused to take any visitors. He gradually drew a following of fellow ascetically- inclined disciples who began living in huts and caves around his mountain. In time, an entire colony formed around him, and the people clamored for him to come lead them in his ways.

He finally gave in to the incessant begging and agreed to be their spiritual leader. After twenty years alone, to the surprise of his disciples, he finally emerged from the fort healthy and fit in all ways.

Until this point, monastic life was a hermit's life (called eremitic monasticism), but that was about to change. By this time, quite a large colony of monks had formed around him in the desert. He took five to six years to organize them into communities and teach them about living a life of self-denial and spirituality. After that, he returned to his desert fort and lived out the rest of his life.[83] Though he was certainly not the first to live an ascetic lifestyle, he seems to have given it momentum in Egypt, and the communities he started spread around the country and abroad. This was the beginning of communal monasticism (called cenobitic monasticism).

The monastic communities that sprang from Anthony may have been disenchanted with the church and people in general, but this was no part-time devotion or passing phase for them—they were in it all the way. Some monks and nuns even took their asceticism to great extremes, living in caves, cemeteries, swamps, solitary cells, and, in one case, a forty-foot-high pillar. One example is Amma Syncletica, a "Desert Mother" from Alexandria. Similar to Anthony, she gave away all her worldly wealth after the death of her parents and took up a hermit's residence in a crypt. She also gained quite the following and was very influential, especially among women joining the monastic movement.

---

[83] Though this time his lifestyle was less solitary. He welcomed visitors and went in and out of nearby cities. In 311 AD, he took a trip to Alexandria to encourage those being persecuted.

Amma Syncletica of Alexandria.
https://www.worldhistory.org/image/5506/amma-syncletica-of-alexandria/

Early on, most of the ascetics were lone figures, but small informal groups soon formed. One was more vulnerable to attacks by the devil when alone, so there was safety in numbers. But as the movement grew in numbers, the need for organization became more important. Enter the monk Pachomius. He saw that the men and women of these small communities needed structure and a standardized way of life. Being a former Roman soldier likely equipped him for the task.

Pachomius set up the first full-fledged monastery, where men and women lived in separate dormitory-like houses. He set up rules and regulations regarding periods of fasting, silence, reading, worship together, and prayer. Instead of following their own random perspectives on food, rest, and other daily activities, monks and nuns had jobs to support themselves in the monastery—weaving baskets, making clothes, and similar jobs.

Life was still far different from the outside, though. No one owned their own property; everything was communal. They put a hooded twist on their simple peasant-like clothes, and meals were not raucous social affairs—they were eaten together but in complete silence. Unlike regular worshippers, those in the monastic communities spent their time in meditation on the scriptures. But what about the many illiterate peasants who wanted a life of devotion in the monasteries? There was good news for them: if they entered the community, there were programs to teach them to read.

Today, many people recognize the words abbot, father, and mother in connection with those in charge of a monastery. This was also the work of Pachomius, the first to designate himself as *abba*. He established a family-like hierarchy, and everyone inside looked after one another's well-being. As appealing as that might have been to newcomers, they weren't automatically in for life. They had a long one-to-three-year probationary period to make sure they were a good fit before being allowed in permanently.

As much work as he did organizing monastic communities, Pachomius wasn't the only "father" of communal monasticism. Basil the Great, mentioned earlier, had a large hand in developing more moderate monastic guidelines to give life in the communities more balance and less austerity.

Before long, there were tens of thousands living in monastic communities. Although these seemed to be little islands unto themselves, thanks to Basil, they were connected to the larger church system. Later, monasteries would fall under the umbrella of a local church bishop. This allowed for more work to be done for the poor and needy, a cause close to Basil's heart and one he devoted much time to.

Some monks like John Chrysostom "the Golden Mouthed" and John Cassian took positions in the mainstream church. Cassian started his monastic career with three years in a hermitage before visiting other monasteries around Egypt. From there, he paved the way for monasticism in Europe.

Several years later, Cassian became involved in a big controversy with Theophilus, Archbishop of Alexandria. Again, the debate over the conception of God raged. This time, it specifically involved Origen's take on the matter. Church bishops and other leaders deemed Origen's ideas heretical as Cassian was preaching them in the West. Angered by their stance on Origen's teachings, Cassian marched to Constantinople to complain to Chrysostom and took a position in the clergy there. After exile and an appeal to Rome, Cassian gladly accepted an invitation to start a monastery in Western Europe.

When he started the first Egypt-inspired monastery in Gaul, he laid out basic rules for life. He tried to help monks in their quest for perfection by outlining their biggest obstacles and the best ways to avoid them.[84] He also took a balanced approach to monasticism. A great example is his approach to hospitality, encouraging even the most anti-social hermits to graciously entertain guests. Cassian's guidelines became the model for other Western monasteries.

The monasteries in Europe made some of the greatest contributions to spreading Christianity across the continent. While most churches were set up in cities and attracted mainly nobility and high society types, many people lived in rural locations and didn't have access to church learning. So, as monasteries popped up in farmlands and other outlying areas, Christianity gradually spread to the common people around the country. By the fourth century, monasteries became well-established and linked to the rest of Christendom.

Once pitted against the Church, monasteries increasingly became part of it. Emperors trying to control the Church founded and built monasteries, some of which became pseudo-mini states of their own. Once places to live a simple life, monasteries began a track that would lead them to become some of the wealthiest and most powerful institutions in the world.

While much of the monastic and Christian expansion had occurred in the eastern part of the Roman world until this time, Christianity was also slowly creeping towards the most western reaches of the empire.

---

[84] His work heavily influenced the monk Benedict of Nursia, founder of the widely-known Benedictine order of monks.

Chapter 14: Western Missionary Expansion and the Papacy

A sweeping trend had developed among the wealthy of large cities in Italy, Greece, Asia Minor, and North Africa. Christianity had, for many, morphed from a spiritual life journey to a faddish movement of the elite. It had become fashionable among the upper class and those looking to move up in society to join the ranks of those professing to be Christians. There was good reason. With the imperial hands in the Church pot, the wealth and prestige of the Church skyrocketed. The allure of a multitude of privileges sent many running for a position among the clergy. Aristocratic women experimented with faddish forms of devotion, much as those trying to set trends in fashion. Yet this was just a small fraction of the population. What about the common people outside high society and the epicenters of the "cultured" world?

Large swaths of rural landscape, filled with people of various cultures, languages, and identities, existed outside the wealth and nobility-filled cities of the Roman and Greek worlds. Although many lands stretching to Great Britain were technically under Roman control, they had avoided Romanization. There were no large cities in these areas at the time—not even what could be considered middle-sized cities. Barely touched by Roman influence, they were also relatively untouched by Christianity.

But as the empire had fractured into Eastern and Western parts, the Church likewise divided. Having benefited from the unification and extensive road-building projects, Christianity now traveled down the spiderweb of paths leading away from Italy and towards Gaul and beyond.[85] Word spread that Christianity welcomed people of any nation or tribe regardless of religious background. That appealed to many who liked being attached to Roman culture but didn't want to fully give up their traditional beliefs. As far as some were concerned, they could worship their gods *and* Jesus—he would make a nice addition to their pantheon of deities.

Some missionaries were making their way west in those days, but the majority of people learned about Christianity through their local grapevine—friends, relatives, and neighbors spreading the word to each other. Though Christianity was not intended to be compatible with pagan worship, the people around the empire adopted it as such.

But who was there to tell them otherwise? Most in the vast expanse of the Roman Empire were far from the educational reaches of the main Church. Thus, Christianity became as diverse as the people scattered around the far corners of the empire. By 410 AD, Christianity had reached the furthest corner—Britain.[86] But not before a few other stops.

Cannibals, beasts, barbarians—these were the ingrained ideas civilized Roman citizens had about the Germanic tribes. Given their history of savage invasion into Roman lands, these perceptions were not wholly unfounded. Bishop Optatus of North Africa expressed the views of many when he said that the "priesthood, chastity, and virginity...would not be safe" among the people of the Germanic tribes. In turn, none wanted or took the task of going out on missions to the barbarian tribes.

But the prestige of the new "Roman" religion was too much for even barbarian tribes to resist. The spread was slower in the outlying areas and was mainly organic. Migrants learned about Christianity in one place and brought it with them when the settled in another. Others learned it from Christians they kidnapped in their raids on Roman lands. Through word of mouth, the news about Christianity got around, and many Germanic people voluntarily converted.

Most preferred the controversial Arian take over the Trinitarian, especially the Goths, who had many times violently butted heads with the Roman Empire over the years. The Goths led the charge to Christianity

---

[85] Late antiquity Gaul encompassed what is now France, Switzerland, Belgium, Luxembourg, and parts of the Netherlands and Germany.

[86] Some evidence shows there might have been a few Christians living in Britain as early as 250 AD.

among the Germanic tribes, and as they adopted it, a dramatic transformation began. Their previous penchant for brutal violence was gradually replaced with what contemporary historian Orosius said was a milder attitude and a tamping down on "savagery."

The conversion to Christianity wasn't without consequence for some in the Germanic world. In a wave of persecution that rivaled that under Emperor Diocletian, converted Goths were persecuted by pagan Gothic kings. The most well-known incident was perpetuated by King Wingurich, who had his men pull a chariot containing a large statue into a town with many Christian Goths. Anyone who worshipped it would be spared. But over 300, including presbyters Wereka and Batwin, refused. The king's men then trapped the Christians inside the tent of worship and set fire to the statue inside, killing everyone, including children and newborns.

Some died under persecution, and others fled to distant parts of the Roman Empire. This wasn't enough to stop the spread among the people, though. In the mid-fourth century, a prominent Christian Goth named Wulfila (who became the first Gothic bishop) worked to translate the Bible from Greek into the eastern Germanic language spoken by the Goths. As Christianity gained a strong foothold among the Goths, they passed their beliefs on to their Germanic cousins of other tribes, such as the Vandals, Franks, and Visigoths.

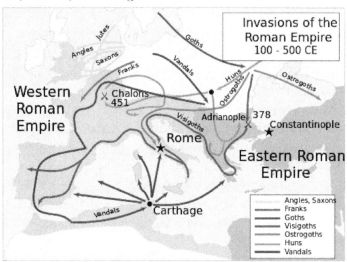

Invasions and migrations from the 2nd to 5th century.
MapMaster, CC BY-SA 2.5 <https://creativecommons.org/licenses/by-sa/2.5>, via Wikimedia Commons; https://commons.wikimedia.org/wiki/File:Invasions_of_the_Roman_Empire.svg

The details of when and how Christianity reached Gaul are a bit murky, but a mid-second-century wave of persecution in Lugdunum shows Christianity had already been established by this time. [87] That's not to say it was flourishing by any means. Surrounded by duel pagan cultures of the Gauls and Greco-Romans, Christianity was discouraged if not downright dangerous to profess, making the Christian population there rather modest.

So was the case with the first church leader of Lugdunum named Pothinus. After a mid-century plague killed thousands in Gaul, the terrified citizens were looking for a reason and someone to blame. Taking a page out of Nero's Christians-as-scapegoats book, the population decided the gods sent the plague because they were angry that the Christians refused to worship them. Pothinus was zeroed in on and promptly arrested. Before he could be tried and legally executed, some took matters into their own hands and swiftly beat him to death. He was the first martyr of Gaul but not the only. After that, church history says that forty-eight other Christians were arrested for refusing to sacrifice to Roman gods and were sent to face wild beasts in the arena.

After the death of Pothinus, Irenaeus took over the reins in Gaul, but the spread of Christianity remained slow. It was tough to make inroads in the local pagan cultures. Many in the upper classes steadfastly clung to old religions and traditions, schools celebrated pagan teachers, and the common people still looked to spells, charms, nature spirits, and divination to cure everyday ills. Many pagan festivals and customs were in place well before the Romans arrived, making them a deeply entrenched part of who the Gauls were.

In the mid-fourth century, Martin of Tours made it his aim to root the pagan idolatry out of the countryside. This became easier among the poorer population as monasteries cropped up. Martin established a "grand monastery," and Cassian later built two more. The close proximity of ascetics living a simple life similar to that of the poor yet freely practicing Christianity fostered the slow spread of Christianity in the area and beyond.

As early as the first century, the apostle Paul at least intended to go to Spain (Romans 15:24), but there is no confirmation that he ever reached the Iberian Peninsula. But sometime between his life and 180 AD, at

---

[87] Many Gallic saints of the period were of Greek origin, so likely Christianity had reached the area through Greek missionaries or migrants.

least a small community of Christians had developed, as Irenaeus made reference to. These had probably reached Spain in the process of fleeing wars in Jerusalem. A hundred years later, Cyprian of Carthage mentioned Christians in at least four cities on the peninsula. As with the rest of Western Europe, Christianity gradually spread through neighbors, families, and friends.

The earlier sporadic Christian persecutions didn't reach the small communities in Iberia, but when Diocletian's fierce sweep came, Iberian Christians suffered with the rest. The first recorded martyr was young Eulalia, said to be about years old. Despite her mother's best efforts to keep her sequestered, Eulalia snuck out and publicly proclaimed herself a Christian. Not content with just that, she also directly insulted the gods and the emperor, declaring:

"Isis, Apollo, and Venus are nothing, Maximian himself is nothing; They are nothing, because they were made by hands, He, because he reveres the works of hands."

Her stand resulted in her being stripped naked, tortured, and tied to the stake to be burned. Defiant to the very end, as the flames kicked up and smoke entered her lungs, she continued to taunt her executioners until her last dying breath.

Iberian Christians weren't the only ones mentioned by Irenaeus. He also spoke about a community among the Celts in Britain. Interestingly, it was probably the Romans themselves who brought Christianity to the furthest reaches of their empire. As early as the first century, Britain was trading with Romee. So, when Roman merchants made their way to the isles for commerce, they also brought stories about Jesus and his disciples.

However, Christianity had hardly gotten a foothold in Britain before it was nearly wiped off the isles. When the Anglo-Saxons invaded Britain in the early 400s AD, they brought their Germanic polytheism and all but replaced Christianity. The few Christians remaining fled into Wales, Ireland, and Scotland, where they continued to thrive virtually undisturbed. But in England, it would take another 200 years before Christianity would again be reestablished.

Back in the thick of the Roman Empire, things were heating up between Rome, Constantinople, Alexandria, Antioch, and Jerusalem, each of which believed they held the right as the primary church. The position of pope didn't officially exist yet, but each bishop threw in his claim as the rightful head of the Church.[88]

As the city where the first Christian congregation was established and the central governing body (council) was housed, Jerusalem was highly important to professed Christians of the early centuries. It was also the city where Jesus died and was resurrected. Many held the city as a beacon of Christian honor and prestige.

Alexandria was a veritable Christian think tank, a key city that believed itself to be the root of Christian theology. From that city, Christianity spread to Europe, but most notably to Africa and Asia. Along with Antioch, Alexandria claimed solid connections to the apostle Peter. Antioch claimed that Peter was the bishop of their city before he even joined the congregation in Rome. In addition to Peter, Alexandria also laid claim to Mark, who was said to have founded the congregation there.

Constantinople, as the newly minted capital of the Eastern Roman Empire (or "New Rome," as it was labeled), was backed by imperial power. In 381, the First Council of Constantinople declared Constantinople just under Rome in the hierarchy of important cities. Rome, nervous about the rising power of Constantinople, took exception to it being so highly honored. At a synod the next year, Damascus I protested the rise of Constantinople. As a relatively young city—only fifty years old—why should it take precedence over the much older cities of Alexandria and Antioch, where Christianity had been established much longer?

By 354, Rome's prominence continued to rise when it was billed "the Apostolic See," a reference to Peter's connection. Damascus used the words of Matthew 16:18, "You are Peter and on this rock I will build my congregation (church)," as a precedent to support the supremacy of the bishop of Rome's position.

Even as Rome's imperial power was declining, its religious power was steadily rising. It was becoming harder to argue with Rome's religious power when it was backed by three emperors. Theodosius II, Valentinian III, and Justinian all positioned the bishop of Rome as "the Rector of the whole Church." There was still no official papal position, but the power of Rome's bishop was being cemented—even more so when Innocent I, a bishop of Rome, claimed that all major decisions should be referred to

---

[88] Although the term "pope" was used as early as the second and third centuries by some churches, the title "pope" for the head of the Roman Catholic Church wasn't official until about the ninth century.

Rome's authority. This gave Damascus I the backing to have himself styled the "Supreme Pontiff" in 380 AD.[89]

Yet with the other cities posing powerful threats to its supremacy, Rome needed to ensure its head position was secured and that the other sees[90] clearly understood it. This was made easier by Rome's close relationship with the emperors, who steadily conferred more and more power to the bishops there. In 440 AD, Roman bishop Leo I used Roman law to his advantage and solidified the position: the bishops of Rome were legally declared the successors of Peter.

When the matter came up again during the Council of Chalcedon in 451 AD, Leo I claimed he was "speaking with the voice of Peter." To quell the discontent of Constantinople, the council again reaffirmed that it stood only second to Rome. However, Rome took exception to this renewed declaration since it did not recognize Rome's authority over Constantinople (or any other see, for that matter). Yet Rome held firm to its position.

The battle for supremacy continued for centuries, coming to a head in the eleventh century. Disagreement over the prime position created the Great Schism of 1054, putting Rome and Constantinople on opposing sides of the divide, each believing they should hold the right to the top position in the Church. Even though Rome's position was well affirmed, debates over the supremacy of the papacy continued throughout the Middle Ages and even into the mid-twentieth century.

---

[89] Or *Pontifus Maximus,* a term used for leaders, particularly emperors, within the Roman Empire's pagan religious order.

[90] From the Latin word *sedes,* meaning "seat," the word see refers to the position of bishop of a city.

Bonus Chapter: Art

Fascinating, storied, and at times bewildering in its meaning, early Christian art melded symbols, classic Greco-Roman imagery, and biblical history into paintings, mosaics, sculptures, and even sarcophagi (coffin-like boxes made of stone).

Many have seen the grand stained-glass depictions and famed Christian-themed art of medieval times, but why is Christian art from the first century never talked about? Because it hardly exists. It's not that early Christians had anything against art, per se, but they had reason not to create it in their early days.

Most early Christians were of Jewish background, and no doubt the words of the Mosaic law were indelibly pressed into their minds, particularly the commandments against forming any images of God, idolatrous depictions of "anything under heaven and earth," and to "be on guard against every form of idolatry." [91]To be fair, much of the Greco-Roman art surrounding first-century Christians had to do with idolatry and pagan worship, so it stands to reason that they would avoid creating any kind of art that could break those commandments.

There was a second practical reason for their silence in the art world: Christianity was not very popular and was even banned for a time. Would people trying to lay low and not make themselves a target for increased persecution be openly painting and sculpting about the things they were outlawed for? Apparently not.

---

[91] There are no artistic images of God in the early Christian art of the Roman Empire.

But their creativity wasn't under wraps for long, as Christians found ways to work around the pesky bans and create art that didn't draw the attention of Roman authorities. Some art simply featured stories from the biblical history of the Jews. Stories such as Noah and the Ark and the prophet Samuel anointing David as king portrayed religious figures that expressed their faith but wouldn't be particularly concerning to the Romans.

Samuel anointing David as king.
https://commons.wikimedia.org/wiki/File:Dura_Synagogue_WC3_David_anointed_by_Samuel.jpg

Sometimes, Christians disguised their beliefs with artistic symbolism. Themes of death and resurrection could not be openly portrayed, but other Bible stories, such as Jonah and the Whale, were used to depict touchier topics.

Jonah being thrown into the sea.

At times, Christians adopted pagan symbols and gave them Christian meaning. Many early works of art contain elements borrowed from ancient pagan religions, like the mother and child, bulls, lions, and peacocks. Why peacocks? It was believed that their flesh never rotted, so many cultures regarded them as a symbol of eternal life.

Not all symbols of Christianity were borrowed from other religions or cultures; some were decidedly their own. The fish symbol was born from an acronym of the words "Jesus Christ God's Son Savior." The first letter of each word in Greek spells out the word Ichthus (ΙΧΘΥΣ), the Greek word for fish.

Another workaround Christians used was to depict figures under classic Roman disguises (think togas and Roman haircuts instead of fake noses and glasses). A great example is a painting called "The Good Shepherd."

Good Shepherd from the Catacomb of Priscilla, 250–300.

As a Jew, Jesus would have worn Jewish garb with fringes and sported a beard, as all Jewish men of the time. But here, he is depicted as a beardless shepherd wearing a toga—two distinctly Greco-Roman features.

Another painting shows Jesus looking like the Greek Orpheus, a demi-god with a supernatural talent for music and writing.

Jesus depicted as Orpheus.
https://commons.wikimedia.org/wiki/File:Christ-Orpheus_from_Rome_catacombe.jpg

Disguise wasn't the only reason Christian art featured things that were out of place for Jews and Christians. They also hadn't developed their own distinct style and borrowed from what they knew of art at the time—classic Greco-Roman features and even characteristics and symbols plucked from ancient Egyptian and Babylonian art. An example is a highly ornate sarcophagus made shortly after the Edict of Milan legalized Christianity. In the middle, Jesus' father Joseph, a Jew, is given a very Roman look. The angels were not immune to a little fine-tuning of their image—they, too, are given togas.

When Christians couldn't openly portray their art above ground, some of the most important works of early Christian art were found underground. The extensive catacombs of Rome held a virtual treasure trove of art in a place easily hidden from public view. [92] Sarcophagi, like the one above, were just the tip of the artistic iceberg. Paintings, mosaics, carvings, and even gold glass were used to portray religious figures and scenes.

---

[92] Underground passages with chambers and insets used for burying the dead.

Often, though, art proclaimed the faith of the deceased, sometimes in engravings of semi-cryptic phrases like "to the well-deserving." Symbolic images might be used alongside the text to express the faith of the dead and their family.

Other times, the faith of the deceased was expressed in painting. An example is the "Veiled Woman," who is depicted with arms outstretched in prayer.

The Veiled Woman.

After Christianity was legalized, there was, understandably, a great shift in Christian art and its content—less disguise and more overt painting depicting Jesus in various scenes from his life.

Jesus healing the woman with the flow of blood.

Mosaic of Jesus preaching, Rome.

As Rome and Christianity grew closer, that relationship also became reflected in Christian art. In a nod to the emperor, Jesus is shown treading on a lion in a style very similar to imperial sculptures.

Christ treading the beasts.

Despite so much upheaval and instability in the world of Christians, the spread of Christianity had unexpected impacts on the creative world. Creations emerged that made a deep and lasting impact on art history, not just in Europe but around the globe. The influence of early Christian art left imprints that could be seen throughout European art into the Renaissance.

Conclusion

Christianity has had a long journey from the beginning of the first century until now. Today, it is one of the major branches of religion in the world with over 2.3 billion people professing to be Christian—that is over a quarter of the world's population. From its origins, it has gone through many changes, some of which Jesus himself prophesied would happen.

Throughout two millennia, Christianity changed the shape of culture, religion, and, in many instances, history, though in many ways that was not the original intention. Early Christianity was not just a religion or a fad but an entire lifestyle, one that thousands eagerly adopted. Those who followed it adhered to tenets such as love, unselfishness, and virtue, among other things, not just during special times or rituals but also as a part of everyday life. They worked to apply the lessons Jesus taught to make real and true changes to themselves for the better. And they shared that message because they wanted others to have a better life and real hope for a better future.

Reading about the progression of Christianity from the first apostles to small groups of disciples to the organization of larger congregations that spread around the Roman Empire is more than just a story; it's the historical heritage of millions. Within that are thousands of real people with many beautiful, heartbreaking, and, at times, terrifying experiences. These stories make up the mosaic of early Christianity.

The message that they preached was based on a strong, enduring hope, not blind faith or wishful thinking. Despite the many changes to Christianity that have come over the centuries, the original teachings of

Jesus and the early Christians still exist within the Bible. That message endures to this day and gives billions of people hope for a better and brighter world.

Part 3: The Crusades

An Enthralling Overview of an Event in Christian History That Took Place in the Middle Ages

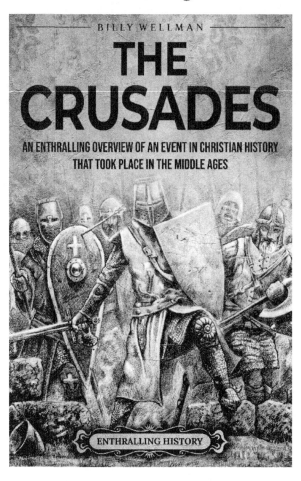

Introduction: Fighting on the Side of God?

"If you are an Arabic-speaking, Greek-Orthodox going to a French school it makes you deeply skeptical if you have to listen to three different accounts of the Crusades—one from the Muslim side, one from the Greek side, and one from the Catholic side."

-Nassim Nicholas Taleb

Over the centuries, there has been endless discussion about what started the Crusades and why they took place. In the earliest rendering of the record, the Crusades were usually explained as a cut-and-dry defensive mission to protect Christian pilgrims to the Holy Land, defend the beleaguered Byzantine Empire (modern-day Turkey), and reclaim the Holy Land, which had been lost to Christendom when Islamic forces seized it in the 7th century.

Of course, such motivations had powerful religious overtones. However, by the 19th century, when the zealous passion for Christianity was in decline and giving way to a host of rationalists, new interpretations were developed. It was around this time that ulterior motives for the Crusades were explored. Those who did this analysis just so happened to live during a period of great European colonization. These were the days of the "Scramble for Africa," in which almost every part of Africa (save Ethiopia and Liberia) was being rapidly colonized by European powers.

Therefore, it is unsurprising that 19th-century scholars put aside religious fervor as a motivating factor and looked at the Crusades differently. To the more rational-minded analysts, the crusaders appeared to be some sort of proto-colonizers.

But was that all the Crusades were about? Nothing more than a bloody land grab of the Middle East? *Hardly.* Anyone who takes the time to thoroughly understand what led to the Crusades and its implications will quickly realize that such rationalizations are utterly absurd.

It might be hard for us today to understand the absolute power that religion had over the masses during the Middle Ages (just as it was for folks in the 19th century), but it would leave any such analysis of the Crusades woefully inaccurate not to take such things into consideration. And considering how violent and utterly bloody the Crusades ended up being, there are those who might not want to consider religion as a motivating factor at all.

But it clearly was. One fateful day in 1095, Pope Urban II gave his clarion call to take up arms to save their Christian brothers and sisters in the East who were being encroached upon by the forces of Islam. It was not colonization that was on the minds of those who heard him. Religious fervor stirred their hearts, and as one, the gathered masses who heard the pope's rallying cry declared, "God wills it!"

For those with a keen understanding of Christian (and Catholic history, in particular), such a phrase is not a coincidence. The phrase stems from the Rule of Saint Augustine. In the 4th century, just prior to the fall of the Western Roman Empire, Saint Augustine hammered out his beliefs as to when the spilling of blood might be God's will.

Before this, Christians in the Roman Empire truly struggled with the notion of partaking in violence. This comes as no surprise since Jesus Christ advocated for nonviolence. This understandably led to pacifist-minded Christians but became a real problem after most of the Roman Empire converted to Christianity. Since the teachings of Christ promoted nonviolent methods, it became harder and harder to find soldiers willing to pick up the sword to defend Rome.

And as this ideological struggle persisted, the Roman Empire became desperate. It needed a strong army to fend off the barbarians who were growing in strength and incessantly pounding at the gates. This dilemma led Augustine to dictate the so-called "just cause" for violence, in which the people would fight because God willed it.

Yes, we can thank Saint Augustine for the rallying cry heard during Pope Urban's speech. And we can also thank him for the mentality that led Christians to believe they were somehow fighting on the side of God.

Section One: The Crusades in the Holy Land

Chapter 1: Origins and Background

"There is nothing intrinsic linking any religion with any act of violence. The crusades don't prove that Christianity was violent. The inquisition doesn't prove that Christianity tortures people. But that Christianity did torture people."

-Salman Rushdie

So, where did it all start? What were the origins of the Crusades? It all starts and stops with the Holy Land. It was actually a Christian Byzantine emperor who first waged a bloody war to keep the Holy Land in his possession; this was certainly a contested piece of real estate! For those of you who don't know, the Byzantines were an offshoot of the Roman Empire. After the Western Roman Empire collapsed in the 4th century, the Eastern half, which included the Levant, survived. Back then, the Byzantines didn't even think of themselves as being part of a different empire; they thought of themselves as *the* Roman Empire.

In the 7th century, the Byzantine emperor lost the Holy Land. He then waged war and recovered it. And then lost it again! The emperor's initial antagonists were not the armies of Islam (although they would come later in the same century). No, the first major opponent of the Byzantine Empire to set its eyes on Jerusalem was the Sasanian Empire, also known as the Neo-Persian Empire. The Persians took Jerusalem in 614 CE. It is believed many Christians died in the siege, and the True Cross (the cross on which Jesus is thought to have died) was captured by the Persians.

Byzantine Emperor Heraclius wrested Jerusalem back from the Persians in 630.

Interestingly enough, if we take a look back in history, this was not the first time the Persian Empire had dominion over Jerusalem. Over a thousand years prior to the Sasanian conquest, King Cyrus the Great of the Achaemenid Empire placed Jerusalem under his control. This event, which is documented in the Old Testament of the Bible, occurred in 539 BCE. Although Cyrus was in control of the region, he proved to be a benevolent monarch. He famously ended the Babylonian Captivity.

Many Jewish exiles, including the great prophets Daniel and Ezekiel, had previously been taken captive by King Nebuchadnezzar of the Babylonian Empire. After the Babylonians were trounced by Cyrus, the Jewish exiles were allowed to return and rebuild their city. Jerusalem would later be dominated by a series of empires.

In 630 CE, Byzantine Emperor Heraclius held the relic of the True Cross high over his head, declaring, "When God wills it, one man will rout a thousand. So let us sacrifice ourselves to God for the salvation of our brothers. May we win the crown of martyrdom that we may be praised in future and receive our recompense from God."

Although we view Pope Urban II's 1095 call for a religious, military campaign as the beginning of the Crusades, one could easily argue that the Crusades were put in motion when Emperor Heraclius of the Byzantine Empire declared these words and then put them into action. One could say that the religious zeal and military onslaught, for which the Crusades would be known, first came together during Heraclius's reign.

Even so, Heraclius's triumph would be short-lived. After the Byzantines drove the Persians out of the Holy Land, the Byzantine Empire and the Persian Empire fought themselves to a standstill. Both sides were thoroughly exhausted. While these two empires were trying to take a breath and recover, the forces of Islam rose up, almost entirely out of left field.

Muhammad had already perished by this time (he died in 632), but before he died, he galvanized his followers to spread Islam to non-Muslim lands. In 636, Muslim forces marched on Jerusalem, just a few years after the Byzantines had painstakingly recovered it from the Persians. Jerusalem was surrendered two years (some say one year) later, and it appears not much blood was shed. The Muslims guaranteed the Christians liberties in exchange for paying the jizya (a tax). Jews were also allowed to come live in the city again; they had not been allowed to settle in Jerusalem for over five hundred years.

The Rashidun Caliphate would also invade Persia. Because of this, Iran (the modern-day name for Persia) is predominantly Muslim instead of embracing its ancestral religion of Zoroastrianism.

Considering the rapid expansion of Islam, the natural question that arises is, why? And in particular, why did Muhammad's successors have an interest in securing the Holy Land under their dominion? First of all, one has to understand the basics of the Islamic faith. Although there is often much confusion and misunderstanding, Islam believes in the same monotheistic God as Judaism and Christianity.

However, there are certainly many religious differences. But even so, it's important to remember that, for Muslims, the term "Allah" is simply another name for the same God to whom Christians and Jews pray. Muhammad grew up in a world that was awash with religious influence, and he was fully immersed in the beliefs of both Judaism and Christianity.

After Muhammad was allegedly visited by the angel Gabriel (rendered as Gibreel in Arabic), he was galvanized to spread a new religious message. Yes, the same Gabriel that stars in the Christmas story and imparts the news of Christ's impending conception and birth to Mary is believed by Muslims to have visited Prophet Muhammad.

The Quran is basically a summary of the events that occurred in the Old Testament and New Testament of the Bible. The names are usually altered in Arabic translations—Moses is Musa, Noah is Nuh, Jesus is Isa, and so on and so forth—but the basic events and characters are the same. However, there is a big difference between Christianity and Islam, as Muhammad stated that Jesus never said he was the son of God.

The angel Gabriel supposedly imparted to Muhammad that the notion Jesus was the son of God was a gross exaggeration. Muhammad was informed that Jesus never said any such thing and that it was a claim fabricated by others after Jesus passed away. To be clear, the Quran states that Jesus was a great prophet and that he performed incredible miracles, just as the New Testament states. Yet, the Quran insists that Jesus was not the son of God.

There is actually a chapter of the Quran that addresses this issue called "The Table." The English rendering of the Arabic title sounds almost comical, and the famous verse of this chapter follows the same vein, as it states, "Isa [Jesus] son of Marium [Mary] used to eat food." This statement sounds absurd, but there is a good reason why this statement was made. It shows that Jesus was an ordinary human being who used to eat food just like everybody else.

An elaboration of this theme can be found in the Quranic verse from "The Table," Surah 5:75:

"The Messiah, son of Marium is but an apostle; apostles before him have indeed passed away; and his mother was a truthful woman; they both used to eat food. See how we make the communications clear to them, then behold, how they are turned away."

Another interesting aspect of focusing on the notion that Jesus used to eat food is the religious tradition that celestial beings, such as angels, do not eat food. The apocryphal Book of Tobit, which can be found in some Christian Bibles, delivers a tale of the angel Raphael that emphasizes this very point. It is said that Raphael disguises himself as a human and, at one point, even has to pretend to eat food to keep his disguise intact.

At any rate, the main thrust of Islam was to correct perceived "errors" such as this and to reaffirm that there was no such thing as the Trinity; there was just one sovereign God. Through the centuries, Muslims would cry out, "Allah Akbar!" ("Allah is greater!").

Muslims truly believed, just like Jews and Christians before them, that they were the ones with the true divine revelation of God. And since they claimed to believe in the same Abrahamic God as the Jews and Christians, they insisted they were the rightful inheritors of the Holy Land. They believed that Jerusalem should be under the stewardship of Muslim administrators.

Islam would indeed prove to be a powerful force to contend with. By the time of Pope Urban II's call to wrest the Holy Land back from the conquering forces of Islam, practically all of the Middle East, Near East, and North Africa were under Muslim dominion. And that was not the end of the story, for Muhammad had taught to continue the fight until the whole world belonged to Dar al Islam, or the House of Islam.

Until then, all nations outside of Muslim control or influence would be considered part of the Dar al Harb, or the House of War. The House of War was viewed as an unenlightened place of chaos; the true light of Islam could not shine there and guide the people. Those living in the House of War were seen as being hostile to the precepts of Islam. It was therefore believed that efforts should be made to allow the revelation of Islam to reach Dar al Harb as well.

Of course, most today do not take such a radical interpretation to heart. But nevertheless, it simply can't be denied that Muhammad's successors and their huge armies pushed forward with the expansion of Islam. They wanted to create an empire that was safe for Muslims to practice their faith and also spread the faith to others. In their minds, everyone should hear about the way of Allah since it was simply the right way to live. This might sound similar, as this was also how Christians viewed their religion at the time.

And so, the Islamic expansion continued. Islamic corsairs from North Africa landed in Spain and took over much of the Iberian Peninsula. Muslim conquerors then pushed on into France. Sicily was seized as well. It's often forgotten how much Christian Europe was on the defensive at the time. Considering all of this, the truth is if the pope had not galvanized the forces of Christendom to stand up to the encroaching armies of Islam, Europe stood a good chance of being overrun.

Christians had long been on the defensive when it came to the Muslims, but with Pope Urban's call for a crusade against Islam in 1095, they would finally go on the offensive. So, along with the pretense of defending the Byzantines and recovering the Holy Land, it wouldn't be too hyperbolic to say the defense of Europe was at stake as well. Even though the Holy Land and the Byzantine Empire would ultimately be lost, Spain, parts of France, and Sicily were recovered for Christendom. Prior to Pope Urban's address, these regions were in a perilous state.

Pope Urban II was not the first pope to consider calling a crusade. His predecessor, Pope Gregory VII mused about as much in 1074 upon seeing the perilous condition of the Mediterranean, declaring that it was time for Christendom "to take up arms against the enemies of God and push forward even to the Sepulcher of the Lord under his supreme leadership." No matter what anyone might say about the later abuses and motivations of the crusaders, there can be no doubt that it was Islamic encroachment that triggered the initial call to arms.

By the time the First Crusade was called, the Muslim forces had been steadily chipping away at the Christian Byzantines in the East. The Byzantine emperor's request for aid against this threat would morph into a larger call to bring glory to Christendom and potentially take back the birthplace of Christianity itself: the Holy Land.

Although some other ulterior motives and events drove the Crusades forward, fighting against Islamic encroachment was indeed the fundamental origin of the Crusades. As the forces of Islam pushed more and more into Christian lands, there were really only one of two possibilities: either the Christian nations crumbled and eagerly submitted to Islam, or a cataclysmic holy war would be triggered. As history can attest, it was the latter that happened.

Chapter 2: The People's Crusade and the First Crusade

"If there ever was a religious war full of terror, it was the Crusades. But you can't blame Christianity because a few adventurers did this."

-Moustapha Akhad

Even before the first professional armies of Europe descended upon the Holy Land, the first to arrive on the scene were not from the knightly or noble classes. Rather, a rabble of impoverished masses led by an itinerant preacher known as Peter the Hermit made their way eastward. This massive tidal wave of peasants would become known as the People's Crusade. In this unofficial crusade, which had been inspired by Pope Urban II's call to arms, the words of a passionate preacher galvanized the poor and huddled masses of western Europe to take up the cross and "fight the good fight."

Just imagine this monk standing around in the middle of a poor medieval village, speaking of how all good Christians needed to take up the struggle against evil. It might be hard for us to fathom it today, but back then, people took the words of this firebrand preacher seriously. Peasants literally dropped everything they were doing to follow this "Pied Piper" wherever he led them.

Farmers left the fields, and bakers left their bread just to follow Peter the Hermit and take on the "infidels" in the Middle East. Even though the pope had ordered the professional soldiers of Europe to take time to prepare themselves before disembarking on the prearranged launch date of August 15th, 1096, those who participated in the People's Crusade were so eager and zealous that they made practically no preparations whatsoever.

They set off of their own accord shortly after the pope's initial call to arms in November 1095. This unorganized mob caused trouble wherever it went. As they passed through central Europe, the People's Crusade viciously assaulted Jewish settlements simply due to the fact that they were of a different faith. This group of marauders also failed to bring adequate supplies with them, so banditry took place, with the people roving the countryside and stealing whatever they could.

Such things hardly seem Christian, yet terror was inflicted upon countless villages as the People's Crusade traveled through Europe. When they reached the Balkans and neared the Byzantine Empire's borders, they caused even more trouble by harassing the locals there. This led to several outright clashes with Byzantine authorities, but somehow, the group eventually made it to the Byzantine capital of Constantinople. The Byzantine emperor, Alexius I Komnenos, quickly washed his hands of them and sent them on to Asia Minor, which was then occupied by Turkish Muslims.

In the vicinity of the once-great Byzantine (but, at that time, Turkish-occupied) city of Nicaea, Sultan Kilij Arslan I of the Seljuk Empire made short work of Peter the Hermit's would-be crusaders. Although the European peasants were good at harassing unarmed villagers, this unsavory group proved entirely ineffective against the professional forces of the Turks. Most of the poorly trained mob of people did not have armor, and some did not even have proper weapons. Imagine folks wielding pots, pans, and broomsticks against a Turkish scimitar! With this image in mind, you can easily understand what an absolute disaster this battle was.

The Turks themselves must have been astonished at the comic absurdity of this bizarre spectacle, of this ragged band of people who had suddenly dropped in on them. At any rate, the People's Crusade was almost entirely annihilated. The First Crusade—as in the first *official* crusade—would be another matter entirely. The people who fought in the First Crusade took their time to prepare. Their campaign would not be launched until the summer of 1096. More importantly, this crusade was made up of professional soldiers

Let's briefly review what led to the First Crusade. In November 1095, in Clermont, France, Pope Urban II gave an impassioned speech to a gathering of French nobility and church clergy, highlighting the perceived threats of Islam and the need to defend the Christian Byzantine Empire and rescue the Holy Land. Breaking with custom, the pope delivered his speech in French rather than Latin. It was a smart move; by speaking in French, Urban was assured that all of those present understood him and the gravity of the situation.

To hear the pope speaking in the local French vernacular would have really helped drive his points home to the audience. He listed a whole litany of grievances that the "enemies of Christianity" had committed. Pope Urban II was known to be an eloquent public speaker, and he was able to perfectly highlight the perceived enemy while calling for a so-called "Truce of God" to unite fellow Christians.

Prior to Urban's call for the First Crusade, there were seemingly non-stop squabbles and skirmishes among Christian principalities. Also, in 1054, the Eastern and Western Churches split away due to differences in doctrine and other issues. For instance, there was a disagreement over the pope's infallibility or whether to use leavened or unleavened bread in ceremonies. These were just two of the items on the churches' long list of grievances with each other. The Great Schism rocked the Christian world, and the split between the Eastern and Western Churches still exists today. It is possible that Urban was hoping to help heal the split and bring the two churches closer together.

Pope Urban II pleaded with the nobles before him to put their differences aside and come together for a common cause and to take a stand against the forces of Islam. As Pope Urban II put it, "Let those who have been accustomed to make private warfare against the faithful carry on to a successful conclusion of war against the infidels, which ought to have begun ere now. Let those who once fought brother and relative now fight against barbarians as they ought."

As it turns out, the crusaders were quite fortunate. As they were putting aside their differences by enacting the "Truce of God," the dominant forces of Islam were, for the most part, in disarray. The Turks, in particular, had been facing a succession crisis ever since the Turkish warlord Sultan Malik Shah passed away in 1092. For the next few years or so, the Middle East would see near-constant fighting between the competing factions of successors who fought for dominance.

In truth, this was not unknown in the West. Pope Urban II had been informed of as much by Byzantine Emperor Alexius Komnenos at the Council of Piacenza in March 1095. The Byzantine emperor had pleaded for military support against the Turks, viewing the sudden dissension in their ranks as a prime opportunity for him to regain lost ground in Asia Minor. Little did Emperor Alexius know that the pope would issue an all-out impassioned plea to not only aid the Byzantines against the Turks but also potentially seize the Holy Land itself.

And the pope's call to arms had the desired effect. Soon, the whole crowd was shouting as one, "Deus lo vult!" ("God wills it!") Those who heard Urban's words were so inspired that they began tearing cloth into makeshift crosses to place on their backs to symbolize their "taking up the cross" to fight for the Holy Land.

The pope even sweetened the deal by offering exemptions from time in Purgatory. According to Catholic belief, an in-between realm called Purgatory exists. It is believed that many will bide their time there before they are able to go to heaven.

But how could the pope even promise such a thing? Well, in the Bible, Christ proclaims to Peter (whom the Catholics cite as the first pope) that "whatever you bind on Earth will also be bound in heaven, and whatever you loose on Earth will be loosed in Heaven." The Catholics believe the pope was given the "keys" to Earth and heaven. Catholics had no issue with popes excommunicating believers; lessening time in Purgatory would be under their purview as well.

It was no small thing for the pope to offer to use his power to lessen one's stay in Purgatory. Although we might be tempted to scoff at such a thing today, such a gesture would have been quite meaningful to Christian believers of this time period. Why wouldn't they jump at the chance to be with God and their loved ones sooner?

In all, it is estimated that some sixty thousand troops were assembled. They were led by European nobles, which included Henry, the brother of King William II of England, and Hugh of Vermandois, the brother of King Philip I of France. The Crusades would establish a long tradition of a king's brother going to war. It was simply far too risky for a sitting monarch to head to war in the Middle East, although it was not unheard of, as we will see later on.

This group of crusaders made their way to the Byzantine capital of Constantinople (modern-day Istanbul) in the summer of 1096, making it to their destination in the early months of 1097 (some began to arrive in November 1096).

They would remain in Constantinople for some time before setting off once again that fall. There was logistical maneuvering to work out, and adequate supplies needed to be obtained. The Byzantine emperor was genuinely grateful to have—if anything else—a major distraction to unleash upon his enemies. He duly provided the crusaders with whatever they needed.

Interestingly enough, the crusaders made a solemn pledge to Alexius Komnenos that they would return any and all territory that had formerly belonged to the Byzantine Empire. This was a rather curious pledge to make since many of the former Byzantine territories, including the Holy Land itself, had been lost long ago. Additionally, keeping this pledge would prove far more difficult than giving it.

At any rate, the crusaders set off for their first real engagement: recovering the city of Nicaea, which had been seized from the Byzantines some twenty years prior. This was the same Nicaea where the People's Crusade (led by Peter the Hermit, who was still alive) met its terrible end at the hands of the Turkish warlord Kilij Arslan.

Fortunately for the crusaders, Kilij Arslan was away on other business at the time, which gave the Europeans an edge over their unprepared opponents. Even without this advantage, this Crusading force was entirely different from Peter the Hermit's force. The crusaders were properly trained and armed; they were an efficient fighting machine. If any of the Turkish defenders who slew Peter the Hermit's followers thought that these outsiders would be just more of the same, they were sorely mistaken.

The crusaders also had the benefit of actively coordinating with Byzantine troops. During the course of the battle, Emperor Alexius made the wise decision to put his naval craft in range of Lake Ascania near Nicaea, effectively blocking off any potential reinforcements. Soon, the crusaders were attacking their opponents on all sides.

Utterly defeated, the Seljuk Turk forces that survived the melee were forced to surrender. Emperor Alexius, who was, of course, much more well-versed in the politics of the region, took over the negotiations. He oversaw the repatriation of Nicaea to the Byzantine Empire. Although Alexius was successful in ensuring that Nicaea was returned, it would not be long before the crusaders began to go back on their pledge of returning lost Byzantine lands.

In many ways, such things are understandable, at least considering them from the viewpoint of the crusaders. Back in those days, land was everything. To be a landed noble meant to be secure. These men had traveled far and had fought hard—save for the most religious—and many undoubtedly began grumbling that they were getting the raw end of the deal. They probably began to question the merits of fighting and dying to restore land to a foreign emperor to whom they had no real allegiance.

Thus, one can easily see why some of them might have begun pushing for some sort of reward of their own. Nevertheless, they allowed the Byzantines to continue guiding them along. They ultimately headed to the mountains of Cappadocia, where they were able to link up with the Armenian resistance. From here, they planned their next major objective: seizing the fabled city of Antioch in the northwestern Levant.

The crusaders reached the gates of Antioch in October 1097. They found themselves in an advantageous position, as they had a constant supply line from their Armenian allies. Even better, an English-led fleet had managed to secure Antioch's port of St. Symeon and was able to open up a direct line to the Byzantine-controlled island of Cyprus.

These open routes of access allowed precious supplies important for siege warfare, such as timber, to be obtained. The supplies were funneled by Genoese sailors, who sailed across the Mediterranean. But even with all of this support and good fortune, the conquest of well-fortified Antioch would be a difficult task. By December, the crusaders were low on food and morale.

A mystic named Peter Bartholomew entered the picture in a big way. Peter was among the main crusader force at Antioch. He gained widespread attention in the camp after he claimed to have had a vision that led him to eventually discover the Holy Lance. This artifact has a long and controversial history. The relic is said to have been the spear that pierced Christ while he was nailed to the cross. It was later known as the Spear of Destiny. There is a whole mythic backstory behind the spear that suggests that whoever has this relic is destined to conquer.

Once the spear was discovered (or perceived to have been discovered, as we don't know for certain if it was *the* spear that pierced Christ), the crusaders were greatly inspired. About ten days later, they finally took the city in June 1098.

In the meantime, the crusaders became angered with the Byzantines. The Byzantines learned the crusade was a lost cause and that the crusaders were on the verge of defeat from a defector from the crusader ranks, Stephen of Blois. It was not true, but the Byzantines accepted this pessimistic and dire forecast and ceased lending aid to the crusaders.

The crusaders nominated their own supreme leader, Bohemond, Prince of Taranto (a Norman principality that was part of the larger Kingdom of Sicily). Since the Byzantines proved so fickle and had turned their backs on the crusaders, Bohemond refused to repatriate Antioch to the Byzantine Empire. Instead, it became part of what would later be known as the Crusader States.

The crusaders hunkered down in Antioch to recover before marching to the gates of Jerusalem, a feat that was reached on June 7th, 1099.

The crusaders knew they were fighting a holy cause, but seeing Jerusalem must have inspired some awe in them. It is easy to imagine the Christians taking a breath and realizing just what they were taking part in. It is said that the following day, priests actually led a barefoot procession around the walls of the city while holding religious relics aloft. This was likely done in imitation of the biblical story about the walls of Jericho. In that story, the high priest led the Israelites around the walls of Jericho just prior to laying siege to the city. According to scripture, the walls miraculously came tumbling down. In the Old Testament, Jericho was one of the first major engagements the children of Israel faced as they established themselves in the "Promised Land."

The crusaders read the biblical stories and hoped for the same outcome. But unlike the biblical description of what happened in Jericho, once the crusaders finished circling the walls of Jerusalem, the city walls still stood as strong as ever. The taking of this fortified city would be no easy task.

Due to deaths and desertions, the crusader force had been whittled down to a fraction of what it had been at the outset. Yet, all the same, a core group of diehard warriors would fulfill the pope's call to seize the city of Jerusalem for Christendom. Interestingly enough, as the Christian crusaders stood just outside the gates of Jerusalem, the Muslim governor of the city, Iftikhar ad-Dawla, issued an order to have all Christian residents kicked out of the city.

Considering the violence of the period, it is probably commendable that the governor did not have the Christians killed outright. But his bid to remove them surely had ulterior motives all the same. The governor probably feared the local Christians might aid the crusaders from within. Just imagine how easy it might have been for a Christian on the inside to open a hidden gate and invite the Christian warriors inside the walls. This fear could have been a motivator for the governor to get the Christians out ahead of the siege.

He also might have wanted to use the expulsion of the local Christians as a major distraction since it created an immediate humanitarian problem for the crusaders. As happy as they might have been to see their Middle Eastern brothers and sisters of the faith, they now had to share their already limited resources to feed the exiled population. The crusaders made do as best they could and settled down right outside the walls of that long-sought-after city.

The governor's decision to expel the Christian citizens would ultimately backfire on the city's defense. A Christian from Jerusalem known as Blessed Gerard, who managed a hospital of sorts for the sick in Jerusalem, came into contact with crusader commanders and offered up his services. Gerard had intimate knowledge of the city's defenses and convinced the crusaders that he could aid them in their siege.

With Gerard's help, the crusaders were able to pinpoint the most vulnerable points of Jerusalem's defenses. The crusaders constructed three siege towers and used them to exploit these vulnerabilities. Nevertheless, the defenders of the city fought back hard and managed to take down two of the siege towers. The third was expertly maneuvered to one of the main gates of the city, giving the crusaders access. They successfully scaled the walls on July 15th, 1099. After a bitter, bloody struggle inside the city, Jerusalem was under crusader control.

By all accounts, what followed next was a terrible, bloody massacre. The crusaders roamed the streets, killing all non-Christians they came across. It is said the streets literally ran with blood. As contemporary chronicler William of Tyre put it, "It was impossible to look on the vast numbers of the slain without horror; everywhere lay the fragments of human bodies. Still more dreadful was it to gaze upon the victors themselves, dripping with blood from head to foot. Then, clad in fresh garments with clean hands and bare feet, in humility they began to make the rounds of the venerable places which the Savior had deigned to sanctify and make glorious with His bodily presence."

The only ones who were spared were those holed up in the city's fortified citadel. One of the leading crusaders, Raymond of Saint Gilles (also known as Raymond IV, Count of Toulouse), opened up a dialogue with those inside and promised them safe conduct out of the city if they surrendered. Despite all of the previous bloodshed, Raymond kept his word. Once the defenders of the citadel put down their arms, they and the few survivors they were defending were allowed to leave Jerusalem in peace.

As terrible as it all was, the Christian crusaders truly believed that God had willed them to take the Holy Land and seize the city for Christianity. They believed they were the instruments of God's wrath. Immediately after the killing of non-believing infidels, the crusaders donned their robes and went on a peaceful pilgrimage to the holy sites, a journey they had long yearned for. It might be hard for us to fathom such things today, but this sort of compartmentalization of actions was quite common during the time of the Crusades.

The crusaders were able to kill for what they believed was a just cause and then put on robes of penance as they visited the venerated sites. Even so, it could very well be that some suffered from what today would be termed "PTSD." As much as they kept telling themselves that God willed it and that they were excused in their actions, many undoubtedly woke up in the middle of the night with nightmares over some of the things they had done.

The objectives of the First Crusade had been achieved. Ironically enough, the man who had instigated all of this to occur in the first place—Pope Urban II—perished two weeks prior to Jerusalem being seized. Pope Urban II did not get the chance (at least on this side of eternity) to see his vision fulfilled. Nevertheless, the wheels had been set in motion, and the subsequent course of history had been determined.

Chapter 3: The Kingdom of Jerusalem

"In the Crusades, getting the Holy Land back was the goal, and any means could be used to achieve it. World War II was a Crusade. The firebombing of Tokyo by Doolittle and the carpet bombing in Germany, especially by the British, showed that."

-Stanley Hauerwas

The crusaders who conquered Jerusalem would soon find out that, in many ways, conquering was the easy part. It was rebuilding the city and holding it that would prove far more difficult. From the outset, there were problems to be addressed. The city walls had been pulverized during the crusader assault, which left the new residents vulnerable to attack. The population of the city was also quite small and quickly dwindling.

Due to the massive slaughter, the local population had been greatly reduced, and the crusaders could not be depended upon to stay. Many had families back home and were eager to leave the Holy Land as soon as possible. Fairly soon after Jerusalem had been conquered, which had been taken at the cost of much blood and treasure, the city was beginning to look more like a ghost town than the center of the Christian faith.

There were barely enough people to man strategic towers and gates, which was necessary for the overall security of Jerusalem. It didn't take much for thieves to waltz right through a crack in the wall in the dead of night. As such, instances of robbery became quite common.

As chronicler William of Tyre explained, "Even within the city walls, in the very houses, there was scarcely a place where one could rest in security. For the inhabitants were few and scattered and the ruinous state of the walls left every place exposed to the enemy. Thieves made stealthy inroads by night. They broke into the deserted cities, whose few inhabitants were scattered far apart, and overpowered many in their very own houses. The result was that some stealthily, and many quite openly, abandoned the holdings which they had won and began to return to their own land."

The crusader-occupied city of Jerusalem desperately needed an infusion of new blood to make up for all the blood that had been lost. So, European pilgrims were incentivized to come to the Holy Land to not only visit but also become permanent residents. The rich and fertile lands were set at an attractive price and were easy to obtain. However, efforts like this have often led to the Crusades being likened to an early attempt at colonization. It is understandable why such a parallel might be made, but the conditions were decidedly different.

Most of those who came to the Holy Land were just passing through and had no intention of settling long-term there. Rather than being colonists intent on putting a stake in the ground, farming, and settling the community, these were primarily religious pilgrims whose main objective was to visit the religious sites, pray, and then go home. Some would end up staying, but many would not.

Along with bringing in some new Christians to the city, the city authorities tried to keep the old Christians—such as Eastern and Armenian Orthodox followers—from leaving. The authorities established the absentee landlord law. This law was an interesting legal development, as it dictated that anyone who owned land could not rent it out and then move away. The legislation stipulated that any landowner had to reside in the city at least once a year, or their property would be considered up for grabs.

These measures were helpful, but the biggest problem the residents of Jerusalem faced was always going to be the threats that confronted them just outside of the city walls. Traveling from Jerusalem to other places in the Levant was always an enterprise filled with considerable risk since there were bandits and hostile armies with which to contend. One never really knew what might happen to them if they stepped outside the walls of Jerusalem.

This fact was clearly demonstrated by an incident that occurred shortly after the city's conquest was complete. On Easter Sunday, a group of some seven hundred Christian pilgrims, who were intent on visiting the Jordan River to observe the famed place where Jesus was baptized, were ruthlessly assaulted. Around three hundred pilgrims were murdered, and about sixty of them were taken as prisoners. They likely suffered a horrendous fate, as it is believed they were sold as slaves. Roughly half survived, fleeing in terror back to the safety of Jerusalem.

The dangers of traveling from one spot in the Holy Land to another led to the establishment of special monastic orders of knights, which would serve as official escorts and protect the Christian pilgrims. The Knights Templar became one of the main honor guards, as they were utilized to escort civilians from one place to another. The Knights Templar may not have been large in number, but they were fierce and efficient to such a degree that just a small group was capable of taking on hundreds of opponents at one time.

The Knights Templar are believed to have been officially founded in 1119 in the early years of the Kingdom of Jerusalem (founded in 1099). The order was established by a French nobleman named Hugues de Payen. The official name of the group was The Poor Fellow-Soldiers of Christ and of the Temple of Solomon. (A mouthful, to be sure!) The name was taken from the Temple Mount in Jerusalem, where the Knights Templar made their headquarters. The mention of being poor is in reference to this monastic order's vow of poverty.

And in the early days, the Knights Templar certainly lived up to this pledge. The knights had a communal lifestyle and dressed in modest, monkish clothing (at least when not regaled in battle armor). Once the Templars became the bankrollers of the Middle Ages, their status would change, although their vows stayed the same.

Although the Knights Templar would become the most famous of the monastic orders, they were preceded by others. Most notably, there was the Knights Hospitaller, an order that was officially founded in 1099, prior to the Templars. However, they had been operating before the founding of the Kingdom of Jerusalem itself. The Knights Hospitaller set up hospitals and shepherded pilgrims to religious sites before Jerusalem was taken. It was only at the dawning of the 1100s that the order took on a more militaristic makeup.

Another order that predates the Knights Templar is a little-known monastic order called the Order of Saint Lazarus. This order, which would later become more commonly known as the Leper Knights, actually began its existence as a hospital for lepers. Some believe this treatment facility actually predated the Islamic conquest of Jerusalem, going all the way back to Roman rule. It is believed the hospital was founded by the Roman Catholic icon Saint Basil. However, the order didn't begin until later, as it was initially a Knights Hospitaller order.

Considering the constant need for warriors, knights afflicted with leprosy were not ordered to retire; instead, they joined the Order of Saint Lazarus. They continued to provide their services even though they were effectively isolated from the rest of the community, relegated to living just outside the gates of Jerusalem in the leper hospital.

At any rate, these Leper Knights were most certainly a fearsome sight. Just imagine a group of knights on horseback, wrapped in bandages that barely hid their terrible open sores, suddenly charging down on you. These guys were virtually immune to pain due to their deadened nerves. As such, the frantic blows of the enemy were barely even felt. Known as the "living dead," these ferocious warriors would raise their broadswords high over their heads and tear their opponents to shreds with no fear whatsoever for their own safety.

These men had the bravery of those who already knew their time was short and figured they might as well go out fighting for what they sincerely felt was a good cause (whether we agree with such notions today or not). All of this made them incredibly formidable fighters. The Leper Knights were dreaded by all, not only because of their ferocious capacity to fight but also out of fear of catching leprosy from being in close contact with them.

There were many other monastic orders that were tasked with providing extra security for those traveling back and forth in the Kingdom of Jerusalem. They also covered the security details for any pilgrims visiting from Europe. But while security is important for a kingdom, a kingdom also needs a king. Surprisingly, the early crusaders were hesitant to take on such a title. Their reverence for Jerusalem was so great that it seemed arrogant to be called the "king of Jerusalem."

This attitude led Godfrey de Bouillon, the first man charged to be the administrator of Jerusalem, to refuse the title altogether. Even though he technically was the first king (he was made ruler on July 22nd, 1099), he insisted on being referred to as simply the "Defender of the Holy Sepulchre." This title was in reference to the Church of the Holy Sepulchre, which was greatly revered by the Christians. It wouldn't be until December 25th, 1100, that the Kingdom of Jerusalem would be overseen by a king. On that date, Godfrey's brother, Baldwin, Count of Edessa (another Crusader state), was crowned.

Godfrey de Bouillon had suffered from a long illness the previous summer. It took some debate to decide who should rule next, but the honor ultimately fell upon Godfrey's brother.

Initially, the Kingdom of Jerusalem was a very basic patchwork of cities that the crusaders had taken. Under Baldwin's reign, this patchwork would expand into a true kingdom, which would make up roughly the boundaries of the modern state of Israel, plus the southernmost regions of Lebanon. Baldwin seized Acre in 1104 and then charged north all the way to Beirut in 1110.

Under the administration of King Baldwin, the population of Jerusalem swelled to a much more comfortable number, at least when compared to the sparsely populated region that existed before. The Kingdom of Jerusalem was fortified into a well-defended Christian state. King Baldwin had already helped shore up relations with the local Christians in the Middle East by marrying an Armenian woman named Arda. This move especially helped him shore up strong relations when he oversaw the County of Edessa, which had a strong Armenian presence.

However, Baldwin was not the most faithful husband. Once Arda had served her purpose, he married a new wife: Adelaide del Vasto. Adelaide was a rich scion of Sicily, so she was a tremendous boon to Baldwin's floundering resources. However, Baldwin was still married to Arda when he married Adelaide. He eventually decided to send Adelaide packing in 1117, upsetting her son, Roger, who was the count of Sicily. Roger would later become the king of Sicily, and even then, he refused to support the Kingdom of Jerusalem.

Baldwin would pass away the following year, 1118, without providing any heirs to take the throne. The crown was initially offered to Baldwin's brother, Eustace III, but Eustace had other plans. So, the crown was handed over to Baldwin of Bourg instead.

The new king was sworn in on Easter Day in 1118. He was crowned by the patriarch of Jerusalem and officially became King Baldwin II of Jerusalem. Baldwin II proved himself to be a formidable defender of the realm. He stood up to incursions from both the Seljuk Turks and the Fatimids of Egypt. However, Baldwin would pay the price for his boldness when he was taken prisoner and captured by his opponents at the infamous Battle of Ager Sanguinis in 1119.

This battle saw a whole host of crusaders, who had been cobbled together in Antioch, annihilated almost to the man. In the aftermath of this terrible exchange, Baldwin was taken hostage. Incredibly enough, King Baldwin would not be released until 1124. It is not entirely clear what Baldwin had to endure during his captivity, but he would prove himself still fit to be king after he was released. The following year, he led his forces to victory in the Battle of Azaz in 1125.

During the reign of King Baldwin II, the formidable monastic order of knights known as the Knights Templar was established. Baldwin II had four daughters, and upon his passing, his oldest daughter, Melisende, would be crowned as the next ruler of the Kingdom of Jerusalem. She would go on to marry Fulk V, Count of Anjou. Fulk proved to be an able leader, but after his abrupt passing in 1143, the Kingdom of Jerusalem faced its first real loss. The County of Edessa was lost to Zengi, an Islamic warlord from Mosul.

The loss of Edessa would lead to the Second Crusade. We will dive more into the Second Crusade in the following chapter, but suffice it to say, it did not go well. At any rate, Fulk and Melisende had a son named Baldwin (later known as King Baldwin III). Baldwin III would perish without an heir, and his brother, Amalric, would ultimately ascend to the throne.

Amalric's son—yet another Baldwin—succeeded him. Baldwin IV, the Leper King, as he would later be known, would not have an easy time with things. Just as his moniker implies, he had leprosy. But despite his terrible sickness, Baldwin IV was a stable hand at the helm. After his death, the Kingdom of Jerusalem, which had long been besieged by adversaries, would fall once again.

Chapter 4: The Second Crusade

"The first two crusades brought the flower of European chivalry to Constantinople and restored that spiritual union between Eastern and Western Christendom that had been interrupted by the great schism of the Greek and Roman Churches."

-Joseph Jacobs

The Second Crusade was a direct call to action after the loss of the Crusader principality of Edessa. After Edessa fell to Islamic forces in 1144, Christians felt compelled to recover it. It had been some fifty years since the First Crusade successfully wrested much of the Holy Land from Islamic control. The first loss of Crusader land came as quite a shock. As soon as word reached western Europe, the situation was presented as a calamity of epic proportions and one that all of Christendom had to address.

On December 1ˢᵗ, 1145, Pope Eugenius III issued the official call for a crusade, encouraging Christians to "take up the cross" and to "live up to the deeds of their forefathers" who had seized the Holy Land during the days of the First Crusade. The pope was basically chiding the new generation of potential warriors not to become ill-begotten stewards and lose the precious lands their ancestors had fought so hard to secure.

This papal call for a crusade was perhaps not quite as attractive as the first since a heavy dose of self-recriminating guilt and heroic ambition laced the dialogue swirling around the Second Crusade. But it was indeed successful enough to at least get the point across. The papal promise to hold up those who died as martyrs, guaranteeing them "a place in heaven," certainly didn't hurt either. For the deeply religious of the Middle Ages, such sentiments meant everything.

And as soon as that mindset is understood, one can understand why folks in western Europe would travel thousands of miles to risk life and limb in the Middle East. The notion that one was "fighting the good fight" and struggling on the side of God was an incredibly powerful motivator for both Christian and Muslim armies.

Back in Europe, King Louis VII of France had been actively recruiting troops on his own. Louis made his own personal call to action around Christmastime, shortly after the pope's address. A popular French theologian, Bernard of Clairvaux, aided the French king. Louis proved pivotal in gathering professional soldiers, so much so that the pope was inspired to issue a renewed call for a crusade on March 1ˢᵗ, 1146, in which he specifically designated Bernard of Clairvaux as a spokesman for the cause.

Bernard gave a powerful sermon on the matter on March 31ˢᵗ (Easter Sunday) to a group of gathered faithful in Vézelay, France. Bernard's sermon, rather than the pope's personal call for a crusade, truly galvanized the masses. The pope accused his audience of letting past conquests slip out of their grasp. Bernard spoke in glowing terms of blessing and hope, preaching how blessed this new generation of Christians was to have the opportunity to seek "such splendid spiritual riches" in their quest to rescue the Holy Land. His sermon was a much more positive and attractive variation of the pope's call to arms and seemed to stir the hearts of those who listened to it.

After Bernard's powerful oratory, the king of France and his queen, Eleanor of Aquitaine, made a pointed show of humility, bowing down before Bernard as they symbolically "took up the cross." Shortly thereafter, King Louis VII led the crusaders from France to Germany. Once in German lands, Bernard gave his blessings to the German king, Conrad III, as well as his nephew (and future Holy Roman emperor), Frederick Barbarossa. It has been said that Conrad was initially hesitant to participate in the Second Crusade, but the words of Bernard of Clairvaux convinced him to partake in the mission.

Bernard had his hands full once the crusade launched, as domestic disturbances began to erupt. Around this time, a French monk, whose name comes down to us as Rudolph, began to cause trouble by inciting mobs to persecute Jewish residents in the Rhineland. As was sadly all too often the case, Rudolph used the rationale that Christians should get rid of non-believers at home prior to waging war against non-believers abroad. But although some diabolical monks and some mobs of so-called Christians engaged in these nefarious acts, such things were never part of official church (as in the Catholic Church) policy.

And to Bernard's credit, he took immediate action as soon as he heard of the disturbance and personally intervened to stop the violence. He met with the riotous monk face to face, ordered him to stand down, and then sent him off to live in quiet exile in a monastery.

In the meantime, The Second Crusade began to take on multiple dimensions. Although the impetus for the Second Crusade was the loss of Edessa in the Holy Land, several side missions began to take shape. Soon after the call for another crusade was made, attention was drawn to the long struggle that had been waged to recover the Iberian Peninsula. The Iberian Peninsula, consisting of modern-day Spain and Portugal, had nearly been overrun by the Muslim forces.

Prior to the Islamic conquest, much of Iberia was under the rule of a European tribe known as the Visigoths. In 711, a group of Muslims known as the Berbers crossed the Strait of Gibraltar from North Africa and stormed into the peninsula. In a stunning defeat, the Visigoths were crushed, and almost all of the Iberian Peninsula became a part of Dar al Islam (The House of Islam.)

However, there were pockets of resistance, small enclaves where Christian kingdoms survived and would continue to do so for centuries. Right around the time of the Second Crusade, a leader of one of these Iberian enclaves, Afonso I Henriques of Portugal, was enlisting aid to recover the port city of Lisbon. With all of this talk of a crusade against the forces of Islam, Alfonso apparently figured it would be as good a time as any to ask for a helping hand.

And he received it. Crusaders from farther afield, such as the Flemings from Flanders, Belgium, who had planned to sail around the Iberian Peninsula, were redirected. Bernard of Clairvaux arranged for them to actually land on the peninsula instead of going around it just so they could hook up with Portuguese troops hellbent on recovering Lisbon. Although this event was viewed as a detour from the main mission, it would prove quite pivotal in the long run.

Islamic armies had been sweeping through the Near East, Middle East, and North Africa. They had been slowly encircling Christian Europe in what was essentially a pincer maneuver. As much as crusaders have been condemned through the years as bloodthirsty, religious zealots (some might even say idiots), if they had not stood up to this advance, one could easily envisage what would have been the result. It is likely that all of Byzantium, Greece, and the Balkans would have been overrun in the East, while Spain and France would have been entirely overtaken in the West. Both sides of the pincer would have then moved forward until the forces of Islam in the East linked up with the forces of Islam in the West, converging together right in the middle of Europe.

Bernard's decision during the Second Crusade to coordinate relief forces to land in Iberia was indeed pivotal in reversing this trend, continuing the long struggle known as the Reconquista.

We will cover the Reconquista itself in more depth a little later on in this book, but for now, just know the Second Crusade ultimately became tied together with this titanic struggle. And the redirection of troops from northern Europe to the frontlines of Iberia would be pivotal in not only reclaiming Lisbon for Portugal (Lisbon was successfully seized on October 24th, 1147) but also for helping to turn the tide against Islamic forces in Iberia.

Another side mission that took great importance during the Second Crusade was the forcible conversion/conquest of pagan Slavs in eastern Europe. This incident would set a precedent for other crusades against the pagan holdouts of eastern and northern Europe.

The main crusader force that had been dispatched for the main mission in the Middle East would largely meet with failure. The crusaders were harried all along the way by the Turks, who seemed to have foreseen their arrival ahead of time. Although there is no proof this was the case, it has long been suggested that the Byzantines forewarned the Turks. Byzantine politics in the region, with their constantly shifting alliances, were indeed complicated, but there is no hard evidence that any such advance notice was given to the Turks stationed in Anatolia.

It must be acknowledged that the Byzantines were often duplicitous and resentful to the Westerners, even when forced to seek out their aid. A lot of this bad blood can be traced directly back to the Great Schism of 1054 when the Catholic Church and the Eastern Orthodox Church excommunicated each other. Politics were also at play within the Byzantine Empire itself, as those with power wanted to make sure they held onto it.

At any rate, the main crusader force beat back several surprise ambushes before they finally made their way to Antioch. All of these ambushes took their toll on the crusaders. Upon arriving at Antioch on March 19th, 1148, King Louis VII led what remained of his crusaders into the city and held an audience with Raymond, the local ruler of Antioch. Almost immediately, there was a disagreement on how to proceed.

Raymond wanted the crusaders to aid him in his struggle against Aleppo, which he viewed as the "gateway" to retaking Edessa. However, King Louis VII wished to head to Jerusalem as soon as possible. The king apparently felt his own personal pilgrimage should take precedence over any further military maneuvers. There was even more drama by way of the king's wife, Eleanor. Eleanor had joined her husband, and it was noticed that she had taken a liking to Raymond. Soon, the court was swirling with gossip that something untoward might be in the works. Louis apparently believed the rumors and had his wife "arrested."

Louis took his wife with him, and he marched on to Jerusalem that April. Conrad and his fellow crusaders arrived shortly thereafter. In Jerusalem, the crusaders received a change of plans, as the plan was now to attack Damascus instead of Aleppo. The city-state of Damascus had been ruled by a string of various Muslim potentates and had previously been an ally of the Kingdom of Jerusalem.

However, Damascus had recently switched sides, becoming friendly with Nur al-Din of Aleppo, and as such, it was now clearly a legitimate target of crusader aggression. The decision to attack Damascus would prove to be a great mistake, as it would come to derail the entire crusade.

The crusaders arrived at Damascus on July 4th, 1148. Initially, the crusaders had the advantage and plowed right through the outer defenses of the city. But once they broke through what has been described as "dense orchards" on the southern outskirts of the city, they found themselves in quite a bind. They had run out of water, and Nur al-Din and some rather heavy reinforcements were on the way to intercept them.

The crusaders were stranded out in the scorching heat and stuck between the walls of Damascus and a huge army with no water. Their position was most certainly not ideal. As such, the crusaders decided to make a hasty retreat. They were practically chased all the way back to the gates of Jerusalem. This utterly inglorious result marked the end of the Second Crusade.

Chapter 5: The Third Crusade

"We, however, place the love of God and his honor above our own and above the acquisition of many regions."

-Richard I of England

As inglorious as much of the Second Crusade might have been, the Third Crusade would come to be known as one of the most heroic. It was also a crusade in which the stakes were much higher since the Third Crusade was launched in the aftermath of the fall of Jerusalem. Yes, Jerusalem had once again fallen, this time after the infamous Battle of Hattin in 1187. The Battle of Hattin was the end result of many years of Islamic attempts to take back Jerusalem.

In the aftermath of the Second Crusade, the Zengid dynasty was able to take control of a united Syria and then proceeded to take on the Fatimids of Egypt. The crusaders used to be rather fond of playing the Syrian faction against the Egyptian faction, and as it turns out, the real key to Islamic domination of the region was uniting Syria and Egypt. The man who managed to achieve this feat was an Islamic warlord and ingenious strategist named Saladin.

Saladin led this united Muslim force to take on the Kingdom of Jerusalem in the year 1187. The condition of the Crusader States also aided Saladin. The last great king of Jerusalem was Baldwin IV, the so-called "Leper King." Even though Baldwin IV was stricken with leprosy, he had proved himself to be an adept and able leader. He was also quite courageous, fearlessly leading armies on horseback, even though most in his condition probably would have been better off staying in bed.

Bandaged and essentially immune to pain due to his leprosy, Baldwin IV struck absolute terror in the hearts of his opponents. But eventually, the Leper King fell, and his nephew, Baldwin V, came to power. Baldwin V was just a child at the time, so the real power behind the throne was his mother, Sibylla, and her husband, Guy of Lusignan. Saladin rallied his mighty forces and struck out against weakened Jerusalem.

Saladin was an able strategist. He developed an ingenious plan that lured the main bulk of the crusader forces out of Jerusalem and into open combat, which, of course, was the very last thing the crusaders should have done. Out by the Horns of Hattin, the crusaders ended up becoming surrounded by enemy forces out in the middle of the scorching desert.

The place was (and still is) referred to as the "Horns of Hattin" because of its stark geographical features. There is an extinct volcano in the region, and the sides of it jut right out of the desert landscape, looking like the horns of some ancient beast stabbing the air. The crusaders fought bravely in the battle, but they ultimately were utterly annihilated.

Saladin then marched on Jerusalem. Although the defenders of the city held out as long as they could, they had to admit defeat. Jerusalem was lost to Christendom once again. Along with Jerusalem, Saladin seized a large chunk of other crusader territories, including the fortified coastal city of Acre. This was a tremendous blow to the crusaders. Therefore, the Third Crusade was called to recover these lost lands.

The Third Crusade is perhaps most notable because of the men who led it. Three of the leading figures of Europe from that age took part in and led this crusade: King Philip II of France, King Richard (otherwise known as Richard the Lionheart) of England, and Holy Roman Emperor Frederick Barbarossa. All but one of these men would make their way to the Holy Land.

Frederick Barbarossa, who was the Holy Roman emperor in addition to many other titles, such as the king of Italy, Germany, and Burgundy, perished on his way there in what was ostensibly a freak accident. He fell off his horse and was pitched into a river. Thanks to the heavy armor he wore, he drowned in the water. Barbarossa's premature death might have been somewhat decisive in the final outcome of the Third Crusade since it meant that most of the men Barbarossa led decided to return home once they learned their commander had died.

Only a small fraction of the troops Barbarossa led were determined enough to follow King Philip or King Richard. Thus, the crusader forces were greatly reduced once they reached the Holy Land. Had Barbarossa lived and led his full contingent, the crusaders would have been a much more formidable force.

It didn't help that Richard the Lionheart was distracted by a side adventure of his own. Prior to reaching the Holy Land, he made a pit stop in Cyprus, where he led his forces to victory and claimed the island.

Upon his arrival in Cyprus, Richard found the island under the control of a Greek despot named Isaac Komnenos, who had seized the territory from the Byzantine Empire in 1184. It serves as a great testament to just how weakened the Byzantines were. A rogue like Komnenos was able to snatch up such prime real estate since the Byzantines were unable to rally a sufficient enough force to take it back.

After Isaac Komnenos had seized both the passengers and cargo of a contingent of shipwrecked crusaders, Richard the Lionheart decided to take a detour and wage war on him. Isaac Komnenos apparently had bit off more than he could chew. When he saw the massive force that Richard had mustered against him, he quickly offered to surrender. He also agreed to pay money for all of the damages he had incurred upon the English subjects who had shipwrecked in Cyprus.

King Richard and those who chose to follow him left Cyprus and headed toward the mainland of the Levant. Richard and his men reached the gates of Acre in 1191, where they linked up with King Philip II of France and his troops.

Although Saladin had been victorious in the past, he apparently had bitten off a bit more than he could chew. He may have taken Acre, but he did not have enough troops left over to defend it. The crusaders found the city sparsely defended and were able to easily conquer it.

After Acre was secured, King Philip quickly lost interest in the crusade, and he and most of his troops decided to ship off for home. However, Richard was not about to turn back as long as Jerusalem remained before him.

King Richard the Lionheart led the crusaders who were brave enough and willing to remain. Before heading for Jerusalem, Richard seized the strategic city of Jaffa, which lay on the road to the holy city. However, Saladin was not far behind and intercepted Richard's army some thirty miles north of the city. Saladin harried the rearguard and attempted to disrupt Richard's progress, but Richard, who was marching in sight of the coastline, was able to keep up a defensive position throughout the harassment. His troop formations did not break.

The final moment of truth came when a contingent of Knights Hospitaller defied Richard's orders to stay on the defensive. The Hospitallers suddenly charged at full speed into Saladin's army, slamming hard into Saladin's right flank. Richard realized he had to act and went ahead and ordered his forces to engage in an all-out attack. The two forces collided with each other near the town of Arsuf.

Richard's forces would prevail at the Battle of Arsuf, causing Saladin's army to retreat. This was a decisive win and cleared the crusaders' way to Jerusalem. Richard made his headquarters in Jaffa and prepared to lay siege to Jerusalem. He led his troops to the gates of the city in November 1191. However, once there, he soon realized that even if he overcame the Islamic defenders of Jerusalem, he would not have enough troops to hold the city. His success would be nothing since the city could very easily be retaken.

Richard realized how useless his position was and decided he might be better off negotiating a peace treaty with Saladin instead. Richard and Saladin had already been in talks through various intermediaries. Despite their ideological differences, the two had come to greatly respect each other as leaders. This alone made the idea of peace much more realistic. But before peace could happen, more fighting would occur.

In July 1192, Saladin attempted to retake Jaffa. Initially, Saladin was successful but faced a crisis when part of his army rebelled against him. Richard sent in reinforcements, and soon, Saladin's troops (those that were still under his control, at least) were pushed back. After this disastrous defeat, Saladin began to seriously consider entering into a peace treaty with Richard.

The final terms of peace were realized when the two men entered into a binding three-year truce, which began in September 1192. The truce ended the fighting; Saladin even guaranteed the free passage of Christians wishing to visit the holy sites of Jerusalem.

Many crusaders were saddened they had been unable to achieve the ultimate objective of taking Jerusalem, but they could at least be appeased that their struggle was not in vain. Saladin died in 1193, but the peace terms of the truce would still stand for some time. It would be right after the end of this three-year truce that the Fourth Crusade would be called.

Chapter 6: The Fourth Crusade

"European merchants supply the best weaponry, contributing to their own defeat."

-Saladin

Richard the Lionheart managed to secure the entire coast of the Levant for Christendom, even though he did not actually retake Jerusalem. Even so, he had secured a respectable three-year truce with Saladin. But after those five years were up, the Fourth Crusade was called. Launched in 1202, the Fourth Crusade was engineered by Pope Innocent III. This crusade was largely just a mission to recoup the land that had been lost and that the Third Crusade had failed to recover. Jerusalem was perhaps the most important item on the crusade's agenda.

The Fourth Crusade, of course, sought to do what the Third Crusade could not: capture Jerusalem. But this crusade would have some serious problems from the very beginning. First of all, the crusaders would receive a pretty significant distraction when they became sidetracked fighting in the Christian city of Zara, located in modern-day Croatia.

Low on funds and morale, the crusaders then became embroiled in Byzantine politics when a claimant to the throne, Alexios Angelos, promised them they would have untold riches if they waged a campaign against the Byzantine Empire. Alexios's father had been the emperor, but Alexios's uncle deposed him. Alexios sought to restore his father to the throne, even though he had been imprisoned and blinded.

But before the crusaders got involved in Zara or the Byzantine Empire, they had to address a problem of their own. They had come up short when paying the Republic of Venice for their services in ferrying the crusaders across the Mediterranean.

The crusaders were supposed to have more men, so the amount they had promised to pay just wasn't possible. Due to their lack of funds, the Venetian doge, Enrico Dandolo, suggested the crusaders could aid him in the capture of the city of Zara as part of the fulfillment of their debt. The doge's desire to take Zara was purely political since the city was occupied by fellow Christian believers. This meant the crusaders were breaking from their ideological convictions and attacking Christians rather than defending them.

It was hard for the crusaders to rationalize this attack as other than a means of making a little money to pay off their debts. This event greatly corrupted the morale of the crusaders, who were now not fighting for a larger-than-life cause but fighting for mere material gain. They had essentially become little more than mercenaries.

The crusaders were successful in seizing Zara for the doge, but as soon as the pope heard about it, he had them all excommunicated. (He would later lift the excommunication but kept the excommunication of the Venetians intact because he believed they were to blame.) Rather than boldly storming into the Holy Land for the cause of Christendom, the crusaders had become a large body of excommunicated heretics.

However, it is important to note that although the leaders of the Fourth Crusade realized they had been excommunicated, the average soldier did not. The excommunication was carefully concealed from the rank-and-file members of the crusader forces, as the leaders knew the men would leave if they found out.

In January 1203, these crestfallen crusaders were contacted by a former Byzantine prince named Alexios Angelos. Alexios sought to suck the crusaders into Byzantine politics, pleading for them to restore his deposed father, Isaac II Angelos, as emperor. It was then that a hare-brained scheme was concocted between the Venetians and the leaders of the crusaders to restore the Byzantine Angelos line to the throne and then use the money from the Byzantine treasury to finance the journey to Jerusalem.

The plans for this plot simmered for several months before the crusaders finally reached the gates of the great Byzantine capital, Constantinople, that June. The battle initially commenced on the outskirts of Constantinople in the suburban areas of Chrysopolis and

Chalcedon. During this engagement, the crusaders were greatly outnumbered but charged the Byzantines on horseback. Surprisingly and against the odds, the crusaders managed to defeat the Byzantines' larger force.

This victory no doubt buoyed their spirits. Riding high on this victory, the crusader forces made use of naval craft to make their way over the Bosporus. Interestingly enough, the crusader fleet soon sailed within sight of Constantinople with the Byzantine prince who had asked for help standing on the deck. To the bewilderment of the crusaders, the citizens of Constantinople did not let out a deafening cry of support. They instead gathered on the walls to jeer and mock the unwanted Byzantine prince. Even though Alexios's uncle was a usurper, the people liked him. Nevertheless, the crusaders were hellbent on installing the proper heir to the Byzantine throne, whether the Byzantines liked it or not.

The Byzantines went on the offensive and unleashed an army of around 8,500 troops. Alexios III, the usurper, led them right through Constantinople's Gate of St. Romanus. The Byzantine army dwarfed the crusader force, which comprised around 3,500 warriors. However, the Byzantines had a problem. For whatever reason, Emperor Alexios III was just not cut out for fighting. He became terribly discouraged and suddenly ordered his troops to retreat. He should have been able to use his mighty force to push back the invaders but instead ended up humiliating himself and his subjects with an unnecessary withdrawal.

In fact, Alexios III was so humiliated that he fled his own kingdom later that night. Demonstrating just how quickly the sands of fate could shift for a Byzantine ruler, Alexios III was deposed, and Isaac II was put back on the throne.

However, there was a problem. Isaac had been blinded to ensure he could not rule. The crusaders insisted that Prince Alexios step up to rule alongside him. Plus, what better way to ensure Alexios followed through on his promise of payment than by making him co-emperor? Prince Alexios became Alexios IV.

And then came the other problem. There just wasn't enough money in the treasury to fully pay what Alexios had promised the crusaders. It was certainly a rough spot to be in; he didn't want to upset the people he ruled too much by draining the treasury and raising taxes, but he also didn't want to upset the crusaders, who could potentially sack the city and wreak havoc because they weren't paid.

Alexios was able to come up with half the money by taking goods from the churches and selling off lands. But the crusaders weren't satisfied with half. And the people weren't satisfied with Alexios's rule. His father also resented sharing the throne with him.

In 1203, violence broke out between the crusaders and the people of the city. Alexios refused to give in to the crusaders' demands, but even this outspokenness against the crusaders failed to gain him favor with the people. In January 1204, a popular uprising dethroned Alexios. He and his father were imprisoned and killed (it is believed Isaac might have died of old age).

Alexios IV's death gave the crusaders the justification to go on the offensive. In April 1204, days after Alexios was murdered, the crusaders ruthlessly occupied the city and drained it of much of its wealth. The Byzantines eventually regrouped around their old capital, Nicaea.

The Byzantines established a strong resistance, and in 1261, under Byzantine Emperor Michael VIII Palaeologus, the crusaders were finally driven out. Even so, the Byzantine Empire would never quite recover from the desolation that had been wrought by the Fourth Crusade. The pope condemned the action, but the damage was done. Orthodox Christians were shocked at what the crusaders had done, and it seemed as if the rift between the two churches would never be patched now (although it is unlikely it would have been patched even if this incident hadn't occurred).

It is ironic that the Fourth Crusade, which began with the same religious fervor and anticipation as the First, Second, and Third crusades, ended without any of the crusaders so much as stepping foot in the Holy Land.

Chapter 7: The Fifth and Sixth Crusades

"In order to avoid contention, never contradict anyone, except in case of sin or some danger to a neighbor; and when necessary to contradict others, and to oppose your opinion to theirs, do it with so much mildness and tact, as not to appear to do violence to their mind, for nothing is ever gained by taking up things with excessive warmth and hastiness."

-*King Louis IX*

The Fifth Crusade was initially called by Pope Innocent III at the Fourth Lateran Council in 1215. You might recognize the name; it was the same pope who called for the Fourth Crusade, which had ended in the disastrous seizure of Constantinople and the excommunication of the crusader force (although by the time of the Fourth Lateran Council, he had revoked the excommunication). Pope Innocent was appalled at what these crusaders had done and actively sought to make amends by calling for yet another crusade.

But in the aftermath of his abrupt passing in 1216, the commencement of this crusade was inherited by the next pope, Honorius III. The Fifth Crusade, predictably enough, had the same intention as the previous two crusades: the recovery of Jerusalem. But even though Jerusalem was the goal, a slight detour was yet again in the works. It had been suggested that perhaps it would be easier to drive through the soft underbelly of Egypt to get there. Interestingly enough, it was none other than Richard the Lionheart who first suggested this all the way back in the Third Crusade.

Few agreed with his strategy back then, but views on this idea had changed by the time of the Fifth Crusade.

So, an all-out assault was launched on the Ayyubid-controlled Egyptian territory of Damietta. On May 27th, 1218, the crusaders landed in Damietta, Egypt. The crusaders then laid siege to the city on June 23rd of the same year. They made use of some eighty ships and a whole host of impressive siege equipment. Some of the siege engines had "revolving ladders" and were covered in flame-resistant furs in case the defenders used Greek fire. This sticky, flammable substance was basically an ancient version of napalm.

The fact the crusaders had planned for such contingencies shows they were not taking this adventure lightly. Even so, the city was heavily fortified, and this first incursion was easily repulsed. The crusaders were relentless and proceeded to attack the city once again. On August 24th, the main tower of the city was seized, and the chains stretched across the Nile to block the intruders were severed.

These developments proved to be too much for the leader of the city, Sultan al-Adil, who perished right after he heard the news of what had happened (it is unknown how he died). He was immediately succeeded by his son and heir, al-Kamil, who made sure that he shored up what remained of the defenses. These measures included wrecking ships in the Nile to create a defensive barrier.

The sultan's ingenious move put off further offensives for some time. The crusaders were forced to wait it out.

In the meantime, relief forces arrived, with the papal legate, Pelagius Galvani, in its train. Pope Innocent III desired for the Roman Catholic Church to take on a more direct role in this crusade in light of the failures of the Fourth Crusade, which had infamously resulted in the whole group getting excommunicated. It was reasoned that if a papal authority led the crusade, the crusaders would stay on track to achieve their actual objectives.

The influx of French soldiers that the legate brought with him did much to bolster the strength of the crusaders. But throughout much of 1219, the two sides were locked in a bloody quagmire of fighting.

It wasn't until November of that year that the crusaders finally managed to prevail and seize the city. But even though the city was taken, the sultan was not defeated; he simply moved his army farther south.

In the end, the crusader victory at Damietta proved to be a costly one and was not really worth the effort. The crusaders found themselves in control of a city surrounded by enemies. They did not have the people or resources to adequately defend Damietta. The Fifth Crusade ultimately came to a close in 1221 by way of a truce. The truce was basically the negotiated surrender of Damietta, in which the defenders were allowed to depart in peace.

Although the Fifth Crusade seemed to accomplish very little, it had its interesting moments, including when a famous monk, Saint Francis of Assisi, arrived in Egypt in 1219 in the midst of the fighting to preach the Gospel to crusaders and Muslims. In fact, it has even been said that he gained an audience with the sultan himself. Not much is known of what was said (some postulate that Francis tried to convert the sultan to Catholicism), but regardless of what was discussed, the sultan was quite intrigued by the boldness of the Christian monk who had come to visit him. It is also theorized that Saint Francis of Assisi perhaps paved the way for a lasting truce between the two warring parties.

The Sixth Crusade was a direct consequence of the failures of the Fifth Crusade. Many historians do not even recognize the Sixth Crusade, as it is sometimes simply referred to as the Crusade of Frederick II since it was largely led and engineered by German Holy Roman Emperor Frederick. Frederick II was largely making up for the fact that he did not take part in the Fifth Crusade.

It was not because he didn't want to fight in the Fifth Crusade. Frederick had pledged to take part but ended up being too late to do so. So, the Sixth Crusade could be seen as the Holy Roman emperor's effort to make amends. Even so, this so-called crusade had hardly any fighting to speak of and largely depended on the political machinations of Frederick II.

Holy Roman Emperor Frederick II successfully negotiated a treaty with al-Kamil that secured peace and granted Christians the control of Jerusalem for a period of ten years as long as the city remained unfortified and the previously demolished walls were not rebuilt. There was also the stipulation that Al-Aqsa Mosque, which the Templars had famously converted into their so-called "Temple of Solomon" headquarters, would remain exclusively under Muslim control.

The terms were a very small price to pay to have Jerusalem back under Christian control. The notion that Jerusalem could be taken without bloodshed was unheard of, yet Fredrick managed to do it.

Even so, his effort was largely unappreciated by Christians and Muslims at the time. In the zero-sum ideological game that was being played, both sides viewed such active cooperation with the supposed enemy as tantamount to treason. Although the peaceful use of Jerusalem by all parties was the result, both sides felt that such a settlement was absurd. And predictably enough, after the ten-year truce was over, the fighting would begin once again.

Chapter 8: The Barons' Crusade

"A crusade is, simply put, something that's bigger than you are. It's a cause with an impact that reaches beyond your personal wants and needs."

-Arthur L. Williams, Jr.

After the Fifth and Sixth Crusades, the numbering of the Crusades gets much harder to keep up with. At this point in history, they branch off into side crusades that had many different names and many different objectives. Among them was the so-called "Barons' Crusade." This particular effort was led by Theobald I (sometimes also known as Thibaut), who was the count of Champagne and the king of Navarre.

And as you might have guessed, the leading lights of the Barons' Crusade were all barons or nobles of some kind or other. It was a veritable who's who of medieval nobility: Hugh IV, Duke of Burgundy; Amaury I of Montfort (son of the famous Simon de Montfort, who also took part); and Richard of Cornwall, just to name a few.

Theobald's army consisted of around 1,500 knights and many infantry units. He led all of them to the Levant. Theobald's troops made their way to the gates of Acre on September 1ˢᵗ, 1239. Here, these nobles were met by homegrown nobles, and the next several weeks would be wasted with frivolous pleasantries.

Nevertheless, the Barons' Crusade would ultimately prove to be much more successful than many that had come before it and any that came after. In November, Theobald led his troops out of Acre and marched to Ascalon, which had been a crusader stronghold since 1153. They erected a fortified castle once they arrived.

However, during the march, one of the nobles, Peter I, Duke of Brittany, broke away from the main group and conducted a punitive raid on a passing Muslim caravan. This was a fairly dreadful act on the part of the crusaders, as the caravan drivers were slaughtered and their goods seized. It was not as much an act of war as it was blatant murder and theft. Nevertheless, the crusader forces were bolstered by the goods that had been taken.

After the crusaders reached Gaza, another faction announced its intention to conduct a raid. This time around, Theobald directly ordered them to stand down. But even after being given direct orders to cease and desist by Theobald and the leaders of the monastic knights who were with them, the men blatantly defied the commands given to them and launched their raid regardless. They headed south toward Gaza, but this time around, the raiders were not successful. Rather than meeting up with a caravan of merchants, they were waylaid by a fully equipped army. The would-be raiders were subsequently annihilated.

The ten-year truce that had given Christians control of Jerusalem was up, and the Muslim forces understandably, considering the sudden onslaught of violence waged against them, retook control of the city. At this point, it must have seemed that yet another crusade was being met with disaster, even if it wasn't an official crusade. But the winds of fate would soon change in the crusaders' favor, as the local Islamic powers began to fight amongst each other.

Sultan al-Kamil had passed away, and the various Ayyubid factions were in chaos while they searched for a successor. The most likely choices were the sultan's sons, al-Adil II and as-Salih Ayuub. But there were also those who backed al-Kamil's brother, as-Salih Ismail, as well as Ismail's son, an-Nasir Dawud. An-Nasir Dawud would momentarily seize control of Jerusalem after the end of the ten-year truce that had been orchestrated by Frederick II.

However, Count Theobald, who was not one to be outdone, indicated that he was ready to try his hand at diplomacy. He entered into negotiations with Sultan an-Nasir Dawud of Damascus and sought to gain an alliance against their mutual enemies in Egypt on the condition that Jerusalem, as well as Sidon, Tiberias, Galilee, and southern Palestine, were returned to the crusaders.

With the sultan of Damascus in his back pocket, Theobald led an army against the Egyptians. The Egyptians ended up standing down at Jaffa. Since Theobald had already hammered out the terms of the treaty with the sultan of Damascus, he saw no reason to take Jaffa. Instead, Theobald secured the terms of his treaty. This meant that Jerusalem was once again in Christian control.

Figuring that his work was done, Theobald then set sail for home in the fall of 1240. Further reinforcements from England would arrive that October when Richard of Cornwall landed in the Holy Land with a significant force. These reinforcements were used to shore up the crusaders' defensive positions.

Even so, it was a rather tenuous grip. Even though Jerusalem was temporarily reclaimed, it would be lost once again in 1244 when a powerful Islamic army led by the Khwarazmians—a Turkish group of warriors fighting for the Egyptians—wrested Jerusalem from the crusaders.

The Khwarazmians, who originated from central Asia, had been displaced by the Mongol invasions that were first sparked by the warlord Genghis Khan. They had since relocated to regions in Iraq and Syria, where they solidified their strength prior to invading the crusader-held territories in and around Jerusalem.

There is an interesting account of what life was like in the city just prior to the Khwarazmian conquest of it. The report comes from an Islamic scholar named Ibn Wasil, who arrived from Cairo to visit the city.

Although Muslims were still granted free access to Jerusalem under Christian occupation, Ibn Wasil was aghast at what he saw. He spoke of his disgust at seeing Christian priests openly preaching and praying inside the Muslim holy site called Dome of the Rock. He was also outraged to see the sacred Al-Aqsa Mosque (which the Knights Templar had previously used as their own headquarters) "decorated with bells." Ibn Wasil had long been critical of Christian control of the city ever since Frederick II diplomatically secured the arrangement back in 1229.

In the summer of 1244, Ibn felt it was high time that someone did something about the Christians controlling Jerusalem. Just a few months later, his prayers were answered. Al-Kamil's son, al-Salih Ayuub, secured a strategic partnership with the newcomers on the scene, the Khwarazmians. On July 11th, 1244, they rolled right into Jerusalem. Just as the Khwarazmians had been displaced by the Mongols, they returned the favor by displacing the Christians of Jerusalem.

The city was quite easy to invade since the city walls had never been rebuilt. And once inside, the Khwarazmians were absolutely ruthless. They cut off the heads of priests and worshipers. They desecrated the Church of the Holy Sepulchre and raided the tombs of crusader kings (save the Leper King, which was left alone).

The military orders of the Knights Templars, Knights Hospitallers, Teutonic Knights, and Leper Knights tried their best to protect civilians. They attempted to establish a corridor through which the people could be led to safety, but the task proved far too difficult against such an onslaught.

An account of the event from a Knight Hospitaller survived. Gerald of Newcastle was one of the lucky ones who lived to tell the tale. As Gerald describes it, "The enemy surrounding them on all sides, attacked them with swords, arrows, stones and other weapons, slew and cut [to] pieces around seven thousand men and women and caused such a massacre that the blood of those of the faith ran down the sides of the mountains like water."

Even so, this was not the end of the struggle against the Khwarazmians. The Christians were not going to allow the city to be taken without a fight. The crusaders rallied their forces and secured auxiliary Muslim troops from the sultan of Damascus, with whom they were allied. This led to a confrontation on October 17th between the crusader and Damascene troops and a contingent of Khwarazmian and Egyptian warriors near Gaza.

Although the town today is known by its Arabic name al-Hiribya, the crusaders knew it as La Forbie. So, the ensuing apocalyptic battle that took place here would be known as the infamous Battle of La Forbie. The crusader and Damascene forces were outnumbered, but they fought so ferociously that it was not at all clear who might come out on top.

However, the fate of the crusaders was sealed when their Damascene allies ultimately became spooked and fled the battle. No matter how hard the crusaders fought, the situation was now utterly impossible. The crusaders' tattered army, which was entirely dwarfed by their opponents, was easily crushed. All hope for a victorious outcome in the Barons' Crusade was dashed.

Chapter 9: Louis IX's and Prince Edward's Crusades

"In prosperity, give thanks to God with humility and fear lest by pride you abuse God's benefits and so offend him."

-*King Louis IX*

In December 1244, the very same year that Jerusalem was lost to the Khwarazmians, the king of France, Louis IX, lay on what was believed to be his deathbed. He had been suffering for some time from a bad case of dysentery. Reduced to skin and bones by the chronic illness, he was so weak that he was barely breathing. Yet, when those in attendance felt that all was lost and were on the verge of giving him up for dead, King Louis made what seemed to be a miraculous recovery.

His eyes suddenly opened wide. He gasped and immediately requested that he be brought his Crusader's cross. King Louis fully believed that he had just been brought back from the brink of death to call for a crusade to reclaim Jerusalem. King Louis IX was ready to lead the latest march to the Holy Land. And he would choose a familiar route to get there.

Louis was unconcerned about the failure of the Fifth Crusade, which ran aground in Damietta, Egypt, as he called for the crusaders to reach Jerusalem again by driving through Egypt. Despite the Barons' Crusade's previous failure, going through Egypt made some strategic sense. The sultan that was behind the Khwarazmian invasion of Jerusalem in 1244, al-Salih, was based out of Egypt. It only made sense that the crusaders would want to take the fight directly to the figure perceived as being their archnemesis at the time.

The sultan turned on his Khwarazmian allies almost as soon as they won the city of Jerusalem for him. Al-Salih no longer had any use for the Khwarazmians, so he rallied his own forces and drove them from the city. If it had been possible, the cleverest move the crusaders could have made at that point would have been to somehow link up with the Khwarazmians.

After all, the Khwarazmians were probably more than ready to seek vengeance against the sultan. An alliance between the crusaders and Khwarazmians would have been a classic case of "an enemy of my enemy is my friend," in which two adversaries temporarily forget their differences to team up against a mutual foe. It would have been interesting to see what the end results of such an unlikely partnership would have been.

However, that is not how history played itself out. The crusaders had no such strategic alliance and instead stormed the beaches (in their own medieval version of D-Day) in June 1249 and took on the enemy by themselves. The sultan and his troops were waiting for them, with horns blaring and drums pounding. If they thought this display would frighten the Christian trespassers, they were mistaken.

King Louis IX was a man of conviction after his near-death experience. And he fearlessly disembarked from his ship as soon as land was in sight, leading his troops to charge the enemy head-on. Accompanying them was Walter of Brienne, who had only recently been ransomed after he was made a prisoner of war in the aftermath of the disastrous Battle of La Forbie.

The sultan had a formidable army that was led by an equally formidable general, Fakhr al-Din. As such, it's a bit surprising that as soon as the crusaders charged, Fakhr al-Din ordered his troops to withdraw instead of crushing the invaders on the shoreline. Even stranger, he ordered Damietta to be evacuated. The crusaders ended up marching into an empty city. For many, it must have seemed as if a divine hand was at work, but their Egyptian opponents had their own reasons for taking these measures.

Fakhr al-Din was a student of history, and he knew how difficult it was for the crusaders to hold the city during the Fifth Crusade. As such, he figured simply letting them have it (and, as a consequence, letting them deal with all of the burdens of upkeep and defense that came with it) would harm them more than it would do them any good.

The Egyptian general regrouped his forces farther up the Nile at the heavily fortified site of al-Mansurah. He patiently waited for the crusaders to meet their doom at this spot. They would either have to march up the Nile to do battle with the Egyptians, which put them at a decided disadvantage, or waste away in Damietta. Each of these was a bad choice; which one they would make was up to them.

In November 1249, the crusader forces determined the Nile had receded enough to continue their invasion farther up the river. This could have been a fortuitous time for them since it was right around this period that Sultan al-Salih abruptly passed away. His general, Fakhr al-Din, wisely kept his death a complete secret as he secured his own grip on power.

Fakhr al-Din also made sure he organized his army into a formidable fighting machine. At the head of his army was a special contingent of warriors known as Bahriyya, which is Arabic for "of the river." This group, which is often likened to an Islamic version of the Knights Templar, was fierce, fearless, and fully dedicated to the cause. This tremendous force waited for the crusaders to arrive.

In December—Christmas Day no less—King Louis IX's forces finally made their way to al-Mansurah, arriving at the opposite side of the Tanis River, where they found themselves facing their opponents. Although separated by water, the two sides began skirmishing. King Louis IX's engineers began vigorously working on pontoon bridges, with which it was hoped that a crossing could be made.

In February 1250, the crusader camp was approached by a local Bedouin man, who convinced them that he could lead them to a narrow portion of the river that could be crossed by horse. He promised to divulge this information for the small price of "five hundred bezants." The crusaders figured this was as good an opportunity as any and took him up on the offer. They were able to cross the river but were easily spotted by a reconnaissance force while doing so.

The reconnaissance force wheeled around and rushed off to inform Fakhr al-Din of the news. The crusaders should have allowed their forces to fully cross and consolidate themselves so they would be better prepared for a pitched battle when it arrived. By doing so, they could have taken advantage of the time lag, as the reconnaissance team had to ride to inform Fakhr.

But instead, the crusaders who had crossed immediately charged at the reconnaissance troops, apparently hoping to annihilate them before they reached Fakhr. They ended up chasing the group all the way to the streets of al-Mansurah. If Fakhr didn't know of their arrival before then, he most certainly would have known by that point. As the crusaders crashed through the city, they very loudly announced their presence.

So, rather than picking the most optimal locale to engage the enemy, the crusaders became bogged down in violent and bloody street fighting. And as the enemy regrouped and reinforced their numbers, the crusaders were easily swarmed in the unfamiliar urban terrain. Hit from all sides, the crusader troops were hacked apart. Hundreds of knights were killed, including some 280 Knights Templar, who seemed to take the brunt of the assault.

Needless to say, the crusaders were pushed back. By April, it seemed that all hope of recovery was lost. An all-out retreat was ordered on April 5th, with the crusaders fleeing down the Nile as they were hacked and hammered by the enemy the whole way. Even worse, in the chaotic melee, King Louis IX himself was captured. His capture brought true meaning to the phrase "a king's ransom," as those holding King Louis demanded a huge amount of money to secure his freedom.

For those who had survived, it was relayed to them that the king would not be released unless 800,000 gold bezants were delivered to the sultan's camp. The king's men did not have that much money on them, but they knew who did: the Knights Templar. The Templars had long served as a kind of banking institution and had enormous wealth. However, the Templars could not just hand over such a huge amount since the money they guarded was deposited by others.

The surviving marshal of the order, Renaud de Vichiers, sympathized with the king of France and wanted him released as much as anyone else. As such, he came up with a crafty ploy to do so without having to break any of his personal vows in the process.

As the king's French troops stood by, Renaud loudly proclaimed that he could not possibly lend any money and that if the French happened to take their money by force, then the Templars would be forced to take reparations upon their return to the crusader stronghold of Acre. The French quickly understood the game the Templar marshal was playing. Although Renaud was bound by oath to safeguard the funds, he would not be held responsible if the French seized it by force.

As such, a small contingent of French troops stormed the Templars' galley and forcibly seized enough money to free their king. While this happened, the Knights Templar stood idly by; they did not break any oath, but they also did not put up any resistance either. As a result of these machinations, King Louis was freed. On May 13th, 1250, he made his way to Acre.

He spent the next few years in that city doing his best to ensure that as many Christian prisoners of war from the Egyptian debacle were freed as possible. For these good works, King Louis IX would later be canonized as a saint. Additionally, many geographical regions would be named after this king and saint (for instance, Saint Louis, Missouri, and the Saint Louis River, both of which are in the US).

Despite this posthumous acclaim, Louis would return home in 1254, greatly disappointed that his mission ended in what he could only see as an abject failure. However, he would try again. Several years later, in 1270, he picked up a powerful ally, Prince Edward of England (the future King Edward I of England). Prince Edward's father, King Henry III, was far too old for such an adventure, but his energetic son was more than up for the challenge.

As soon as all of the papal blessings and financial arrangements were made, Edward was ready to embark for the Holy Land. But King Louis, who was again leading the charge, once again had his sights set on North Africa instead. This time, he wanted to seize the Muslim-controlled city of Tunis and make it his forward base of operations. It was believed that Tunis could be used as a Mediterranean supply depot and a launching point for an overland march through Egypt and then on into the Holy Land.

But as fate would have it, King Louis would perish that August while Prince Edward was en route. After Louis's death, a truce was negotiated with the emir of Tunis. Ironically enough, by the time Edward landed, he was informed that the crusade was over. Unsure of what else to do, Edward and his troops sailed from Tunis and landed in Sicily, where they spent the winter. They then headed to that last great bastion of the Crusader States in the Levant: Acre.

Prince Edward arrived at the city of Acre on May 9th, 1271. The situation was a fairly desperate one for the crusaders, as they struggled to hang onto their remaining toehold in the Holy Land. In fact, just prior to Edward's landing, the once-mighty French castle, which had long stood just outside of Acre, known as Krak des Chevaliers, had just been taken by Islamic forces.

The crusaders' main antagonist at this time was a local sultan named al-Malik al-Zahir Baibars (also spelled Baybars). Shortly after Edward's arrival, the sultan rode to the gates of Acre with a large force, not to fight but to openly mock and taunt the crusaders holed up inside the city. Although Prince Edward came with a small army that numbered only in the hundreds, his arrival boosted morale. However, he and his troops would not be enough to turn the tide. Prince Edward quickly realized that open combat would spell disaster. Nevertheless, he wanted to do what he could to strike out against the antagonists of Christendom, so he began to conduct hit-and-run raids. However, these attacks were not carried out against soldiers; they were being conducted against civilian targets, making them little more than terrorist-styled attacks. These attacks were undoubtedly cowardly, as the only real reason Edward targeted civilians was that they were much easier to subdue.

Deep down, Edward must have known that such acts were certainly not befitting of a Christian prince of his stature. Yet, it seemed that such petty, punitive actions were all that he was capable of carrying out. But he soon had bigger fish to fry. He began to engineer an outright collaboration with one of Islam's greatest foes: the Mongols. Edward sent an envoy to the Mongol warlord Abaqa Khan and persuaded the Mongols to attack the city of Aleppo, located in modern-day Syria. This would put the Mongol forces just northeast of Acre.

The plan was to use the Mongol attack on Aleppo as a distraction. So, when the Mongols attacked, the crusaders could march right up to an undefended Jerusalem. But the crusaders first had to take out an important fortress called Qaqun, which stood as a watchtower between Acre and Jerusalem.

Edward and his troops, along with a group of Knights Hospitaller and Knights Templar, marched on the fortress. The group was only able to reach the very edge of the citadel before they were waylaid by enemy forces. Their opponents proved too formidable, and they had to retreat. This humiliating retreat led to nothing but mockery from Sultan Baibars.

It has been said that the sultan proclaimed, "If so many men cannot take a house [the fortress of Qaqun], it seems unlikely that they will conquer the kingdom of Jerusalem." Even so, Edward still attempted to come up with a plan for a renewed assault. But after he was very nearly killed by one of Baibars's infamous assassins, he finally admitted defeat and began his long trek back to England.

However, he did not leave before gaining Baibars's pledge to agree to a ten-year truce. Baibars would perish five years later. Some have theorized that he was poisoned by one of his own assassins. At any rate, the last remnants of the Crusader States would soon be in jeopardy once again.

Chapter 10: The Fall of the Crusader States

"Every war is its own excuse. That's why they're all surrounded with ideals. That's why they're all crusades."

-Karl Shapiro

The year 1291 would be an infamous one, for this would be the year that the final toehold of the Crusader States in the Holy Land would be lost. The successor of Baibars—Sultan al-Ashraf Khalil—would deal the crusaders their final blow.

By 1291, much of Europe had put the Crusades on the back burner. It just was not a priority for most of the European leaders at the time. With no large crusader force from Europe forthcoming, the main defenders of the city of Acre were the resident military orders: the Templars, Hospitallers, and Teutonic Knights. There were even a handful of Leper Knights from the Order of Saint Lazarus. All of these knights were willing to give their lives for the city of Acre and its forty thousand residents. Many of them ultimately did.

The new sultan began to plan what would be the final assault on the city in March 1291. The sultan's forces surrounded Acre and made their camp right outside the city's walls. They began their assault on April 5th but not before providing an opportunity for those inside to surrender. It had long been a part of Islamic tradition to allow a city's inhabitants a chance to voluntarily submit to Islam.

This does not mean the residents had to convert. Rather, the residents had to accept the authority of Islam. Christians would remain unharmed as long as they paid the jizya (a religious tax) and submitted to the terms that went with being a second-class citizen. However, the defenders of Acre had not spent their whole lives struggling to maintain their hold on the Holy Land just to give up now.

There was also no real guarantee that their conquerors would hold up their part of the bargain. Although these were the general rules of Islamic warfare, there was so much hatred and antagonism between the two camps by this point that it would have been hard to say whether such terms would have been held up even if the crusaders laid down their arms and agreed to them. The chivalrous days of Richard the Lionheart and Saladin were long gone and had been replaced by two hundred or so years of endless animosity.

The crusaders felt they had only one option—to fight on. So, when they received word the sultan was willing to discuss the terms of their surrender, the crusaders answered by hurling arrows, stones, and garbage at the sultan's messengers.

The crusaders then fortified their defenses and prepared for the inevitable assault. They also attempted to sabotage the Muslims. In the middle of the night, a group of knights from the Order of Saint Lazarus actually snuck out of Acre and attempted to destroy the sultan's siege engines. If they had been successful, this would have significantly diminished the sultan's ability to wage war. However, these leper-stricken knights ultimately failed in their efforts, as their horses got tripped up in the tent rope lines that crisscrossed all over the sultan's camp.

The resulting tumult brought the enemy down upon the Leper Knights, and they were quickly dispatched. Just a few weeks later, on May 14th, the sultan led his final assault on Acre. His siege engines tore through the city walls as planned, and his troops poured into the city. Hospitallers, Templars, Teutonic Knights, and Leper Knights all engaged the enemy and fought with everything they had. The only real reinforcements were a handful of knights sent from England. But this was just a drop in the bucket, and their opponents' larger numbers would overwhelm them soon enough.

The small group of tattered knights who survived made their way to the Templar fortress known as the "Templar House." They safeguarded civilians who ran to the fortress for refuge. The sultan initially promised safe passage for the civilians who remained, promising to escort them to a nearby port with his own men so that they could be evacuated from the city. Many had already attempted to make their way to the port only to be trodden by the hooves of the invaders' horses.

The chaotic conditions were quite dangerous. For example, the patriarch of Jerusalem, Nicolas of Hanapes, lost his life simply slipping off a boat and perishing in the waters. But feeling as if this was the only chance they had to shepherd the remaining civilians out of Acre, the Templars agreed to the proposition. But after they opened the gates to the citadel and their Muslim escorts entered the Templar House, it is said they began mistreating the women and children.

Some accounts dispute the notion that the women and children were mistreated or harassed, but something seems to have provoked the Templars, as it seems unlikely they would attack for no reason after giving their word. For whatever reason, the enraged marshal, Peter de Sevrey, decided to go back on the agreement, slamming the gates shut and locking a few hundred enemy combatants inside. The surviving Templars, Hospitallers, Teutons, and Leper Knights tore into their enemies, making short work of them.

The sultan was very weary of the prolonged struggle and wished to put an end to it. He ordered his engineers to plant explosives around the foundation of the Templar House.

The explosives managed to tear through the walls of the compound. The sultan's forces then stormed into the building. But as soon as they did, the whole building collapsed down upon them. Everyone inside was killed when the roof caved in. The crusaders and those under their charge had perished. This was the end of the crusader stronghold of Acre, and with its fall came an end to the Crusader States.

Section Two: Other Crusades

Chapter 11: The Northern Crusades

"Any crusade requires optimism and the ambition to aim high."

-Paul Allen

The Northern Crusades were actually a series of expeditions against the pagan holdouts in northeastern Europe. The Northern Crusades relied upon the precedent of battling pagans that had been established during the Wendish Crusade, as well as the efforts of Holy Roman Emperor Charlemagne the Great, who had waged war on the pagans of Saxony (modern-day Denmark). The actual starting point of what has been lumped together as the Northern Crusades is believed to be when Pope Celestine III called for action in 1195.

The call to arms was issued, and the Livonian Knights, or Brothers of the Sword, found themselves knee-deep in warfare with the remnants of European paganism in the early 1200s. Livonia made up much of the eastern shores of the Baltic Sea in northeastern Europe, which today makes up the modern-day nations of Latvia, Lithuania, and Estonia. This region became ground zero for Christian missionaries wishing to convert the local pagans. It also saw increased settlement by western (predominantly German-speaking) European peoples.

As the inevitable conflict between Christians and pagans escalated, it was determined that the region would benefit from a permanent military order entrusted with the protection of Christians and the active conversion of pagans. Albert, Bishop of Riga, founded the Livonian

Order in 1202. Shortly thereafter, the Livonian Knights were locked into increasingly hostile combat with (predominantly Lithuanian) pagan warriors.

The order itself had many early victories but was nearly annihilated in 1236 during the Battle of Saule, in which the Lithuanians rallied and unleashed a ferocious onslaught upon them. Many of their number, including their grand master, were killed in battle. After this incident, the remnants of the Livonian Knights were subsequently absorbed into the Teutonic Knights. The merger appears to have been completed by 1237.

The Teutonic Knights have an interesting history that should be addressed in some greater depth. The order began its existence in the Holy Land as the guardians of the Hospital of Saint Mary. After the initial loss of Jerusalem in 1187, they shifted focus to Acre. But after the fall of Acre, they were forced to shift gears once again. And once the Holy Land had been lost completely, the vast majority of Teutonic Knights ended up redeploying to Livonia.

The pope decreed that a new crusade against the pagans of Livonia was in the works and even declared that Livonia was the "land of the Mother of God." Such things sound a bit bizarre, considering the fact the northeastern European lands of the Baltic are fairly far away from the Middle East, but in those days, the pope's words were powerful. And if he declared it to be so, it must be. Additionally, the pope's words added to the mystique and attraction of crusading and potentially dying in an effort to subdue pagan lands.

But the Teutonic Knights would not only butt heads with the pagans. They also got into the bad graces of the Russian Orthodox Christians. The Russians were part of the Christian family, but the family had broken apart back in 1054, with Eastern Orthodoxy on one side and the Catholic Church on the other. The animosity over their religious differences and perhaps the fear that the Eastern Orthodox members would convert the Livonian pagans before the Catholics had the chance would lead to an armed confrontation.

The most famous of these confrontations has to be the famed Battle on the Ice in 1242, in which a whole regiment of Teutonic Knights was decimated by the forces of Russian Prince Alexander Nevsky. The knights were lured out onto a frozen lake before they were hemmed in and subsequently hammered into submission by the Russian forces. A retreat was attempted, but the knights were barely able to keep from falling down on the ice in the melee. The entire affair became an utterly devastating debacle for the Teutonic Knights.

This event kept the Teutonic Knights away from the Russian frontiers. Instead, they refocused their efforts on the Baltic coast and a region known as Pomerania, which today constitutes much of Poland and part of Germany. In the same fateful year that the Battle on the Ice took place, Polish Duke Swietopelk II of Pomerania began to take issue with the Teutonic Knights stationed in the region. To get rid of them, he decided to align himself with the local warlords so that he could push them out.

In the past, the Poles had aligned themselves with the Teutonic Knights against the pagans, as was the case when the Teutonic Knights were recruited in the 1220s to aid the Poles in their struggle against the pagans of Prussia. The Teutonic Order had aligned themselves with the Polish Duke Konrad of Masovia. The Poles had recently taken a beating from Prussian warriors who had engaged in terrorist-styled attacks, killing civilians and razing religious buildings to the ground.

Prussia (not to be confused with the later Kingdom of Prussia) is yet another Baltic principality that no longer exists but, at the time, consisted of the southeastern reaches of the Baltic. The pope had famously issued a Golden Bull in regard to the Prussian attacks, sanctioning a crusade in 1230. The Teutonic Knights, the Poles, and loyal Pomeranians joined forces to slam into the pagan Prussians. The Teutonic Knights were successful in their charge and drove the Prussians out.

But every few miles the Teutonic Knights advanced, they would stop and build a fortress. By doing this, the Teutonic Knights were putting down permanent roots. Although the Polish duke was happy the Teutonic Knights helped him get rid of the Prussians, he now had to contend with a permanent army of Teutonic Knights camped out in his land.

Additionally, German immigrants from the Holy Roman Empire began to come in droves, settling the land surrounding Teutonic castles under the assumption that they were under the full protection of the Teutonic Knights. Decades later, Duke Swietopelk of Pomerania sought to remedy Poland of this situation by aligning himself with bands of Pomeranians to dispatch the Teutonic Knights.

The duke fully understood the Teutonic Knights were at their best when they could charge out of their fortresses to launch rapid strikes before returning to the refuge of their castle walls. So, the duke began to relentlessly harass and harry the knights, hoping to catch them out in the open. He led a series of successful ambush attacks, attempting to catch the knights off-guard.

Duke Swietopelk also laid siege to many of their fortresses. By 1244, the Teutonic Knights only had three fortresses left in their possession that were still fully intact. The crafty duke ended up surrounding these remaining strongholds by erecting counterforts all around the beleaguered Teutonic castles. The Teutonic Knights were able to rally their strength, and they took out the counterforts one by one.

However, in 1247, the duke had to admit that his cause was lost. At this point, the pope entered the picture, insisting the two sides come to a peaceful resolution. In 1249, the Treaty of Christburg was enacted.

Decades later, in 1308, the Teutonic Knights once again came to blows with the Polish powers, this time over the German enclave of Danzig (Poland's modern-day Gdańsk). The Teutonic Knights were victorious, but they left a veritable massacre in their wake. The devastation was apparently so bad that even the pope condemned the order. It is not known exactly how many people died, but historians agree that mass killings took place.

The Teutonic Knights would lumber on for some time, but their reputation was in shreds. This terrible event would prove to be one of the final footnotes of the Northern Crusades. Historians have deemed the Northern Crusades to be far more successful than the crusades to the Holy Land.

Chapter 12: Crusades against Heretics

"The surest way to work up a crusade in favor of some good cause is to promise people they will have a chance of maltreating someone. To be able to destroy with good conscience, to be able to behave badly and call your bad behavior 'righteous indignation'—this is the height of psychological luxury, the most delicious of moral treats."

-Aldous Huxley

The Christian Gnostics practiced a mystical variation of Christianity. It had first come to the forefront in the 2nd century before it was ruthlessly suppressed by the supporters of mainstream Christianity.

The Christian Gnostics and the Cathars envisioned a world of dualism in which there was an equally good God and an equally evil one. To the Catholic Church, this seemed to be equating Satan with being somehow on par with God. This belief was considered heresy by church leaders since official Christian doctrine teaches that Satan is the fallen angel Lucifer, a being created by God. Thus, it would be logically argued that the two could not be equated. The created is not equal to the creator.

The Cathars were heavily influenced by the Gnostics who came before them. Both sects believed the world was inherently evil and that the goal of humanity was to shed their human bodies so that their souls would be free of the evil physical world. This is also contrary to church teaching since the fundamental teaching of Christianity is that the dead will be resurrected to live in a glorified (and entirely physical) body.

In the course of their religious evolution, the Cathars managed to pick up some strains of Hinduism in their teachings, as the Cathars believed in a form of reincarnation and transmigration of souls. They believed that people were continually reborn in physical form until they could finally be "freed" to roam as disembodied spirits. Such contrary teachings from those who called themselves "Christians" was more worrying to the pope than the advancing Muslim forces.

As such, a crusade was called in 1208, and the crusaders dutifully stormed into the heart of France to destroy the Cathars and those who sheltered them. Interestingly enough, this mission was considered so important that the pope's personal legate—Arnald Amalric—literally led the charge. This papal representative was on the ground, directing the carnage. Arnald Amalric wrote some rather astonishingly gleeful accounts of the bloodshed being inflicted.

At one point during the melee, he fired off a missive in which he gloated, "Today, your Holiness, twenty thousand citizens were put to the sword, regardless of age or sex." It is quite shocking to people today to hear of anyone, let alone religious leaders, casually speaking of wholesale slaughter in this fashion. But in those days, religion had become militant. Christians who were perceived to have fallen away from the mainstream faith were viewed as corrupted and akin to being a plague. It was feared that if these Christians went unchecked, their "heretical" beliefs could spread to other Christians.

In response to the news of the destruction of the Cathars, the pope wrote, "Praise and thanks to God for that which he hath mercifully wrought through thee and through these others whom zeal for the orthodox faith hath kindled to this work against his most pestilential enemies."

Here, the pope is clearly referring to the heretics as a "pestilence," as if they were some sort of virus that needed to be snuffed out. And this same mentality was in place when the Bosnian Crusade erupted in the Balkans in 1235. A hearty dose of conquest was also present, as the Kingdom of Hungary sought to add vast tracts of territory to its kingdom. This makes sense, as the leader of the Bosnian Crusade was the crown prince of Hungary, Prince Coloman.

Even though conquest was the main drive behind this crusade, religion played a role. In fact, the Bosnian Crusade was directly linked to the Albigensian Crusade, which took place years prior.

It had been rumored that a Cathar antipope named Nicetas had taken up residence in Bosnia. Today, scholars are unsure if this figure ever even existed. Nevertheless, there was very little reason to justify the terrible fighting that ensued. Beyond accusations of Bosnia harboring Nicetas, more general accusations were made that the Bosnians embraced a sect called Bogomilism. Adherents of Bogomilism believed in the duality of good and evil and were similar to the Cathars.

After all of the bloodshed ran its course, the crusaders achieved very little; they only succeeded in seizing very small sections of Bosnian territory.

The greater threat of the Mongols soon took precedence over petty squabbles among Christians. Right in the midst of the Bosnian Crusade, the Mongol armies threatened to invade the Balkans. And before it was all said and done, Prince Coloman himself would perish.

Chapter 13: The Alexandrian and Savoyard Crusades

"Any crusade requires optimism and the ambition to aim high."

-Paul Allen

The Alexandrian Crusade, also sometimes known as the sacking of Alexandria, took place when the potentate of Cyprus, Peter I, decided it would be profitable for him to invade Alexandria, Egypt. Although often considered part of the Crusades, it has been widely noted that this particular military operation lacked much of the religious ideals that were trademarks of its predecessors.

In many ways, the Alexandrian Crusade was more or less just a preemptive strike against a foreign adversary. Peter had received some startling intelligence information indicating that the Egyptians were planning an assault on Cyprus. So, Peter raised up troops of his own to take the fight directly to Alexandria, Egypt. Peter I of Cyprus spent the better part of three years raising an army. His forces were joined by the famed Knights Hospitaller, who were holed up on the island of Rhodes.

Peter and his men met up with the knights at Rhodes in the fall of 1365. His fleet was said to have consisted of around 165 ships. The armada descended upon Alexandria on October 9th, 1365. Peter and his men stormed the city, and over the next few days, thousands were killed, and even more were taken as prisoners of war. Peter's men burned the city, razing mosques and churches alike to the ground. Egypt had—and still does have—a sizeable Christian population, but it seems even they did not fare much better than their Muslim countrymen in Peter's onslaught.

Besides robbing and murdering the inhabitants of Alexandria, Peter was apparently eager to turn the situation into another Damietta, as he believed he could use the city as a forward base for future crusades into the Middle East. But his fellow captains realized how vulnerable they were. Or perhaps they knew the history of previous ill-fated campaigns in the region. Regardless, they convinced Peter they should leave while they were still ahead.

And that was precisely what they did. Rather than sticking around to hold the city and inevitably face wrathful reinforcements, Peter's men looted as many valuables as they possibly could and killed anyone who stood in their way before hopping back onto their ships and setting sail for Cyprus. Thus, the Alexandrian Crusade is often said to be more akin to the sacking of a city than an actual ideological crusade.

But however you may quantify it, the daring raid would be remembered. It would later end up getting a mention in the famed medieval text *The Canterbury Tales*.

The Savoyard Crusade commenced on the heels of the Alexandrian Crusade. Officially sanctioned by Pope Urban V, the Savoyard Crusade was launched in the Balkans in an attempt to offset the growing threat of the Ottoman Empire. This particular crusade gets its name due to the fact that it was led by Amadeus VI, Count of Savoy.

The Savoyard Crusade saw Westerners actively collaborating with Hungary and the Byzantine Empire, the latter of which was becoming increasingly harried and hounded by the Ottomans. The pope first convinced Louis I of Hungary to take part, persuading him to take a stand against Turkish encroachment in the region. The pope was also in frequent contact with Byzantine Emperor John V Palaeologus about the terms of cooperation between the Christian West and the Christian East.

At the center of these talks were plans to heal the schism that had erupted between Latin Catholics and Orthodox Christians. The Byzantine emperor was considering reuniting with the Catholic Church and even recognizing papal authority over the Greek Orthodox Church if he were aided in driving the Turks from the Balkans. Emperor John V seemed true to his word. In 1366, he even made his way to the court of the Hungarian king, where he swore an oath that he and his family would personally convert to Catholicism.

All of this was music to the pope's ears, and he eagerly did what he could to coordinate the crusader forces to conduct the Byzantine Empire's much-needed relief operation in the Balkans to check the expansion of the Ottoman Turks. Shortly thereafter, Amadeus led a considerable force by boat straight to the Dardanelles to attack Turkish positions in Gallipoli.

The crusaders captured the city that August after the Turks fled, and the city's residents flung open the gates. Unlike other medieval seizures of cities, the taking of Gallipoli appears to be one of liberation rather than conquest. It makes sense; this city had only recently been overrun by the Turks. The Byzantine residents certainly appreciated being rescued.

Controlling Gallipoli was of crucial importance strategically since it gave the crusaders control over what had been the main weigh station of the Turks as they crossed over into Europe. The Savoyard force reached Constantinople on September 4th, 1366, and then launched an expedition against another of Byzantium's enemies: the Bulgarians. The crusaders laid hold of the strategic settlements of Mesembria and Sozopolis that October.

The crusaders also attempted to take Varna. They hoped the citizens would just open the gates and let them in, but this was not the case. Instead, an embittered stalemate ensued.

Amadeus VI of Savoy soon found himself running out of money and was forced to return home. However, before they left, the Greeks showed their appreciation to the crusaders for aiding them against the Turks and Bulgarians. According to Savoyard chroniclers, "all orders of religion, gentlemen, citizens, merchants, people, women, and children, and [they] all went to the seaside to meet the count, crying 'Long live the count of Savoy, who has delivered Greece from the Turks and the Emperor, our Lord, from the hands of the Emperor of Bulgaria.'"

Despite all of the gratitude, the Byzantines did not convert to Catholicism, instead allowing Byzantine politics to prevail. The emperor was kind enough to fork out some fifteen thousand florins to help pay for the costs incurred by Amadeus of Savoy and his crusader force.

Chapter 14: The Ottoman Crusades

"The Ottoman Empire ... The rulers in Turkey were fortunately so corrupt that they left people alone pretty much. [They] were mostly interested in robbing them. And they left them alone to run their own affairs. With a lot of local self-determination."

-*Noam Chomsky*

The Ottoman Empire, the largest contiguous empire in the history of Islam, would rise up in central Europe to shake the former giant of Asia Minor—the Byzantine Empire—to its core. The Ottomans began as various Turkic tribes that migrated into Anatolia during the tumult of Mongolian expansion. These bands of warriors eventually coalesced under one dynamic leader: Osman.

The Ottoman Empire rose up under Osman (the empire actually gets its name from Osman, whose name is Uthman in Arabic). Under Osman, the Turks struck out against the Byzantines in 1301, advancing toward Nicaea on the Byzantine Empire's southern flank. The Byzantines went into action and sent an army to intercept the intruders, but the Turks rallied and dealt the Byzantines a stunning defeat.

Many refugees poured out of Nicaea (now the Turkish city of Iznik) and fled to the higher ground of Nicomedia (the modern-day Turkish town of Izmit). The fighting would continue even after Osman perished. In 1326, the Turks managed to seize the Byzantine city of Bursa. This outpost would become the first capital city of the rapidly expanding

Ottoman Empire.

The Turks would use Bursa as a forward base. They finally captured the city of Nicaea in 1331. Further advancements were made when nearby Nicomedia was taken just a few years later, in 1337. The Ottomans pushed closer and closer toward the isthmus—the thin strip of land—that connected Asia Minor to southeastern Europe, and the Byzantines seemed practically powerless to stop their advance.

The Ottomans would soon push into the Balkans and make a lasting impact on places like Serbia, Bulgaria, and Bosnia, impacts that can still be felt to this day.

In the meantime, the Byzantine Empire was in a state of panic. A disastrous conflict broke out in 1342 between two different Byzantine claimants to the throne, making matters even worse.

The drama was over the succession of a young Byzantine prince, John V Palaeologus, being contested by his regent, John Kantakozenos. During the course of the struggle, Kantakozenos became desperate enough to make friends with the Byzantine Empire's natural enemy: the Turks. He aligned himself with a Turkish warlord named Orkhan (also spelled as Orhan). With the aid of his Turkish allies, John was successful in his bid and ultimately went on to become Byzantine emperor John VI.

The Turks had greatly aided Kantakozenos in his quest, but they were now camped practically right outside of Constantinople's mighty walls. The Ottomans would continue to be enlisted as auxiliary troops, periodically fending off Bulgarian invasions. These engagements led the Turks to eventually set up camp right on the Gallipoli Peninsula. The seizure of this territory was rightfully viewed with deep suspicion by the Byzantines since it would have allowed their "allies" an easy path to strike out at the heart of the Byzantine Empire.

The situation became even worse in 1354 when an earthquake knocked down the fortified walls of several Byzantine settlements in the region. With the medieval mindset being what it was, this was not seen as a coincidence. The Turks took it as a divine invitation to seize the towns that had been "miraculously" rendered defenseless.

After this event, the Ottoman Turks were deeply rooted in what had previously been the southern heartland of the Byzantines. The Byzantines were so outraged by these developments that they seemingly placed all of the blame on the political machinations of their emperor and forced John VI Kantakozenos to resign in 1354.

About ten years later, in 1362, the Ottomans gained a powerful leader named Murad I, a figure who would serve as a unifying force for the Ottomans until his death in 1389 during the Battle of Kosovo. Murad I first began the process of utterly surrounding the Byzantine capital of Constantinople by seizing control of both sides of the isthmus on which the great metropolis sat. The Byzantines faced very little hope of succeeding on the military front, so they resorted to diplomacy and signed a treaty with the Ottoman sultan.

For a time, there would be peace, but the Byzantines were made subservient to the Ottomans and forced to pay tribute. This sense of desperation led to renewed talk in inner Byzantine circles to break out of the bind in which they found themselves.

In the meantime, the Serbs in the Balkans had grown in strength. In 1363, they managed to join forces with Hungarian, Wallachian, and Bosnian troops to wage war against Turkish positions in Adrianople. The push was successful at first, but in one of the most ridiculous reversals in history, this coalition of forces proceeded to celebrate their gains right there in the field. They camped out near the Maritza River and drank themselves into oblivion. While they were sleeping off the effects of their festivities, the Ottomans launched an assault against them. These hungover warriors were in no shape to fight and were forced to flee. Many of them perished in the process.

The Turks would solidify their gains and make Adrianople (Edirne) their official capital. It was due to all of these developments that the pope called for the Savoyard Crusade. As mentioned in the previous chapter, the Savoyard Crusade involved Duke Amadeus of Savoy, who just so happened to be the cousin of the Byzantine emperor.

The crusade was fairly successful in rolling back Turkish gains, resulting in the seizure of Gallipoli from the Turks. The Turks continued to make inroads in the Balkans, and on September 26th, 1371, they came to blows with yet another Balkan coalition led by the Serbs. This battle would go down in Turkish history as *Sirf Sindigi* ("The Destruction of the Serbs").

The name of this battle is not mere hyperbole since an army was annihilated and much of the Serbian nobility was destroyed in this catastrophic onslaught. In the aftermath, large chunks of Serbia and other Balkan territories were occupied by the Ottomans.

A champion would soon rise up in the form of Lazar of Serbia. He would attempt to push the Ottoman advance back once again. Lazar created yet another coalition, this time mostly consisting of Bulgarians, Bosnians, Serbians, Wallachians, Albanians, and Hungarians.

Murad I quickly responded to this incursion, and the two sides met for a climactic round of warfare in 1389 that would become known as the Battle of Kosovo. The Turks were once again victorious, but their victory would be bittersweet, for their leader, the great Murad I, perished.

But Murad was not killed in combat. A Serb by the name of Miloš Oblić snuck into the Ottoman encampment and assassinated Murad. After this event, Lazar of Serbia, who had been captured and made a prisoner of war during the Battle of Kosovo, was himself executed in retribution. His son, Stefan Lazarević, succeeded the throne, but he had no stomach for crusades and ultimately became an obedient puppet of the Turks while the Balkans were slowly carved up by the Ottoman state.

In 1391, the Turks seized Bosnia, and just a couple of years later, in 1393, Bulgaria found itself under Turkish dominion. With the Balkans under their thumb, the Turkish war machine then turned its attention once again to the Byzantines. Just a few years after the fall of Bulgaria, the Turks laid siege to the Byzantine city of Nicopolis and succeeded in taking it. Prince Mircea of Wallachia led a new coalition of Christian crusaders down the Danube River. They made their way to Nicopolis to face the Turks head-on.

This confrontation would later become known as the Battle of Nicopolis, which took place in 1396. The Turks had heavily fortified the city, and it soon became quite clear to the crusaders that taking it would not be an easy feat. The crusaders lacked even the most basic aspects of siege equipment.

Sultan Bayezid I, who came to the throne in 1389, had been alerted to what was happening and arrived on the scene with a formidable force. However, the Turks did not immediately attack the crusaders. Instead, they camped nearby, daring the crusaders to be the first to strike. The crusaders took the bait and soon charged right into the enemy. The strike was premature, and those who had charged headlong into the enemy found themselves in an extremely vulnerable position. The Turks were able to close in and annihilate them.

The rest of the battle was a rout, as the disorganized crusader army began to retreat in utter chaos. Most of those who fell behind were killed, but some were taken captive. Johann Schiltberger, who was a participant on the side of the crusaders, noted his version of the event.

Schiltberger stated, "Then each was ordered to kill his own prisoners, and for those who did not wish to do so, the [sultan] appointed others in their place. Then they took my companions and cut off their heads, and when it came to my turn, the [sultan's] son saw me and ordered that I should be left alive, and I was taken to the other boys, because none under 20 years of age were killed, and I was scarcely 16 years old." This testimony is indicative of the Turkish habit of sparing young men since they could be forced into serving the Ottoman army.

By this point, the situation in Constantinople was entirely untenable. The Byzantines were surrounded, and they knew their metropolis, nestled right in the midst of a vast Turkish empire, would be swallowed up soon. The Byzantine emperor actually "snuck" out of his own kingdom to make a trip to the West to plead for aid and yet another crusade.

However, no serious efforts would be made until a few decades later. Another crusading coalition was cobbled together in 1444. This time around, a scheme had been concocted to have the main vanguard of the crusader army march down the Danube River to meet the Turks while Venetian naval craft would be sent to blockade the straits, preventing reinforcements from flowing into the Balkans. And if this wasn't enough, it was planned to have the Greeks stage a diversionary attack in southern Greece.

It was believed that if all of these operations were successful, then a small group of a few thousand Turks would be left stranded in the Balkans. It would be easy for the crusaders to take down such a paltry number. It was hoped this grand strategy would succeed in driving the Turks away for good and give Constantinople some much-needed breathing space. But as they say, the best-laid plans of mice and men often go awry.

As the strategy unfolded, the Greeks did their part, creating a distraction in the Peloponnese, but the Venetians proved unable to blockade the straits of the Bosporus due to bad weather. Their ships would remain in port. The sultan's army was able to cross into the Balkans to reinforce the residual force that had been left there. This meant the crusaders faced a very large and formidable army when the two sides finally came face to face in the vicinity of Varna in November 1444.

Realizing they were grossly outnumbered, the crusaders hunkered down and literally circled their wagons as they moved into a defensive position to sustain the heavy assault that awaited them. Initially, the crusaders' tactics served them well enough. When the Turks advanced, the crusaders were able to pick quite a few of them off by launching a heavy rain of arrows in their direction.

The crusaders learned that a top Turkish commander had been killed during the first melee, which greatly heartened them. Nevertheless, the Ottomans continued their relentless advance against the beleaguered crusaders. The crusaders attempted to rally and charge their opponents but were routed in what turned into an unmitigated disaster.

In the middle of this carnage, the king of Hungary was killed. His head was placed on the tip of a spear. The Turks proudly waved this trophy high into the air for all of the crusaders to see. For them, the message was quite clear—their bold commander had fallen, and it would not be long before the rest of them would succumb as well.

Geopolitically speaking, the Greeks of the Peloponnese would suffer the most from this debacle since they were immediately subjugated and subjected to reprisals for their role in the crusade.

The Ottoman Empire was a true juggernaut and military powerhouse. It seemed as if all efforts to dislodge it would prove impossible. Nevertheless, Pope Nicholas V was ready to call for yet another crusade as a consequence of the losses that had been incurred. His biggest backer was George Skanderbeg of Albania.

This leading figure of Christendom cobbled together a suitable force of crusaders, but in doing so, he incurred the wrath of Sultan Murad II, who immediately struck out at Albania. Hungary's crusading champion John Hunyadi and a coalition of Hungarians and Wallachians sent troops to aid the beleaguered Albanians. The forces then collided in Kosovo, leading to the 1448 Second Battle of Kosovo.

The crusade would meet its end here, as it was a decisive Ottoman victory. The Turks were able to consolidate their gains in the Balkans and turn their focus toward toppling the Byzantine Empire.

This feat was achieved just a few years later by Murad II's son, Mehmed II. After a protracted siege, Constantinople fell to the Ottoman Turks in 1453. It was pleas from Constantinople that had kickstarted the Crusades in the first place, and now the once-mighty Christian capital of the East had fallen. The shock of Constantinople's fall was profound, not only to Christendom but also to the world.

Chapter 15: The Reconquista — Setting the Stage for Things to Come

"The Sultan Abd-er-Rahman was one of the Heaven-sent rulers of men. Prompt yet cautious in council and in war, unscrupulous, overbearing and proud, he was as ready to wreak terrible vengeance, as he was politic to forgive when it suited him. Berber and Yamanite alike acknowledged that at last they had found their master. He ruled until his death, in 788, with the tempered severity, wisdom, and justice which made his domain the best organized in Europe, and his capital the most splendid in the world."

-S. P. Scott

The Iberian Peninsula stands as one of the most unique geographical regions in the crusading period. As mentioned earlier, the Visigothic Christian kings ruled Spain in the early 700s, but they began to be harassed and harried by Islamic forces arriving from North Africa. It was just a hop, skip, and jump to cross the Strait of Gibraltar and lay siege to the southern beaches of Spain. And during this period, the assaults were happening more and more frequently.

All of this led to a massive incursion by a Muslim warlord whose name comes down to us as Tariq in 711 CE. Tariq's forces were victorious. They crushed the Visigoths and took over nearly all of the Iberian Peninsula. The invaders even pushed into France until they were stopped by the mighty ruler known as the Hammer—Charles Martel (better known as Charlemagne).

Back in conquered Iberia, the entire peninsula had been overrun, save for the remote mountainous enclaves where a Christian resistance was kept on life support. However, this small Christian holdout would one day march forth from the corner it had been backed into and revive Christian Iberia (which its Muslim conquerors referred to as al-Andalus).

In the first stages of the conquest, al-Andalus was overseen by administrators who hailed from the Umayyad dynasty, which was based out of Damascus, Syria. The Umayyads were overthrown and displaced by another group, the Abbasids, in the 740s, which changed the course of Iberian history. For one thing, the capital of the Abbasid dynasty was Baghdad, Iraq. This meant those who were tasked with running the Iberian Peninsula were quite far from the peninsula itself.

The drama between the Abbasids and the Umayyads was not yet over, though. Even though the ruthless Abbasids had killed much of the former Umayyad nobility in their pursuit of power, a young prince by the name of Abd al-Rahman had escaped their clutches. Like a king in exile, Rahman grew up with a fire in his belly and a determination in his heart to take back his kingdom.

He eventually made his way to Córdoba, Spain, in 756, where he declared himself to be a sovereign ruler of an independent Umayyad state. Perhaps considering how brutal (as well as apathetic due to their faraway administrative posts in Baghdad) the Abbasids had been, the residents of Iberia jumped at the chance to rally behind Abd al-Rahman. The Abbasids apparently did not put up much resistance to this takeover (if they noticed at all), and Iberia remained an independent emirate for a time.

Eventually, those tasked with running al-Andalus would find the greatest danger they faced was not from rival Muslim powers but from the Christian enclaves in the northern mountains. They had been patiently waiting for just the right time to come down and take back what had once belonged to them.

A ruthless Muslim leader who seized power in al-Andalus took center stage of this struggle in the 980s. His name comes down to us as al-Mansur. He proved himself to be an excellent military strategist and managed to keep the Christians in the north in check. He also gained ground on the North African coast of Morocco.

Al-Mansur's rule was essentially a dictatorship, and while he was crushing external enemies, he was also quelling internal opponents. He managed to clean house so thoroughly that he decimated the internal bureaucratic machinery that had allowed the Muslims to control Iberia efficiently. Al-Mansur would pass away in 1002, leaving a corrupt and chaotic legacy of governance in his wake. The name given to this period was *fitna*, which means "anarchy."

Al-Andalus went from a united peninsula, with territories spilling into North Africa, to several warlord states. The division of al-Andalus would be crucial for the Christian reconquest of the peninsula since it was much easier to take a piece of Spain back at a time. Toppling minor kingdoms was an easier goal than standing up to a united and powerful peninsula-wide regime.

Interestingly enough, many of the weaker warlord states realized just how precarious of a situation they were in and began paying tribute to some of the most powerful Christian kings in northern Iberia to keep them from attacking.

As the Christians' foes became more fractured, the two Christian powers of León and Castile merged together when Ferdinand the Great of Castile wed the sister (and ultimately the heir) of the king of León. Due to the tribute they received from Muslim states, León and Castile began to slowly become quite wealthy. Rather than being vagabond kings hiding in the wilderness, these Christian states grew financially and militarily strong.

But these petty warlords soon began to groan under the strain of the *fitna* system. After the Christians seized control of Toledo, they finally sought help. In what was essentially an Islamic call for a crusade against the Christians, aid was requested from the powerful Almoravids, who had taken over Morocco. In 1086—about a decade prior to Urban II's first call for a Christian crusade—the Almoravids sailed to Iberia and engaged the Iberian Christians in battle.

The Islamic forces scored a victory, and the Christian troops were driven out. The Almoravids quickly realized the weakness of the fractured system that had existed in Iberia and attempted to reinstate a more unified form of governance. But it did not last. In just a matter of years, the Almoravids were losing power, and around 1120, they had to concede defeat and give up al-Andalus outright.

The Christian kingdoms were on the rise and began to unite increasingly more with each other. León and Castile were ultimately absorbed by a rising power known as the Kingdom of Pamplona. After Pamplona gained the Kingdom of Aragon, it became the much larger Principality of Catalonia.

However, at the dawning of the 1100s, the kingdom retracted, and Navarre became the main focal point of Christian Iberia. During the Second Crusade in the 1140s, the pope took notice of what was happening in Iberia and coordinated to have significant manpower sent to the peninsula.

At the behest of Alfonso I Henriques of Portugal, Flemish soldiers and a batch of Anglo-Norman warriors, who were on their way to the Holy Land, made a pit stop in Iberia. They joined forces with the Portuguese to seize the important Iberian port city (and ultimately the capital of Portugal), Lisbon.

Although much of the Second Crusade is remembered as a dismal failure, this side mission proved to be a stunning success. Lisbon was ultimately reclaimed for Christendom on October 24th, 1147. Christian knights continued to be summoned to Iberia to support the reconquest of vast tracts of land. These lands began to define the boundaries of what would become Portugal and Spain.

One interesting development was the establishment of a unique Iberian monastic order of knights, which would become known as the Order of Santiago. Santiago is actually the Spanish name for Saint James. It was believed the remains of Saint James had been miraculously discovered in northern Spain.

According to Catholic tradition, James had conducted missionary work in Spain before heading back to Jerusalem to lead the early church. Since James's alleged visit is not mentioned in scripture, it is not entirely clear where this account comes from. However, the Bible documents that James was in Jerusalem when he was martyred. The Spanish legend insists that his body was shipped off to Spain.

This order of knights would often be on the frontlines of the conflict to reconquer Iberia. Prior to Iberian-based orders, the Knights Templar had some limited participation in the region, but it proved much more practical to have monastic orders native to the peninsula to permanently safeguard the gains being made in the Reconquista.

The southward push against the Muslim settlements continued, resulting in a major exchange between Christian and Muslim forces in 1195 at the Battle of Alarcos. At the fortress of Alarcos, the beaten and battered Castilian troops sought refuge. In the end, the Castilians had to admit defeat and surrender, which led to the loss of several strategic fortresses and further incursions by their adversary.

But even so, just a couple of years later, in 1212, another tremendous battle between the two sides was waged in Iberia. The Battle of Las Navas de Tolosa would completely alter the course of history.

A force led by the unified Spanish kingdoms of Castile, Aragon, and Navarre hooked up with a contingent of Portuguese troops and delivered their opponents a stunning blow. Prior to this, Muslim forces had regained some territory and appeared to be on the rise. After this major defeat, though, much of their gains would be lost.

Most historians believe the Battle of Las Navas de Tolosa was the turning point for the entire Reconquista. After this decisive victory, Christian forces were able to push farther south. As it pertains to the Portuguese, a rapid advance to the Algarve region in 1249 led to the complete seizure of the territory that would come to define modern-day Portugal.

However, not all of these territorial gains went without their moment of controversy. One must consider how difficult it would have been for some of these Christian kings to determine who would get what. As it turns out, the king of Castile was not happy with the Portuguese claims in the Algarve, leading to a lengthy dispute between the two powers.

The pope proved to be a useful diplomat in this disagreement, as he diffused a potentially deadly dispute through negotiations. The Treaty of Alcañices was signed in the year 1297. It was in this treaty that the exact boundaries between Castile and Portugal would be sorted out.

This mediation by the pope set a precedent that would be followed in later years. The papacy would again play the vital role of mediator when Portugal and Spain divvied up much of the New World (the Americas) between each other.

As the Spanish and Portuguese reclaimed their territory in Iberia, the Muslim settlements in the peninsula were being squeezed more and more until they were pigeonholed into the southernmost enclaves of the Iberian Peninsula. Soon, all that would remain of al-Andalus was just one southern corner of Iberia, which would become known as Granada.

The Christian expansion would not go unanswered. A new Muslim power from North Africa, the Marinids, would arrive on the scene. The Marinids showed up around the year 1275 and offered their aid to the besieged region of Granada. Their aid was not always appreciated by the Granadans, though. As was the case before, when "outside help" arrived, there was almost certainly disruption and oppression at the local level.

After the Marinids arrived to strengthen the position of the enclave, the Christian kings came to realize the importance of gaining control of the narrow strait that flowed between the North African coast and the southern tip of Spain. Until the connection between Granada and the North African coast was severed, there would always be a threat of incursions and reinforcements being sent from Muslim strongholds in Morocco. As such, securing the strait became the Christians' main objective.

The Christian kingdoms of Iberia waged war against the Marinid newcomers. In 1292, the Christians managed to seize Tarifa. Then, in 1310, even greater success occurred with the seizure of Gibraltar. Gibraltar is the island that lies in the strait between North Africa and Spain. It was a convenient stop for invasion forces and was of strategic importance for the Christian kings. The Christians temporarily lost Gibraltar in the back-and-forth struggle that followed, but by 1350, the Christian dominance of the strait was complete. Grenada was effectively surrounded with no hope of reinforcements.

In the end, it would be the mighty Spanish power couple of Ferdinand II of Aragon and Isabella I of Castile who managed to seize Granada in 1491. They finished the Reconquista, securing the entire Iberian Peninsula in 1492. And as anyone who has ever read a history book might know, that fateful year of 1492 saw a man named Christopher Columbus sail the ocean blue on behalf of the Spanish Crown.

Although Columbus didn't realize it at the time, he had stumbled upon a whole new continent. And since the victorious armies of Christian Europe had finished the Reconquista, they were looking for something new to do. Heading to the New World and conquering it for their countries sounded appealing.

But why did Columbus even sail westward? Well, the fall of Constantinople and the subsequent closure of the old roads to the East led Columbus and other explorers to look for an alternate route to India. Columbus believed India could be found by sailing westward, but he accidentally "discovered" the Americas (for those who don't know, Leif Erikson was the first European to discover the Americas, although native tribes had lived there even before Erikson made his journey).

The Crusades and the Reconquista were also major factors in exploring the New World. The Portuguese and Spaniards had spent centuries trying to reclaim Iberia, so they had become understandably militant about their faith. They had fought hundreds of years of religious wars. With this in mind, it is easier to understand the mindset conquistadors had when confronted with the Maya, Aztecs, and Inca, civilizations that had not been introduced to the Christian God.

When the Spanish conquistador Hernán Cortés beheld the Aztecs conducting human sacrifices, with Aztec priests ripping out the hearts of their sacrificial victims, his reaction was both understandable and predictable. The Spaniards and Portuguese were determined to conquer this new land for Christ, just as they had done in Iberia.

For better or for worse, these battle-hardened Christian crusaders, riding high on the waves of the victorious conclusion of Iberia's Reconquista, were ready to stake their claims in the New World. As much as we tend to condemn these men today (and there is certainly plenty of reason to do so), one can only imagine what might have occurred if the forces of Islam were the victors rather than the Christians. If that were the case, would a Muslim version of Columbus have sailed from the Islamic stronghold of Iberia and discovered the New World? Would the armies of Islam have given the Native Americans a choice—submit to Islam or go to war? Rather than having a staunchly Catholic Mexico, Cuba, Colombia, and Brazil, would these countries have mosques on every corner?

So, what is the point of mentioning all this? The point is that those who engaged in the Reconquista were militant, brutal, and aggressive, but they were no more so than their Islamic opponents. It is impossible to say for sure, but if the Muslims were the ones to travel to the New World, their conquest of the Americas would have likely resulted in the same dislocation of Native American civilizations. It is safe to say, though, that much blood has been spilled in the name of religion throughout history.

Conclusion: The Lasting Legacy of the Crusades

Whether we like it or not, the Crusades are a crucial lynchpin in history. Without them, the world today would be a much different place. As much as we might be tempted to demonize one side, we are missing the bigger picture if we do. The Crusades were not launched on the mere whims of some pope who wanted to be mean and nasty and colonize the Middle East. The Crusades were a defensive operation aimed at aiding the Greek Byzantines.

And whether we agree with it or not, the subsequent seizure of the Holy Land was also viewed as a kind of Reconquista since all of the Levant had been controlled by Christians until it was forcibly seized by the forces of Islam in the 7th century. By the time of the Crusades, the question of who had control of these lands was seen through the brutal lens of the Middle Ages, in which property rights fell to whoever was willing to fight for them.

If a clear and balanced portrayal of the Crusades and what led up to them were presented, we would see that both sides used the same fanatical ideology to justify their uncompromising brutality. There were no "good guys" and "bad guys" in these religious wars. Each side thought they were justified. And more often than not, each side felt the ends justified the means. This is indeed the ultimate legacy of what would become known as the Crusades.

Part 4: The Knights Templar

An Enthralling History of the Rise and Fall of the Most Influential Catholic Military Order

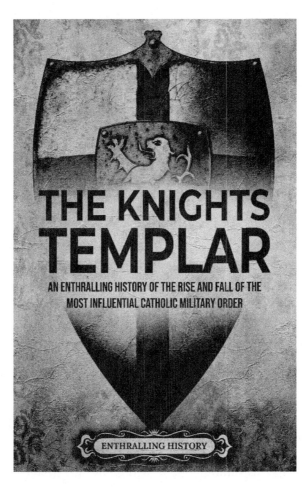

Introduction

The Knights Templar is certainly one of the most intriguing organizations that ever existed. It was a military order at first, created to protect the Christian-controlled Holy Land after the First Crusade, but it became much more than a group of devout Christians who wished to fight in the name of God. Throughout a somewhat short but still very powerful period of its existence, the Knights Templar established itself as a dominant military group with distinct customs, traditions, and rules, and it was respected all over Europe. It would receive countless gifts and donations from European rulers and political figures, who would try to honor the holy and graceful deeds of the order. Members of the order would be admired among both commoners, who would almost make them living legends based on the stories they heard, and among the powerful, who would give them command of their armies, grant them strongholds and castles, and make them their advisors. For about two hundred years, the Knights Templar played a big role in the power politics of the known world and continued to stay influential even after its demise.

However, the great popularity and status that the order held in the Christian world would ultimately cause its downfall. At the dawn of the 14th century, after the unsuccessful final attempts of the Crusaders to regain control of the Holy Land, the Templars would be brought down by the ones who once adored them so much. King Philip IV of France sought to increase his influence and dominate the papacy at the height of the Inquisition's power, and the Templars would be declared criminals. King Philip would start the purge of the Templars, hunting them down and putting them on corrupt ecclesiastical trials, where they would be condemned for being heretics, traitors to the church, and sodomites. By 1314, the Knights Templar had virtually lost all the power that it once held and would soon be destroyed. It is still one of the most fascinating orders, both for the people who admire them and historians who are compelled to find out more about its mysterious nature.

And mystery has surrounded the order since its creation. It always carried this sense of secrecy, of not fully disclosing what was going on behind closed doors, which raised suspicion about the true nature of its deeds. Throughout the years, the Templar Order has been linked to various secret societies, like the Freemasons, with some claiming that the surviving Templars went underground and continued living as the Freemasons. Conspiracies about its connections to different kinds of heresies are also common. According to many, Templars conducted secret, forbidden rituals and gathered powerful artifacts from the Holy Land, which granted them their power. Whether or not these allegations are true (and most of them probably aren't), one thing is for certain—the legacy of the Knights Templar still continues to live on today and manifests in different ways.

This book is for those curious readers who want to know more about the amazing history of the Knights Templar. It is truly a one-of-its-kind topic that continues to excite historians to this day due to the flawed, limited, and common misconceptions and ideas of the order. This book will mainly cover the outstanding two-hundred-year-long history of the Knights Templar. It will dive deep into how the order was created after the First Crusade, how it rose to dominance and stayed in power for all those years, and the causes of its downfall from being the most influential military organization to essentially a myth. In addition, it will also focus on the structure of the order to better explain what kept it so well organized throughout the years. Finally, it will describe some of the figures who played key parts in its history. And, of course, we will talk about the twisted legacy of the Knights Templar.

Section One: Origins of the Order

Chapter 1: The First Crusade

The First Crusade was a defining moment in world history. Of course, it did not only have immense religious consequences. The First Crusade also completely transformed the political landscape of the known world and disrupted the balance of power that existed prior to it. Ultimately, however, it led to the creation of the Knights Templar; thus, the First Crusade is pivotal in understanding how the order came to exist. This chapter will cover the history of the First Crusade and explain its significance in relation to the formation of the Order of the Templars.

An Unstable Europe

The dawn of the new millennium saw Europe in the midst of all kinds of power struggles and crises. The continent was as divided as ever and was still trying to form its own identity. In Iberia, the *Reconquista* was still underway, with the Catholics trying to reclaim the lost peninsula from the Muslims. The British Isles were unstable due to constant invasions from Scandinavia. The Normans had even found their way into the Mediterranean, having arrived in southern Italy and Sicily, where they established a foothold in these regions as fierce fighters and mercenaries, ready to seek gold and adventure. Germany and France perhaps had the least problems, but even there, constant uprisings plagued the monarchs. In the East, what was once the great and powerful Eastern Roman Empire was struggling to keep the territories that it had left together, as it was under constant threat from all sides.

Amidst all these major actors was another player in Europe that sought to increase his influence over the continent. That was, of course, the pope. The papacy was constantly trying to remind everyone that it was the highest authority in the Christian world, only second to God himself. It considered itself an institution to which the rulers of all the Christian kingdoms should answer. While the European monarchs were not exactly keen on this idea, there was virtually nothing that they could do about it. The papacy was, in many cases, a thorn in the side of many rulers. Though they all respected the papacy as an institution and recognized its holy nature, this loyalty would prove to be an inconvenience from time to time. The pope would often excommunicate those he believed disobeyed his direct orders or violated the general principles of Christianity.

One of the best examples of this is what happened between Henry IV of Germany and Pope Gregory VII. The pope was a pragmatist who wanted to reform the church and wipe out the corruption that existed within the highest ranks. King Henry, on the other hand, was tired of the papacy's involvement with the internal affairs of Germany. An additional reason behind the escalation of the tension between the two is that Henry controlled most of northern Italy, including Rome, where the papacy was located. Thus, Henry was not content when the pope wanted to centralize Rome's power even more. The disputes eventually led to the excommunication of Henry from the church in 1074 and further instabilities surrounding the power struggles of the papacy.

Henry IV and his supporters were shocked by Pope Gregory's decision to excommunicate the king. Henry's ancestor, Otto I, was crowned by Pope John XII as the emperor in 962 in Rome. Henry had a unique position of power, and he would not give it up easily. Thus, when the bishops of Germany and northern Italy were summoned to a council at Brixen in 1080, they declared that Pope Gregory had abused the powers given to him by God and proposed that he should be removed from the position. They also nominated the next pope, Wibert, Archbishop of Ravenna, who would eventually be crowned Pope Clement III some four years later in 1084, when Henry IV was finally able to march on Rome and take the city from the papacy's control. He then became the Holy Roman emperor.

Of course, the papacy was not just willing to give up without a fight either. Henry had made it clear that he was ready to take the necessary steps to keep the institution in check. The members that fled the city after its conquest first elected Victor III as the new legitimate pope, one who was independent of Henry or Clement III. But the untimely death of Victor III just a year and a half later made them elect a new pope yet again. This time, it was Cardinal Bishop Odo of Ostia, who would be known as Urban II. However, he still would not be recognized in the lands of the Holy Roman Empire as the legitimate pope, as the German and northern Italian bishops fully supported Clement III.

The Two Popes

Thus, the situation in Europe prior to the start of the First Crusade was pretty messy overall. In a period of uncertainty and instability, the two popes—Clement III and Urban II—coexisted in a weird environment. The former was backed by the most powerful man in Europe at the time, Henry IV. The latter, on the other hand, was elected by the weakened papacy that believed Henry IV had committed a crime against the holiest institution in the world and, therefore, the whole religion.

These differences between the two popes made the Christian world very confused. Clement III was trying his best to reinforce his position as the true pope. He resided in Rome under the protection of Emperor Henry and was very much leading the Catholic Church. He was acting as the pope should; he contacted different rulers and offered his help, support, and advice. For example, he communicated with the archbishop of Canterbury in England and invited him for a visit to Rome. He also made contact with the Serbs, sending one of their archbishops a traditional pallium—an ecclesiastic vestment worn by the highest-ranking officials of the church. In short, he was acting as the pope should have acted. He had ongoing conversations with different parts of the Christian world and did not interfere too much in internal affairs—something that he had learned was not the wisest thing to do from Pope Gregory.

Urban II, on the other hand, could not even safely enter Rome. He did visit the city on a couple of occasions during the Christmases of 1091 and 1092, but he was forced to stay outside of the walls for most of his visit and departed the city quickly, eager not to overstay his welcome. Plus, he did not have the support of Henry or the bishops of Germany and northern Italy. Urban's efforts to contact the Christian world were more small-scale and, thus, inconsequential. He would occasionally send letters of support and encouragement with his blessings, like in Iberia, where the process of kicking out the Muslims was beginning to be more and more successful. However, Urban could not gain a strong foothold as the legitimate pope, especially when compared to his rival counterpart.

Surprisingly, Urban found a different, rather unusual ally to strengthen his position. That was the Eastern Orthodox Church. An important thing to remember is that the Great Schism saw the division of the Christian Church into the Western Catholic and Eastern Orthodox Churches. The separation, which happened in 1054, was a culmination of the already deteriorating relations between Rome and Constantinople—the two pillars of the Christian world that were still under Christian control. Because of different distinctions that existed between the Latin and Greek cultures and their respective practices of the religion, which were sometimes as petty as whether or not unleavened bread should be used in the sacrament of communion, the Christian Church split in two, forever damaging the relations between the East and the West.

Thus, when Urban II realized that he was not really gaining any considerable progress with Catholic Europe, he turned his attention to the east to try to repair relations with Constantinople as much as possible to have someone back him up. His efforts were met with relative warmth, considering the fact that Urban was effectively the first pope to try and communicate with the Eastern Church after the Great Schism. Both the Byzantine emperor, Alexios I, and the patriarch of Constantinople, Nikephoros III Grammatikos, expressed their sympathies with Urban's wishes to civilly discuss the differences that existed between the two branches. The emperor even invited the pope to Constantinople and proposed that a united council be convened. It would be attended by the senior clergy from both sides to further clarify the distinctions and resolve the existing disputes. The patriarch, on his part, offered his full support to the efforts of reuniting the church, declaring in a private letter to Urban that he desired "with all [his] heart...the unity of the Church."

Urban's move was pretty successful. The relations started to heal and promised a hopeful future with the Western and the Eastern Churches united. Urban now had won the hearts of the Byzantines, even lifting the excommunication of the Byzantine emperor that had been passed in 1081—another sign that their alliance was not something one could just easily look over. Pope Clement could do nothing but watch from the sidelines as his rival slowly achieved a feat that no one had even thought of. When Clement found out about the frequent letters between Urban and Nikephoros, it was too late to act. Urban was victorious in the battle of the two popes, as he repaired the relations with the East and the West and established himself as the leader of the Christian world.

Trouble in the East

While Urban was busy reinforcing his position as the legitimate pope by repairing the relations with the Eastern Church and, therefore, the Byzantine Empire, Emperor Alexios was struggling to keep his vast lands under his control. Once upon a time, the Eastern Roman Empire was the richest, biggest, and most powerful empire in the known world, stretching from the Balkans to the Middle East. It even controlled parts of North Africa. In addition, four out of the five Christian holy sites were under its control. The Byzantines were proud because holding Constantinople, Antioch, Alexandria, and Jerusalem was a pretty big achievement, especially since the West only had Rome, the so-called "Eternal City," which had lost most of its glory after the collapse of the Western Roman Empire.

However, the Byzantine Empire was under constant threat from all sides, which eventually caused its decline. The Byzantines were overextended and could not effectively contain all the invasions. Thus, by 1095, it had lost most of its territories, only being able to hold on to the core regions in eastern Europe, as well as the western parts of Anatolia and some of the lands that bordered the Black Sea. Most importantly, by the 7th century, the empire had lost three of the four holy sites that it once held, with only Constantinople, the capital of the empire, standing strong.

Prophet Muhammad's successors swarmed the Byzantine positions in Asia Minor and the Middle East. While the Byzantines were occupied with defending their territories against invasions from the Bulgars in the north, the Muslims conquered Persia, then Syria, Palestine, and Egypt, seizing Jerusalem, Antioch, and Alexandria in the process. The dominating Umayyad Caliphate managed to conquer all of North Africa and Spain—the lands that were once part of the great Roman Empire and were predominantly occupied by Christians. The Europeans only responded when the threat of the Muslims invading mainland Europe became too close for comfort. After the Muslim forces sacked the city of Bordeaux in 732, the French forces were able to halt their advance at the Battle of Poitiers and drive them back to Iberia. Despite this, the Muslim naval attacks continued in Sicily and parts of southern Italy. The idea of a united Christian effort to stop the Muslims did not exist back then, and it would take some 350 more years for it to develop. Only with the help of the Norman mercenaries were the Christians able to start fighting back in Spain and Sicily.

The Umayyads and their successors—the Abbasids—did treat those they conquered with respect. The rulers permitted the practice of different religions as long as those people paid a special tax. They also did not forbid the pilgrims who wished to visit the Holy Land. However, this would all change with the arrival of the Seljuk Turks. They came from the Eurasian Steppe, and they conquered the caliphate, converting to Islam shortly afterward. The Seljuks were different from the Umayyads and the Abbasids since they were far more vicious when it came to treating people of other religions and cultures. When they seized Jerusalem in 1065, they massacred the Christian population of the city, publicly shaming the patriarch and killing those who opposed them. After that, they proceeded to defeat the Byzantine forces in the decisive Battle of Manzikert in 1071, driving the Christians out of most of Anatolia and conquering the Byzantine city of Nicaea.

Losing Nicaea was disastrous for the Byzantines. Not only was it one of the biggest cities in the empire, but it was also very close to Constantinople, lying some ninety-five kilometers (sixty miles) southwest. There was no doubt that if they weren't stopped, the Turks would continue advancing until they arrived at the capital. Still, Emperor Alexios had not lost all hope. He knew that if Constantinople fell, the Muslims would have another direct gateway to Europe, which, in a way, would have been worse than when they controlled Iberia. At this time, the eastern European nations were not nearly as organized or powerful as the French, who stopped the Arab threat at Poitiers. Realizing the true scale of the imminent threat, Alexios turned to get aid from the West, sending a desperate letter in early 1095 to Pope Urban, asking for Europe to answer the call to arms.

Deus Vult

Fortunately for Alexios, when the messenger arrived at the Council of Piacenza in March of 1095, Pope Urban had managed to further consolidate his position as the true pope. The biggest development in that regard was the fact that Prince Conrad, heir to Henry IV of Germany, had sworn his loyalty toward Urban and denounced Clement III. Prince Conrad was one of many "defectors" from Henry's (and therefore Clement III's) camp. Many prestigious priests and Henry's own wife had switched sides and declared their support for Pope Urban. So, when Urban called the meeting at Piacenza in German-controlled territory to discuss an array of ecclesiastical issues, it seemed that he had finally grasped the victory in his rivalry with Clement III.

This was the situation with Urban when the Byzantine envoys unexpectedly arrived at Piacenza to deliver the news of the struggling Byzantine Empire and to ask for help from the pope. The whole council was shocked to hear the news. According to the messengers, the Byzantine Empire would not be able to hold off the Turks for long and was in need of immediate help. Urban carefully listened as the envoys delivered the message. He was quick to realize that there was a decision for him to make. He could try to urge the Europeans to go to Alexios's aid and defend against the Turks. This would be a graceful act and would definitely improve his already great relations with the Byzantines. More importantly, however, it was an opportunity for Urban to cement himself as the true leader of the Christian world and unite the church once and for all.

Urban knew that he had a near-impossible task. Assembling Europe's forces was quite a feat to achieve. He did want to help Alexios, but he needed the armies of different rulers, who would be skeptical of funding an expedition thousands of miles in the east in unknown lands against an unknown foe. This was what was going on in Urban's mind on his way to Clermont, France, in mid-1095. Over the course of the summer, he set out to recruit different powerful Italian and French leaders to his cause. He also sent out envoys to assemble a council of virtually unseen levels of importance at Clermont, which would focus on the ongoing political matters as well as ecclesiastical issues.

When the council assembled in November of 1095, Urban had already managed to sway Raymond of Toulouse, a powerful sponsor, to aid in the campaign. Urban hoped Raymond's help would motivate others to join him. At the council with the clergy and many French knights, whom the pope had also asked to assemble. Urban waited for the end of the council to deliver his speech, in which he described the situation in Anatolia and discussed the importance of Europe's answer to Byzantium's cause. In fact, his description was so terrifying that it almost felt like an over-exaggeration. He urged the Europeans to unite and fight for the same cause. "So let all feuds between you cease, quarrels fall silent, battles end and the conflicts of all disagreements fall to rest. Set out on the road to the Holy Sepulchre and deliver that land from a wicked race!"[93]

---

[93] Somerville, R. (1974).

The pope's message was so powerful that it was met with a loud response from the assembled. "Deus vult!" the crowd shouted. "God wills it!" The council would be dismissed after this grand finale, still mesmerized by the power of the pope's speech. Urban was pretty content with the outcome too. At Clermont, he did not propose a plan of attack, the route the Europeans should take to the Holy Land, or any other logistical issue for that matter. All those details could wait. He did, however, promise eternal salvation to those who participated and incited his audience, motivating them to follow God's will. After the council, envoys would be sent all over Europe to spread the pope's message. They claimed that those who would answer his call would forever be remembered as heroes.

The March to the Holy Land

Soon enough, the Christian world started answering the pope's call. About thirty thousand people, a pretty sizeable force, were assembled in the end, and they were all motivated by one purpose: cleansing the Holy Land of the Muslim conquerors and reclaiming what had been taken from them. The First Crusade consisted of people of all ages, statuses, and professions, and they all took part for different reasons. A lot of the participants were knights who were there for the glory. They loved adventure and a challenge, and they wanted to make a name for themselves. There were also many commoners, those who had nothing to lose and hoped to get rich or die trying. The others were dedicated Christians. They understood what lay ahead of them and the risks that were involved with journeying to distant lands, but they were willing to sacrifice everything for the sake of their religion and their loyalty to the pope. To all these Crusaders, the First Crusade was like a divine mission, their destiny even, and all of them embraced it in a way that suited them the most.

Still, despite the fact that the assembled force was quite sizeable and deeply motivated to venture to these unknown lands, the problems the Crusaders encountered were difficult to deal with. The most obvious of these problems were the aforementioned logistical issues. For instance, the first wave of the Crusaders, led by French priest Peter the Hermit, consisted mostly of ordinary, poor citizens. They ravaged the German lands and assaulted Jewish communities that lived in the Rhineland region. Of course, those who were massacred and looted had nothing to do with the Crusade, nor did they pose any threat to Peter the Hermit's men. The People's Crusade, as it became known later, was ultimately pretty unsuccessful, and it is not hard to understand why. Upon their entry into Anatolia in October of 1096, they were quickly defeated by the Seljuk forces.

The map of the First Crusade

However, the disastrous People's Crusade would be followed by an effort known as the Princes' Crusade. This time, a more organized force that consisted of trained soldiers and was led by a group of European nobles took on the challenge. Raymond of Toulouse was in charge of the southern French forces, Bohemond of Taranto led a smaller force of Normans from Italy, and Godfrey de Bouillon had assembled the men from Upper and Lower Lorraine. These princes were also joined by several other powerful nobles like Robert Curthose, the son of England's William the Conqueror, and Robert II, Count of Flanders. Together, the army counted almost 100,000 men—a force of unseen size and strength.

The Crusaders saw initial success after they crossed into the Muslim-occupied territory, taking the city of Nicaea with the help of Byzantine ships in June 1097. Then, they successfully defended against an attack at the Battle of Dorylaeum, allowing them to strengthen their position in Anatolia. However, the worst part of their journey was still ahead of them, as the march to the Holy Land was very slow and difficult. The lack of organization and the huge size of the army was disadvantageous. The Crusaders were ill-supplied and suffered thousands of desertions due to starvation and disease. Thus, when they reached the city of Antioch in October 1097, the Crusaders did not fancy their chances of taking it with a frontal assault. Antioch was one of the largest and most defended Muslim cities, so the Crusaders decided to starve it out and prepared the siege in late October. The siege of Antioch would be one of the most tumultuous endeavors of the Crusades, with the city surviving for months while the attackers struggled to maintain high morale and discipline. They continued to lose numbers due to attrition.

The indecisiveness of the Crusaders, paired with misinformation from Stephen de Blois, the son of William the Conqueror who would eventually desert, who claimed that there was no hope of taking the city, caused Emperor Alexios to halt his reinforcements and not come to the aid of the Crusaders. When the Crusaders eventually entered the city in June 1098 after help from the Christian population inside, they decimated the Muslim inhabitants and sacked Antioch to the ground. Just days afterward, they sallied out of the city to defend against the Muslim relief forces and completely routed them. At that point, it became clearer than ever that the Crusaders were ready to move on to their next and final target: the holy city of Jerusalem.

The march to Jerusalem would be even more difficult, with the Crusaders reaching it one year after they had taken Antioch, in June 1099. The Muslims, who were aware of the imminent attack, made the journey to Jerusalem hell for the Christians, evacuating everyone they could from the towns on the way and destroying potential supplies by poisoning the wells and burning down trees. By the time the Crusaders laid siege to the city, they had even fewer means of attacking it than Antioch. They only counted about fifteen thousand men, had little food and water, and not enough supplies to build good siege equipment. Thus, the initial assault in mid-June failed, and the Crusaders were forced to retreat back to their positions. Crucially, in late June, Genoese sailors would arrive at the port of Jaffa, delivering much-needed wood and food to the attackers.

At that point, the Crusaders were fed up with their failed attempts at capturing the city, as well as being ridiculed and taunted by the Muslim defenders, who would often raise crosses on the city walls and mock them. Filled with hatred and further motivated by preachers to take back the city of God, the Crusaders went on to fiercely attack Jerusalem with new siege towers they had constructed with the help of the Genoese. They did not stop their efforts even after they managed to get into the city on July 15th, 1099. The Crusaders were not content with just capturing Jerusalem. They went on to sack it to the best of their ability, massacring all the non-Christians they came across. They showed no mercy to the defeated Muslims. They burned down the mosques, believing that dealing with the Muslims ruthlessly was the only right way of cleansing the Holy City. Overwhelmed with what victory felt like, many of the Crusaders fell on their knees and started praying in the Holy Sepulchre, thanking God for empowering them to fulfill their divine mission. After four very long years, the First Crusade was finally over.

The Aftermath of the First Crusade

The First Crusade was a unique campaign. A united European force had never really been seen before, let alone traveled thousands of miles east to unknown lands, motivated by a holy cause. It is remarkable enough that the effort was made, let alone that it was ultimately successful. In a way, the First Crusade's success was also helped by the relative weakness of their enemy. By the time the Crusaders reached Anatolia, the Muslims were divided and could not set aside their differences to assemble competent enough armies to fight off the invaders. Jerusalem, for example, was held by the Egyptian Fatimids, who were Shi'a Muslims and rivals with the Sunni Turkish Muslims who controlled much of Anatolia. However, the Turkish Muslims were separated into smaller warring kingdoms. Because of this disunity, which was caused by the cultural differences between the Muslim kingdoms, and the inability to produce a united war effort, the Crusaders established four Catholic kingdoms in the conquered lands: the County of Edessa, the Principality of Antioch, the County of Tripoli, and the Kingdom of Jerusalem. Godfrey de Bouillon was the first ruler of the Kingdom of Jerusalem, but he refused to call himself king

instead preferring the title of Protector of the Holy Sepulchre. After his death just one year later, he would be succeeded by his brother, Baldwin I. He would become the first true king of the Kingdom of Jerusalem, and he was crowned at the Church of the Nativity. A Catholic patriarch was also installed in the Holy City, signaling that the newly established territories were independent of any Byzantine influence and were, therefore, European.[94]

The victory obtained in the First Crusade would be celebrated all over the Christian world. People believed that the will of God had been fulfilled. The ones who succeeded and returned home safely would be crowned as legends, while the deserters would forever be damned. Crucially, in the years following the capture of Jerusalem, waves of pilgrims would start venturing out to the Holy Land to experience its divinity firsthand. However, despite the victory of the Crusaders, the route to the Holy Land was still not safe. The pilgrims would be attacked on their way to the holy sites, sparking a need for a force to defend those who wished to visit Jerusalem. What the Latin kingdoms of the East needed was a group of individuals who would devote their lives to the cause of defending all Christians in the Holy Land.

---

[94] Frankopan, P. (2012). The First Crusade: The Call from the East. Belknap Press of Harvard University Press. Chapters: 1, 7, 11-12. Napier, G. (2011). The Rise and Fall of the Knights Templar. History Press. Chapter 1.Somerville, R. (1974). The Council of Clermont (1095), and Latin Christian Society." Archivum Historiae Pontificiae, 12, 55-90.

Chapter 2: Not-so Humble Beginnings

Despite the seemingly impossible challenge, the First Crusade was ultimately successful. The Christians had successfully managed to reclaim the Holy Land and even established European-led kingdoms in the Middle East. It was a proud achievement for all of the Christian world, and it opened up the opportunity for European pilgrims to travel to the lands. However, that task would require much more than sheer will. It would require a force to protect those who wished to pray in the Holy Land. This need led to the creation of the Order of the Templars. This chapter will explore exactly how the Knights Templar originated.

Hugues de Payens

Establishing a foothold in the Holy Land was a pretty significant feat for Europe. After all, it was the fulfillment of God's will; the Christians were destined to return to Jerusalem. Thus, when the news of the triumph reached Europe, there was a wave of pilgrims that wished to travel to the Holy Land. Before the First Crusade, different Muslim rulers would treat the Christian pilgrims differently, with some being more tolerant than others when it came to letting them travel, let alone practice their religion and culture. But the victory in the First Crusade was an opportunity for the Christians to permanently reclaim what had been lost to the Muslims.

However, there was one problem. More than half of all the Crusaders who managed to survive the campaign had returned home, taking back all the riches they could with them. Those who returned home would be celebrated as heroes and be respected in their communities. Unfortunately for those who wished to stay in the newly conquered Holy Land or travel to it after the Crusade, there was a big issue. There was a shortage of men to defend the Latin kingdoms. The four kingdoms amounted to a small Christian state surrounded by a hostile Muslim world. The Turks, despite their somewhat weakened position, still controlled most of Anatolia, the only path overland that connected the two continents.

Thus, the pilgrims were mistaken when they thought that their "grand return" to the Holy Land would be guaranteed after the victory. Yes, those who wished to take a more expensive sea route from the ports of Venice and Genoa could get to Jerusalem and the other kingdoms relatively safely, but those who wished to travel overland almost always fell prey to the Turks, who were less friendly with the traveling Christians and understandably so. Even those who traveled by sea would encounter all sorts of bandits on their way from the port of Jaffa to the Holy City. These bandits would strip them from all the possessions they had and then oftentimes massacre them.

All in all, there was a need for some kind of a police force to be created to ensure a safer route for the pilgrims. After all, this was the whole reason the Crusade had taken place—to connect the Christians back to their roots. A now-legendary French knight, Hugues (Hugh) de Payens, would take the initiative into his own hands. Not much is known about Hugues de Payens. He was a vassal of the count of Champagne and probably visited Jerusalem while in the count's entourage in 1104. There is speculation that he had been to the Holy Land prior to that visit, but whether or not he actually participated in the First Crusade is not known. He would be the crucial factor in creating the Order of the Templars.

The creation of the order is described as a very noble decision by William of Tyre, a Levantine bishop who wrote about the Templars about sixty years later. According to him, the nine knights, who were led by Hugues de Payens, approached King Baldwin II of Jerusalem in 1118 with a request to grant them the right to protect the "roads and routes against the attacks of robbers and brigands." The nine knights gave away all of their material possessions and devoted themselves to the service of God and the good of all Christians. They would become warrior monks, living together in poverty and vowing to be chaste.[95] These nine knights further developed the concept of the "ideal" or "chivalrous" Christian knight that was so prevalent in the Middle Ages. A lot of European knights had done similar things at the beginning of the First Crusade, such as giving away all of their possessions to the poor to fully dedicate themselves to a greater cause. Hugues de Payens and his companions, in a way, embodied the spirits of those knights, as they sacrificed everything for a noble cause that would not only prove their allegiance to the powerful upper class but also help the poor.

Thus, King Baldwin II of Jerusalem was instantly taken up by the idea of a force of noble individuals that wanted to protect the traveling pilgrims. He granted Hugues de Payens and his men the former Al-Aqsa Mosque as their headquarters. The Al-Aqsa Mosque was one of the biggest and the most sacred mosques in all of the Muslim world, and giving it to the brotherhood whose goal was to directly oppose the Muslims was symbolically significant. There, at the Temple Mount, Hugues de Payens would officially become the leader of the brotherhood. He would be the Master of the Temple, and the nine knights would come to be known as the first Templars. The brotherhood would be called the Poor Knights of Christ and the Temple of Solomon, but they are best known as the Knights Templar. Together, they vowed their loyalty to the patriarch of Jerusalem, to live as monks, and fight against those who disturbed the travelers wishing to reach the Holy City.

The First Templars

Besides Hugues de Payens, there is little known about the other founding members of the brotherhood. The most famous was Godfrey de Saint-Omer from Picardy. The others were André de Montbard, Payen de Montdidier, Geoffrey Bisol, Roland, Gondomar, and the final member, whose name we do not know. These nine men were the first Templars. They dwelled in the Al-Aqsa Mosque, living as monks in extreme poverty. It is for this reason that their knighthood is even more impressive, especially when compared to traditional European knights.

The word of the order spread quickly throughout the Christian world. For the first decade of their existence, Templars lived as monks and defended the pilgrims from Jaffa to Jerusalem, just as they had vowed to do. They quickly impressed those who traveled to the Holy Land and

---

[95] Napier, G. (2011).

even attracted supporters from the West. For example, the Templars came across Fulk V, Count of Anjou, who visited the Holy Land in 1120. The count was very impressed with the noble deeds of the order and offered to show his support by annually gifting them silver. Fulk V was one of the first associates of the Templar Order, with other European nobles following his example.

Thus, by 1127, the Templars had already gained much recognition not only in Outremer (the land of the Crusader States) but also in mainland Europe. This was one of the reasons for their diplomatic mission to France. Organized by Baldwin II, the Templars traveled to Anjou to convince their trusted friend, Fulk V, to marry Baldwin's daughter, Melisende. The count of Anjou was a very powerful noble, which shows the significance of the mission that was entrusted to the Templars. Not only that, but Melisende was also the heiress to the throne of the Kingdom of Jerusalem, meaning that Baldwin was offering Fulk the opportunity to become the next ruler of the kingdom.

In addition to this mission, Grand Master Hugues, who was leading the delegation, had another task to accomplish during his visit to Europe. He needed to recruit more knights to join the order. Baldwin had told Hugues his plans of expanding the Crusader States, and he needed men to fight in what was supposed to be the next Crusade against Damascus. It is not exactly clear whether or not the order had grown or not by this point. While some sources say that there were already around thirty knights in the order, others claim that it still consisted of the original nine. Either way, new recruits would be pretty useful. It would ensure that the order remained strong after the service of the original nine Templars while also providing for a better force to combat the ongoing problem of the endangered traveling pilgrims.

The seal of the Grand Master of the Order of the Knights Templar. Courtesy of Andrew Simsky
https://commons.wikimedia.org/wiki/File:Seal_of_Templars.jpg

It is widely believed that during their visit to Europe, the Templars showed they were not as poor as when they had started out. They had sworn to live in austerity, but the extent to which they went to keep this promise in the early years is truly remarkable. Sources recount the early Templars wearing borrowed, torn clothes since they had given away everything that they owned prior to joining the order. Some speculate that it is why the seal of the Grand Master features two men sharing a horse since it symbolizes their extreme austerity. Despite the fact that the word "poor" would remain in the official name of the order, by the time King Baldwin had sent them on the diplomatic mission to Europe, they had managed to start accumulating some material possessions. They were by no means poor.

The Templar delegation met with many different powerful men of Europe, and each of them was kind enough to donate generous gifts to the order. For instance, Theobald, Count of Blois, and William Clito, Count of Flanders, gifted the order some lands and the right to feudal reliefs on their territories. Others followed the example of Fulk of Anjou and donated gold and silver to Hugues and his companions. Even commoners, who were astonished by the stories of the Templars, which depicted them almost like popular heroes who defended the pilgrims in Outremer, would give them whatever they could, such as clothes and food. A number of people even offered to willingly join the ranks of the Templars, as they were fascinated with the idea of traveling to the city of God and doing the right thing.

All in all, the tour of Europe proved to be pretty successful for the order. By late 1127, they had traveled all over the continent and met the most important figures of the time while also collecting gracious donations and being joined by more men who wished to practice the Templar life. This boosted the popularity of the Knights Templar massively, spreading their name throughout the Christian world and organizing crucial connections that would last for many years to come.

Bernard of Clairvaux and the Council of Troyes

There was one other man who the Templars met that would influence their legacy forever. That man was Bernard of Clairvaux, an abbot who was already known for his charisma and passion for practicing the Christian religion his own way. According to some stories, for example, he jumped in a pool of freezing water when he was a young man to "cool from the heat of carnal longing." After becoming a monk, Bernard joined the famous Cistercian Order at Citeaux with about thirty more of his fellow Burgundian followers. The amazing nature in which he preached, as well as how he led the Cistercians, earned him a name in France. In fact, Hugh of Champagne, after returning home from his second visit to the Holy Land when he came across the Templars, gifted Bernard a piece of his land to establish a new monastery and further expand the Cistercian Order. They renamed the place Clairvaux, Valley of Light, and attracted passionate people from all over France to join them. The Cistercians are also known as the Bernardines, further implying the abbot's significance on the order.

Bernard of Clairvaux

Bernard of Clairvaux and the Cistercian Order firmly believed that true purity could only be achieved by severe austerity and chastity. Thus, he and his followers strictly followed the Rule of Saint Benedict, unlike the majority of the clergy and the ecclesiastic world of the time, which were more associated with luxury. Bernard believed that sacrificing material possessions and struggling was the right way to achieve purity. Therefore, whenever he met the Templars, it was no surprise that he was instantly impressed by them. It is possible that King Baldwin had sent a letter to Bernard prior to Hugues de Payens's visit to Europe, where Hugues asked the abbot to help him devise the official rules of living for the Templars, as well as gain more support in the West. Bernard could have also been aware of the situation in Outremer through Hugh de Champagne since he often contacted the count, who was gracious enough to build the monasteries of the Cistercians and donate to them on many occasions. In addition, André de Montbard, one of the original nine Templars, was Bernard's uncle. Either way, he knew of the troubles in Outremer.

Bernard of Clairvaux would play a crucial role in cementing the Templars' position in Europe and help them finally obtain the recognition that they (or at least King Baldwin) sought in the apostolic world. Thus, on January 13th, 1129, after about a year and a half of the Templar delegation traveling all over Europe and making acquaintances with most of the powerful nobles of the continent, the Council of Troyes would be convened. It would change the fate of the Knights Templar forever. It could be argued that this council was the most significant meeting after the origin of the First Crusade. It was presided by Cardinal Bishop Andrew of Albano, who represented Pope Honorius II. Other influential members of the Christian world were present, such as the archbishops of Sens and Rheims with their own small delegations of bishops. Bernard was also present, despite reportedly suffering from fever, as well as Stephen Harding, who was the new abbot of Citeaux. Theobald of Blois attended the council, and he had very sympathetic views of the Templars and Bernard. Of course, the Templar delegation was also there, with Hugues de Payens as its head.

The Latin Rule of the Templars

Hugues de Payens would be given the honor of giving a speech at the Council of Troyes. In his speech, he would tell of the origins of the Templar Order. At first, he described the grim situation of Outremer, how the devout pilgrims who wished to visit the Holy City suffered on their way to Jerusalem and how the Latin kingdoms of the East were surrounded by swarms of enemies. He spoke of how the Templars lived, of their austere ways of wearing plain clothes and being allowed only one horse. He also spoke of the Templars sharing everything that they owned. They ate together and tried to avoid any contact with women. Finally, Hugues briefly told them of the hierarchy within the order, saying that the Templars answered to him, the Grand Master, while the order was loyal to the patriarch of Jerusalem.

The council was impressed by Hugues. However, despite the fact that they mostly praised the Templar practices that the Grand Master described, everyone agreed that in order for the Knights Templar to be fully accepted in the Catholic Church as a religious order, they needed a written set of rules that would be ratified by the members of the council. This would ensure the Templars' official "enrollment" as a religious order.

Bernard of Clairvaux would propose drawing up a new official written version of the Templars' way of life. The seventy-three-clause document would become known as the Latin Rule of the Templars. It contained virtually everything about the Knights Templar, from their daily activities to the deeper concepts in which they believed. The Latin Rule of the Templars regulated nearly every aspect of a Templar's life, giving the men a concrete structure they had to follow. With its introduction, the Templar Order would transform its lifestyle to be more Benedictine (following the rule of Saint Benedict). This was due to the influence of Bernard, who himself was a devout Benedictine. Before the Latin Rule, the Knights Templar was considered to have been following the rule of Saint Augustine.

The Latin Rule recognized white as the main color of the Templars' clothing, symbolizing the fact that the Templars had put the darkness of their life behind them. The white habit became synonymous with the Templars, even though the iconic red cross was not added until later. White should have only been worn by the actual members of the order, while their sergeants and squires were required to wear either black or brown clothing. Only those who were deemed "Knights of Christ" were worthy of wearing white, at least according to the Latin Rule. In addition to this, everything the Templars wore needed to be easy to put on and take off; for example, it should not have any additional laces. This detail further underlined the simplicity of their life.

Knights Templar in their typical attire
https://commons.wikimedia.org/wiki/File:Knights-templar.jpg

The Latin Rule also regulated how the order should treat newcomers, saying that boys should not be accepted until they were able to wield weapons and bear arms. It also underlined that brothers should only serve until the end of their fixed term and be allowed to return to secular life afterward. There were rules about the misconduct of the Templars and how they should be dealt with. Generally, the Latin Rule was pretty strict. It treated nearly all misdemeanors, from deserting the battlefield to leaving the castle without permission, with the same severity: expulsion. A lot has been said about the discipline and the strict hierarchy within the order. The Grand Master was the true, supreme leader of the Templars. He oversaw every possible thing that was concerned with the order. He had virtually unrestricted power, and every Templar would have respected him. Not only that but his word was almost thought to have been as important as the word of God himself, showing the allegiance that the Templars had toward their leader.

The physical appearance of the Templars was also noted. Beards and monks' tonsures were mandatory to further promote the sense of equality and brotherhood in the order. The Latin Rule proposed two meals a day that should be silent and communal—one at noon and the other at dusk—with meat only being allowed three times a week. Of course, any physical relationships with women were prohibited. The Latin Rule also underlined that Templars should be occupied with something at all times; chatting and just relaxing during their free time was forbidden. Instead, they should pray, organize clothing and equipment, or work in the stables. The number of horses for each Templar was also increased to three.

The Latin Rule organized the daily routine of the Knights Templar. It pointed out what the brethren should do at different hours of the day. The routine was pretty similar to the normal routine of a regular Catholic monk. This detail is important to understand in a wider context. Since most of the members of the council who drew up the Latin Rule were members of the clergy, the Latin Rule focused heavily on the matters that they were more aware of, which means they did not include much about the military aspects of the order. The Knights Templar was not, after all, a traditional religious order. The whole reason behind its creation was to deal with military matters. Templars were as much knights as they were monks. This was a unique combination that had never been seen before; thus, it was not understood very well.

Over time, new rules would be added, and the document would be expanded to include up to seven hundred clauses in total by the end of the 13th century. These new rules would contain more details about the different aspects of a Templar's life, including more emphasis on the military side of things. It would also be translated into French to be more accessible to the Templars. This was also an unprecedented development, taking into consideration the "superiority" of the Latin language over the other European languages in the Middle Ages, especially in ecclesiastical matters.

Transforming the Concept of Knighthood

All in all, the Templars' visit to Europe turned out to be more successful than they could have imagined. They managed to gain the international recognition that they so desperately needed, with many of the most powerful men in Europe fully supporting their existence. In addition, thanks to Bernard of Clairvaux and the Council of Troyes, they were officially accepted into the Catholic Church and had the backing of important members of the faith. Not only that, but they had also grown their ranks, returning home with men who wished to journey to

Outremer and serve in the order. King Baldwin had also accomplished his goal of swaying the count of Anjou, and it was almost certain that he would get the help that he needed from the West to help him fight off the Muslims in the Holy Land.

Spreading the word about the incorporation of the Knights Templar into the Catholic Church meant that there would be, without a doubt, some criticisms aimed toward the order. The most famous one was a letter signed by Hugo Peccator or Hugh the Sinner. While the exact author of this letter is not known, it is thought to be the work of theologian Hugh of Saint Victor. The author seemed to be skeptical about the nature of the order, calling the members people with "no wisdom." He criticized the role of the warrior monk and the implications that might come with it. Hugh warned the Templars not to be tempted by the Devil since he had the power to twist their will and corrupt them. He wanted the Templars to constantly be working on themselves, to try to understand their inner state and strive for personal salvation. For him, killing and hating one's enemies were devilish temptations, and he was worried the Templars might not be able to protect themselves from letting the Devil enter their hearts.

Similar criticisms came from other religious personas. Prior Guigo of the Carthusian Order, for example, also sent a letter to Hugues de Payens sometime in 1129, reminding the Grand Master not to mix the military side of the Knights Templar with the religious side. He stressed that in order for the Templars' killings to be justified, they should first "purge [their] souls of vices, then the lands from the barbarians."

These criticisms were defended by none other than Bernard of Clairvaux in his work called *In Praise of the New Knighthood* (*De laude novae militia*). In fact, he had been asked by Hugues de Payens to write such a document in light of the criticisms. It was originally written in Latin sometime after the Council of Troyes, presumably in the first part of the 1130s. The document strongly supported the idea of the warrior monk and praised the deeds of the Knights Templar. Bernard called the Templars and Hugues the "knights of Christ" and "Grand Master of the knights of Christ," respectively. He recognized the Templars as being a new separate form of knighthood, at least in comparison with the old concept that had originated in Europe after the collapse of the Roman Empire. He claimed that the Templars were the embodiment of the new ideal of knighthood, combining the monastic with the military and fighting in the name of God.

Traditionally, knights would serve their masters and get payment in return, which they would spend to either purchase lands and rise up in the ranks or get better, flashier equipment. Many knights who ventured to the Holy Land during the First Crusade searched for glory and praise, and they were hoping that reclaiming Jerusalem would bring them that. While they were certainly not wrong, Bernard claimed that the purpose of the Templars stood higher than all of them. There was nothing wrong with killing in the name of Christ. He distinguished between the "regular" form of killing, which would be murder, and the killing of evil. The former was undoubtedly a sin, while the latter was not. It was justified. Bernard even went as far as to say that not only those who would die for Christ could attain salvation but also those who killed in his name. In other words, he tried to prove that the Knights Templar was not only an honorable organization due to its exceptional monastic lifestyle but also because of its military side.

This distinction of the Templars representing a new higher form of knighthood played a vital role in the order's developing stages. In some sense, the Templars fully embraced the status that Bernard of Clairvaux had granted them. After all, the differences between the old and the new knights were apparent. The purpose of the old knight can clearly be seen even from his appearance: colorfully painted shields and lances, silk cloths and expensive armor for their horses, excessive attention to detail, and expensive gold or silver-plated ornaments all over their equipment. This appearance expressed their prior success, wealth, and status as knights. The flashy appearance of a traditional knight can be considered a sign of his innate motives, which, more often than not, had nothing to do with serving God. Bernard even compared knights to women due to their focus on appearances.

Templars were, in a way, the next step in the evolution of the image of the knight. They did not exist to fight for those who paid them the most or to rise up in the ranks or buy better equipment as a sort of upgrade. They did not perform actions for praise. Instead, they were warriors of God. They were the representation of what a Christian knight should be. The idea that had been mentioned by Pope Urban II at the Council of Clermont was further underlined and supported by Bernard. The pope had remarked that war against evil was just, while Bernard claimed that the true warriors of justice were the Knights Templar, as they fought against the looming evil in Outremer.

The pope was right to assume that the Crusading knights would be motivated to fight for a noble, pious cause. And while a good portion of the Crusading knights did genuinely go to war to reclaim the Holy Land, it was apparent that their initial motivations were overshadowed by their lust and greed, whereas the Templars had no such feelings since they lived the life of a monk. The introduction of the Knights Templar was followed by a subtle paradigm shift that affected both the church and the aristocracy of Europe. Templars were respected because of their devotion to their distinct, never-before-seen warrior monk lifestyle. After their appearance on the international scene, other knights were also expected to live by the Christian code of ethics as well.

Thus, those who were critical of the Templar Order's purpose and structure, although relatively few in number, were met with quite a fierce defense from one of the biggest allies of the Templars. With *In the Praise of the New Knighthood*, Bernard of Clairvaux further justified the creation of the Knights Templar. Instead of perceiving the "job" of a warrior monk as being nearly impossible to successfully pursue, he saw it as a noble cause that was only meant for the strongest in mind and body. His differentiation of "homicide" (sinful killing) and "malecide" (the killing of evil) was also crucial. It meant that the deeds of the Templars were not up to interpretation; they should not be judged by others because of their purpose. After all, the Templars had received blessings from King Baldwin, who granted them one of the most important holy sites in Jerusalem, as well as from the patriarch of Jerusalem. And now, they were backed by the majority of the Catholic Church in the West.

The trip to Europe was a stunning success. As the Templar delegation sailed back to Outremer, having established strong connections with the most powerful men of the West, the future of the order looked promising—and it certainly would be.[96]

---

[96] Napier, G. (2011). *The Rise and Fall of the Knights Templar*. History Press. Chapter 2.

Hill, P. (2018). *The Knights Templar at War, 1120-1312*. Pen & Sword Military. Chapter 1.

Barber, M. C. (1984). "The Social Context of the Templars." *Transactions of the Royal Historical Society*, 34, 27–46.

Martin, S. (2011). *The Knights Templar*. Oldcastle Books.

Chapter 3: The Return to Outremer

This chapter looks to explore the period after the Templars' visit to Europe up to the Second Crusade. By that time, the Knights Templar had managed to become pretty successful. It was now officially recognized in the West and was supported by the Christian world. The years that followed would only see the power of the Templars increase almost exponentially. They would become more and more involved in the important affairs of Outremer.

Damascus

The Templar delegation returned to Outremer in May 1129. Count Fulk of Anjou was also with them, having agreed to marry Melisende, King Baldwin's heiress. The king was fascinated by the success of the European tour. The Templars had achieved everything that he had desired. Through the recognition of the Templars, Baldwin also managed to raise the West's awareness of the situation in the Holy Land. He desperately needed men to fight for him, but the fight was not necessarily going to be defensive. Yes, attacks on Christian lands were still happening, but Baldwin had different goals in mind. He had his eyes fixed on Damascus.

Not only was the ancient city of Damascus one of the richest in the Near East, but it was also strategically very important. It was located about fifty miles from the Mediterranean, making it too close for comfort to the narrow stretch of Crusader-controlled lands. With enough effort and coordination, whoever ruled Damascus could control the land supply chains between the northern and southern parts of the Crusader States. The Muslim world was still not unified back then, and King Baldwin looked closely for a potential opportunity to take the city, as it would be a good outpost against future threats that came from Syria. Crucially, Tughtigin, the atabeg of Damascus, had passed away a year before the Templars' return to Outremer. The city was under the control of his son, Buri, who was not nearly as proficient at ruling as his father.

Buri had bad relations with a very important organization in Damascus: the Assassins. The Order of the Assassins was a secular sect of Shi'a Islam, and its aim was the elimination of powerful individuals who were considered potential threats. The problem was that Damascus was predominantly a Sunni Muslim city; thus, the Assassins were often frowned upon by the population. Atabeg Tughtigin had dealt with this issue by granting the Assassins control of the fortress of Banias, from which they conducted their operations. Buri, perhaps succumbing to the pressure due to being a young and inexperienced leader, started a purge of the Assassins in the autumn of 1129, causing unrest and riots throughout the province. The leader of the Assassins, Ismail, approached King Baldwin for help and offered him the fortress of Banias for protection.

Baldwin, of course, could not let this perfect opportunity get away. He called for help from the rest of the Latin kingdoms of the East and assembled an army with the count of Tripoli, the count of Edessa, and the prince of Antioch in late 1129. A squadron of Templars, including those recruited from Europe by Hugues de Payens, was also in the army. King Baldwin marched to Banias in November, where he came across the forces from Damascus. Atabeg Buri had stationed his army between Baldwin and the fortress and was waiting for the Crusaders to come to him. Baldwin, however, was hesitant to advance and stalled the stand-off.

The action started when a small force led by William of Bures decided to start pillaging the settlements near the fortress. They were ambushed by the Damascene vanguard about twenty miles from the main Crusader camp. The Damascene cavalrymen, who knew the landscape, destroyed the breakaway force, with only forty-five men surviving. Baldwin decided to advance quickly on the enemy forces after he heard the news of the ambush from the survivors. Unfortunately for him, heavy rain made it impossible for his army to go farther, and the attackers were forced to retreat.

This assault was King Baldwin's second failed attempt to capture Damascus. He had only managed to raid the surroundings of the city in 1126, and he was now forced to go back. Also, after crossing back to the Christian-controlled lands, the reinforcements that he had from the other Latin kingdoms also returned to their homes. This meant that Baldwin's chances of snatching Damascus had faded, as assembling a competent enough force would be more difficult as time passed. All in all, the failure to capture Damascus would prove to be fatal for the Crusaders in the long run.

The Three Papal Bulls

The failure to take Damascus did not really affect the Knights Templar. In a way, it further cemented their status as warriors against the forces of evil. We should not forget that the original goal of the Templars was to protect the pilgrims on their way to Jerusalem from the swarms of bandits that ambushed them. However, their transition from that role to fighters for the king of Jerusalem seemed very natural. It is as though it was a given from the very beginning. Although their exact identity is unknown, the Templars who participated in the Damascus campaign were skilled warriors.

The Damascenes had technically nothing to do with the pilgrims traveling to Outremer. Thus, the Templars technically should have had nothing to do with the Damascenes. But they did go to fight against them, signaling that their duties were not limited to dealing with bandits and thieves. Plus, it was still a noble cause. It can be argued that the Templars joined Baldwin's forces because they already considered the Muslims at Damascus as a threat, and the fact they fought against them made the Damascenes a legitimate "evil." Therefore, the actions of the Templars were justified back then, even if Baldwin's motivations included capturing the rich city just to expand his power in Outremer, not for defensive purposes.

After Damascus, the Templars' wealth started growing exponentially, thanks to the gracious donations the order received from all over the world. Gifting money, lands, castles, and different resources became a pretty common way for the givers to prove their piety. In fact, it was considered just as pious of a deed as contributing to building churches and directly supporting the clergy. The Templars themselves, of course, never really asked for donations since they followed the Benedictine lifestyle as outlined in the Latin Rule.

Among these avid supporters of the order was Pope Innocent II. Despite the fact that, in the 1130s, he still was not the one true, legitimate pope (he did not even dwell in Rome, unlike his rival, Pope Anacletus II), Innocent made sure that he showed his gratitude. After the Council of Pisa, which he had called in 1135, Pope Innocent collected a mark of gold and silver from the clergy each year and sent it to Outremer.

Pope Innocent's support would become even clearer with the issue of the first of three papal bulls that were concerned with the Knights Templar. In 1138, his rival, Anacletus, died. Innocent's supremacy was not to be challenged. A year later, he issued the first bull, named *Omne datum optimum*, a document that gave a list of privileges to the order. It was the first official, written evidence of papal support for the Templars. The first bull underlined the fact that the Templars were fighting in the name of Christ and were the defenders of the Christian faith. It also made it clear that the Grand Master of the Templar Order was to be elected by the brothers themselves without any outside interference, and it expanded his duties and rights as the head of the order.

This may have been the result of the influence of the newly elected Templar Grand Master, Robert de Craon, who succeeded Hugues de Payens after his passing in 1136. Robert de Craon was not only a great warrior. He was also known for his organizational skills. After his election, the new Grand Master would make it his goal to find official support for the order with help from the papacy. It could be argued that the first papal bull was a fruitful result of his efforts.

Alongside these points, the bull exempted the Templar Order from paying tithes and promised the order it could keep all spoils that were retrieved from the Muslims during their fighting. In addition, the bull granted the order the right to build chapels and churches and recruit members of the clergy to come and reside there. The leaders of the order were able to offer the clergy to stay as permanent members of the brotherhood after one year of serving, but they also had the right to expel them as they saw fit. In short, the papal bull gave the Templars an amazing opportunity to further grow their order, and it underlined how the order could boost its income and ensure stability.

The privileges of the Knights Templar would increase in the following years, as the new popes would introduce two more papal bulls. After *Omne datum optimum*, Pope Celestine II would issue *Milites Templi* in 1144, urging the clergy to collect resources for the Templars in exchange for one-seventh of their penance's remittal. Furthermore, it gave the Templars further access to the Christian churches of the world and made sure that they were received and treated with respect and care. *Militia Dei*, which was issued by Pope Eugenius III a year later, further consolidated the Templars' position. It gave them the right to collect their own tithes from the properties they owned, as well as bury their dead in their churches unless they had been excommunicated.

The three papal bulls put the Knights Templar at the center of the Christian world. It legitimized the order and gave them unseen levels of respect and privilege. By 1145, the Order of the Templars stood higher than virtually any other similar organization. It even had the firm backing of the papacy. Though there were some criticisms about granting the Templars this much independence and exclusive rights, there was nothing the critics could do to reverse the changes that had already been made and legitimized by the bulls. Due to the popes' efforts to show their support, the order would keep growing in size and wealth from other sources. The Templars participated in numerous military campaigns in Outremer for the good of Christianity, and they were generously rewarded for their noble efforts. The three bulls were issued to build on the previous successes of the order, with donations and funding swarming in.

The Templars in Iberia

The Templars would gain a strong foothold in the Iberian Peninsula, which began in the early years of their existence. Iberia was dominated by the Moors (which was a term Christians used to call Muslims, primarily those who were in Iberia or North Africa). They controlled the southern part of the peninsula by the 12th century. The Christians, however, had already started a (somewhat) united offensive to drive the Muslims out of the lands, which they considered to be Christian. The *Reconquista* was one of the most significant yet drawn-out and disoriented war efforts in history, and it lasted for centuries. Over time, progress was made by the Christian kingdoms to reconquer the lost lands. By 1085, King Alfonso VI of Castile had captured the central city of Toledo, weakening the Muslims' position.

Alongside the Kingdom of Castile and León—an entity that would change from time to time to include the names of both or just one of the two provinces until it finally united in the 13th century—there was the Kingdom of Aragon and the smaller but just as fierce counties of

Barcelona and Portugal (which became a kingdom in 1139). These states fought to drive the Muslims out of the peninsula, but oftentimes, they had internal problems and even challenged each other for supremacy in the region. The fight for Iberia became very important, almost like another Crusade, with Pope Paschal II even declaring that the sins of those who fought for the reinstitution of Christianity in Iberia would be remitted, just like in the First Crusade.

The Iberian kingdoms had already organized military orders or rather confraternities of knights to combat the Muslim threat at the beginning of the 12th century. After the rapid expansion of retrieving lands, Alfonso I of Aragon founded the Confraternity of Belchite in 1122 and the Order of Monreal in 1124. These confraternities were similar to the Knights Templar in the sense that their purpose was to combat the existing Muslim threat. The main difference is that they were not composed of warrior monks, and the knights who wished to join them did not have to live monastic lives. They were not Christian orders. Rather, they were communities of Christian knights that were employed by King Alfonso to fight the Moors in the south. Similar to the Templars, they were given different fortresses and small towns to conduct their operations from, and while they saw initial success, both confraternities would soon meet their end, as they could not deal with the overwhelming Muslim forces. Still, the main purpose of the confraternities was to provide military support to the king's forces and to patrol strategic lands, like narrow passes and valleys.

The appearance of the Templars in Iberia would prove to be a pivotal point for the *Reconquista*. It is logical to assume that the Templars first entered the peninsula during their visit to Europe when they had traveled all over the continent to spread the word about the formation of their order and gather any type of support they could. Interestingly, they first became involved in Portugal rather than in other Spanish kingdoms. At the time of their arrival, sometime in 1128, Portugal was not in the best of situations. There was a political crisis going on between Queen Teresa and her son, Afonso Henriques. Young Afonso had gathered support from Galician nobles, and he wanted independence from his mother. After a period of struggle and the important Battle of São Mamede, this would be granted to him in June of the same year. A couple of months before that, in March, Queen (technically Countess) Teresa would grant the Templars their first documented holding in Iberia: the Castle of Soure, which was located about fifty miles south of the town of Coimbra.

Prince Afonso would regift the castle to the Templars after he seized power from his mother. While this action may seem a bit unnecessary, by doing so, Afonso could confirm his support to the Templars.

Gifting the Castle of Soure to the Templars was not, of course, only a matter of showing gratitude for their deeds in Outremer or simply a pious act by young Afonso. It also hinted that he wanted the order to stay in his lands and grow and possibly even help him in future wars against the Muslims. The Templars, however, at that point in time, simply did not have enough members to properly run the castle, let alone reinforce Afonso's army with their elite skills.

Still, Iberia was in an all-out war. The Christian kings in the peninsula did not have enough resources to spare some for the Templars, who would just take them back to Outremer. Although gathering support and donations to take back to the Holy Land was the initial intent of the Templars, the ongoing situation in Iberia would have made them stay and take part in the *Reconquista*. Plus, Soure was a castle of strategic importance, located right on the front lines, further encouraging the order to set up, search and recruit more brothers, and actively defend their position. In addition, the confirmation of the fact that Soure was Templar property, paired with Afonso's declaration of brotherhood to the order, meant that he would have more reasons for the legitimization of his rule. After all, he had rebelled against his mother and made himself the ruler. All in all, it would create a good image for the young prince, as well as encourage the Templars to fight with him or for him in upcoming battles.

The remains of Castle
This file is licensed under the Creative Commons Attribution 2.0 Generic license; it is free to share, copy, and modify. https://commons.wikimedia.org/w/index.php?curid=627601

The Templars' presence in Portugal would only increase after that. There are documents that confirm more lands were granted to them in the region. However, the Templars would not actively get involved in battle before 1144. The main explanation for this is that the expansionist Afonso was mainly concentrated on pushing his borders against other Christian states. Thus, the Templars would not agree to fight with him against other Christians, as it would go against their code. It is logical to think that they only grew their numbers and power from 1128 until they finally joined the *Reconquista* in 1144 after the Moors attacked their castle at Soure. Unfortunately, they were defeated, as the Muslims heavily outnumbered the brothers, who did not get much help from King Afonso.

But this did not stop the Knights Templar from continuing to spread their influence in Portugal; it just means that the Templars were not directly involved in major campaigns in the *Reconquista* until 1147. At this time, King Afonso fully consolidated his power at home and started going on the offensive against the Moors. The Templars would assist the king at the Battle of Santarém in March 1147 and then, with the combined forces of the Second Crusade, join him in capturing Lisbon. This would further boost their position in Iberia. King Afonso granted them the churches of Santarém, and later on, they would gain control of the Castle of Cera. All in all, the Templars would gain a significant foothold in Portugal, and over the years, they increased their presence as they fought for Christian Portugal against the Muslim threat.

In Spain, the Templars appear to have gained their first bit of land in 1130, two years later after they did so in Portugal. Raymond Berenguer III, Count of Barcelona, granted the order the Castle of Granyena in July and also joined them as an associate member. His son, Raymond Berenguer IV, would continue what his father had started and form a pretty warm relationship with the Templars over the years in Barcelona— something that would prove to be vital in the years to come.

An extraordinary development for the Knights Templar occurred when King Alfonso I of Aragon had the order mentioned in his will. King Alfonso, fittingly nicknamed "The Battler," had expanded the lands of Aragon significantly during his rule and weakened the power of the Muslims in the region. We should also not forget his love for the military orders, which he would establish to help him defend the newly conquered lands from those who wished to take them back. Unfortunately, Alfonso of Aragon had no heirs, and when he died in

1134, securing the whole of his kingdom proved to be a problem. Knowing that various Spanish nobles would seek to take over parts of his lands and wanting to avoid the dissolution of the kingdom that he had created, Alfonso declared in his will that he left the Kingdom of Aragon and Navarre to "the Orders of the Temple, St. John of Jerusalem and the Holy Sepulcher."[97]

This move was certainly ambitious and, in some sense, reckless, and it certainly confused his kingdom. A military order could not rule a whole kingdom. Alfonso's younger brother, a monk named Ramiro, would save the Kingdom of Aragon and Navarre from collapse. Ramiro realized that someone needed to act for the future of the kingdom, so he came out of the monastery and raised a child that would later be betrothed to Raymond Berenguer IV, who was already the count of Barcelona at the time. With this move, Raymond Berenguer managed to become a legitimate king of Aragon in 1150.

Raymond Berenguer would play an important part in resolving the matter of Alfonso's will. The late king had left the whole kingdom to the Christian orders of the East, not only the Templars but also the Knights Hospitaller (although the latter was not nearly as present in Iberia as the former). Raymond knew that he could not just ignore these orders, believing that would be an unjust act. However, he also recognized that he would need them in the fight for the peninsula. This was where his tight relations with the Knights Templar came in. Because of his family's history with the order, Raymond was able to come to an agreement with the Templars in November of 1143. Grand Master Robert of Craon attended the ceremony in Girona, where the Templar Order would receive six important castles in Aragonese lands, along with the territories that surrounded them.

This was, by far, the biggest amount of land the order had received by that point. The six castles of Monzon, Mongay, Barbara, Chalamera, Belchite, and Remolins were, in a way, an investment from Raymond. He needed the Templars to stay and reinforce his armies, and with this act, he established a sense of trust and permanent connection between the order and the throne. Along with the lands, he promised the order a tithe of all royal revenue, a fifth of all lands conquered from the Muslims, and several other yearly payments and economic benefits, like exemption from taxes and customs. He hoped all of this would motivate the

[97] Lourie, E. (1975).

338

Templars to build up their possessions in Iberia and fight in the *Reconquista.*

The Templars became a force to be reckoned with in the Iberian Peninsula, even though they were thousands of miles away from their home base in Jerusalem. Unlike the rest of Europe, the Iberian lords actually needed the help of the Templars; other European nobles gave them donations for their goodwill and piety. After all, the Iberians were in a war against the Muslims to take back what was once theirs, and the order fit their requirements perfectly. The castles the Templars received in the peninsula were of strategic importance and almost forced the Templars to the front lines.

And the Templars certainly delivered. They aided the Iberian lords numerous times during the *Reconquista,* further boosting their popularity. With their success came more lands, more privileges, and more respect, so much so that it can be argued that by the time of their downfall in the late 13th century, the Templars were significantly present in Iberia. We shall return to the order's ever-increasing role in the peninsula later on, but before that, it is important not to forget about contemporary developments in Outremer, where the Templars would be needed against an emerging threat.[98]

---

[98] Valente, J. (1998). "The New Frontier: The Role of the Knights Templar in the Establishment of Portugal as an Independent Kingdom." *Mediterranean Studies*, 7, 49–65. http://www.jstor.org/stable/41166860.

Lourie, E. (1975). "The Will of Alfonso I, 'El Batallador,' King of Aragon and Navarre: A Reassessment." *Speculum*, 50(4), 635–651. https://doi.org/10.2307/2855471.

Hill, P. (2018). *The Knights Templar at War, 1120-1312.* Pen & Sword Military. Chapter 3.

Martin, S. (2011). *The Knights Templar.* Oldcastle Books. Chapter 1.

Chapter 4: The Second Crusade

We have now looked at the early period of the Templars' existence. Due to the exceptional premise of the organization, which included the merging of two different lifestyles of the monk and the knight, the Templars managed to gain a significant following pretty early on. They earned their name in the Christian world with the help of powerful Europeans and members of the church, which boosted their popularity higher and higher, eventually making them the most well-known Christian order. In this chapter, we shall take a look at a historical development that can be considered the final step to the Knights Templar finally cementing their position as the most important military organization. The Templars played a pretty big role throughout the course of the Second Crusade. All in all, their involvement would take them to highs that nobody could have expected.

The New Possessions

Robert de Craon, the new Grand Master of the Templars, was a much more administratively-minded leader than his predecessor, Hugues de Payens. Robert had taken the position in 1136, and since his election, the Templars' power seemed to increase exponentially. Under Robert de Craon's leadership, the Templars realized the potential their order had. We have already discussed their gains in Iberia, where the Templars would grow stronger and stronger. A partial reason for this was the need for experienced fighters against the Muslims during the *Reconquista*, and it was a role that was perfect for the Templar Order. The Templars became a valuable asset for Iberian lords against the Moors, and over time, they would be granted more and more possessions.

Robert de Craon was directly involved in much of the process of forming relations with the Iberian kingdoms from the very beginning. He was present at Girona when King Alfonso's will was discussed. So, we can assume that he believed the order could benefit in a similar way in the Holy Land as it did in Iberia. In the mid-1130s, the Templars received more castles in Outremer, the first of which were situated north of their center of operations in Jerusalem in the Principality of Antioch.

Sometime around 1136 to 1137, the order received its first holdings in the Amanus Mountains, some sixteen miles from the city of Antioch. It was a strategically important location. The place was known as the Belen Pass, and it connected Antioch with Cilician Armenia. The Templars were assigned to guard the pass, which

Ruins of Baghras, viewed from the west side

was originally used by the First Crusaders to cross from Armenia into the Holy Land. The fortress of Gaston, originally known as Baghras, which the Templars received, was one of the gateways to Syria. Along with Gaston, the Order would also gain possession of La Roche-Guillaume and La Roche de Roussel, which were both important fortresses built in mountainous regions to patrol the passes to the Latin kingdoms. The Templars would also be granted the castle at Darbask and the Port of Bonnel on the Gulf of Ayas later on.

The order would also see some love from the new king of Jerusalem, Fulk, who succeeded Baldwin in 1131. In his efforts to consolidate his position in the south against the Fatimid Caliphate of Egypt, he made sure to mobilize the military orders in his possession and entrust them with the running of strategically important points. The Templars already held the Castle of Latrun, which they used to patrol the way from Jaffa to Jerusalem. It was an important road that was used by the pilgrims to travel to the Holy Land. In 1139, King Fulk also gave them the castle in Gaza. In short, their presence would increase in Outremer, as the lords of the Latin kingdoms realized their potential in defending the Holy Land against the Muslims.

Since their creation, the Crusader States were almost fully (with the exception of Cilician Armenia) surrounded by Muslim lands that were hostile to them. Fortunately for the Christians, for some time, the Muslims were divided amongst themselves and did not pose as big of a threat to the newly established Christian kingdoms. However, as the Crusader States observed their enemies mobilize, they started counting more on whatever help they could get, and the Knights Templar was one of the best solutions to their problems.

A New Threat

The Latin kingdoms would not face much resistance directly after their formation at the end of the First Crusade. Again, this was caused by the disunity of the Muslims in Anatolia and the Middle East and their inability to find some kind of an agreement between the Shi'as and the Sunnis. Baldwin's campaigns against the Damascenes were, as we already remarked, more of a wish to expand rather than an answer to direct aggression.

The situation would change in the late 1130s, however, as much of the Muslim world would start to unite under one leader. His name was Imal al-Din Zengi, the Atabeg of Mosul. In 1128, he managed to capture the city of Aleppo, challenging the supremacy of the Damascenes in Syria. In fact, just like King Baldwin of Jerusalem, he wanted to take Damascus for himself to consolidate his power in the region and emerge as the leader of the Sunni Muslims. King Fulk and the other leaders of the Latin kingdoms in Outremer observed Zengi carefully, eventually recognizing him as the biggest threat to the integrity of the Christian lands, and rightfully so. Zengi was thirsty for war. He had correctly assessed the power vacuum that existed in the region and wanted to take full advantage of it.

The Latin kingdoms' efforts to fight against Zengi were very disoriented. At first, Count Raymond II of Tripoli ventured out to meet Zengi's forces in battle while they were besieging Damascene territory. He was defeated, and Zengi now turned his attention toward the Christians. Count Raymond, who lost most of his men in the battle, knew that he would not be able to defeat the Muslims. He approached King Fulk for help.

King Fulk answered the call and marched north with whatever men he could assemble, including a contingent of Templars. His efforts were unsuccessful, though, as he was ambushed by Zengi's forces and forced to retreat to Castle Montferrand in Tripoli. There, Zengi laid siege to the entrapped Christian forces. The situation seemed dire. King Fulk sent messengers to Antioch and Edessa for aid. While the remaining Latin kingdoms started to assemble their armies to help, Fulk managed to negotiate a ransom with the besiegers. In exchange for his and his men's safety, the Christians gave Zengi possession of Castle Montferrand in July of 1137, which further increased his power in the region.

This defeat would demoralize the Christians, although it was a great success for Zengi. Even though Zengi was now in an open war against the Latin kingdoms, he knew that he was much more powerful for one simple reason: the Christians lacked the manpower. That's why he continued to attack the Christian cities in Outremer and took them one by one, eventually reaching Edessa in 1144.

The Christian effort had become even more disjointed by that point. For one thing, King Fulk had passed away in an accident in 1143, and the Kingdom of Jerusalem was left to his young son, Baldwin III, who ruled with his mother, Melisende, since he was not old enough to rule alone. In addition, Joscelin II, Count of Edessa, did not have a good relationship with the rest of the Christian kingdoms. He had been in an alliance with Jerusalem, but the future seemed uncertain after Fulk's death. The young count was not that experienced when it came to military matters, which explains why he was outclassed so much at Edessa.

In late 1144, Joscelin II, who was allied with the Turkish Artuqids, rode out to besiege the city of Aleppo—one of the most important cities

Zengi possessed. He left Edessa in the hands of mercenaries, but he was not able to pay them sufficiently for months. This decision would turn out to be fatal for the young count. Knowing that the capital of the county was poorly defended, Zengi besieged the city for a month, building siege equipment and digging under the walls. He finally captured it in December 1144. His armies ravaged the city, massacring soldiers and members of the clergy and selling the women into slavery.

The fall of Edessa was disastrous for the Latin kingdoms. Still, they could not, or did not, send help to Joscelin, who, in a desperate attempt, tried to retake the capital in October 1146. Before that, he ruled the remnants of his county, those that were still untouched by the Muslims. It was a valiant effort by the count, who was acting quickly after Zengi had been murdered in his sleep by a slave. Unfortunately, Joscelin could not recapture the city, as the forces under Zengi's son, Nur ad-Din, drove him out.

Nur ad-Din was Zengi's second son, the self-proclaimed sultan of Aleppo. While similar to his father in his mercilessness, Nur ad-Din was also a devout Muslim. It was his firm belief in Islam that made him wise. He was not like other rulers who indulged themselves in wine and women. Instead, he preferred to spend his time studying the holy texts. Nur ad-Din promoted his wars as holy wars, or jihads, where those who died sacrificed themselves to God or Allah. And even though he had lost some territories to his brother in Iraq, he was eager to recruit experienced mercenaries from every region in the East. Eventually, he bolstered his army so much that he was basically continuing his father's legacy as a threat to be feared. And feared he was.

The Call for the Second Crusade

The situation in Outremer was becoming more and more desperate. The Latin kingdoms had never been as weak since the end of the First Crusade. Edessa, the northernmost kingdom, had fallen almost completely to the Muslims, including the city of Edessa itself. It was not looking too good for the Christians. Thus, when the pilgrims returned to Europe from Outremer with the news of Edessa's fall the next autumn, Pope Eugenius knew that he needed to act quickly. He wanted the Christian kingdoms to venture to the Holy Land once again and help take back Edessa, reinforcing Outremer with fresh warriors from Europe. He wrote to King Louis VII of France, asking him about the possibility of a potential Second Crusade. King Louis saw the journey to Outremer as an opportunity to redeem himself, as he had lost popularity in the eyes of his people when he unrightfully claimed the lands from his Burgundian vassal. The king was excited to hear the pope's concerns and helped him organize a council at Vézelay in the spring of 1146. More importantly, he invited the one man he knew for certain would be in favor of the new Crusade: Bernard of Clairvaux.

The Council of Vézelay proceeded similarly as the Council of Clermont. Everyone knew ahead of the gathering why the pope had called them to assemble. The audience was curious to see Bernard of Clairvaux preach too, as they all remembered his powerful words at Troyes, which had caused the Knights Templar to ascend to unseen levels of popularity. His charisma caused a similar result as what had happened with Pope Urban about fifty years prior. The gathered members of the council were instantly taken up by the idea of going to Outremer to reclaim the lost lands. King Louis and his younger brother Robert were the first ones to vow to venture out. Hundreds soon followed. Many were the descendants of the previous generation that took part in the First Crusade. For those people, it was as much about taking back Edessa and the spiritual salvation that the Second Crusade promised as it was about continuing the legacy of their families and maintaining the prestigious status their fathers had attained. Germany's Conrad III was also convinced to join the Crusade, making it the first time that monarchs of European states led the Crusaders. A group of Crusaders from England would also start their journey to Outremer, but they would divert from their path and end up in Portugal to take part in the *Reconquista*, which we will discuss later.

In late April of the same year, after the news of the new Crusade had spread throughout the continent, the pope and King Louis met at the Paris Temple. The meeting, which had been organized by the new Grand Master of the Knights Templar in France, Everard des Barres, was also attended by about 130 Templars and their sergeants and squires. (Everard would be "officially" elected after the passing of Robert de Craon in Outremer, although the exact date of his death is unknown. Some sources say that Everard held an important role in the order in France, but it is unclear when Everard succeeded Robert.)

The meeting would prove to be vital for both the Templars and the Crusaders. It is thought that this was when the Crusaders received the pope's blessing to wear the iconic red cross on their clothes. The pope would also allow the Templar treasurer to collect taxes from the church to offer financial support to the Crusade. Most importantly, it was decided that Grand Master Everard, with a group of other Templars, was to follow the French army during the Crusade. Over the course of the Crusade, Everard would play a bigger role, becoming, in essence, the military advisor of Louis VII.

The Journey to Outremer

Thus, the two main forces were on their way to Outremer. It has to be said that Conrad III of Germany's forces were not nearly as professional as those of King Louis VII. The biggest factor that determined the overall discipline of the French was the presence of the Knights Templar. King Louis was very impressed by the Templars and their way of life, which they strictly followed. He considered them to be role models for his troops. His trust in the Templars is further shown when he sent Grand Master Everard to the Byzantines to negotiate their passage through Anatolia.

Emperor Manuel Comnenus (Komnenos) was somewhat hesitant to grant the Crusaders military access for two main reasons. Firstly, he had not called for help and did not expect anything for himself should the Crusade be successful, unlike Emperor Alexios in the First Crusade. Secondly, since he was busy fighting in Sicily, he had made peace with the Seljuk Turks and thought that his actions might damage his already-wavering relations with the Muslims. It was due to this that the Byzantine emperor was not liked by the Crusaders.

Matters got worse in November 1147 when the news of Conrad's defeat reached the French forces who had arrived in Nicaea and were planning to cross to the Holy Land. Conrad's army was separated from the French army. In fact, he had reached Constantinople sometime earlier than Louis and had decided to proceed through Anatolia alone. In late October, however, the Germans were ambushed by the Turks at their camp. They were overwhelmed by the light Turkish cavalry, who swarmed their positions. The king and about a tenth of his forces managed to survive and retreat back to the Byzantine territories, but the Germans would partially blame the emperor for not providing military support to the journeying Crusaders.

Conrad and Louis would meet in Nicaea after the disastrous German defeat to discuss how they would continue their march. The two kings decided to take a route that went through the coastline of Anatolia all the way to the port of Antalya. Unfortunately, Conrad soon fell ill and was forced to return to Constantinople; he was only able to reach the Holy Land in 1148.

The route to the Holy Land would prove to be much more problematic to King Louis than to his predecessors in the First Crusade. The French were constantly under attack from the Turkish forces. Usually, the Turks did not have large numbers. Instead, the Turkish mounted archers quickly harassed the French army, which was moving slowly in a long column from the flanks. It was very difficult for the French to effectively answer the "hit and run" style of the Turks. To reduce the number of casualties and further increase discipline in his forces, King Louis asked Grand Master Everard for his advice. Everard divided the army into smaller contingents that were each led by a Templar. This approach seemed to work; the Crusaders successfully repelled the Turks, first at Ephesus in late December 1147 and then at the valley of Meander, where the Crusaders would be ambushed trying to cross the river but would come out victorious. They even captured a number of the enemy forces.

After Meander, Louis only had to get to the port of Antalya, where he hoped he would be able to transfer the rest of his forces by sea. They would have to endure many difficulties during their final leg of the journey to Antalya, however. At that point, the Crusaders had sparse supplies and not a lot of horses. The heavy cavalry that they did have was of no use in the mountainous regions of southern Anatolia. Thus, as the French passed through the narrow passes of the Cadmus Mountains, they would suffer many casualties from the Turks, who used the terrain to their advantage to constantly harass and disrupt the French forces.

It was at this point that the Templars really showed their military expertise. They understood that the main objective was for the French to get out of the narrow pass and reach Antalya. The Templars started to enforce their discipline harder than before, making the Crusaders follow their lead. The Crusaders developed a deep sense of respect toward the Templars after they managed to up the morale and save Christians from deserting or fleeing.

Finally, after days of struggling, the Crusaders arrived at Antalya. There, with help from the Byzantines, King Louis boarded the ships with his best forces and headed for Port Saint Symeon in the Principality of Antioch. The rest of the forces under the command of the remaining French nobles would soon follow. The rest of the forces, those who did not manage to get on the ships, would have to pass overland to Antioch, and they would almost be fully wiped out by the Turks in the process.

The Fiasco at Damascus

It can be argued that the journey to Antioch was much more difficult for Louis than it was for the First Crusaders. The Crusader army had lost the majority of its forces. In addition, Louis had run out of money, and even if he did have it, what direction the Crusade would go after Antioch was still under question. However, he would receive a lot of help during his stay in Antioch. For one thing, his army got some time to rest after a tiresome and brutal journey. More importantly, though, Grand Master Everard would step up once again to help the Crusaders, this time financially. As the remaining Crusader forces arrived in Antioch throughout the spring, Everard sailed to Acre, a Templar stronghold. There, he raised the necessary amount to help fund the rest of the expedition. It is logical to assume that Everard got the money directly from the order's treasury, showing, once again, the sheer financial growth the Knights Templar had undergone since their early days. It is also possible that Everard borrowed the money and used the vast riches of the order as insurance.

In any way, Louis was humbled by this action so much that he vowed to repay the Templars as soon as he could, ordering his subjects to raise insane amounts of money for his debts to the order. The French Crown and the Templar Order would become closer than ever after this gracious act from Everard, although he did technically loan the French the money. With this, as well as the pope's decision to entrust many important matters to the Templars in France, the order would basically run the French treasury for the next century and a half.

There was still a question of what was next for the Crusaders. Conrad had finally reached the Holy Land in the spring with the remnants of his force. It was agreed that the plan of action would be decided during an assembly near Acre. Everyone would attend. Alongside the European kings Louis and Conrad, there were the nobility and high-ranking officers of their armies. Young Baldwin III, King of Jerusalem, also attended with his mother, Melisende. The patriarch of Jerusalem was there as well, accompanied by a couple of archbishops from Nazareth and Caesarea. The Knights Templar were also there, represented by Everard, as well as, according to some sources, Robert de Craon, the Grand Master. (Robert is thought to have been still alive by the time of the assembly, but he surely passed away soon after.) Finally, there was the Grand Master of the Knights Hospitaller, Raymond du Puy.

The assembly decided with little to no opposition that the target of the Crusaders should be Damascus. This is a decision that has been frowned upon by modern historians, and for good reason. Damascus's strategic importance is certainly undeniable. So is the fact that the city itself was pretty rich and prosperous, and its surrounding lands were fertile. However, it was also not that wise to attack it then. The Damascenes were Shi'a Muslims, unlike the surrounding Muslim factions, like the one under Nur ad-Din. Thus, the two factions did not really have friendly relations, and the Damascenes had previously sided with the Christians under King Fulk in their efforts to stop Zengi's invasions. Therefore, attacking the only buffer state and a potential ally was not certainly the best idea. Plus, the city itself was heavily guarded, and it was not easy to approach.

Many historians and some contemporaries, like Raymond of Antioch, thought the wiser target was Aleppo—the heart of Nur ad-Din's kingdom— or Edessa, the city that had been lost to the Muslim invaders prior to the Second Crusade. This city was supposed to be the "original target" of the Second Crusade. The main argument that might have overpowered these two options was the fear of Nur ad-Din conquering the city himself. If that happened, he would become the most dominant power in Syria and pose a greater threat to the Latin kingdoms.

Whatever the reasoning was, the target was set, and the Crusaders started preparing. The army was led by the king of Jerusalem, who assembled quite a number of men. King Louis and King Conrad also joined King Baldwin with whatever forces they had left, altogether composing an army of no more than fifty thousand men. It has to be said that the role of the Templars was not as big as in the journey leading up to the final assault on Damascus, although it is safe to assume that they were present in the army. The Crusaders rode out from the coastline through Banias in the summer, arriving near Damascus in late July.

The Crusaders set up camp south of the city in the orchards that bordered it. It was a good location since it provided the attackers with reliable food and water supplies. The orchards were also not that far from the city; they were located about four miles away. On July 24th, the Crusaders started their assault through the orchards. This proved to be a difficult task since the defenders had scattered their vanguard in the trees and had them constantly fire upon the attackers as they advanced. However, this defense was not enough, and the Crusaders managed to successfully go on the offensive and push the majority of the Muslims back to the other side of the Barada River.

There, thanks to the bravery of King Conrad, who fought on foot, and his German troops, the Crusaders overcame the Muslim defenses of the river. They passed over to the other bank and drove them all the way back to the city. Then, they started to use the wood found in the orchards to build palisades and siege equipment. It all seemed dire for the Damascenes until relief forces arrived in the city. Unur, the ruler of Damascus, had called for help from the atabeg of Mosul and Nur ad-Din. By the time the Crusaders had crossed the river, the Damascenes had assembled enough reinforcements for a counterattack, which halted the progress of the Christians.

Still, since the beginning of the siege, the Crusaders were pretty successful. However, for some reason, the attackers would make the fatal mistake of abandoning their position at the orchards and moving the camp to the eastern side of the city on the plains. There is no real explanation for this. It was a foolish move for many reasons, including the scarcity of supplies at the new camp. When the defenders realized that the Crusaders had moved, they sent reinforcements to the orchards, where they built barricades and mounted more defenses, making it impossible for the attackers to return to their original camp. The Damascenes knew that the Crusaders had made a mistake and did not really force a fight upon them, especially once they knew that even more help from Nur ad-Din was on the way.

The Crusaders understood that they had put themselves at a massive disadvantage and that they needed to act quickly before they ran out of food and water and before the defenders would get new forces. The Crusaders decided to abandon the siege and retreated on July 28th, just five days after their arrival. Their shameful retreat was accompanied by constant harassment from the Muslim forces, which followed the Crusaders as far as they could, inflicting many casualties.

The failure to capture Damascus was catastrophic. Not only was it demoralizing for the Latin kingdoms, which knew their position in the region had weakened, but it was also a disaster for the rest of the Christian world. The Second Crusade was a complete fiasco from start to finish, as the Crusaders were unable to achieve anything of importance.

This is why, after Damascus, the different parties started blaming each other to justify their loss. For some, the failed siege at Damascus was the fault of local Christian barons, who were known for making deals with the Muslims. When discussing who would be put in charge of Damascus once it was taken, the local barons had completely been left out, leaving some to suspect that they had conspired with the Muslims, giving them information ahead of time. Others thought that Raymond of Antioch's unwillingness to support the Crusaders led to their failure. Raymond, unlike the others, did not support the assault on Damascus. All in all, there is a lot of speculation as to whose fault the failure at Damascus really was.

Later sources also partially put the blame on the Templars. A couple of German monks who traveled to Outremer in the 1160s wrote that the order was to blame for the fiasco of the Second Crusade. They accused the Templars of conspiring against the Christians, even saying that they were paid by the Damascenes not only for information but also for the deliberate sabotage or disruption of the Crusaders' ranks.

These and other accusations toward the order have never actually been proven, however. What is clear is the fact that the Templars played an influential role in the Second Crusade. King Louis trusted the brothers very much, and the Templars helped increase the discipline and professionalism of the army. Plus, we should not forget about the funding that the Templars raised for the Crusaders after their arrival in the Holy Land. During the Second Crusade, the Templars were involved in events in Iberia. There, the Crusader forces would join the Spanish and the Portuguese in the *Reconquista*.

The Iberian Crusade

Along with their role in the main Crusader campaign, the Templars would also see some action in Iberia during the Second Crusade. It is important to remember that the Second Crusade, despite being caused by the loss of Edessa in Outremer, did not really serve its original purpose. After the arrival of the Franco-German forces in the Holy Land, the Crusaders did not even try to recapture Edessa or engage in defensive warfare. Instead, they chose to expand the Christian territories with their assault on Damascus, which failed miserably. All in all, it was a disjointed effort, with wars being fought in three different regions in the name of the Crusade.

The first, as we already discussed, was the main campaign in Outremer. The other two were the so-called Wendish Crusade, where the northern European Crusaders ventured out against the Slavs, and the Crusade in Iberia as part of the *Reconquista*. Due to the involvement of the Templars in the latter, we shall focus on the Crusader efforts in Spain and Portugal, which were rather successful.

By the time the Second Crusade was called, the *Reconquista* had been well underway, with the Iberian kingdoms seeing more and more success in driving the Muslims out of the peninsula. The Knights Templar was an established organization in both Spain and Portugal by then, with the brothers being in possession of dozens of fortresses to aid in their fight against the Moors. In a way, the *Reconquista* was already an unofficial Crusade, but the actual Crusaders would get involved in the fight until sometime in 1147.

This group of Crusaders set sail from the British Isles, planning to circle the continent and arrive at the Holy Land by sea instead of crossing the English Channel to France and going overland. Consisting of warriors from England and Scotland, as well as parts of northern France, Germany, Flanders, and Frisia, the Crusaders started their journey from Dartmouth in May of 1147. This group did not have a monarch or a prince to lead it, which was different from the main forces under Louis and Conrad. Instead, different groups would be led by different counts and barons, like Arnout IV of Aarschot leading the German contingent and Hervey de Glanvill of Suffolk leading the Crusaders from England. Still, it was a pretty sizeable force of about two hundred ships.

The Crusaders landed at Porto in June of 1147. It is logical to assume that they were forced to stop in Portugal due to bad weather and to resupply before they continued their journey to Outremer. However, contemporary developments in the Christian world also have some historians convinced that the Crusaders came to Iberia to assist the Spanish and the Portuguese in the *Reconquista*. It is believed that Bernard of Clairvaux motivated these groups from the Low Countries to come to the aid of the Iberian Christians. Also, Pope Eugene had given his blessings to King Alfonso VII of León-Castile in his efforts against the Muslims, basically authorizing the Crusade in Iberia. Previously, Pope Paschal II had told the Iberians that their fight against the Muslims served the same purpose as the Crusaders' efforts in the Holy Land, giving the *Reconquista* the status of a holy war. Thus, if Bernard and Pope Eugene planned for a part of the Crusader forces to journey to Iberia to help against the Moors, the Second Crusade can be seen as a general holy war on all non-Christians.

Whatever it was that made the northern European Crusaders land at Porto, they would prove to be of great help against the Muslims. After their arrival, the Crusaders quickly met with Alfonso I of Portugal (who was technically not a king at the time). With the help of the Templars, Alfonso had already managed to expand his territories and drive the Muslims out. At the meeting, the two parties discussed a potential offensive on Lisbon, which was one of the richest and most important cities in Iberia. The Crusaders were initially reluctant to participate. This was because they knew of the previously failed siege of Lisbon, which had taken place in 1142. However, after much discussion, they agreed. In return, Alfonso promised them much of the loot from the city, as well as lands and exemption from taxes in the conquered territories.

The Siege of Lisbon. By Joaquim Rodrigues Braga - Joaquim Rodrigues Braga
https://commons.wikimedia.org/w/index.php?curid=1596202

The combined forces of the Crusaders and the Portuguese laid siege to Lisbon on July 1ˢᵗ. There was a total of about twenty thousand men, including a contingent of Templars who had become regulars in the Portuguese armies. At the time, Lisbon was thought to have had a population of about 150,000 people, many of them refugees from Santarém and other newly conquered Portuguese towns near the River Tagus. Unlike their hasty approach at Damascus, the Crusaders decided to wait and blockade the city. Eventually, after four months, the Moors surrendered in late October due to the lack of supplies in the city, which had caused a mass famine.

The capture of the city was relatively peaceful, with the Christians allowing the civilians to leave after they entered. The capture of Lisbon would be a pivotal victory for the *Reconquista*. The victory solidified the Portuguese position against the Muslims and swung the balance of power in favor of the Christians. It was also one of the more significant victories for the Crusaders during the Second Crusade, especially since they did not really achieve anything of importance in Outremer.

The Aftermath of the Second Crusade

Overall, the Second Crusade was not nearly as successful as the first one. The main campaign had failed, and the victory in Iberia was the only silver lining. However, the Templars' role throughout the whole Crusade cannot be understated. The Second Crusade boosted the popularity and status of the Templars even more. Because of their close involvement with King Louis's army, they gained much respect in France, playing a significant role in France's financial affairs. The funds the Templars managed to assemble after the Crusaders' arrival at Outremer also show the power they had accumulated since their creation. Many Crusaders who stayed in the Holy Land and Iberia would join the Templar Order and reside in one of their numerous castles as sergeants or squires. The Templars sought to build on their successful participation in the Second Crusade. They were looking at a bright future ahead of them, and what followed was a period where they were at the height of their power, as they were regarded as the most respected organization in the Christian world.[99]

[99] Napier, G. (2011). *The Rise and Fall of the Knights Templar*. History Press. Chapter 4.

Hill, P. (2018). *The Knights Templar at War, 1120-1312*. Pen & Sword Military.

Forey, A. (2004). "The Siege of Lisbon and the Second Crusade." *Portuguese Studies*, 20, 1-13. http://www.jstor.org/stable/41105214.

Martin, S. (2011). *The Knights Templar*. Oldcastle Books. Chapter 2.

Constable, G. (1953). "The Second Crusade as Seen by Contemporaries." *Traditio*, 9, 213-279. http://www.jstor.org/stable/27830277.

Section Two: The Rise of The Knights Templar

Chapter 5: The Rich Knights of Christ

We have already covered the origin story of the Knights Templar. The order became much more than a brotherhood of nine knights who pledged to protect the pilgrims traveling to the Holy Land. From the creation of the order in the early 12th century up to the Second Crusade, the whole Christian world got to know what the Templars stood for. Starting from the second half of the 1100s, the Templars slowly rose to the peak of their power, expanding the order all over the continent. This chapter looks to explore a different side of the Templars, one that is often forgotten, as it is often overshadowed by their warrior monk lifestyle.

Rags to Riches

The official name of the Knights Templar is technically the Order of the Poor Knights of Christ and the Temple of Solomon. As we have remarked many times, the word "poor" did not accurately reflect the order's status. The Templars were becoming more and more popular, which meant there were more and more of those who wanted to donate. And although the brothers followed a strict Benedictine lifestyle, they were in possession of a small kingdom's worth of wealth. This fact would be recognized by the Christian world soon enough.

One of the pivotal moments in the process of the order's establishment as a fully-fledged, strong financial institution was the Second Crusade. After the arrival of King Louis's forces in Outremer, Grand Master Everard would singlehandedly raise enough money for the campaign to continue. Funding a whole Crusade was not an easy task; in fact, many rulers would decide not to take part in the Crusades because of the massive costs associated with it. However, Everard managed to gather all the money needed for an expedition to Damascus for about fifty thousand men, either getting it directly from Templar reserves or borrowing it and using Templar possessions as insurance. While it is not known how he raised money, it is believed that Everard gave King Louis about thirty thousand French livres and two thousand marks of silver. Of course, this was a loan; the Templar Grand Master did not simply gift the French king this much money. If Everard had been kind enough to gift the king this huge sum, Louis would surely have been embarrassed.

The Templars' financial involvement in France was also boosted by the pope's initiative for the members of the order to become treasurers of the state. This tradition, which would evolve over time, would continue for more than a century and a half until the complete demise of the Templars. The order operating from the Paris Temple, which was the headquarters of the Templars not only in France but also unofficially in mainland Europe, would be in charge of the French treasury. They would do everything from collecting taxes to giving out loans. They assisted the French monarchs in financial matters and did so pretty effectively. For instance, they helped Philip II restructure the tax collection system and significantly increased his overall revenue. After Louis VII, the French kings would select one of the Templars to serve the throne for their lifetime. This allowed the monarch to form a close relationship with the order, which was not only limited to financial advice.

The system the Templars pioneered was much like a modern bank. Banks did not exist in Europe back then, making it even more impressive how neatly the order was able to handle the different fiscal issues. Perhaps their general devotion to order and discipline, which was, in turn, based on the Benedictine lifestyle, helped the Templars establish one of the first and most effective early banking systems in Europe. For example, the Templars realized there were a lot of people in different locations willing to borrow money from the order or deposit their possessions in their hands. So, they came up with a credit note system. When a person deposited money to a Templar location, they would be given a special official document with the details of the transaction. This document could be redeemed at any other Templar site with no additional costs or difficulties. In the meantime, before the deposited money was taken out, the order could loan to another party or use it to invest in its own development, as the knights were confident that it would be returned because of the influx of money the order saw on a regular basis. This system would last until the order disbanded, and various individuals, from European nobles to members of the Catholic Church, would use it regularly. The Templars would be open for business on most days, and they usually agreed with their clients about the transaction details beforehand.

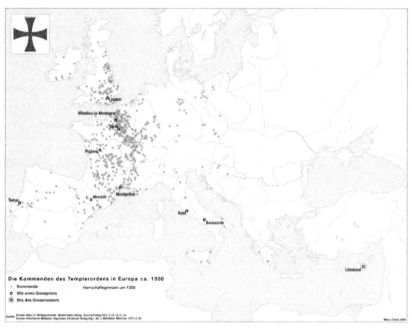

Templar holdings in Europe

In their financial endeavors in Europe, the Knights Templar would see a lot of support from the papacy. By the time the Templars started implementing their convenient fiscal system, different popes had already shown how much they valued the order; the papal bulls are perhaps the best example of this. They also made the Grand Master of the Templar Order one of the most powerful men in all of the Christian world by giving him the privilege of "directly answering" to the pope and not any other monarch or lord. Because of the close relationship between two of the most respected organizations in all of Christianity, the papacy would use the services provided by the order just as much as lords from different kingdoms.

In the early 1160s, the Templars were performing a similar role for Pope Alexander III as they had in France; they effectively managed the papacy's treasury. Most of the papacy's financial matters would see the involvement of the Templars in one way or another. For example, Pope Innocent III heavily relied on the Templars when he tried to raise funds for the Fourth Crusade, which began in 1202. Not only did the pope directly borrow from the Order and later repay his loans, but once he had the opportunity, he also gave the Templars additional privileges of collecting taxes from members of the clergy to better organize the upcoming war effort. The Templars, along with the Knights Hospitaller, were responsible for transferring the actual funds to the Holy Land during the Crusade, as well as dealing with all of the fiscal issues that might have arisen during the process. This way, the Knights Templar continued to further cement itself as the biggest and most influential Christian organization after the papacy.

Financial Ties with the English Crown

The role of the Templars as (proto) bankers would increase in Europe as time went by. Besides their main center of operations at the Paris Temple, they would be very successful in the British Isles. They even started to conduct business with the British Crown itself. The Templars' involvement with fiscal matters in England and the whole of Europe can be attributed to increasing levels of globalization, which was accelerated by the events of the 12th century.

At the time, more and more European kingdoms began to emerge as sovereign states with clearly defined territories. Due to this, the importance of international trade began to rise. The development of the concept of mercantilism was also a contributing factor, as wealth slowly shifted from the hands of the feudal lords (who, by all means, still held the majority of resources) into the hands of merchants, traders, farmers, and people of other professions. These people were more willing to contribute to the building of markets and roads, which bolstered their income even more. They paid more taxes to their rulers, with the money then being reinvested to increase the economic landscapes in which they all coexisted. It was all a big chain reaction, and the Templars managed to find their own niche in the developing world.

England was one of the most progressive and economically advanced places in Europe at the time. It was only natural for the Templars to find their footing there. This would play into the formation of England as an economic power and London, therefore, as an economic hub. Starting in the late 12th century, English people from all social classes are documented as having deposited their possessions at the London Temple. Again, people would entrust the order with everything from actual currency to pots of gold and silver to other miscellaneous valuable items. The order's temples were one of the safest places at the time to keep one's money. They had been built by clever engineers, and all of them were designed as fortifications. Most of them were even designed to have secret passes and keeps underground. They were also well guarded by tens, if not hundreds, of knights, squires, and sergeants.

Another prominent reason, as already partially discussed above, was the convenience of the transactions. The client was able to confidently leave their possessions in the hands of the Templars with the ability to retrieve them from any Templar location at any time without too many complications. The people felt respect for the order, which made the organization trustworthy. And not even kings (in most cases) would dare to mess with an internationally well-respected and sacred institution. The order essentially guaranteed safety, security, and secrecy, and as the records show, the English rulers saw its importance from the very start.

On many occasions, different kings would use the riches of the temples to their own advantage, as they were aware of the availability of funds. In times of need, they would take large amounts of money from the Templars and repay the order over time from other treasuries of the state, such as Westminster or the Tower of London. In 1276, Edward I would withdraw one thousand marks. Henry III would seize forty thousand marks from the temple as a way to confiscate the money from Falkes de Bréauté, a Norman adventurer who entrusted the money to the Templars but was then accused of treachery and conspiracy. One of the most popular ways for kings to repay the Templars was by granting them all sorts of additional privileges, like exemption of different kinds of taxes or providing help to the order in building new holdings.

Thus, the Knights Templar was seen as a reliable financial institution in England. In turn, this accumulated a similar sense of trust between the order and the English Crown. Members of the order were often employed by the English monarchs to oversee a myriad of fiscal issues, such as the collection of taxes. They were not only limited to conducting private business in the name of the Templars. Instead, they were made official ambassadors of the Crown and assigned to different missions. For example, a group of Templars would oversee the transportation of money from England to Ireland. In exchange, the English rulers agreed to pay for any injuries on the road or reimburse them for their troubles. The Templars also acted as third-party trustees. The most notable example of this was when they were entrusted with the ownership of castles that were supposed to be a part of a dowry from Louis VII's daughter to Henry II's son during their arranged marriage. Because the two kings agreed to marry their children when they were still very young, the castles went into the Templars' possession until the children were old enough to marry and, thus, receive them.

These and a dozen more fiscal services were performed by the Knights Templar on a regular basis in England from the late 12th to the end of the 13th century. They were effectively the best financial institution in the kingdom until the wealthy Italian merchant organizations became more prominent in Europe. The English monarchs trusted the Templars on many occasions, and the Templars never disappointed. They continued to carry out different sorts of transactions for the Crown for more than a year and earned an amicable reputation with the English kings. The Templars not only ensured the safety of the funds but were also very flexible in their agreements, developing the first fully-functioning banking system in Europe. The Templars' ways of handling money so effectively, as well as their integrity and administrative capacity, are certainly impressive. It certainly helped send the Templars to the height of their power.

New Holdings

Perhaps one of the best indications of the Templars' rise to power was the extensive number of new holdings they either received or built during the second half of the 12th century. Of course, the order had several headquarters in different regions, which were both the most fortified and the richest. However, the Templars also built countless buildings that served a myriad of purposes. For example, they built churches, mills, and bridges. With time, they also extended whatever they had already acquired. For example, by the 1170s, the Templars are thought to have expanded their main holding at the time, the former Al-Aqsa Mosque at Mount Temple. They completely renovated the old building and added new underground vaults and halls, where they allegedly kept their most precious possessions.

Other castles in Outremer also received love from the order. In fact, it is estimated that the Templars spent the most money and resources on their architectural projects, either repairing those castles and fortresses or building completely new holdings. These castles were heavily guarded since they were located at various strategic points all over Jordan and Palestine. Most of their walls were over 150 feet high and accompanied by a set of defensive towers at every possible point. The costs associated with maintaining, let alone building, such grand structures are truly remarkable, especially when we take into account that they were always manned by hundreds of soldiers.

The Templar fortresses of Outremer were so big that they had the capability of sheltering thousands of people in case they were ever driven out of their towns during an invasion. The Templars had stocked the castles with more weapons than the garrison needed, as well as food and other provisions for potential sieges. The impressive Templar holdings of the East include Atlit Castle, also known as Pilgrim Castle, on the northern coast of Israel; it was built during the Fifth Crusade and capable of supporting about forty thousand soldiers during a siege. Near Antioch, the order was in possession of the famous Baghras (Bagras) Castle, renamed Gaston by the Templars. It was initially abandoned by the Byzantines but repaired and used by the order. Alongside these, the order was in control of Acre, Jaffa, and Sidon, which were all heavily fortified and of great importance.

Castle Almourol

Iberia was another region where most of the Templar holdings were giant castles. Perhaps the reason behind this was the existence of an imminent threat: the Muslims. After all, they were present both in Outremer and Iberia. Just like in the Holy Land, the Templars would be granted a lot of their fortresses. In fact, it can be argued that the order was more favored by the Iberian lords than by their Latin counterparts in the East due to the number of holdings they donated to the Templars. The Castle of Soure was the first one to be awarded to them, and by the 1170s, other Portuguese castles, such as Almourol and Longroiva, would also be in their possession.

Out of these two, the Castle of Almourol, situated on a rocky island in the Tagus River Valley, was heavily damaged when the order got hold of it. However, the Templars repaired and extended the castle, adding ten additional defensive towers and a more fortified inner keep.

The Master of the Templar Order in Portugal at the time, Gualdim Pais, also personally oversaw the construction of two more castles, Pombal and Tomar, with the latter becoming the Portuguese headquarters of the Knights Templar. In Spain, alongside the six major castles the order received from King Alfonso's will, the Templars possessed Miravet, one of the best fortresses in all of Iberia. Despite the fact that the later lords of Aragon and Castile were more favorable toward the Knights Hospitaller and not as gracious toward the Templars, the order managed to hold on to their precious possessions until it met its demise. The Knights Templar continued to play a major role in the *Reconquista* and was a force to be reckoned with in Iberia.

Of course, Templar holdings were not only heavily fortified and strategically important castles. In most of Europe, Templars were in charge of churches, monastery complexes, a variety of agricultural and industrial buildings, and sometimes even small towns. Despite the fact that the Templars had several big castles, the absence of a direct threat and a potential enemy meant the Templars were not needed to man these huge fortresses, unlike in the Holy Land or Iberia. Instead, to show their gratitude, European lords became more and more creative when they granted the order new possessions. The Templars would proudly take over whatever lands they could and make the most of them. Over time, as more members joined the Knights Templar, the skills of the order also increased, which meant they were perfectly capable of conducting agricultural or industrial processes and competent enough to run small towns.

The Templars were already established after their initial visit to Europe in 1127, as they had received enough estates through donations from different European lords. Later on, these estates, which mostly comprised of farms or manors, would be grown to include a network of Templar-built houses, from where the brothers would collect taxes and fund future expansion efforts. These became known as preceptories, which were subordinate houses and communities of the Knights Templar.

One of the main reasons behind the Templars' enthusiasm for building was their relationship with the secretive medieval and now-famous guild of the Masons. In fact, there seems to have been a special unit composed of the brothers, who were a separate class of "Templar Masons." Nowadays, the guild of the Masons is often associated with secret societies and conspiracy theories. Even though most of it is made up, it is true that the members of the guild did not like the involvement of outside parties in their affairs. Even so, they could be easily identified due to the use of excessive geometric shapes in their buildings.

The Paris Temple can be considered one of the most focal examples. It was built in the 12th century by the order and served as its main headquarters in Europe. Although the Paris Temple was demolished in the 19th century by Napoleon, it was described as having tall walls with corner towers and sharp edges, resembling the work of the Templar Masons. While the Templar architecture of the time was still confined to Benedictine standards—without any complex ornaments and details—it was still very unique compared to everything else from the period. We shall return to the matter of potential Templar involvement with the guild of the Masons later on.[100]

[100] Martin, S. (2011). *The Knights Templar.* Oldcastle Books. Chapter 2.

Ferris, E. (1902). "The Financial Relations of the Knights Templars to the English Crown." *The American Historical Review,* 8 (1), 1–17.

Hill, P. (2018). *The Knights Templar at War, 1120–1312.* Pen & Sword Military. Part 2.

Faith, J. (2011). *The Knights Templar in Somerset.* History Press.

Napier, G. (2011). *The Rise and Fall of the Knights Templar.* History Press.

Chapter 6: Templar Military Power in the Holy Land

The Second Crusade ended terribly for the Crusaders. The kings of Europe had invested a lot into their eastward campaigns, but they ultimately failed to achieve any sort of meaningful progress in Outremer. The Second Crusade, however, as we have already remarked, was not as disastrous for the Knights Templar. In the years following the Second Crusade, the Templars' military involvement in the Holy Land would only increase. This chapter will explore further military endeavors of the Templars in the East and how its successes and sometimes failures put the Knights Templar at the height of their power.

Following the Second Crusade

In a way, the failure of the Second Crusade increased the need for a stronger Christian presence in the Holy Land. Edessa was completely destroyed, and those Latin kingdoms that remained were not really in a position to challenge the supremacy of the Muslims on their own. Therefore, the years that followed the Second Crusade would be crucial in determining the future of Christianity in Outremer.

As we have already mentioned, it is not exactly clear when Everard des Barres officially became the Grand Master of the Templars. His heavy involvement in the Second Crusade was more than enough proof of his competence as a reliable and experienced leader. Over the course of the campaign, his expertise bailed the Crusaders out of what would have been doomed situations, such as when he reorganized the French army to increase morale and discipline to pass through Anatolia or when he singlehandedly raised enough money for the continuation of the Crusade in Outremer. He was already a well-known and respected figure during the Crusaders' council near Acre, probably hinting at the fact that he was the de-facto Grand Master of the Templar Order by then. Robert de Craon, the second Grand Master of the Templar and the successor to Hugues de Payens, is thought to have passed away in January 1149. It is believed that this was the time when Everard was officially elected as the new Grand Master.

However, instead of staying in the Holy Land, which was the typical dwelling place for the Grand Master, Everard chose to return to France with King Louis. The reason behind this might be the prestige he had accumulated during the Crusade with the king, as well as his nostalgia and love of his home. In any case, he left André de Montbard, one of the nine founding knights of the order and an equally experienced and competent leader, in charge. Around 1150, Everard, as the Grand Master of the Templars, received a letter in France from André, who requested reinforcements and additional funds for the well-being of the order.

There was another much more concerning point made in André's letter. The Second Crusade had somehow managed to increase the Muslim threat instead of diminishing it. Nur ad-Din was on an absolute rampage, having established firm control over all of Syria, and he had his eyes fixed on the Latin kingdoms. After Edessa, Antioch was his next target, and Raymond, Prince of Antioch, knew it. He had seen initial success in repelling Nur ad-Din, but as time went by, the situation seemed more and more dire for Antioch.

Due to Raymond's somewhat poor relationship with the rest of the Latin kingdoms, he had allied with the Kurdish Assassins in a desperate effort to stop the sultan's advance. It was all in vain. Nur ad-Din ran over Antioch, defeating the alliance first at Baghras and then at Inab. Eventually, the Muslims ambushed Raymond's camp in late June 1149, slaying the prince and destroying the majority of Antioch's forces in one night. It was a sweeping victory for Nur ad-Din, who cut Raymond's head off. He sent it to his rival, the caliph of Baghdad.

Nur ad-Din's success was a signal for the Christians to unify. Responding to the letter from the patriarch of Antioch, André de Montbard assembled more than a thousand Templars and Templar squires to join King Baldwin of Jerusalem's relief force. Although the army was, in theory, not large enough to defeat Nur ad-Din in a head-to-head battle, their quick response to the call and appearance in the north forced the Muslims to negotiate. In the treaty, most of Antioch's lands were seized by Nur ad-Din, but it was the best the Christians could manage. At least they had avoided a complete collapse of the principality and had hope that, as time went by, their chances of fighting back would increase.

Help did arrive in the form of Everard des Barres and other Templars sometime in late 1151 or early 1152. However, after his return to Outremer, Everard resigned from the position of Grand Master, choosing to return to France, where he appears to have joined the Cistercians at Clairvaux, living the rest of his days as a monk. Bernard de Tremelay was elected as the new Grand Master, who, despite his short time as the head of the order, was pretty successful. Most notably, in 1152, the forces of Jerusalem somehow managed to defeat a much larger invading Artuqid Turkish force that had camped close to the Holy City. In a miraculous victory, the Christians slew five thousand Muslims, giving them some much-needed good news. While the victory over the Artuqids was not as significant in the grand scheme of things, it was still a motivating factor for the Christians. It eventually resulted in their rally and a new war effort in Egypt.

The Siege of Ascalon

Ascalon was one of the most important cities in the East. It was located on the Palestinian coast of the Mediterranean, and it was surrounded by Christian-controlled lands from all sides. The Kingdom of Jerusalem controlled the lands on its north and east, while the Templars were in charge of Gaza, some ten miles south of the city. The order had received the area as a gift in 1149/1150, and it spent many resources in building the deserted Gaza into one of the most well-defended strongholds in all of Outremer. The Templars had reconstructed the destroyed lands and fortified Gaza beyond belief. In fact, the order had established such a firm position in Gaza and the southeastern areas of Ascalon that the Egyptians had given up trying to reinforce the city. While the Egyptians had tried to take Gaza back due to its importance in their access to Ascalon, the Templars had defended their fortress with much enthusiasm, impressing even William of Tyre, one of the most vocal critics of the Knights Templar.

Nevertheless, Ascalon was still a very difficult place to attack. The fact that it was deep in the Christian territories meant the Egyptians had to make quite an effort over the years to supply it with weapons, provisions, and men. It was surrounded by thick stone walls and had multiple towers, which were always manned by the defenders. Still, the victory over the Artuqids near Jerusalem, when paired with the rise of King Baldwin III from the shadow of his mother, Melisende, as the legitimate king of Jerusalem, as well as the fact that the Templar efforts had decreased the Fatimid presence in the region, gave the Christians the confidence to organize an attack on Ascalon.

Baldwin III called for reinforcements from all over his kingdom, and his call was sufficiently answered. Of course, Templar Grand Master Bernard de Tremelay and the Grand Master of the Knights Hospitaller, Raymond du Puy, were there with whatever brothers they could assemble for the siege. In addition to the military orders, most of the Jerusalem nobility were present with their smaller forces. The united force arrived at Ascalon in January 1153 and camped outside the city. During their march, they witnessed the Fatimid settlers who lived outside of the city walls retreating back to the fortress. This made the Christians' journey relatively smooth without any real complications.

The siege was also accompanied by a naval blockade, led by Gerard of Sidon, who commanded fifteen ships and patrolled the seas. This fleet did not allow resources to reach Ascalon or let anyone flee from the city. In addition to this, new reinforcements would be received in the form of pilgrims who arrived in the Holy Land by sea during Easter. King Baldwin offered to pay those who wished to join the siege and bought some of their ships to dismantle and construct more siege equipment.

The siege of Ascalon continued for five months. The attackers tried to stall the siege for as long as they could, hoping to starve the defenders out and force them to give up. By then, only small skirmishes had been carried out between the two sides, and King Baldwin wanted to minimize his casualties as much as he could. However, a sizeable Egyptian fleet would eventually arrive to relieve Ascalon, carrying about seventy galleys' worth of supplies and men. The massive Egyptian fleet met with little resistance from the blockading Christian fleet under Gerard of Sidon, who correctly realized that his forces would have been defeated in all-out naval combat and retreated.

Still, despite this, the Christians were seeing some progress. They had managed to move closer to the city and were slowly advancing. The defenders tried to harass the sieging troops with arrows and pieces of debris they would light on fire, but they did not see any significant success. Finally, in August, a part of the city's wall collapsed, as it had been under constant bombardment from Baldwin's forces. Suddenly, the attackers had an opening. Grand Master Bernard realized this and rushed to the gap with a small force of forty Templars, which was separated from the rest of the attacking forces. The Templars tried to advance by themselves without help from the main army, and while they did manage to get inside the walls, they were eventually cut down by the defending forces. This somewhat careless move cost Bernard his life, and the bodies of the dead Templars were hung from the city walls to intimidate the Christians.

However, Baldwin was convinced that his armies were still in a commanding position. A breach had been made, and the attackers were not about to give up after five months of slow progress. Instead, they retreated for a day and held a council, where they decided to continue the attack. Instead of using the breach to enter the city, the attackers continued to bombard Ascalon, forcing the defenders to surrender about a week later, on August 22nd, 1153. Baldwin agreed to let the Muslims leave in peace, and he proudly entered the city. He entrusted its governance to his brother Amalric. This marked one of the biggest victories of the Latin kingdoms in Outremer.

The Templars' peculiar move during the siege has been explained by different historians. Some, like William of Tyre, believed that the Grand Master and his small squad wanted to be the first ones to loot whatever parts of the city they could. They underestimated the strength of the defenders. According to William, the Templars knew that if a full-on assault was ordered by Baldwin, his men would pillage whatever was the most valuable in Ascalon. He essentially attributes their action to their innate greed. Other records are similar, but they do not really blame the Templars for being motivated by their own gains. Instead, other chronicles say that the Templars managed to make an impressive push toward the city's center but were eventually cut off and slain deep inside the city. Some even tell of the treachery of those nobles who accompanied the Templars but refused to follow them inside the city. In any case, the Grand Master's hasty decision mostly likely caused the contingent of Templars to be separated from the main army, which was not under the command of Bernard, unlike his knights. Whatever the truth may be, Ascalon was still a success for the Christians, meaning that it was also a success for the Templar Order in the long run.

Nur-ad Din's Retaliation

The years following the siege of Ascalon saw a shift in the balance of power in the East. While Baldwin III successfully captured the last of the Fatimid cities in the Holy Land, the Muslim states continued to mobilize. Not one year had passed since the capture of Ascalon before Nur ad-Din laid siege to Damascus, a city whose value we have already remarked upon. By then, the Damascene leaders, afraid of Nur ad-Din's might, had allied with the Latin kingdoms on a couple of occasions, thinking that their alliance would be an effective deterrent. Still, Nur ad-Din seized the city relatively easily in just a week with help from the inside, and even though he returned to Aleppo with his forces, taking Damascus was one more step closer to the doorstep of the Christian Holy Land.

With Damascus under his belt, Nur ad-Din and the Christians continued to stare each other down, and a series of skirmishes would break out here and there, although they were mostly smaller raids. Surprisingly, the Templars would be pretty involved in these conflicts, patrolling different trade routes and attacking hostile Muslim caravans that wished to cut their path short by entering the Holy Land. The Templars would not only disturb the travelers but also often take their valuables to add to their own treasures, further increasing their riches. Most notably, the Templars struck gold when they managed to capture a wanted Egyptian outcast vizier and his son, who were trying to flee to Cairo during a period of instability in Egypt. In fact, the vizier and his son had conspired against the caliph and were charged with the murder of the caliph's brothers. Unfortunately for them, they were ambushed by a contingent of Templars, who slew the vizier and sold his son to the Egyptians for sixty thousand pieces of gold.

In May 1157, Nur ad-Din would continue his advance with an assault on Castle Banias, which was controlled by Humphrey of Toron. This happened because King Baldwin III had violated an agreement that had previously been reached by the Christians and Nur ad-Din by ordering a raid on some Turkish-occupied areas in the region. Humphrey and a contingent of Knights Hospitaller, who dwelled in Banias after the castle had been granted to them by Baldwin some time beforehand, managed to hold out for as long as they could. They fought valiantly while waiting for relief forces from the king. After hearing that Baldwin's cavalry was on its way, Nur ad-Din decided to abandon the siege and instead raze Banias to the ground before retreating.

In fact, Baldwin's vanguard just missed the Muslim forces that were ordered to fall back. The king's army decided to camp by a nearby lake, but the men were as careless as ever, thinking that Nur ad-Din had gone all the way back to Damascus. The Muslims ambushed the Christian camp, running over the unorganized forces, which could not mobilize amid the attack. While Baldwin himself managed to escape, Nur ad-Din's forces captured a lot of prisoners, including Templar Grand Master Bertrand de Blanchefort (who had succeeded André de Montbard) and the future Grand Master Odo of Saint-Amand. The latter would be released in March 1159, while Bertrand was ransomed by the Byzantine emperor in May of that year. After their defeat at Banias, Bertrand added new points to the Latin Rule of the Templars that talked about discipline during camping while on a mission.

This defeat at the hands of Nur ad-Din was disastrous for King Baldwin III. As for the Templars, while their reaction to the absence of the Grand Master is not known, they seem to have continued existing as before, staying true to the hierarchy of the order and answering to the brother who was now in charge. Still, it seems that they were more reserved when it came to making big decisions, such as going to war in Baldwin's army between 1157 and 1159. They were absent in the Battle of Butaiha, for example, which ended in a victory for the Christians.

Baldwin III died in February of 1162 and was succeeded by his younger brother, Amalric, the one who had been granted the city of Ascalon after the Christians' triumph against the Fatimids. King Amalric of Jerusalem was perhaps the most different out of all the previous kings due to the fact that he had his eyes fixed on the southwest. He wished to conquer the rich Egyptian territories instead of putting up a fight in the north, where Nur-ed Din was still a big problem. Maybe the reason behind his desire for Egypt was the ongoing political crisis of the Fatimids, as well as the friendly relations between the king and the Byzantine emperor, which gave him leeway to focus his attention on the south.

By the start of the 1160s, Egypt was deep into a period of turmoil and did not really have the power or resources to contest other major actors in the region, most notably Jerusalem. The power was not really in the hands of the Fatimid Caliph. Instead, the vizier, Shawar, was in control behind the scenes. However, Shawar was quickly ousted by another man by the name of Dirgham, who forced the former vizier to flee north to Syria. This struggle was quickly noted by both young King Amalric and Nur ad-Din, with both rulers wishing to take over the remnants of the once-great Fatimid Caliphate for themselves and solidify their position as the sole power in the Middle East.

Amalric was the first to strike. In September 1163, the king's forces marched on Egypt, demanding that the Egyptians continue paying the yearly tribute. At first, Amalric and his army were victorious when they confronted Dirgham's forces near Pelusium, forcing them to retreat to the city. However, when the Christians laid siege, the Egyptians decided to destroy the dams on the Nile River, flooding the lands and forcing Amalric to give up. Grand Master Bertrand, who had been released from captivity by then, accompanied his king with a group of Templars. He played a role in the negotiation between the two sides, with the Egyptians promising to continue paying tribute to Jerusalem.

In the meantime, Nur ad-Din was still unstoppable in the north. While Amalric was busy fighting with the Fatimids and making no real progress in capturing more territory, Nur ad-Din decided to attack Tripoli and weaken the Christian positions in the north. Here, however, the Templars proved their worth once again, scouting out the enemy's positions ahead of time and ambushing them at night. The Templars, who were fewer in numbers and led by Gilbert de Lacy, an experienced English warrior who had joined the order some years prior, quickly routed Nur ad-Din's army. They even forced the sultan to flee for his life barefoot from his camp. Although this encounter did delay Nur ad-Din for quite some time, an interesting development that followed his defeat would change the history of the Middle East forever.

After suffering a defeat against Gilbert de Lacy and the Templars, Nur ad-Din retreated and started building his forces back up to renew his assault on the Christian lands. It was then that the sultan received an unexpected visitor from the south: Shawar, the ousted vizier of Egypt, who had fled to Syria. Shawar approached Nur ad-Din with a proposal. He offered to march his armies down to Egypt and overthrow Dirgham. If they succeeded, Shawar promised to pay the sultan an annual tribute in return for his help. Nur ad-Din instantly liked the idea of attacking Egypt. In fact, he had been thinking about it himself for quite some time, since the start of the unstable period in the region. Instead of riding south himself, he sent Shirkuh, one of his trusted generals, with a sizeable force.

In the meantime, he would focus on the Latin kingdoms in the north. An up-and-coming young man by the name of Salah ad-Din Yusuf ibn Ayyub would accompany Shirkuh in the Egyptian campaign and play a big role in the following events. He eventually became known as Saladin.

The Syrians saw great success against the Egyptians. Shirkuh confronted Dirgham's forces near Pelusium and defeated them with relative ease, killing their leader. Even though Shawar was back in power by the spring of 1164, thanks to the effort of Nur ad-Din's forces, he demanded that they quickly leave the Egyptian lands, declaring that they posed a potential threat to his kingdom. Shirkuh, however, had other plans in mind. He took the town of Bilbeis and fortified it, while Shawar sent an envoy to Jerusalem for help, promising the king, as well as his military order, huge sums of money and an array of gifts in return. King Amalric, realizing that he had the opportunity to wipe out a big chunk of Nur ad-Din's forces, assembled an army mainly comprised of Templars and marched south to lay siege to Shirkuh's position. The Syrians held out for more than three months in the fortified town, after which Amalric decided to break off the siege since Nur ad-Din had renewed the attack on the Christian factions in the north. The king of Jerusalem believed that the northern threat was more imminent and dangerous than helping Shawar in Egypt, so he turned back with his army to help defend against Nur ad-Din in the siege of Harenc (Harim) in Antioch.

Before Amalric was able to get to Antioch, a Christian alliance of Antioch, Tripoli, Armenia, and even the Byzantine Empire, led by Prince Bohemond III of Antioch, had assembled its troops to defend the region. It has to be noted that Bohemond had more than six hundred Templars with him, which made up the main punching power of his army. At first, the Christians forced the Muslims to retreat, but the Christians chased them forward, charging straight into an ambush and suffering a decisive defeat. All the leaders of the Christian forces, including Prince Bohemond, Count Raymond of Tripoli, and Byzantine General Constantine Coloman, were captured. It was a disaster and yet another victory for the Muslims against the Latin kingdoms. King Amalric could not help his fellow Christians in the north and was also unsuccessful against the Syrians in Egypt. He was only able to negotiate for Shirkuh to evacuate the territory immediately with the remainder of his forces.

A Change of Heart

Surprisingly, soon after these events, the relationship between the Templar Order and King Amalric of Jerusalem would start to worsen, according to William of Tyre, although he does not dive too deeply into the details. Apparently, Shirkuh continued to attack the Christian positions after his exit from Egypt. He assaulted two cave fortifications that were under the control of the Templars, who surrendered to the Muslim general without putting up a fight. In the meantime, Amalric had heard of Shirkuh's plan and tried to pursue him throughout Jordan to contest his move on the Templar positions. However, the king was late, as the news of the fall of the fortified territories reached him before he could catch up with the invaders. According to William of Tyre, twelve Templars who had fled from the site encountered the king and his small relief force. Amalric was infuriated with the Templars, claiming that they did not care about the kingdom's integrity and accused them of treachery. The king ordered the twelve Templars to be publicly hanged at the gallows and returned back to Jerusalem. This act, justifiable or not, caused the order and the king to frown upon each other, marking one of the most significant turns the relationship between the two parties had taken since the order's creation.

Because of this incident, the Templars would not join King Amalric in the future expeditions in Egypt, which lasted for the remainder of the 1160s. The king was really keen on taking over the Egyptian lands, and he would continue his campaigns with or without the Templars' help. Still, perhaps the lowest point in his relationship with the order happened five years after the first development. This time, it was more complicated.

The Assassins—a secretive military Shi'a organization that had originated from Castle Alamut in Persia but had established a somewhat strong foothold in Outremer by the 1170s—were continuing to be a thorn in the side of the Sunni Muslims. They opposed the bloodthirsty nature of the jihad, which had been used by many rulers to justify their war effort against the Christians. With the rise of Nur ad-Din and the decline of Fatimid Egypt, the Assassins had correctly recognized that their position in northeastern Syria was under threat from the Sunnis.

The main headquarters of the Assassins was the fortress of Masyaf in the mountainous Jebel al-Sariya region. From there, they would conduct their secretive operations of assassinating powerful individuals who they thought were a threat to the organization and disturbed peace and stability in the region. For example, they murdered Count Raymond II of Tripoli because the count wanted to take their castle for himself. This policy of murdering tyrannical leaders was due to the Assassins' inability to field armies or squads, unlike the Templars, due to their relatively smaller size. By increasing their notoriety, however, the Assassins forged a rivalry with the Knights Templar, which held strong fortifications near the Shi'a organization and was constantly trying to limit its activity.

Starting from late 1153, the balance of power shifted in favor of the Templars, as they were granted more and more castles and continued to build up their possessions, forcing the Assassins to pay an annual amount of two thousand bezants (Byzantine gold coins). The murder of an Assassin envoy in the early 1170s would see the relationship between the Templar Order and the Assassins deteriorate completely, with the two officially becoming enemies. This also worsened the already poor relationship between the Templars and King Amalric.

Sometime in 1173, an Assassin envoy was sent to King Amalric, according to William of Tyre. The messenger had been sent to Jerusalem to negotiate the terms of tribute to the Templars. According to William of Tyre, the Assassins were ready to convert to Christianity if the Templars agreed to exempt them from paying the tribute and not disturb their actions. The implications of this agreement were huge. In a way, it made sense for the Assassins to convert since they were the only party practicing Shi'a Islam in the region and were frowned upon by Nur ad-Din and the rest of the Sunni world. Also, their conversion would make their relations more favorable with the Latin kingdoms, with both sides using each other's experience and expertise in overcoming a common enemy.

William of Tyre suggests that their wish to convert to Christianity was propagated by the newly elected leader of the Assassins, whose name he does not mention in his account, although he calls him an "eloquent man of very sharp brain."[101] The new leader had collected different sacred writings of other religions and compared them to Islam. He came to the conclusion that the Shi'a ways of living were not optimal. He even encouraged his men to break basic Muslim traditions like drinking alcohol and eating pork.

---

[101] Hill (2018), p. 76.

So, when the envoy arrived at King Amalric's court, he was happily received, as the king saw the potential that lay in the agreement. To not upset the Templars, Amalric proposed that he would pay the two thousand bezants to the order from his own treasury as compensation. The talks went smoothly, and the messenger was set to return back to Castle Masyaf to finalize the agreement. He was to be accompanied by a member of the king's guard; however, he was murdered by the Templars just outside of Tripoli.

King Amalric had guaranteed the envoy's safety, granting him royal protection and respecting his status as a diplomat. This meant that the murder was a treacherous act, jeopardizing everything that had been agreed upon by the two parties. It was also seen as a shameful display, and the Assassins severed the agreement and refused to contact Jerusalem following the incident. But why exactly did the Templars do it? While the exact motive is not known, a chronicler named Walter Map writes about the greed of the Templars influencing this decision. He claims the Knights Templar, being a military organization and thriving on war, could not allow for the cessation of hostilities in the region. There was also the matter of greed, a common Templar motivator according to both Walter Map and William of Tyre. The two thousand bezants that had been paid by the Assassins every year was certainly nice for the order, and giving it up would have been very difficult, even if Amalric partially compensated what the Templars would have lost.

On the other hand, the Grand Master at the time, Odo of Saint-Amand, sent a letter to King Amalric, apologizing on behalf of his brother, who, as Odo claimed, was reckless in his actions and did not have approval. He promised the king that the Templar who had committed the crime, a knight by the name of Walter of Mesnil, would be sent to the pope to be tried, underlining the fact that the king had no authority over punishing the brother since the order only answered to the papacy. Later on, the Templars would claim that the Assassins did not deserve to be given the chance of conversion to Christianity and that they would contribute nothing to the defense of the Latin kingdoms. They supported this idea by saying that the secret organization had abandoned the idea of accepting the new religion once the news of their envoy reached them.

Whatever the case, the murder of the Assassin envoy was horrific, and it strained the relations between King Amalric and the Knights Templar even more.[102]

[102] Napier, G. (2011). *The Rise and Fall of the Knights Templar*. History Press. Chapter 4.

Hill, P. (2018). *The Knights Templar at War, 1120-1312*. Pen & Sword Military. Part 2.

Martin, S. (2011). *The Knights Templar*. Oldcastle Books. Chapter 2.

Nowell, C. E. (1947). "The Old Man of the Mountain." *Speculum*, 22(4), 497–519.

Chapter 7: The Rise of Saladin

Saladin has become one of the most recognized names in military history. So far, we have only mentioned him as a young warrior who accompanied the Syrian general Shirkuh in Egypt. However, as time would show, Saladin would rise to become a powerful, feared, and well-respected man not only in the Middle East but also in Europe. In response to Saladin's rise, the Knights Templar would demonstrate the full might of the order. This chapter will cover how Saladin became a threat to the Templars and how the brothers struggled to overcome the challenge he posed to the Christian world.

Montgisard

King Amalric died in 1174, leaving the kingdom in the hands of his young leper son Baldwin IV. The teenage Baldwin was, as one would imagine, not competent enough in ruling when he was put in the position of king. In addition, his kingdom was in shambles, as the greedy Frankish lords had been squabbling over territories in the lands controlled by the Kingdom of Jerusalem. A similar situation was going on in Nur ad-Din's sultanate. The great sultan had died the same year as Amalric, making internal politics very complicated. Rival Muslim atabegs from Mosul, Aleppo, Cairo, and Damascus fought each other for superiority.

It was at this time that the young Saladin, an experienced general who had proven his worth in the Egyptian campaigns and against the Christians, managed to unify most of the rival atabegs under his rule, convincing them to join him and continue the jihad against the Christians instead of fighting between themselves. It is thought that he succeeded in doing this because of his reputation as a pious, god-fearing man. He was respected all throughout the Muslim world for his manners and ethics. These traits complemented his amazing fighting prowess, a skill for which he was known amongst the Franks. It must be said that, unlike the other Muslim leaders who had risen to prominence before him, such as Zengi and Nur ad-Din, Saladin was not as ruthless and bloodthirsty, especially when comparing his attitude toward the Christians. While he believed that they should be driven out of Outremer, he also understood why the Crusaders were motivated to fight. He thought their cause was just as noble as the Muslims. Thus, a new era of rival rulers was about to start in the East, with Saladin as the main leader of the Muslim world on one side and young Baldwin IV on the other, who was perhaps not as experienced as his counterpart but had the entourage and the support of the Templars and the other nobles of Outremer.

Saladin

The first encounter between Saladin and the Christians would occur in 1177. For the first three years as the true sultan of the Muslim world, Saladin tried to unify his realms. He had taken Damascus and nearly succeeded in the siege of Aleppo but had to retreat. Still, he managed to unite the Muslims in most of Syria and established firm control over

Egypt. Cairo was used as his main city. In 1177, his sultanate stretched from the Nile to Mesopotamia, which was an impressive feat that no Muslim ruler was able to achieve after the arrival of the Crusaders.

After the reunification of the Muslim lands, Saladin decided to turn his attention to the Christians and finish the process of driving them out of the Holy Land. Saladin's actions were closely monitored in the Latin kingdoms, and everyone realized the threat he would pose if he was able to launch an offensive with unified Syria and Egypt strengthening his back. So, when Saladin entered the lands controlled by the Christians in northern Sinai with a large army, King Baldwin IV was quick to answer. According to the accounts of William of Tyre, Saladin's army was huge, counting more than twenty-five thousand troops, most of which were experienced cavalry divisions. Saladin's entourage was the elite Mamluk contingent; the Mamluks were heavily armored shock cavalry from Egypt and were thought to be unstoppable on an open field.

It was logical that Saladin would attack either the city of Ascalon or the Castle of Gaza as his first target. King Baldwin, who had received intelligence of Saladin's moves, had fortified Ascalon, as he believed Gaza was in the safe hands of the Templars and could be quickly reinforced in case of a siege. The young king had anticipated correctly, for Saladin soon appeared at the doorstep of Ascalon. He chose to avoid a confrontation at Gaza, which was located closer to the Egyptian border. Baldwin sallied out with his forces, eager to meet Saladin in battle, but he was advised to retreat to the city since the opposing army was much larger than what he had expected.

The Muslims realized that they had effectively cornered the Christian army in Ascalon. They knew they would be relatively unopposed if they entered the heart of the kingdom, so they started to march toward the poorly defended Jerusalem and raided the lands along the way. King Baldwin realized the situation would be desperate if Saladin's army reached the Holy City, so he decided to chase after the enemy with a small force of his most elite troops, which would allow him to move quickly to catch up with Saladin. He sent to Gaza for help, assembling a small but very professional force of about four hundred mounted knights, plus eighty Templars led by Grand Master Odo of Saint-Amand. In addition, the king brought about two thousand infantrymen who would support his elite vanguard. The king planned to surprise the Muslim forces, which were slowly moving toward Jerusalem, from the north and disrupt their advance until more reinforcements showed up.

King Baldwin caught up with Saladin on November 25th, 1177. The Muslim army was crossing a narrow mountainous pass southeast of Ramla at Montgisard, causing them to stretch their numbers. Due to the disadvantage of the terrain, the Muslims' numerical superiority was ineffective. The Christians decided to act quickly and decisively, knowing that if the enemy managed to get out of the area, they would struggle in a head-to-head battle. Before their offensive, William of Tyre wrote that the Christian forces "arranged their lines according to military rules, disposing in proper order those who to make the first attack and the reserves who were to come to their aid."[103] This probably hints at the Templars' role of heading the organization of the troops and leading them into battle.

Then Baldwin's troops charged Saladin's northern flank headfirst without any hesitation, aiming to break through the front lines and get to the sultan himself. According to one chronicler, Ralph of Diss, the Templar contingent bonded together "as one man...turning neither left nor right...recognizing the battalion in which Saladin commanded many knights and manfully approached it."[104] The Templars slaughtered their way into the heart of Saladin's army, which was slow to mobilize against the surprise attack. Although Saladin managed to escape, leaving much of his equipment behind in order to run away faster with a small number of his Mamluk knights, most of the Muslim forces were chased down and slain.

It was a huge victory for the Christians; in fact, it was one of the most significant during the existence of the Crusader States. With it, King Baldwin narrowly managed to avoid the loss of Jerusalem and forced Saladin to retreat to Egypt. For days, the scattered Muslim soldiers would be cut down, with the Christian forces looting their corpses and taking the loot back to their king. All in all, the victory at Montgisard brought a sigh of relief to King Baldwin, as it gave him a chance to regroup and rethink his strategy against Saladin, who he knew would eventually return. The king had also, in effect, repaired the damaged relations between the crown and the Knights Templar. The Templars were praised for a long time after the battle because of their bravery and fighting at Montgisard, as they had been the ones who led the king's forces to victory. Still, despite this decisive victory, Baldwin IV had lost quite a few of his troops in the

---

[103] Hill (2018), p. 81.
[104] Hill (2018), p. 81.

encounter, and while he had, for the time, driven Saladin out, the war was not over. The victory at Montgisard helped boost the morale of the Christians, but the years that followed would prove to be difficult to endure, as a succession crisis and an array of internal problems destabilized the kingdom, giving Saladin a chance to retaliate.

Jerusalem's Succession Crisis

After the Battle of Montgisard, Saladin and Baldwin agreed to a truce, which was very much needed by both sides. For Saladin, it would give him more time to regroup after his defeat against the Christians and think of a new plan of action. For Baldwin, peace would relieve his kingdom from the constant pressure Saladin's sultanate exerted, giving him time to organize a better defense. However, a new Templar castle, Chastelet, located in a strategically important location near Jacob's Ford about ten miles southwest of Damascus, was taken by Saladin in violation of the agreement. The sultan claimed that Baldwin had agreed not to fortify the Jacob's Ford area since it was very close to the city of Damascus and posed a threat to the safety of the Muslims in Syria.

Chastelet was an impressive fortification located at the narrow crossing point of the ford. By early 1179, even though the Templars were not done building the castle, it had been constructed to the point where it could have been used defensively in case of an attack. All in all, the establishment of the Knights Templar in the area at Castle of Chastelet would have meant that caravans traveling from Egypt to Syria would have to go under the observation of the Christians, making the route unreliable. Saladin initially offered Baldwin 60,000 dinars to abandon the construction, an amount he later increased to 100,000 dinars. Still, Baldwin refused, making Saladin launch an offensive on Chastelet.

He arrived at the castle in May but was forced to retreat when one of his emirs was killed by Templar archers. In June, the Christians would mount an assault on Saladin, led by Templar Grand Master Odo and Raymond of Tripoli. This time, Saladin reigned supreme, defeating the Christians and capturing Odo of Saint-Amand. It was the second time the Templar Grand Master had been a captive of a Syrian sultan, as he had been captured years earlier in 1156 with Bertrand de Blanchefort, who was the Grand Master of the order at the time. The two were quickly released from captivity thanks to the ransom paid by the Byzantine emperor. This time, however, Odo declined to be exchanged for a captured Muslim general, and he eventually died in prison in 1180.

Arnold of Torroja would replace him as the new Templar Grand Master. He had previously been the Master of the Templars in Spain and Provence. Arnold was an experienced man and quick to indulge himself in the administrative matters of the East, urging the Latin kingdoms to unite and face the threat of Saladin. His time as the Grand Master of the order was unfortunately cut short. In 1184, he decided to travel to Italy with Patriarch Heraclius and the Grand Master of the Knights Hospitaller, Roger des Moulins. They wanted to spread the word of Saladin's rise and ask for Western help.

Arnold could not deliver the message himself, however, as he died during the journey. He was replaced by Gerard de Ridefort, a charismatic person and the former marshal of Jerusalem, who would be remembered as arguably one of the worst Grand Masters at making big decisions. Around the same time, King Baldwin IV died of leprosy at the age of twenty-four. The years that followed would see the Grand Master and the Knights Templar as a whole becoming involved in the succession crisis of the Kingdom of Jerusalem.

The late leper king had no heir, so his ten-year-old nephew, Baldwin V, ascended to the throne under the patronage of Count Raymond of Tripoli. Unfortunately, the bad genes of the family showed once again, as young Baldwin soon fell ill and died, only lasting one year as the king of Jerusalem. Baldwin IV, however, had thought ahead. He had stated in his will that if his heir died at a young age, the rule of the Kingdom of Jerusalem would be entrusted to Count Raymond until a suitable new king could be found, preferably someone from Europe. Count Raymond, in fact, was already an experienced leader, so having him remain as regent after Baldwin V's death was a good idea, even more so because he managed to renegotiate a ceasefire agreement and a four-year non-aggression pact with Saladin.

Still, a power vacuum existed in the kingdom, with the Frankish nobles of Outremer soon recognizing that Raymond had not found a replacement by late 1186. In September of 1186, Baldwin IV's sister, Sybil, would claim that she was the legitimate heir to the throne, even though succession laws at the time excluded females. She revolted against Count Raymond and declared her husband, Guy of Lusignan, the new king. Interestingly, Grand Master Gerard was an avid supporter of this move, leading some historians to believe that Sybil and Guy had promised the Templars more power for their support.

Unsurprisingly, Guy of Lusignan was not exactly loved by his subjects. For one thing, he was seen as a usurper by the Frankish nobles, who believed that his claim to the throne of Jerusalem was weak. In addition, he was not really considered high nobility since he did not have an impressive background like the other possible choices. The only ones who sided with him, besides the Templar Grand Master, were power-hungry nobles, such as Reginald (Raynald) of Chatillon, who had a terrible reputation. Reginald was an unpredictable person, having been imprisoned by the Syrians for about sixteen years, which had probably caused his hatred toward the Muslims. After his release in 1176, he would set out on several anti-Muslim expeditions outside of Jerusalem-controlled territories and raided trade caravans that were trying to reach Syria from Egypt. In 1182, he had gone even further by raiding merchant ships in the Red Sea and Muslims who were traveling to the city of Mecca. Needless to say, the fact that King Guy had surrounded himself with people like Reginald of Chatillon and a rather rash Templar Grand Master was not a great sign.

The Fall of Jerusalem

It can be argued the recklessness of these two singlehandedly sabotaged any potential talks of peace with Saladin and angered the sultan beyond belief. First, in 1186, the peace between the Muslims and the Latin kingdoms, which had been finally agreed upon by Count Raymond, was jeopardized when Reginald attacked a Muslim merchant caravan. He killed the Egyptian entourage and looted their goods. Saladin was furious and turned to Count Raymond for an explanation. The count had nothing to do with Reginald's actions and told the sultan this.

Then, he brokered another peace agreement between his lands in Tripoli and his wife's domains in Galilee, giving Saladin his word that nothing like this would be repeated again in exchange for mercy for himself. Over the years, Count Raymond had grown pretty close to the Muslim ways of life and understood their customs fairly well. He had been a prisoner in Syria, but instead of hating the Muslims, he developed a respectful attitude toward them, which explains his relative success in the talks with Saladin. However, little did Count Raymond know that his efforts would once again be for nothing.

Soon after the incident, Raymond, on one side, and Guy and his entourage, on the other, decided to meet in the count's lands to talk about the ongoing situation in the Holy Land and settle on some sort of an agreement to improve their relations. They all realized that petty infighting would only speed up the doom of the Christians in the East. They agreed to meet at the town of Tiberias on the Sea of Galilee. The delegation, which included the Grand Masters of both the Templars and the Hospitallers, had marched out of Jerusalem and decided to stay at Templar Le Féve for the night. Before their arrival, however, Raymond had received word from Saladin's envoy to let some Muslim troops pass through his lands, a proposition he accepted because of his truce with the sultan. Unfortunately for the count, he was too slow to let the arriving delegation know about the Muslim troops.

The Templar squad under Grand Master Gerard, which counted only ninety brothers, as well as fifty more from the Hospitallers and secular knights, decided to attack. Their small force, however, was nothing in comparison to Saladin's seven-thousand men. Although Gerard decided to confront the Muslims on May 1st, 1187, at the Spring of Cresson, Grand Master Roger of the Hospitallers advised him not to proceed with the attack. The ensuing battle was a complete massacre, with the Muslims winning easily over the Christian knights. Grand Master Gerard managed to escape with two other knights while everyone else, including the Grand Master of the Hospitallers, was slain on the battlefield.

Saladin was not content with the victory at Cresson. His encounter with the Christians at Cresson was yet another instance of a broken peace agreement from the Latins. He was fed up with the untrustworthiness of the Franks and continued his march to Tiberias, besieging the city. Count Raymond realized that his treaty with Saladin was once again dead, and he had ridden out of the city before the arrival of the Muslim forces to meet with King Guy in Jerusalem and make up with him. By the end of June, King Guy had called for reinforcements from all over his realm and assembled a force of more than twelve thousand troops, which included large contingents from the Templars, Hospitallers, Turkish mercenaries, and infantrymen from the Frankish lords. By answering the call, the Templars and Hospitallers had summoned most of the brothers who were fit for fighting, leaving most of their fortifications relatively unattended. Saladin, on the other hand, had received even more reinforcements at Tiberias, with his numbers reaching about twenty thousand men. Tiberias would quickly fall to the sultan, and the countess of Tripoli would be trapped inside the castle.

It was looking desperate for the Franks, who, despite assembling an army, were hesitant to launch an offensive against the Mamluks. It was the middle of summer, and attacking in the extreme heat would put the Christians at a disadvantage. Plus, they correctly assumed that they would be outnumbered. Count Raymond advised King Guy to take a defensive position, even though his wife was a prisoner of the sultan and his lands were directly under threat from the Muslims. At first, the king listened. However, Grand Master Gerard thought otherwise. While the Christian army was encamped at Sephoria, he persuaded King Guy not to listen to the cowardly Count Raymond. The Grand Master told the king that losing Tiberias and allowing the Muslim force to move around and raid his lands freely was a shameful display. This was all Guy needed to hear. A day later, on July 3rd, 1187, he and his army rode out of Sephoria to meet Saladin at Tiberias.

The Christians decided to approach Saladin's position from the north through the hills of Galilee, arriving at the village of Lubya. They marched in the traditional column formation, with Count Raymond at the front, followed by the heart of the army with King Guy, and the Templar and Hospitaller contingents at the very back. Saladin had heard of the Christian offensive and sent out mounted archer divisions to harass the enemy and prolong their march. This had a devastating effect on the Christians, who would come under fire from the smaller Muslim squadrons again and again. They were never able to chase them down. Finally, the king received word from the Templars at the back, urging him to stop his advance. The king was forced to camp in the hilly region known as the Horns of Hattin.

Their situation was looking doomed. The Christians had no reliable water supply nearby. They were exhausted from the constant harassment and marching in the heat, and they were encamped in an uncomfortable position. Allegedly, Count Raymond realized what was going on and said aloud, "The war is over. We are dead men. The Kingdom is done for."[105] During the night, Saladin reached the Christians from the south. His men made a great fire, and in the morning, the breeze took the smoke over to the Christian camp in the north, making their lives even more difficult. As dawn broke on July 4th, Saladin's men attacked the Christians, splitting the army in half. King Guy's demoralized troops fought as hard as they could but were quickly overwhelmed by the might of Saladin's army. The Horns made it even more difficult for them to escape, as the Muslims overran their positions.

---

[105] Martin, (2011), p. 69.

The Muslims claimed a decisive victory and slew most of the Franks. The Muslims walked away from the battle with an array of valuable prisoners, including Grand Master Gerard, King Guy, and Reginald of Chatillon. They also claimed an invaluable Christian relic for themselves, the True Cross, which had been transported from the Church of the Holy Sepulchre to boost the morale of the fighters and remind them of their cause of fighting for Jesus.

The Battle of Hattin was the final decisive blow. The prisoners were taken to Damascus, where the sultan spared the lives of the king and the Grand Master but publicly executed Reginald, who was hated. As for the captured Templars, he forced them to either convert to Islam or die. The Templars, to nobody's surprise, refused to give up Christianity, bravely offering themselves to be hanged or beheaded, believing they were dying as martyrs in the name of Jesus for a greater cause. This almost fanatical devotion of the Templars to their religion was one of the main reasons for Saladin's negative attitude toward the order. In Damascus, he executed more than two hundred Templars, only sparing their Grand Master.

Saladin then turned his attention to the now undefended lands of the Kingdom of Jerusalem. As we have already mentioned, the remaining Christian cities were left with no real garrisons since they had been sent to support the main army, which made it very easy for Saladin to take the Holy Land by storm. One by one, the cities and fortresses for which the Christians had sacrificed a lot, like Ascalon, Gaza, and Acre, fell into the hands of the sultan without any opposition. He finally reached the most important city of them all—Jerusalem—in October of 1187 and marched into the city.

Even though Saladin was tolerant and respectful toward the Christian population of the town and allowed the Church of the Holy Sepulchre to continue existing as a Christian monastery, he forced the Templars to abandon the Al-Aqsa Mosque, the place where the order had been founded. In fact, no Templar would ever be able to set foot in the place of their origin ever again. However, the Christians were far from done when it came to fighting for the Holy Land.[106]

---

[106] Hill, P. (2018). *The Knights Templar at War, 1120-1312.* Pen & Sword Military. Part 2.

Martin, S. (2011). *The Knights Templar.* Oldcastle Books. Chapter 2.

Humphreys, R. S. (1977). *From Saladin to the Mongols: The Ayyubids of Damascus, 1193-1260.*

Chapter 8: The Third Crusade

If it had been unclear before, the fall of Jerusalem signaled that the balance of power in the East had shifted heavily in favor of the Muslims. While the sultan had not completely wiped out the Christian presence in Outremer, he had substantially weakened it by taking key cities and fortresses in the Holy Land. The scattered Christians were in a panic, and just as they had done before when times were tough, they requested help from the West. This chapter will explore the response of the Christian world to the fall of Jerusalem in 1187 and take a closer look at the pivotal role the Knights Templar played in the effort to take back the lost lands.

The News Reaches Europe

By 1189, the only meaningful victory of the Christians versus Saladin had been the Battle of Montgisard. As we have already remarked, however, the victory at Montgisard only postponed the inevitable collapse of Jerusalem, which was struggling with internal problems while having to deal with the sultan at the same time. Despite the best efforts of the Templars, even their professionalism and military prowess were not enough to keep the Muslims at bay.

One of the biggest and, in a way, accidental problems with the Knights Templar as an institution was that there was no good way of replenishing the casualties the brothers suffered on the battlefield. While many people were willing to join the order, most of them were occupied with non-military matters, like running the numerous Templar holdings or financial affairs, while a minority of the Templars were knights who served in the armies. In addition, the fact that the Templars had embraced celibacy made it impossible for them to have children, which means they did not produce sons who could follow in their footsteps.

Over the years, due to the countless encounters with the Muslims, the Templars had exhausted their numbers, making it very easy for Saladin to overwhelm them in their own castles. Still, this did not diminish the role of the Templars; in fact, it made them even more valuable. Grand Master Gerard's influence in the succession crisis of Jerusalem describes the power the Templar Order held even when the situation in Outremer was dire. And even though Gerard could and should be criticized for the hasty and unwise decisions he took to exert his influence over King Guy, it could be argued that Jerusalem was doomed either way.

After the Battle of Hattin, Brother Terrence, the Templar Grand Commander, took charge of the order since Gerard had been taken as a prisoner by Saladin. Terrence was quick to realize that the remaining Christian forces were far from enough to put up a fight against Saladin. So, he wrote two letters and sent them to the pope and Count Philip of Flanders, who had recently visited the Holy Land. The Templar brother described the disastrous situation in the East and urged Europe to start a new Crusade. Pope Urban III, after receiving the letter in the spring of 1188 in Verona, reportedly had a heart attack due to the grave content of the letter and died on the spot. Gregory VII replaced Urban III, and although he only served as the new pope for no more than three months, he managed to circulate the letter among the European lords, spreading the news of the fall of Jerusalem around the continent. The pope urged the European kings to stop fighting each other and concentrate their attention and resources on a new expedition to the Holy Land. This would be the Third Crusade.

Interestingly, all of Europe suddenly swung into the Crusading spirit, much like the first time after the Council of Clermont. European lords from all over started to mobilize and answer the pope's call. Arguably, their motivation was not so much divine (they did not seek to remit their sins by fighting in the name of Christ). Instead, they wanted to prove themselves on the battlefield since the rival kings of Europe had not gained anything significant after years of warfare.

The Third Crusade presented a new opportunity. It could be a way to prove a ruler's worth not only to their subjects but also to the pope.

Gaining more favor with the papacy could only prove to be advantageous. King William II of Sicily, for example, who was one of the first to receive the news, immediately sent a small fleet to Antioch to offer support and a potential escape mechanism for the Christians of the city. Eventually, England's King Richard I "the Lionheart," France's King Philip II, and Holy Roman Emperor Frederick Barbarossa would start the main campaign to the Holy Land.

The Kings' Crusade

The Kings' Crusade, as the effort would fittingly come to be known, would, much like the Second Crusade, be two separate journeys to the Holy Land. Emperor Frederick I of the Holy Roman Empire was the first to set out to Outremer, doing so sometime in early 1188. He had about twelve thousand men at his disposal. All the major German dukes, as well as his own son, followed the lead of the sixty-six-year-old emperor. Before the Germans started their march, however, the emperor sent envoys to the Hungarians, Byzantines, and Turks, asking them for military access, as his forces would have had to go through their lands. Frederick also sent an emissary to Sultan Saladin himself, as he had made a treaty with him earlier and thought it would have been only just to let him know of the end of the non-aggression pact.

The emperor's forces crossed Hungary without any losses, and they were welcomed by the locals, who let them pass peacefully. Anatolia would prove to be much more challenging for Emperor Frederick. Even though he had asked for military access, the Turkish mounted archers were problematic to deal with, just as they had been during the First and Second Crusades. Unlike his ancestor Conrad, Emperor Frederick was able to successfully repel the attack of the Turks, first at the Battle of Philomelion, where about two thousand Crusaders decisively defeated a ten-thousand-strong Turkish army, and then at the capital city of Iconium in May, sacking the city and killing about three thousand Turks in the process.

It all looked very promising for the German Crusaders, as they had approached the Latin kingdoms without having suffered any significant casualties. Unfortunately, the old emperor was not destined to take back the Holy Land. In June, Emperor Frederick Barbarossa's horse slipped while crossing the Saleph River, drowning the emperor. This heavily demoralized the German army, causing most men to return home to the pending election of the new Holy Roman emperor. Those who remained, about five thousand men in total, were led by Frederick's son, Frederick of Swabia, to Antioch, where they would eventually join up with the other Crusader army.

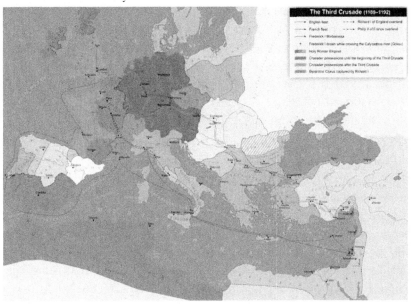

The route of the Third Crusade

The second and the main Crusader army was led by Richard I and Philip II. In fact, the two had stopped their war to unite for the Crusaders' cause and started mobilizing in January 1188. Their combined army was larger than Frederick's, counting upward of twenty thousand men, including a sizeable contingent of Templars led by their new Grand Master and a dear friend of Richard, Robert de Sable. The two kings agreed to muster their troops and meet at Sicily, from where they would set sail to the Holy Land. Unfortunately, Richard and Philip's relationship would suffer throughout the campaign, as the two kings would fall out over the issue of Richard's marriage. He had decided to break his betrothal with Philip's sister, Alys. For this reason, Philip left Sicily in March 1191 without waiting for the English to arrive. They would set out for Outremer a month later.

By the time King Richard arrived in the Holy Land, only Tripoli and Antioch were under firm Christian control. All the other possessions had been lost to Saladin. The Crusaders reunited at Acre in June, complete with the English and the French, as well as the remainder of the German troops (now under Leopold V of Austria since Frederick of Swabia had died) and an Armenian force under King Leo. Richard put himself in charge of the assault on the city. Taking Acre would be a significant achievement for the Christians if they wished to continue further military operations in the south. Acre fell a month later on July 12th. The Crusaders' inability to properly negotiate who should be put in charge of the city caused Richard to once again fall out with Philip and Leopold, who both decided to return to Europe with much of their forces. Still, this did not really affect King Richard. He had made it clear that he was capable of achieving more in the Holy Land.

After Acre, Richard took his men to Jaffa since taking the coastal city would make a potential assault on Jerusalem much easier. The Crusaders, however, were intercepted by the Muslim army in early September at Arsuf, which was about thirty miles away from the city. There, Saladin's men would suffer another decisive defeat by the Crusaders, who, despite being heavily outnumbered, managed to gain victory due to the tactical genius of Richard. The Templars also made up a significant portion of the army, so their efforts deserve recognition as well. Arsuf was Saladin's first major defeat after Montgisard, with Richard effectively taking control of the coastline and posing a serious threat to Jerusalem.

However, despite the successes at Acre and Arsuf, Richard and the Crusaders would never manage to take back the Holy City. Even though he had an open path to Jerusalem and came close enough to the city to see its walls, he decided to take the Templars' advice and not proceed any further. The order believed that even if the Crusaders managed to capture Jerusalem, it would be a near-impossible task to keep it, as it would require much effort and manpower. The Templars argued that most of the Crusaders would sail back to Europe instead of staying in Jerusalem, making it difficult to defend the Holy City. Richard listened to his advisors and chose to retreat to Ascalon. There, he rebuilt the city, which had been razed to the ground by Saladin, and chose to negotiate with the sultan instead, seeking to allow the free practice of Christianity to the pilgrims inside the city.

The king stayed at Ascalon for four months and then returned to Acre, only to hear the news that Saladin had taken Jaffa in just three days. In response, Richard decided to organize a counterattack and took the city back with the help of a small Templar force. After that, the negotiations with Saladin came to an end. The sultan recognized the Christian territories along the coast and agreed to a truce, while Richard agreed to dismantle the fortifications he had rebuilt in Ascalon. In early October 1192, Richard the Lionheart set sail to England, accompanied by a Templar entourage. He had achieved some progress during the Crusade.

The Aftermath of the Third Crusade

Before Richard left for England, he made sure to indulge himself in one more important matter—the succession of the Kingdom of Jerusalem. By the time the Crusaders reached the Holy Land, King Guy had been released by Saladin. Still, the nobility of Jerusalem was not exactly keen on his return, and when he tried to take power back, he was refused. Instead, the Frankish lords of Outremer favored Conrad de Montferrat, the German prince who had arrived in Outremer to support the Crusader States in 1188. Richard I endorsed Guy and wanted to install him as king. The matter would eventually be decided by a vote, with the Frankish nobility voting unanimously for Conrad. In theory, this made a lot of sense, judging by the fact that Conrad was of European descent and Guy's previous reign could not be characterized as successful.

Unfortunately, however, Conrad would be murdered by the Assassins just two days before he was to be crowned king. The barons of Jerusalem agreed to make King Richard's nephew, Henry of Champagne, the new king of Jerusalem. There still are doubts over whether Richard ordered the murder of Conrad, but nothing has ever been proven. As for Guy of Lusignan, Richard entrusted him with the control of the island of Cyprus, which he had actually conquered on his way to Outremer. In fact, in 1191, when Richard stopped at the island with his ships to resupply, he aided the people of Cyprus in getting rid of their Byzantine ruler, who was unpopular due to his positive relations with Saladin. After driving him out, Richard sold the island to the Templars for 100,000 bezants, who then sold it back to Richard and, therefore, Guy a year later. Choosing Guy as the leader of Cyprus meant that he was officially out of contention for the throne of Jerusalem. The island was a much more suitable place for him to rule since it was not nearly as strong or important as other Christian holdings in the East.

With the Third Crusade, the Christians managed to reclaim some of the lost territories in the Holy Land. Most importantly, they had now regained control of the coastline, making it more accessible for pilgrims and potential reinforcements to arrive from the West. In addition, they had significantly weakened Saladin's position, and the sultan would pass away soon after the end of the Third Crusade.

All in all, this Crusade was not nearly as unsuccessful as the second one. It can be argued that, in a way, the Crusaders were unlucky. Who knows what would have happened if Emperor Frederick Barbarossa had made it to the Holy Land with most of his army. Still, despite the infighting amongst the leaders of the Crusade and the relative lack of resources they had to work with, they achieved quite a lot, more than one would expect. Even though they did not capture Jerusalem, the Crusaders were probably right not to try an assault on the city, as it would result in more casualties and would be difficult to hold once the majority of the army returned home.

As for the Templars, just like the rest of the Christians of the East, they were given some breathing room after their struggles with Saladin. The new Grand Master, Robert de Sable, had proven to be a much more competent leader than Gerard, who was eventually beheaded by Saladin in 1189. After the Third Crusade, the Templars took their time to rebuild and regain their strength. They moved their headquarters to Acre and quickly started fortifying it, transforming it into the wealthiest and most important Christian city of the East. The brothers also contributed to the reconstruction of the destroyed castles that had been in their possession.

Most importantly, the Templars tried to regain the lost fortresses in the Amanus March, like Castle Gaston, which had been abandoned by the Muslims after being conquered in the 1180s. The Templars fought over Gaston with Leo of Armenia for more than two decades until, finally, the king decided to turn it and other Templar holdings over after being excommunicated by the pope.

Templar involvement in the Third Crusade was just as, if not more, prevalent than during the Second Crusade. The Templars were the driving force of King Richard's army, and they helped the king navigate the Holy Land. Grand Master Robert had played a similar role to Everard des Barres, advising and guiding the leader of the Crusade and striving for discipline and excellence in his army.

One very important development that followed the Third Crusade was the establishment of the Teutonic Order—one of the three major Christian military orders in history, alongside the Templars and the Hospitallers. Out of the three, the Hospitallers were the oldest, founded in 1070, some fifty years before the Knights Templar.

The Hospitallers' original purpose was not fighting. Founded by a group of merchants from Amalfi, the Hospital, as the name suggests, served as a place for the traveling pilgrims in the Holy Land to stay and be treated. The Hospital had close ties with the Church of the Holy Sepulchre, providing the pilgrims with any sort of humanitarian aid they might need. The order was highly popular from the very beginning and began receiving lands all over Outremer after the success of the First Crusade. In fact, it was officially recognized by the pope in the early 1110s, with Saint John the Baptist as their patron saint. After the election of their second Grand Master, Raymond du Puy, the Hospitallers adopted a military aspect as part of their lifestyle. This development coincided with the formation and rise of the Templars, which was a Christian military organization at the very beginning.

It is thought that the Templars would often guard the holdings of the Hospitallers in the early years since the Hospitallers had not yet incorporated militarism. However, under Grand Master Raymond, the organization came up with a new name: "the Order of the Knights of the Hospital of Saint John of Jerusalem." This name was inspired by their Templar counterparts, and the two became more and more alike. Just like the Templars, the Hospitallers would also make a name for themselves, and while their possessions and overall wealth and power were not as excessive as the Knights Templar, they were deeply trusted by the kings of Jerusalem and even rose to prominence in Europe. In fact, the order would continue its operations long after the dissolution of the Knights Templar, a matter we shall discuss further down the line.

As noted previously, the foundations laid by the Templars and the Hospitallers led to the creation of another very important Christian military order: the Order of the Teutonic Knights. The Teutons would be formed by those German Crusaders who chose to stay in the Holy Land after the Third Crusade (as you might recall, a large number of the German troops chose to return home after the death of their emperor). Those German knights who decided to stay joined a field hospital set up by a group of German pilgrims and merchants from Lubeck and Bremen. The headquarters were not nearly as impressive as those of the Templars and the Hospitallers. It was a tent made from sails located in the city of Acre. The Hospitallers had chosen Saint Mary as their patron, and when the German knights joined, they were named the Teutonic Knights of Saint Mary's Hospital of Jerusalem.

The Teutonic Order would officially be recognized by the Templars in 1198 at the Temple of Acre, incorporating it into the Christian Church. Over time, the Teutonic Knights would shift their base of operations from the Holy Land to northern and eastern Europe, becoming heavily involved in the politics of the Holy Roman Empire, Lithuania, Hungary, and other major European states. In fact, at the height of their power, they would establish their own state off the coast of the Baltic Sea and become a major actor in Europe.[107]

[107] Brand, C. M. (1962). "The Byzantines and Saladin, 1185-1192: Opponents of the Third Crusade." *Speculum*, 37 (2), 167-181.

Martin, S. (2011). *The Knights Templar*. Oldcastle Books. Chapter 2.

Hill, P. (2018). *The Knights Templar at War, 1120-1312*. Pen & Sword Military. Part 2.

Lotan, S. (2015). "The Teutonic Knights and their Attitude about Muslims: Saracens in the Latin Kingdom of Jerusalem and in the Baltic Region." *Fear and Loathing in the North: Jews and Muslims in Medieval Scandinavia and the Baltic Region*, 313-328.

Willoughby, J. (2012). "A Templar Chronicle of the Third Crusade: Origin and Transmission." *Medium Ævum, 81*(1), 126-134.

Section Three: The Fall of the Knights Templar

Chapter 9: The Final Days in the East

Overall, even though the Christians managed to consolidate some of the lost territories thanks to the efforts of the Templars and King Richard in the Third Crusade, many questions still needed to be answered. Most importantly, how long would the "peace" between the Latin kingdoms and the Muslim world continue? In addition, there was also the issue of Jerusalem, as the Holy City was not under the control of the Christians.

As for the Templars, even though the order would manage to reclaim much of its strength, it was no surprise that it would not reach the level it had before. While the Knights Templar continued to build up their resources, expanding in Europe and reinforcing the frontlines in the East, the order would start declining in the decades following the recapture of Acre. This chapter will explore how the order was confronted with different challenges throughout the 13ᵗʰ century, starting an almost one-hundred-year period of instability and chaos that would eventually see the end of the Knights Templar.

The Fifth Crusade

The world was split over whether or not the Third Crusade had been a success. It has to be said that King Richard had made significant improvements for the Christians in the Holy Land. Perhaps if he had had the backing of the full Crusader force, he might have even gained even more than he did. As it stood, after Richard's departure from Outremer, Jerusalem was still in Saladin's hands. This was perceived as a viable reason for a new Crusade by Pope Innocent, whose efforts eventually resulted in the shameful events of the Fourth Crusade. Instead of arriving in the Holy Land, the Europeans sacked the city of Constantinople, which at that time was still under the Byzantine Empire's control.

Due to this, the Templar involvement in the Fourth Crusade was basically nonexistent. After all, the main purpose of the order was to fight against the Muslims and protect the interests of the Christian world. Warring with their Greek Orthodox Christian brothers did not fall on the Templar agenda. However, not long after the Fourth Crusade, in 1216, Pope Honorius III would finally make Pope Innocent's dream come true.

By then, Guillaume (William) de Chartres was the Grand Master of the Templars. The heavy Templar involvement in the Fifth Crusade was due to a letter he received from the pope, in which he was asked to meet with the leaders of the new Crusade to discuss the plan and oversee the operations. The same letter was received by the Hospitaller Grand Master, Guérin de Montaigu. Together, the two Grand Masters met with King Andrew of Hungary and Duke Leopold of Austria on the island of Cyprus. The funding of the expedition was also overseen by the Templars, as the money would be collected at the Paris Temple by Brother Haimard, the Templar treasurer, and be transported and accompanied by the knights of the order.

After much consideration, the Crusaders decided to launch an assault on the city of Damietta – a key Egyptian city located in the Nile Delta. Surprisingly, after some initial struggles the Crusaders experienced during landing, Damietta was easily captured in mid-1218. By then, John of Brienne, King of Jerusalem, and Hugh I of Cyprus had also joined up with the rest of the forces. The Crusaders would be impressed by the skill of the Templars, especially given the fact that they were fighting in difficult conditions. Navigating the swamps and marshes of the Nile Delta was not easy, but the Templars were able to maneuver effectively both on horseback and on foot in difficult terrain. Their bravery was remarked upon by Oliver of Paderborn, who accounts much of the Crusaders' success to the Templars.

Unfortunately for the Templars, Guillaume de Chartres would die during the siege in late August. He was replaced by Peter de Montaigu— the brother of Guérin de Montaigu, the Grand Master of the Hospitallers. In an extraordinary circumstance in the history of these military orders, the same family was in charge of both the Templars and the Hospitallers.

The loss of Damietta prompted the Egyptian Sultan al-Kamil to send an interesting offer to the Crusaders in the autumn of 1219. In the letter, he offered to give Jerusalem and the True Cross back to the Christians in exchange for the recently captured Damietta. Perhaps the sultan thought that the establishment of a Crusader holding so close to the heart of his sultanate posed a serious threat. However, the Crusaders declined the offer for the same reason King Richard had done so decades earlier; they knew holding onto Jerusalem would take a lot of resources that Outremer still did not have.

In true Crusader fashion, the victory at Damietta would be followed by internal quarrels over who should be put in charge of the city, causing many of the men to hop on ships and abandon the Crusade. In addition, the Templars had their own problems in the north, as their Atlit Castle was under siege by the Muslims, who maintained the siege until November of 1220. For this reason, Peter de Montaigu had to send a number of his men northward, taking much of the strength and wisdom away from the Crusader army.

At that point, Cardinal Pelagius, the de-facto leader of the Crusade who had been sent from Rome by the pope himself, was considering a new assault on Cairo, the capital of the Egyptians. However, the two Grand Masters would argue that stretching the Crusader resources from Damietta to Cairo would be challenging, as they were not aware of the potential strength of the Egyptians. In fact, when the sultan realized that an attack on Cairo was imminent, he offered the Christians a ceasefire for a second time, now guaranteeing them a thirty-year truce and control over the city of Jerusalem and the lands that acted as a buffer between the Holy City and Egypt.

However, even though this offer seemed logical to accept, and Pelagius had been ordered by the pope to discuss any peace agreements, the cardinal denied the offer and set his eyes on Cairo. He did not listen to the advice of the Templar and Hospitaller Grand Masters. Cardinal Pelagius was banking on German reinforcements led by the newly elected Emperor Frederick II, the grandson of Frederick Barbarossa. Unfortunately for Pelagius, the Germans were nowhere to be seen, and he had already committed to an offensive on Cairo. This caused the Christians to overextend and be cut down by the Egyptian hit-and-run forces. This defeat eventually caused the cardinal to give up, forcing him to surrender Damietta back to the Egyptians. The Fifth Crusade was over.

Frederick II

Some Crusaders blamed the failure of the Fifth Crusade on Emperor Frederick II's absence. He had vowed to join the Crusade in 1212 at his coronation. Still, Frederick II was a very interesting figure who would come to define most of the future matters of Outremer. From an early age, Frederick II had an interest in studying the East and was fascinated with Arab culture. So much so, in fact, that he ruled as close to the Arabs as possible, residing in Sicily (which was, at the time, a part of the Holy Roman Empire). His personal bodyguard was composed entirely of local Muslim Saracens. His curious nature and obsession with finding a connection between science and God also led to many believing the young emperor was an atheist. He would indulge himself in unruly experiments, as he would try to observe a man's soul leaving his body or how the organs of a dead man may have been affected by the evil or good things he had done in his lifetime. In short, Frederick II was not an ordinary ruler, and his motivations for taking up the cross and joining the Crusade were certainly different from his predecessors. It is clear he was not motivated by recapturing Jerusalem and did not believe the Muslims were his enemies.

His difficult character had, in fact, caused his delay in joining the Fifth Crusade. Pope Gregory had waited for him to journey to the Holy Land for a long time and, seeing that the emperor was stalling, excommunicated him. In a weird decision, Frederick took up the cross after being excommunicated, prompting the pope to excommunicate him a second time, even though he still had not recovered from his previous excommunication. Thus, it is not surprising to understand why not everybody in Outremer was exactly keen on the appearance of the double-excommunicated, weird, and potentially atheist Emperor Frederick when he finally landed at Acre in September of 1228. The news had already reached the Holy Land, and not everyone was looking forward to collaborating with the emperor.

This caused a big division in the ranks of the Christians, with most of the Frankish lords of Jerusalem, the Hospitallers, and the Templars all choosing to side with the pope's decision and not support Emperor Frederick. On the other hand, the Teutonic Knights were willing to help Frederick in his upcoming military endeavors due to their German ties. An important detail to understand is that Frederick's decision to come to

Outremer was also because he had a legitimate claim to the throne of Jerusalem through his wife Isabella, who was the only child of King John de Brienne of Jerusalem. However, Isabella had recently passed away during childbirth, making Frederick a regent for his newborn son Conrad, who was next in line for Jerusalem's throne.

Soon after the arrival of Frederick, the Templars found themselves in a quarrel with the Holy Roman emperor. The emperor demanded loyalty from the Templars when he showed up with his forces at the Templar Atlit Castle. The Templars denied forfeiting the castle to the emperor but agreed, somewhat reluctantly, to join his Crusade. But to distance themselves, they stated they would only accompany Frederick because of their own goodwill and eagerness to reclaim the Holy Land. They also marched about a day's distance behind the emperor. The Hospitallers did the same. Surprisingly, even though Frederick's army was not large, only counting a couple of thousand men at best, his first move to Jaffa was very successful. Through diplomacy, Frederick managed to negotiate the control of Jerusalem.

With Jerusalem secured, Frederick had definitely made a statement to those who opposed him in Outremer, including the military orders, the patriarch, and the majority of the Frankish nobility. However, it can be argued that recapturing the Holy City was not a significant improvement for the Christian positions. Frederick had only managed to cede control of the actual city itself, not the lands surrounding it. This was important as, effectively, Jerusalem was on the southern border with Egypt, with no real buffer separating it from the Muslims, leaving it an easy target for potential invaders. In addition, the city was still isolated from the rest of the Holy Land; there was only a tiny, narrow corridor to the coastal cities, which could be easily exploited to cut off supply lines. Moreover, the whole agreement had been achieved due to the internal fighting of the Egyptians, who had no real time or resources to spend on defending Jerusalem from a potential Christian attack.

In fact, the talks about the control of Jerusalem are thought to have been started way before Frederick arrived in Outremer, as he had received an envoy from Sultan al-Kamil, who first proposed ceding the city in exchange for Frederick's help against Damascus. However, the two sides had not come to terms, but they laid down a basis for the talks that took place at Jaffa. And even though the alliance between Frederick and the Muslims against Damascus was not part of the deal, Frederick let the Muslims retain control of the Al-Aqsa Mosque. He allowed the practice of Islam in the city and banned the Templars from entering their historical headquarters.

Overall, it was still a victory for Frederick, despite the fact that he over-glorified his achievement. But what he did next was an even more politically motivated move to show his superiority over his opposition. On March 17th, 1229, after taking control of Jerusalem, Emperor Frederick entered the Church of the Holy Sepulchre and crowned himself the king of Jerusalem, a title that most of the Holy Land thought he had no right to. What makes this move even more ridiculous is the fact that Gerold of Lausanne, Patriarch of Jerusalem, who had been one of the fiercest critics of the emperor thus far, had ordered all the members of the church from practicing their religion as long as Frederick was in the city. This meant that there was no one in the Holy Sepulchre to crown Frederick, causing him to put the crown upon his own head. He literally crowned himself. Then, in the presence of the loyal Teutonic Knights who had accompanied the emperor, the new king of Jerusalem announced that he forgave the pope for excommunicating him and declared himself "God's Vicar on Earth," a title only held by the pope before.

The vast majority of the Christian world, both in the East and the West, was appalled by Frederick's actions. He had made a lot of powerful enemies in the Holy Land, including the Templars and the Hospitallers, who refused to follow the emperor any longer and returned to Acre, where the anti-Frederick sentiment was the strongest. The city was reportedly outraged by the emperor's actions. No one supported his claim, with most of the people believing that the rightful heir to the throne was Conrad, Frederick's son, who had still not come of age. Even as the father to the king, he was despised for his arrogance.

The relations between the Templars and the Crown of Jerusalem, an institution that was historically one of the closest allies of the order, deteriorated, reaching an all-time low because of Frederick's illegitimacy. It got so bad that there were eventually rumors going around that the brothers (the Grand Masters of the Templars and Hospitallers) wanted to assassinate the emperor and place somebody else on the throne. When Frederick arrived at Acre with his force, demanding those inside to surrender the city and declare their loyalty to their new king, he was swiftly denied by Grand Master Peter. The stand-off between the two sides continued for more than a month, with Frederick surrounding Acre and the Templar Atlit Castle with his forces, ordering them to shoot anyone who tried to enter or leave, especially the Templars.

Eventually, however, in late April 1229, Frederick learned of his lands in Europe being besieged by none other than John of Brienne, the former king of Jerusalem, who was now leading a papal army to punish Frederick's actions. (John had been pushed aside by Frederick after Frederick married John's daughter.) This news shocked Frederick and forced him to quickly return to Italy, abandoning Acre in early May. When the emperor left, the crowd threw rotten meat at him, once again demonstrating their hatred toward the self-proclaimed king. Still, Frederick's departure was not the end of his involvement in the East, as the Holy Roman emperor first left two of his trustees in the Holy Land and later sent Richard Filangieri, an imperial marshal, with a sizeable force to oversee his affairs. Filangieri and the rest of the supporters would settle in Tyre in 1231, while the rest of Outremer continued to oppose the emperor and refused to recognize him.

After Frederick's return to Italy, he continued posing a problem for the Templars, confiscating many of their possessions and refusing to hand them over, even after being ordered to do so by the pope, causing him to be excommunicated once again. The effects of Frederick's peculiar endeavors would be felt by the Templars and the rest of the East in the years to come, as outside involvement from the West had once again left the Holy Land destabilized and weakened.

The Conflict between the Orders

Despite the ongoing dispute about the succession of the Kingdom of Jerusalem, by some miracle, the Christians were still holding onto their lands. The truce that had been agreed upon by Frederick and al-Kamil would last for ten years until 1239, giving the Christians of the East a small window to build up their forces for a potential assault on their positions. Instead of that, however, as they had done before on many occasions, they could not come to terms with each other. Rival camps continued coexisting throughout the 1230s, with Richard Filangieri and the imperial supporters on one side and the Templars, Hospitallers, the patriarch, and the Franks on the other.

While it is true that during this period, some effort was made to weaken the Muslims, mostly through the combined efforts of the military orders, nothing significant was achieved. The Templars and the Hospitallers suffered several defeats, first at Hama and then at Atlit. It was becoming clear that the Latin kingdoms were losing their grasp on the Holy Land quicker than ever. In 1239, Pope Gregory urged the leaders of Europe to unite once again for a new Crusade, but no major powerhouse was interested in sending the resources necessary to conduct an expedition. As they most likely realized, due to past examples, it was doomed to achieve little anyway.

The only noble that answered the call was Theobald, King of Navarre and Count of Champagne, who arrived at Acre in September of 1239 with a laughable force of no more than a thousand men. Still, any amount of help was welcome for the struggling Christians of the region, who, just like in the old days, immediately started drawing up plans for what was next. Theobald had incorrectly assumed the complexity of the politics of the East. Upon his arrival, he was convinced to launch an offensive in the south on Gaza and Ascalon. This decision was heavily influenced by the Templars, who had managed to negotiate a deal with Damascus by offering help in the war against the Egyptians (who held Gaza and Ascalon) in exchange for the Damascenes ceding control of the Templar castles that had been conquered by Saladin decades earlier.

However, before Theobald was able to muster up enough men to form a competent force, Count Henry of Bar decided to take matters into his own hands. He embarked on a secret expedition to Gaza with about 1,500 men of his own. Henry had not told any major baron of Outremer of this endeavor, hoping to capture Gaza by himself, which he incorrectly thought to be poorly defended. He did ask the Templars and Hospitallers for reinforcements, but this request was instantly rejected by the military orders. They knew this sort of an attack was foolish.

The orders were proven to be right when Henry's much smaller force was ambushed deep into Egyptian territory. The Muslims slew the Crusaders, killing Henry in the process and capturing more than six hundred men. It was a disaster for the Christians, whose chances of solidifying their positions were further reduced by Henry's reckless actions. However, surprisingly, the blame fell on the Templars and the Hospitallers, who were accused of treachery because they did not help the count in his campaign. This detail is thought to have been an incinerating factor for the increasingly poor relations between the West and the Templars, with the Templars being blamed for acting solely according to their own interests instead of doing what was right for the greater good.

The Western Christians, who would later put the Templars on trial for this and many other reasons (a topic that will be covered in the following chapters), did not understand why the order would deny an opportunity to fight against the Muslims—the people the Templars had sworn to fight in the name of Christ. The truth of the matter was that the military orders correctly recognized the unwise plan of attacking Gaza and saved themselves from an impending defeat. But the fact that they would involve themselves in the politics of the East on such a deep level, choosing sides and even dealing with the Muslims for their own benefit, created a level of suspicion surrounding the purpose of their existence—a suspicion that would be exploited in the coming decades.

The Templars would face even more complicated matters after the arrival of Richard of Cornwall, brother of King Henry III of England and the brother-in-law of Emperor Frederick II. Richard landed in the Holy Land in the autumn of 1240, and he immediately started a series of negotiations with the Muslims, as well as with the nobility of the East. The aim of his visit was to check Frederick's claims of the East; after all, the emperor was still the "king" of Jerusalem, but he had been away from his kingdom for a long time. The Englishman found the military orders, for the first time in a while, split regarding what was best for the good of the Holy Land, with the Hospitallers preferring a more diplomatic approach with the Egyptians in light of the Templars' decision to ally with the Damascenes to reclaim their long-lost castles. In fact, Richard was able to successfully negotiate the southern lands of Belvoir and Tiberias, as well as the release of the previously captured Christians at Gaza with the Egyptians, thanks to an earlier agreement the sultan had approved with the Knights Hospitaller. With this, even though some southern cities like Gaza, Nablus, and Hebron still stayed under Muslim control, Richard took charge of the surrounding territories, establishing the long-deserved buffer near the Holy City.

The brother-in-law of Frederick II was certainly content with himself when he set sail for England a year later in 1241, as he had reclaimed a sizeable landmass for the Christians while also undermining the Templars' influence in the region (remember, the order and the emperor hated each other). By siding with the Hospitallers, Richard had effectively swayed them more to the imperial side, forging a rivalry between them and the anti-Frederick Templars.

Still, the Templars did not sit back and watch Richard and the Hospitallers gain more influence. Templar Grand Master Armand of Perigord did not want to give up his order's alliance with the Damascenes, who had promised him the return of the old castles in the north. So, after the departure of Richard, a Templar force attacked the Egyptian town of Hebron and then successfully proceeded onto Nablus, achieving victory and sacking the city.

There was no denying that a wedge had been driven deep between the Knights Templar and the Knights Hospitaller, with both orders becoming each other's rivals in the following years. Both of them would be involved in the succession struggle of Jerusalem once again. This happened not long after the sacking of Nablus, after the arrival of Thomas of Aquino, who was supposed to accept the throne of Jerusalem in place of Prince Conrad, the son of Frederick II, who had finally come of age to become king. The Templars, however, perceived Thomas's arrival as the final step to their loss in the East. They thought that if he were to convince the Franks of Outremer to accept him as king, the order would lose much of its prominence to both the imperialist camp and the Hospitallers.

Thus, the Templars proceeded to do everything in their power to reduce Conrad's influence, claiming that Dowager Queen of Cyprus, Alice, was the person to whom the throne of Jerusalem really belonged. Then, in the summer of 1243, they were able to drive Conrad's supporters out of the Holy Land with some help from Italian merchants, who had their own unsettled grudges against the emperor. The Templars had triumphed over their long-time enemy. Despite their success, however, Grand Master Armand's concerns would eventually come true, as the whole of Eastern Christendom was not ready to fend off a new Muslim invasion that awaited them in the following decades.

The Battle of La Forbie

Decades of instability and internal struggles had greatly affected the Latin kingdoms. Two of their biggest competitors in the East—Cairo and Damascus—went to war in 1244. For the Latins, the situation was looking dire, as Egypt had made a close alliance with the Khwarazmians (Khwarezmians), a Sunni Turkish people who were fierce and brutal warriors. The Templars had allied themselves with the Damascenes, but even they knew that stopping Egypt would be very difficult once the Khwarazmians reinforced them. So, waiting for an inevitable offensive on their positions, the Templars, now with the help of the Hospitallers and the Teutons, with whom they had somewhat repaired their relations due to the impending threat, started building up fortifications in the major Christian cities of the East.

The Khwarazmians proved to be even more ruthless than they had anticipated. On their way to Egypt, they ran over every attempt of resistance by the Damascenes, destroying every villa and town on their way, including Tiberias and Nablus. In June 1244, about ten thousand of them had reached Jerusalem, which was thought to be their final stop before reaching Cairo and joining their forces with Egypt. The invaders laid siege on Jerusalem, which, to no one's surprise, was not able to hold. After a month, the city had fallen, and the defenses prepared by the military orders were not enough. The Khwarazmians stormed the city, massacring the local Christian population as they attempted to flee to Jaffa. The invaders then proceeded to violate the remains of the previous kings of Jerusalem at the Holy Sepulchre and set the city ablaze, only then deciding to continue their march to Egypt.

The Christians of Outremer were shocked by the news. A decision was taken to assemble what forces they could to meet the Khwarazmians before they reached their reinforcements. At Acre, the Franks called for their own reinforcements from Damascus, who arrived under the Damascene leader al-Nasir. The Templars, Hospitallers, and the Teutons assembled a combined force of about one thousand knights from all of the orders, which acted as the elite part of the Christian army. About six hundred secular knights were also present under Walter, Count of Jaffa, and Philip de Montfort of Tyre. Several other important figures of the East were also there, with the full army counting about ten thousand troops in total—the largest force the Christians had assembled since Hattin. In October, the Christians started their march south, hoping to catch the Khwarazmian army near Gaza and confront them in battle.

On October 17th, 1244, the combined army of the Christian nobility, the military orders, and the Damascene allies met the Khwarazmians in battle a couple of miles northeast of Gaza at the village of La Forbie. Unfortunately for the allies, the enemy had managed to meet up with the Egyptians, so their numbers were higher than what the Christians had expected. The battle, which lasted for two days, saw both sides fighting fiercely against each other. For the Latins, it was their final stand, as they had committed most of their capable men into the army. For the Egyptians and the Khwarazmians, it was a chance to break the Christians and overwhelm them in later encounters.

The first day ended with no major improvements for either side. The Templars, Hospitallers, and Teutons ensured high morale and discipline for the Christian infantry and were able to repel the enemy's cavalry charges. However, on the second day, the Damascene flank was hit, with the Egyptians and Khwarazmians managing to quickly break the Muslim allies of the Latins, forcing them to run for their lives. This, in turn, caused the Christian flank to become exposed, with the enemies taking swift advantage and running them down, killing as many men as they could.

The Christian army was almost fully destroyed. No more than fifty Templar and Hospitaller knights managed to escape from La Forbie. Grand Master Armand of Perigord, along with the count of Jaffa and several other important Latin figures, were captured, never to be seen again. La Forbie had shattered the dreams of the reunification of the Holy Land, as the Latin kingdoms would never be able to recover from their biggest loss since the Battle of Hattin.

After the battle, the supporters of Conrad and the imperialist camp put the blame on the Templars, claiming that the Damascenes' retreat was their fault since it had been the Templars' decision to ally with them in the first place. And while the order had played a crucial role in keeping Outremer together for so many years, there was no time for any failure, especially at this hour. Still, despite their criticism, the new Grand Master, Guillaume of Sonnac, who was elected three years later in 1247, probably because the order was unsuccessfully negotiating the release of Armand, continued to build up Templar holdings and ensure that a disaster like La Forbie never occurred again. Little did he know, much tougher times still lay ahead for the Knights Templar.

The Fall of Acre

Suffering another major defeat at La Forbie naturally prompted the West to answer with another Crusade. However, as was the case before, no one was really keen on venturing out to the Holy Land, as they did not believe their efforts would save the Latin kingdoms from falling. To make matters worse, Damascus fell to the Egyptians soon after their victory at La Forbie, meaning that the more unified Muslims now posed a bigger threat to the Christian positions than before. In addition, the succession crisis of Jerusalem and the internal fighting that came with it had not only deprived the Latin kingdoms of valuable manpower and experienced leaders but also made it even more difficult to find a potential reason for reunification, as different actors acted on their own personal interests and did not prioritize the greater good of the Christian East.

It did not look good for the Templars and the rest of the military orders that had been fighting for years to protect the Holy Land from their enemies. As we have already mentioned, it was becoming more and more difficult for them to replace their ranks, and they had lost much of their prized possessions throughout the 13th century. The Templars did not hold as many castles in strategic locations as they once did, and of those that they did control, few were garrisoned sufficiently enough to hold off a potential invasion. It was looking doomed for the Latin kingdoms.

Only King Louis IX of France answered the call for what would be known as the Seventh Crusade. Louis was a famously pious man and had vowed to venture out to the Holy Land once he recovered from his illness. In the end, the king arrived at Cyprus in September of 1248, where he was met by the new Templar Grand Master, Guillaume de Sonnac, and King Henry of Cyprus. The parties discussed the plan of action, finally deciding to mount an assault on the city of Damietta. King Louis was confident that he had learned enough from the past Crusader mistakes at the Egyptian city and hoped not to repeat them.

The Crusaders' stay at Cyprus was drawn out, however, as King Louis faced transportation problems, which halted his advance for seven months. This, paired with the lack of supplies, lowered the morale of the troops, with a good number of them deserting. Louis had to launch his offensive with less than half of the army he had started with. Even though the Crusaders had thought they would surprise the Egyptians with an attack on Damietta, the sultan had learned of the stationed Crusader army in Cyprus and had mobilized against them by sending reinforcements to the Egyptian heartland and evacuating the city. So, when King Louis and the Crusaders landed on the beaches in June 1249, after being met with some resistance from the Egyptian forces, they were surprised to see Damietta undefended. They walked into the city and claimed it for themselves. After much consideration, a follow-up assault on Cairo was agreed upon.

However, just as in the case of the Fifth Crusade, the geographic challenges would prove to be a fatal enemy for the Christians, who got separated while trying to cross the Nile River in February 1250. The Egyptians, who had tried to avoid hand-to-hand combat as much as they could, saw an opening and quickly mobilized their troops. The part of the Christians that had crossed the river under Louis's brother, Richard of Artois, forced the Muslims to retreat to the town of Mansoura. Richard was adamant about chasing down the retreating forces, and he did not wait for the majority of the Crusader army to cross the river and be in range to support. This caused Richard's vanguard to be lured into more heavily fortified Egyptian positions. The Muslims were more aware of the geography of the region and outmaneuvered the Christians, leading them into a trap and massacring their front contingent. Nearly three hundred Templars lost their lives in the ensuing encounter, which was a heavy loss considering how much the members of the order contributed to the overall strength of the army. Guillaume de Sonnac was also wounded, losing an eye.

Three days later, when the rest of the Crusader force was in a position to attack, they managed to defeat whatever resistance the Muslims had put up outside the town of Mansoura. However, they were reluctant to continue with a siege, having suffered lots of casualties, including Grand Master Guillaume, who died on February 11th, 1250. This caused a lot of chaos and uncertainty in the ranks of the French. King Louis could not decide what to do and chose to wait outside the city, a decision that proved to be another mistake. The Egyptians quickly cut off the Crusaders' supply lines and made them heavily suffer from attrition and disease. In early April, Louis finally gave up and ordered a retreat. The Egyptians chased the Crusaders down, massacring nearly the whole army and capturing King Louis. The Seventh Crusade was yet another failure.

King Louis would eventually be released in exchange for the city of Damietta. The Crusaders, however, lacked the funds for the ransom of their king and asked the Templars for a massive sum of thirty thousand French livres, a demand that was first refused by the order on the grounds that Louis had not deposited money in the Temple, making the loan impossible. In the end, however, the Templars, under Marshal Reginald de Vichiers, were convinced to provide the necessary amount, realizing the urgency of the situation and making an exception for the king. King Louis, after his release, would form a good relationship with the Templars. He stayed in the Holy Land until 1254 and helped reunite the squabbling barons of the Latin kingdoms. With his endorsement, Reginald was elected as the new Grand Master of the Templars, and the king vowed to repay his debts to the order. In fact, Louis did much more for the development of Outremer than many previous kings had done in the past. He invested a lot of money into building up the defenses at towns like Jaffa and Acre and led the Holy Land into a relative period of stability, which was helped by the ten-year truce agreed with the Egyptians upon his release.

However, when King Louis departed, the Holy Land would once again descend into an unstable period, one characterized by war and internal power struggles. This time, the problem lay in the newly emerging threats both from the south in the form of the Mamluks gaining power in Egypt over the Ayyubid dynasty and in the northeast, as Outremer was about to be overrun by the Mongols.

The Christians of the East were very much aware of the Mamluks' capabilities; they had been elite slave warriors who had fought in the ranks of the Egyptians since the reign of Saladin. Over time, however, they had accumulated enough power to rise up and trample the dynasty, becoming the rulers of Egypt and posing a direct threat to the Holy Land. Their military supremacy would once again be proven when, in 1260, the Mamluks crushed the Mongol forces that had arrived at their doorstep near Nazareth. For some, this was a surprising development, as their two major enemies were fighting each other. However, the Templars had long been aware of the Mongols' activity and had correctly observed that they were fighting everyone they encountered on their way to the West, despite their religion or culture. In the late 1250s, some Templars in the region had urged for a build-up of fortifications of some of the cities, like Jaffa, and to abandon those sites that could not withhold a Mongol invasion. The order had also sent multiple envoys to Europe, describing the doom that was about to descend on the Holy Land in the form of the Mongol invasion.

With the victory against the Mongols and the accession to the throne of the Mamluk leader Baybars, Outremer was bound to be a target for the new sultan, who believed that the Christians had no right to exist in the East. He had also shown the Mongols how capable the Mamluk army was, forcing them to watch from the sidelines as he went on a campaign to rampage through the Christian lands. In the 1260s, Baybars ran over the Latin kingdoms, capturing one town after the other. The Christian military orders, which had bonded together despite their differences in internal political struggles, were unable to mount a significant resistance to the Mamluk advance. Arsuf, one of the most heavily fortified Hospitaller holdings, fell to the Egyptians, which was soon followed by the Templar castle of Safed.

The Templars tried to spend more and more resources in the desperate defense of their holdings, using their connections with King

Louis to receive generous aid from France. However, it was not enough. Before the arrival of England's Prince Edward in 1272, the Latin kingdoms were almost completely conquered by their enemies. After Arsuf and Safed, the Mamluks had taken nearly all the coastal cities of the Holy Land, including Jaffa and Caesarea, as well as major fortifications in the region, like the Templar Castle of Beaufort and the Hospitaller Krak des Chevaliers. The situation looked dire, especially after the fall of Antioch in 1268 and the evacuation of the Templar castles in the Amanus March, a location the order had possessed since the very beginning of its days.

Thus, the arrival of Prince Edward, who had heard of the atrocities of the Mamluks and the Mongols from a Templar messenger in London and came to the Holy Land with reinforcements, gave some hope to the Christians of the Holy Land. However, the Englishman did not manage to improve the positions of the Latin kingdoms. He negotiated a ten-year truce with the Mamluks, as he had to return to London to be crowned as king in the wake of the passing of his father, Henry III.

Edward brought the news of the desperation of the Holy Land to Europe. The continent was shocked, and the talks for a new Crusade started. The new Templar Grand Master, William of Beaujeu, had realized that the future of the region was not looking too good, prompting him to go on a tour of Europe to gather whatever support he could for Outremer. In 1273, in a journey reminiscent of that of Hugues de Payens a century and a half prior, Grand Master William visited all the major European rulers to convince them to join a new Crusade. In 1274, a council assembled in Lyon to discuss the matter; however, in the end, no one decided to take up the cross, and William returned to Outremer empty-handed.

The following years saw heavy Templar involvement in the internal matters of the ongoing succession disputes in Tripoli and Jerusalem, with King Hugh of Cyprus being crowned the king of Jerusalem in 1269. He did not care to rule his kingdom from the Holy City and was instead isolated on his island. From there, Hugh observed as the rest of the Latin kingdoms were caught up in a civil war, blaming the order for being ignorant of what was good for the Christians. His distrust toward the Templars culminated in his assault on the Templar castle of Gastria on the island of Cyprus. As for the order, Grand Master William was trying to hold things together, but his involvement in the disputes of Tripoli was of no use. He managed to negotiate another truce with the Mamluks in

1282, but the peace was broken by the Egyptians, who had no more intention of dealing with the Christians.

The new Mamluk Sultan Qalawun embarked upon his quest of driving the Christians out of the Holy Land once and for all as soon as he ascended the throne of Egypt in mid-1285. The sultan stormed the Latin lands one by one, taking the port of Latakia and capturing the Hospitaller castle at al-Marqab by 1287. Learning of the sultan's intentions from an agent, Templar Grand Master William warned Tripoli twice about a potential invasion of the city, but the Tripolitans refused to listen. They had grown increasingly weary of the Grand Master after his involvement during the civil war, which lasted from 1277 to 1282. Consequently, Tripoli fell to Qalawun in the spring of 1289. Then, the Grand Master got intel about the next target of the Mamluks, the city of Acre, which was arguably the most heavily defended Christian holding of the East. But it was bound to fall without support, which was nowhere to be seen. William advised the people to evacuate the city or offer Qalawun something else, like a generous payment, in return, but he was once again denied. The Mamluks laid siege to Acre in early April 1291.

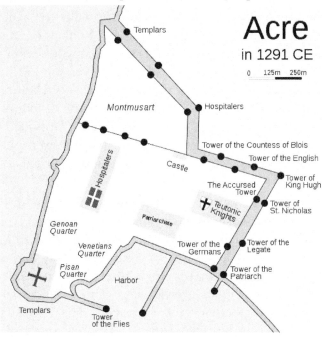

Acre in 1291

Although Qalawun died in the early stages of the siege, his son, al-Ashraf Khalil, pledged to take the city and kill every Christian in it for his dying father, and the Mamluks rallied behind their new sultan. The Muslims started a long siege, building siege equipment for the assault and receiving reinforcements every day. With their backs against the wall, the Christians tried to negotiate, but their envoy was executed by the sultan. Even though Acre was heavily defended and well-supplied because the Christians still controlled the sea and were able to supply provisions, it was clear that they simply did not have enough men to repel an all-out Muslim attack.

Grand Master William realized this and decided to sally out of the city with a small but elite force to try and catch the besiegers off-guard and inflict at least some casualties. It was all in vain, however, as the Templars and the Hospitallers had to retreat because their horses were entangled in the enemy camp. They lost about twenty knights.

By mid-May, the bombardment was well underway, and its toll was being felt inside the city's walls. King Henry had arrived with about two thousand men from Cyprus, but it was still not enough. On May 18th, the Muslims were finally able to break through after three days of fierce fighting with the Templars and the Hospitallers at Saint Andrew's gate. The Muslims overwhelmed the Christian defenses by sheer numbers. Grand Master William died fighting. King Henry and a large part of the city's population managed to evacuate on ships, leaving the rest of the soldiers behind to fight until the last man. Soon, the Muslims were able to break the defenders at the city's center and were met with fierce resistance at the Templar headquarters, where the brothers put up a final stand. Eventually, the Templar commander, Theobald Gaudin, decided to flee with whatever wealth he could gather from the temple at Acre. The city was lost. The Crusaders, who had held the Holy Land for nearly two hundred years, were finally defeated.[108]

---

[108] Powell, J. M. (2007). "Church and Crusade: Frederick II and Louis IX." *The Catholic Historical Review*, 93(2), vi–264.

Martin, S. (2011). *The Knights Templar*. Oldcastle Books. Chapter 2.

Hill, P. (2018). *The Knights Templar at War, 1120–1312*. Pen & Sword Military. Part 2.

Welsh, W. E. (2016). "Crusader Catastrophe: The Battle of La Forbie." *Medieval Warfare*, 6(5), 26–33.

Jackson, P. (1987). "The Crusades of 1239–41 and Their Aftermath." *Bulletin of the School of Oriental and African Studies*, University of London, 50 (1), 32–60.

Chapter 10: The Trial of the Knights Templar

After decades of fighting for the good of the Christians in the Holy Land, the Templars and, for that matter, the rest of the Latin kingdoms were finally defeated once and for all at Acre in 1291. The future, for the first time, seemed uncertain for the Knights Templar. Even though the order still held a lot of possessions and power in Europe, Outremer had always been their main base of operations, as well as their birthplace. While the Templars wanted to continue their existence in the West, the kings of Europe had other plans in mind. This chapter will look at the fate of the Knights Templar after the fall of Acre, diving deep into the final years of the order's existence in Europe, where a change of heart would prove to be fatal for the Templars.

After Acre

Theobald Gaudin fled to Sidon, taking with him what Templar wealth he could gather from the compound at Acre. There, he was elected as the new Grand Master, and the Templars tried to devise a plan of action against the Mamluks. However, they had no time. The invaders did not stop their offensive at Acre. After taking the city, they continued their advance on whatever Christian positions remained, capturing one Templar castle after another. The Muslims swept the remainder of the Holy Land throughout the summer of 1291, and Grand Master Theobald and the rest of the brothers were forced to flee to Cyprus, the only place in the East that remained somewhat out of reach from their enemies. By autumn, all of the famous Templar holdings were abandoned, with the brothers taking whatever they could with them and destroying whatever they could not. The Mamluks swiftly entered Sidon, then Haifa, and then took the castles of Tortosa and Atlit—a task no other invader had been able to successfully accomplish. By the end of 1291, the Templars were effectively out of Outremer. They would never again step foot in the Holy Land.

Limassol, a Templar fortress in Cyprus, was chosen as the new headquarters for the order, and the following year, Jacques de Molay succeeded Theobald as the new Grand Master. Jacques had spent about thirty years as a member of the order, and he would spend his time as the Grand Master wholeheartedly trying to restore the position of the Knights Templar in Outremer.

Grand Master Jacques de Molay
https://commons.wikimedia.org/w/index.php?curid=2612812

Unlike some of the previous leaders of the order, who were more concerned with gaining power for themselves by getting involved in the complex politics and acting from behind the scenes, Grand Master Jacques had much clearer motivations. In addition to Cyprus, the order held the small island of Ruad just off the coast of Palestine, which the Grand Master thought to be a valuable resource in conducting new operations in Outremer. He did not want to give up on the dream of the Christians returning to the Holy Land, but he was disappointed when he was informed of the island's loss to the Mamluks, who had realized the importance of the Templar holding there and stormed it in 1302. In a way, this was the final blow to any hope of regaining the lost territories. Jacques de Molay had tried getting help from the West in the mid-1290s during his visit to Europe, but he had been unsuccessful. No major European power wanted to contribute to the restoration of the Holy Land, as they were well aware of the costs of a potential expedition.

On the surface, however, Europe was still sympathetic to the Templar Order. In 1294, during his visit, Jacques de Molay had spoken to Pope Boniface VIII, and his holiness granted him and the rest of the Templars the same privileges they had held in Jerusalem. Essentially, the pope tried to make it clear that the order was still respected, despite the loss of the Holy Land. Some subtle help also came from different European kings, who offered benefits like exemption from certain taxes to help the struggling Templars. Unfortunately for Jacques de Molay, the biggest supporter of the Templars, Edward I of England, was occupied on two fronts, as he was fighting with France and Scotland at the time and could not offer reinforcements to the Grand Master, although he did promise similar economic benefits. All in all, it seemed clear that the *Reconquista* of the Holy Land or another Crusade was only possible in the distant future—a future the Templars would not be able to see.

The Templars were not the only ones unsure of their future. The other two military orders, the Hospitallers and the Teutons, were also forced to abandon their possessions in the Holy Land and escape to the West. It seemed that all three orders had lost their original purpose since there were no more Christians in the East for them to defend. They all adapted to the situation differently. The Hospitallers, for example, adopted the previously overlooked responsibility of patrolling the seas and played an important role in the maritime matters of the Mediterranean. At first, they followed the Templars and dwelled in Cyprus, but they quickly made the island of Rhodes their main base of operations and slowly started building up their resources both on the sea and on land. As for the Teutons, they relocated north to the port city of Marienburg in Prussia. From there, they spent centuries fighting against the pagans in eastern Europe, becoming increasingly involved in the politics of the region. They eventually established their own sovereign state. Thus, the three military orders continued their existence.

Philip against the Templars

Due to the shadow that was cast over the future of the military orders right after the fall of Acre, there were talks of a potential merge of the Knights Templar and Knights Hospitaller. The argument for the unification of the two institutions was mainly the fact that they would be more competent at conducting their future affairs since both orders had been significantly weakened by the loss of the Holy Land. The Teutons were not a part of this conversation, perhaps because of the way they had always distinguished themselves from the Hospitallers and Templars due to their Germanic origin. However, immediately after the fall of Acre, no one really had time to consider a unification of the orders, and, thus, the matter was mostly ignored by all parties.

In 1305, the talks would commence once again of a potential merge of the Templars and the Hospitallers. This time, Pope Clement V was the initiator. The pope invited Jacques de Molay and his Hospitaller counterpart, Foulques de Villaret, to discuss the issue. Jacques de Molay was still not sold on the idea, claiming that the two orders were separate entities, and although their functions often intertwined, they would better function if left separate. In fact, when he arrived in Paris in late 1306 to discuss the matter, he made a sound argument, but the pope was still not convinced. The two waited for Grand Master Foulques to arrive before decisively deciding anything. The Hospitaller had been delayed in Rhodes because of some domestic issues.

At that time, another matter popped up on the agenda. Pope Clement was curious about the allegations he had heard about the Templar Order. According to the rumors, behind the image of a virtuous Christian military order was actually a sinful institution that secretly conducted sinful and inappropriate practices. There were even allegations of heresy and sodomy. The Grand Master, of course, denied everything the pope said to him and told the pope that he would allow the papacy to investigate the order to clear up any doubts. In turn, the pope sent a letter to Philip IV of France, requesting the king to conduct a thorough inquiry.

The anti-Templar sentiment had grown the strongest in France.

However, the matter was much more serious than either the pope or Jacques de Molay had thought. On Friday, October 13th, 1307, all the Templars in France were arrested, including their Grand Master. It was a move that shocked Christendom and forever changed the legacy of the Knights Templar.

But why exactly did King Philip IV of France, the ruler who would come to be known as Philip the Fair, arrest the Templars? At the time of the arrest, nobody was sure, and Europe did not know how to react. The order had been a well-respected organization that had always served the interests of Christians. Not only that, but they were under the direct protection of the pope. No monarch had the authority to prosecute the Templars without permission from the papacy. In any case, some thought that this unexpected move from Philip was unjustified. It is true that Philip was an extraordinarily pious ruler, but he was also arrogant and power-hungry. The Templars, at the time of his ascension to the throne, were one of the wealthiest actors in the whole of Europe. Thus, his motivations may have been to seize the valuable Templar possessions he knew existed in his country.

In fact, King Philip is known to have overexercised his power on a couple of occasions. For example, he had seized the assets of the French Jews just a year earlier in 1306 to gather more funds for the French economy, which had been deprived of income due to warring with England. Later on, he would do the same thing with the Italian bankers from Lombardy. In addition to all of this, in 1303, because of his "pious" nature, he tried to kidnap Pope Boniface VIII and bring him to France to make the pope face virtually the same charges the Templars later faced. In any case, although the move was unexpected, Philip was prone to making extraordinary decisions. It appears that he had sent out the plan for the arrest of the Templars in September. Therefore, he must have been prepared for what was about to happen.

The main charges set against the Templars were heresy, blasphemy, and sodomy—a combination of words that had never been associated with the order. However, the Inquisition was already well underway, so Christians were aware of the consequences if one was to be found guilty of those charges. Europe was very fearful of the alleged witches who practiced magic and had witnessed the Inquisitors publicly burn and hang every heretic they could find. The accusations against the Templars were nothing new to the people, partially because Philip had used similar accusations against Pope Boniface. The public had a mixed reaction to the Templars' arrest. Pope Clement, for example, condemned Philip's actions in a letter he sent to the king on October 25th, saying that the Templars were under the protection of the papacy and that he had no right to arrest them without proof.

However, by the time the pope wrote the letter, the Templars had already been put on trial at the University of Paris. At the assembly, the arrested Templars, including Jacques de Molay, confessed to the crimes they had committed. The Grand Master confessed to denying Christ and spitting on the cross, shocking the assembly and starting a public upheaval in Paris. The people took to the streets and demanded the execution of the Templars. Pope Clement, who was now pressured to act because the Templars had admitted their guilt, signed a bull a month later, ordering the arrest of all brothers throughout Europe. This, in turn, prompted different reactions in different kingdoms. For instance, England, Portugal, and Aragon were reluctant to prosecute the Templars because of the close ties the rulers held with the order. The whole of the Catholic world was in disbelief but complied with the pope's orders. In the following months, most of the Templars were sent to prisons.

Depiction of Baphomet
https://commons.wikimedia.org/w/index.php?curid=45656

In the prisons, the brothers would be forced to confess their sins, often through torture. By then, the Inquisition was involved, and despite it being a structure under the papacy, it very much served the interests of the French king. Thus, the Templars were tortured, and not a lot of them could endure it. In the end, when they finally broke, they spoke of unheard atrocities they had practiced in secret in different Templar compounds around the world. Many brothers admitted to taking part in the violation of the cross by spitting and urinating on it, followed by denying Christ as the Messiah; they recognized him as nothing more than a prophet. Templars also spoke of acts of sodomy, which took place during their reception ceremonies and included requiring the brothers to kiss each other on erotic parts of the body in order to be fully accepted into the order. Some also spoke of breaking celibacy and having indulged in sex with women. Perhaps the most heretical act confessed by a number of Templar brothers was praying to a demonic deity called Baphomet. This creature's description varied according to different Templars but is largely depicted as a goat-headed man with wings and has become associated with satanic rituals.

The Trials

Months after the start of the Templars' imprisonment, Pope Clement finally requested the Templars to be heard in front of him and a papal committee. On December 24th, 1307, the court was convened, and Jacques de Molay and several high-ranking Templars were brought forth to discuss their charges. However, unlike before, Grand Master Jacques and the rest of the brothers retracted their confessions, claiming that they had only confessed to the Inquisition to escape torture. This was a crucial development, and it confused the assembled audience, including King Philip and his righthand man Guillaume de Nogaret, a man with just as fanatical views as the French king. By retracting their confessions, the Templars stalled the hearings, forcing the pope to suspend the proceedings for the foreseeable future until further proof could be collected.

Philip was furious. He had hoped for the order's quick capitulation, as he could then seize the wealth of the Templars for himself and solve his financial troubles. After the suspension of the hearings, he was desperate to regain public support. He even assembled the Estates General for the first time in history to see how the people felt about the trials, but he was disappointed to see that the majority of the assembled population was still very sympathetic toward the Templars. By then, the king hardly tried to hide the fact that he was exerting influence over the papacy, forcing the pope and his lawyers to reside in Paris, where they worked meticulously on the matter. From time to time, Philip would send several Templars he knew had confessed to the pope, but the official hearings would not continue until November of 1309.

The renewal of the official papal hearings on November 26th saw Grand Master Jacques de Molay speak once again to the assembly. This time, however, it was completely different than what he had said a year earlier. The Templar Grand Master publicly expressed that he was unfit to defend the order against the charges, saying that he had no legal training or counseling. Philip saw this as a victory and made sure to spread the word that the Grand Master had refused to defend his brethren, going as far as to shame him in front of the imprisoned Templars.

The following February, however, two Templar brothers by the names of Reginald of Provins and Peter de Bologna stepped up to defend the order; they were the only ones with a legal background among the brothers. In April, after yet another renewal of the hearings, the two Templars made quite a case of the order's innocence. They told the court that the allegations against them were all made-up. It was just a part of Philip's cunning scheme to undermine the Templars' power and gain their wealth for himself. In addition, they spoke of the torture they had to endure, claiming that the Inquisitors would only be done once they heard what they wanted to hear.

This caused outrage in France. After the end of the hearings, Philip realized he was in a desperate situation. His plan had failed, and he needed an alternative, which for him, being the arrogant king that he was, was a more tyrannical approach. Philip received more legal counseling and carefully weighed the stakes. On May 11th, 1310, he declared that all Templars who had retracted their confessions were to be found guilty, accusing them of being relapsed heretics. The following day, fifty-four Templars were sentenced to death. Since they were considered heretics, they received the most painful and dreadful punishment: death by fire. Still, this was not the end since the hearings were still planned to continue.

The following year, in 1311, the Council of Vienne convened. The Templar matter would finally be decided once and for all. It is important to mention that the pope and the assembled clergy were under immense pressure from King Philip, with the French king sending a small armed contingent to "oversee" and "protect" the pope in case anything went wrong. Seven Templars were brought forth and given a chance to speak and defend their order. However, it was all in vain.

Despite the pressure the pope faced from the king, his next decisions did not fully please Philip. On October 20ᵗʰ, 1311, he signed a new bull titled *Vox in excelso* and formally dissolved the order. However, according to the pope, the Templars were not found guilty of the charges set against them. Clement would issue another bull in the following spring, *Ad providam*, where he declared that all Templar possessions should be given to the Knights Hospitaller, shattering Philip's hopes of seizing the fortune for himself. Finally, the third papal bull, *Considerantes dudum*, allowed separate provinces to prosecute the Templars separately, restating that the charges were not to be discussed as a whole but instead according to whichever Templars had been captured. By doing this, the prosecution of the Templars was a papal matter, and the Inquisition was to handle the rest of it. Little did he know that the Inquisition, despite being a papal institution, had become increasingly independent and had developed similar fanatical Christian views as King Philip and his henchmen.

There was still the question of what should be done with Jacques de Molay and the three other high-ranking Templars who had been imprisoned with him. In December 1313, the question was finally addressed when Clement and the clergy started yet another series of meetings. It had been almost seven years since the Grand Master had been captured at the Paris Temple. By March 1314, time had certainly taken its toll on Jacques de Molay. The Grand Master, Geoffroi (Geoffrey) de Charney, Hugues de Pairaud, and Geoffroi de Gonneville were brought forward on a special platform at Notre Dame, where the inquisitors read out the council's decision. All four of them were sentenced to indefinite imprisonment. The Templars were publicly shamed once again for being heretics, only being saved from death by the grace of the pope.

Before they could be brought back to the cells, however, Jacques de Molay had a final thing to say. Without permission from the guards who accompanied him, he lashed out, shouting out a retraction of the confessions he had made earlier and speaking of the order's innocence. He adamantly defended his brethren, something he had failed to do for all these years. Motivated by the Grand Master, Geoffroi de Charney joined in and claimed that he was innocent, while the rest were swiftly taken back to their cells. Of course, the guards eventually reacted and seized both Jacques and Geoffroi. It was a desperate move, and arguably, both Templars knew that by publicly retracting their confessions, they were signing their own death warrants. King Philip was quick to act, as everyone had heard of the spectacle at Notre Dame. He assembled his council and declared the two Templars to be relapsed heretics.

At Ile aux Javiaux, in front of a crowd that had gathered to witness the final moments of the Templars, Grand Master Jacques de Molay and Preceptor of Normandy Geoffroi de Charney were publicly stripped of their clothes, tied to wooden stakes, and set ablaze. As the Templars burned, their whole order collapsed with them. Jacques de Molay wished both Pope Clement and King Philip to meet him before God within a year, while Geoffroi de Charney continued to shout of his innocence and loyalty to his Grand Master. The Knights Templar had fallen.[109]

[109] Martin, S. (2011). *The Knights Templar*. Oldcastle Books. Chapter 3.

Julien Théry. (2013). "A Heresy of State: Philip the Fair, the Trial of the 'Perfidious Templars,' and the Pontificalization of the French Monarchy." *Journal of Medieval Religious Cultures*, 39 (2), 117–148.

Perkins, C. (1909). "The Trial of the Knights Templars in England." *The English Historical Review*, 24 (95), 432–447.

Nicholson, H. J. (2011). *The Knights Templar on Trial: The Trial of the Templars in the British Isles, 1308–11*. History Press.

Field, S. L. (2016). "Torture and Confession in the Templar Interrogations at Caen, 28-29 October 1307." *Speculum*, 91 (2), 297–327.

Chapter 11: Templar Secrets and Legacy

Thus, after nearly two hundred years of existence, the Knights Templar was destroyed. Jacques de Molay was the last Grand Master, and the order would never see the light of day ever again. Most Templars in Europe were imprisoned, and over time, the image of the Knights Templar would transform into a myth. This chapter will briefly cover the twisted legacy of the Templar Order, taking a look at the rumors and secrets that have been associated with the order since the very beginning. We will also try to explain why the Templars became such a mythicized phenomenon.

After 1314

The Templar Order was officially disbanded, and its Grand Master was publicly executed by 1314. However, in some parts of the world, the brothers who still roamed free tried to overcome the challenges presented to them in different ways. Despite the formal dissolution of the order, King Philip was deprived of its wealth and numerous invaluable possessions. The king's agents were disappointed to find out that most of the Templar records, which were held in the Paris Temple, had disappeared, as had a lot of the wealth the king knew was located there.

La Rochelle

In fact, it is believed that somehow the Templars knew about their grim future before 1307, as most of the order's treasure seems to have been evacuated by the time the trials began. Before the arrests, most documents in the Templars' possession are believed to have been burned by Jacques de Molay, and the riches are thought to have been taken to the Templar holding of La Rochelle, which acted as the main naval base of operations for the order. Located on the coast of the Atlantic in southeastern France, Templar ships frequently sailed to La Rochelle; however, what they carried has never been identified. Even after the fall of the order, the castle contained nothing suspicious and certainly nothing valuable. Plus, there was no sign of the Templar navy.

As for the members of the order, they continued living in different parts of Europe. Most Templars may have been arrested and tortured throughout France, Germany, and parts of Italy, but Iberia and Britain still remained relatively friendly toward the brothers. In Portugal and Aragon, where the Templars were not found guilty after the trials, the Templars took a new name, Knights of Christ, and continued serving in a military role as they had before. In fact, over time, the Knights of Christ became increasingly involved in exploration, funding many expeditions to the New World. Famous explorers like Vasco da Gama and Christopher Columbus both had connections to this order (a fact that might explain the red cross on many of Columbus's ships that sailed to the Americas). Although the theory that says the Templars discovered the Americas is still seen as far-fetched and has never been proven, those Templars who did survive and transformed into the Knights of Christ continued to exist.

In other parts of the world, the Templars adapted to the situation differently. Some are thought to have joined the Hospitallers and the Teutons due to the closeness between these organizations. Not long after the fall of the Templar Order, the Templars are believed to have even fought in Scotland, as several sources tell of their involvement with the Scottish Robert the Bruce, which eventually led to the founding of the Scots Guards and, later on, the Freemasons.

Templar involvement has also been speculated in Switzerland, a state that quickly managed to become one of the strongest military powers in the 14th century, despite its small size. The Templars are thought to have bolstered the Swiss army, making it a small but elite and disciplined force. This theory is further supported by the idea of the Templars sharing their banking knowledge in Switzerland, laying the foundations for the famous Swiss banking traditions. All in all, those Templars who survived the purge did not just cease to exist. As the brothers had done countless times in the past, they adapted to the challenges they faced.

The Mysterious Knights of Solomon

In addition to their extraordinary two-hundred-year history, during which the Templars became the biggest military order and one of the most influential actors in Crusader world politics, the order has also risen to popularity because of the mysterious nature that surrounds it. In fact, many contemporary chroniclers and historical figures, as well as modern historians and scholars, firmly believe that even though King Philip's main motive was to seize the riches of the Templars for himself, there must have been some truth in the allegations made against the Knights Templar. Although not a lot of evidence of their heretical activities has been found, it is unwise to imagine that the suspicions were not based on anything.

Perhaps this sense of mystery about the order is caused by the lack of reliable written sources, which, in turn, technically makes everything we have mentioned up to this point questionable. Still, the Templars were mysterious in every aspect of their lives, with the subtle exception being their role in the politics of the time and their military actions. For instance, there is even a debate surrounding the origins of the order, as many believe that it originated much earlier than 1119. Different chronicles tell of different years and events at the beginning of the order's existence, making it unclear when exactly it was founded and how many members there were initially. In addition, the lack of official Templar documents before the Council of Troyes is highly suspicious due to the fact that the Templars were a Christian organization, making some believe that the order was, at first, a military institution and only became Christian after Hugues de Payens's visit to Europe. In any case, the actual dates and the conflicting details about the Templars' early days are the least mysterious thing about them.

There seem to be more intriguing details that have never really been explained. One of those is certainly the mystery surrounding the Temple Mount and the alleged excavations of the Templars at their headquarters. The Al-Aqsa Mosque has always been a subject of much speculation. Some believed that there was great treasure buried below the Templar headquarters and that they started out there because they knew of the treasure. In addition, by the time the king of Jerusalem gave them the Temple Mount, it was not in good shape and had been partially destroyed. Why would the Templars accept such a place? Did they want to spend years and countless resources rebuilding it? Some believe that they were looking for something, maybe an ancient Christian relic, some document about the origins of Christianity, or even the Ark of the Covenant. Maybe they found it; nobody knows for sure.

A stained-glass depiction of the Holy Grail

After all, various relics have been connected to the Templars. For example, the Holy Grail, the cup from which Jesus drank at the Last Supper, has come to be associated with the order. Some think it may have been because of Troyes, the city where the first fables about the magic nature of the grail were written and where the Templars got their start. Still, this connection has never been proven, and the myth of the Holy Grail pops up all throughout Europe with different explanations for its powers and origins.

As for the alleged Templar practices of heresy, there is still the question of what is logical to believe and what is not. Close Templar ties to Catharism, a Gnostic movement in southern France that originated in the 12th century, is seen as a reason to believe the order was open to heretical tendencies. The Cathars were recognized as a heretical sect and the enemies of the papacy, but the Templars openly accepted them in their ranks, especially at places like Languedoc, where the Cathars, according to some accounts, even outnumbered the brothers. Grand Master Bertrand de Blanchefort also came from a Cathar background, making it feasible that there was a much deeper connection between the sect and the order. The Templars have also been linked with other less prominent heresies, like the Johannites and the Cult of Mary Magdalene and the Virgin Mary, underlining their potential keenness for John the Baptist. The members of the Johannites saw him as the real messiah, and the two women were also thought to have been the faces of God, making its members goddess-worshipers.

Most often, however, the Templar connections with the Muslim world have been underlined as a reason to believe that the members of the order had diverged from Christianity. The brothers were suspiciously close to the Muslims. After all, the Templars often made alliances with different Muslim rulers to strengthen their own power in the region. Still, over time, they became more and more open toward the Muslims and did not outright see them as enemies as they had in the beginning. They exchanged knowledge and became more and more aware of Muslim traditions and their lifestyle, sometimes even adopting parts of it. For this reason, the Christians confronted the brothers countless times, believing that they had developed a much deeper, intimate relationship with the Muslim world than was acceptable.

Some say the order was conducting secret satanic rituals, including worshiping demonic deities, in their holdings. This is probably the most trumped-up charge set against the Templars by King Philip. We have mentioned Baphomet, a mysterious creature that was associated with a satanic cult. What has been speculated is that, despite its various descriptions by different captured Templars, Baphomet may have just been a life-sized head with magical powers to make the lands fertile. The Templars are known to have kept heads in their compounds, like that of Saint Euphemia of Chalcedon, which was preserved in Cyprus. This "obsession" with heads may have originated from the Muslim world, namely the Assassins, who are known to have buried the new members of their organization up to their heads as part of their reception ceremony. On the other hand, Baphomet may have just been a translation error from the word Mahomet—the French for Prophet Muhammad. Still, whether or not the Templars actually worshiped Baphomet in the first place has not been proven, and stretching this theory to assume that Baphomet was actually Muhammad is even more unwise if we want to maintain historical objectivity.

Out of all the charges set against the Templars, the one with the most backing was denying Christ—a practice that was remarked in the Chinon Parchment, a papal document from 1308 that describes some of the confessions of the imprisoned Templars. According to the document, the Templars admitted that spitting, urinating and spitting on the cross, and denouncing Christ was part of the reception ceremony for a new member, but it was only done to imitate the torture the brothers would have to endure if they ever fell in the hands of the Muslims. Whether or not this is true, it was certainly not a good look for the order and gave rise to further suspicions about its mysterious nature.

Conclusion

Overall, the Knights Templar found its own unique place in history. Over the course of its short existence, the order managed to become much more than a group of Christian knights devoted to the noble cause of protecting traveling pilgrims. The ongoing processes reshaped the order's purpose so much that, at first glance, one can be astonished at why the Templars diverged from the simple path that had been chosen by Hugues de Payens. While this remark is logical, we should not forget that the Templars existed in a complex political landscape and had to adapt to the ever-changing power struggles of the Christian and Muslim worlds. The truth of the matter is that the privileges granted to the order signify its distinct, almost invaluable nature and, if nothing else, shows that the Templars deserved whatever praise and love they received in their lifetime.

As for the secrets surrounding the order, the Knights Templar just cannot be separated from its mystery, despite the efforts of numerous historians and scholars. In fact, it is the mythical nature of the Templars that makes them so interesting. We do not really know if the members of the order were just ordinary men or part of a larger secret society that continued to exist even after 1314. The various myths and theories about the darker side of the Templars define their uniqueness and provide an intriguing point of view to look at and analyze the order.

All in all, throughout the course of this book, we have observed the two-hundred-year history of the Knights Templar and analyzed how the order transformed during this period in response to the events that happened. From just nine knights to a global superpower, it is safe to say that the Templars were successfully able to overcome the challenges they were presented with until they were dissolved.

The brothers were pioneers in many aspects of life. They were not only spectacular warriors but also exemplary Christians, inventing a completely new standard for medieval knights. Their contributions to socio-economic life should also not be forgotten, as the Templars were way ahead of their time, essentially becoming the first bankers of Europe. For these reasons, we may never see an organization quite like the Knights Templar again.

Here's another book by Enthralling History that you might like

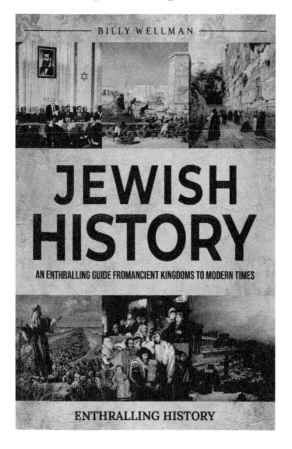

Free limited time bonus

Stop for a moment. We have a free bonus set up for you. The problem is this: we forget 90% of everything that we read after 7 days. Crazy fact, right? Here's the solution: we've created a printable, 1-page pdf summary for this book that you're reading now. All you have to do to get your free pdf summary is to go to the following website:

https://livetolearn.lpages.co/enthrallinghistory/

Once you do, it will be intuitive. Enjoy, and thank you!

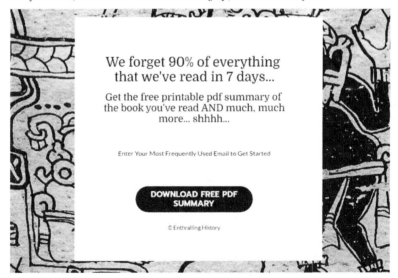

We forget 90% of everything
that we've read in 7 days...

Get the free printable pdf summary of
the book you've read AND much, much
more... shhhh...

Enter Your Most Frequently Used Email to Get Started

**DOWNLOAD FREE PDF
SUMMARY**

© Enthralling History

Appendix A: Further Reading and Reference

Holland, Tom. *Dominion: How the Christian Revolution Remade the World.* 2019.

MacCulloch, Diarmaid. *A History of Christianity: The First Three Thousand Years.* 2009.

Mullin, Bruce Robert. *A Short World History of Christianity.* 2006.

Shelley, Bruce. *Christian Theology in Plain Language.* 1982.

Ware, Kalistos. *The Orthodox Church.* 1963.

Edersheim, Alfred (1904) *The Life and Times of Jesus the Messiah.* London: Longmans, Green and Co.

Insight on the Scriptures, Volume 2 p. 387. Messiah. Watchtower Bible and Tract Society of Pennsylvania. https://wol.jw.org

Encyclopedia Judaica Vol.05 (2007) Fred Skolnik, Editor in Chief Michael Berenbaum, Executive Editor

Judaism in the First Century (2009) Yale Courses. The Jews, Hellenization, and the Maccabees

https://www.jewishvirtuallibrary.org/the-ancient-greeks-and-the-jews-jewish-virtual-library

https://www.historytoday.com/archive/jews-greeks-and-romans

The Hellenization of the Jews. GH Gilbert. American Journal of Theology (1909) https://www.journals.uchicago.edu/doi/pdf/10.1086/478870

A Historical Atlas of the Jewish People: From the Time of the Patriarchs to the Present. Eli Barnavi (Editor). Schocken Books.

Knight, George Angus Fulton. "Maccabees". *Encyclopedia Britannica,* https://www.britannica.com/topic/Maccabees. Accessed 20 July 2022.

Pompey's Siege of Jerusalem. Jona Lendering. https://www.livius.org/articles/concept/roman-jewish-wars/

Flavius Josephus, Jewish War Volume 2

The Jewish Encyclopedia. (1976, Vol. VIII, p. 508)

Britannica, The Editors of Encyclopedia. "Gospel According to Matthew". Encyclopedia Britannica, https://www.britannica.com/topic/Gospel-According-to-Matthew. Accessed 21 July 2022.

All Scripture Is Inspired of God and Beneficial. Watchtower Bible and Tract Society of Pennsylvania.

The Ecclesiastical History, Eusebius, of Caesarea, Bishop of Caesarea. Published 1942 Cambridge, Mass.: Harvard University Press

The Cyclopedia of Biblical, Theological, and Ecclesiastical Literature. James Strong and John McClintock; Haper and Brothers; NY https://www.biblicalcyclopedia.com/

The Slaughter of the Innocents https://biblearchaeology.org/research/new-testament-era/2411-the-slaughter-of-the-innocents-historical-fact-or-legendary-fiction

w12 4/1 pp. 18-19 ◻ Apocryphal Gospels—Hidden Truths About Jesus?

Caesar Augustus: An Archaeological Biography December 13, 2019 Bryan Windle https://biblearchaeologyreport.com/2019/12/13/caesar-augustus-an-archaeological-biography/

New Catholic Encyclopedia (1967) page 918. New York: McGraw-Hill Book Company

The Greatest Man Who Ever Lived. Watchtower Bible and Tract Society of Pennsylvania

Herod Archelaus https://en.wikipedia.org/wiki/Herod_Archelaus last edited on 21 August 2022

Bible Translations:

New World Translation

Byington Version

Kingdom Interlinear Version

King James Version

"Sea of Galilee Boat (Jesus Boat)". Madain Project. Retrieved 1 September 2022. https://web.archive.org/web/20200929210904/https://madainproject.com/boat_of_jesus

The Imperial Bible Dictionary (1866) Cross, Crucify page 376. London: Blackie and Son.

"Bearing Thorough Witness" About God's Kingdom. Watchtower Bible and Tract Society of Pennsylvania

The Germans of Galacia
https://sites.ualberta.ca/~german/AlbertaHistory/Galicians.htm

Britannica, The Editors of Encyclopedia. "Phrygia". Encyclopedia Britannica, https://www.britannica.com/place/Phrygia. Accessed 9 October 2022.

Macedonian History https://macedonian.org/our-culture/macedonian-history/

Konstan, David, "Epicurus", *The Stanford Encyclopedia of Philosophy* (Fall 2022 Edition), Edward N. Zalta & Uri Nodelman (eds.)
https://plato.stanford.edu/archives/fall2022/entries/epicurus/

Baltzly, Dirk, "Stoicism", *The Stanford Encyclopedia of Philosophy* (Spring 2019 Edition), Edward N. Zalta (ed.)
https://plato.stanford.edu/archives/spr2019/entries/stoicism/

Christopher W. Blackwell, "The Council of the Areopagus," in C.W. Blackwell, ed., *Dēmos: Classical Athenian Democracy* (A. Mahoney and R. Scaife, ed., *The Stoa: A Consortium for Electronic Publication in the Humanities* [http://www.stoa.org]) edition of January 26, 2003.

Cartwright, M. (2009, September 02). Corinth. *World History Encyclopedia.* Retrieved from https://www.worldhistory.org/corinth/ October 3, 2022.

Lystra https://www.allaboutturkey.com/lystra.html

Cartwright, M. (2016, May 04). Philippi. *World History Encyclopedia.* Retrieved from https://www.worldhistory.org/Philippi/ October 3, 2022.

Cartwright, M. (2016, May 01). Thessalonica. *World History Encyclopedia.* Retrieved from https://www.worldhistory.org/Thessalonica/ October 3, 2022

"Greek Language, Early Christian and Byzantine." New Catholic Encyclopedia. Retrieved February 04, 2023 from Encyclopedia.com:
https://www.encyclopedia.com/religion/encyclopedias-almanacs-transcripts-and-maps/greek-language-early-christian-and-byzantin

Kelly, John N.D. "Apologist". Encyclopedia
https://www.britannica.com/topic/Apologist. Accessed 1 February 2023.

Lévy, Carlos, "Philo of Alexandria", *The Stanford Encyclopedia of Philosophy* (Fall 2022 Edition), Edward N. Zalta & Uri Nodelman (eds.), URL = <https://plato.stanford.edu/archives/fall2022/entries/philo/>.

Santrac, Aleksandar S. (2013). Three I know not what: The influence of Greek philosophy on the doctrine of Trinity. In die Skriflig, 47(1), 1-7. Retrieved February 11, 2023, from http://www.scielo.org.za/scielo.php?script=sci_arttext&pid=S2305-08532013000100059&lng=en&tlng=en.

Ruben Ortega | 9 June, 2016 | Chronology, Expansion of Christianity, The Life of Early Christians https://www.earlychristians.org/the-life-of-early-christians/

J. Warner Wallace Published May 18, 2020 Lessons for Today's Church from the Life of the Early Church https://coldcasechristianity.com/writings/lessons-for-todays-church-from-the-life-of-the-early-church/.

Jonas, Hans "Gnosticism. " Encyclopedia of Philosophy. Retrieved March 04, 2023 from Encyclopedia.com: https://www.encyclopedia.com/humanities/encyclopedias-almanacs-transcripts-and-maps/gnosticism

"Gnosticism" by Edward Moore, *The Internet Encyclopedia of Philosophy*, ISSN 2161-0002, https://iep.utm.edu/, March 4, 2023

Britannica, T. Editors of Encyclopedia *Ebionite. Encyclopedia Britannica.* https://www.britannica.com/topic/Ebionites

Arendzen, J. (1909). Ebionites. In The Catholic Encyclopedia. New York: Robert Appleton Company. Retrieved March 12, 2023 from New Advent: http://www.newadvent.org/cathen/05242c.htm

Krauss, Samuel. "Nazarenes". *Jewish Encyclopedia*. Retrieved 2023-03-23. *jewishencyclopedia.com.*

David Eastman (Translations & Introductions). *The Ancient Martyrdom Accounts of Peter and Paul.* (SBL Press: Atlanta, 2015).

Britannica, T. Editors of Encyclopedia). *St. Clement I. Encyclopedia Britannica.* https://www.britannica.com/biography/Saint-Clement-I

Catholic Online, Pope St. Clement I https://www.catholic.org/saints/saint.php?saint_id=37

Catholic Encyclopedia (1913) Pope St. Clement I by Henry Palmer Chapman, https://en.wikisource.org/wiki/Catholic_Encyclopedia_(1913)/Pope_St._Clement_I

John Malham, Foxs Book of Martyrs (1856)

The Martyrdom of Polycarp. Translated by J.B. Lightfoot. Abridged and modernized by Stephen Tomkins. Edited and prepared for the web by Dan Graves. https://christianhistoryinstitute.org/study/module/polycarp

Watchtower Bible and Tract Society 'Away with the Godless!' w89 11/15 pp. 21-23

Wingren, G. (April 8, 2023). St. Irenaeus. Encyclopedia Britannica. https://www.britannica.com/biography/Irenaeus

Irenaeus of Lyons, Grant, Robert M. (Robert McQueen), 1917-2014 London ; New York : Routledge

Britannica, T. Editors of Encyclopedia (Invalid Date). *Saint Hippolytus of Rome. Encyclopedia Britannica*. https://www.britannica.com/biography/Saint-Hippolytus-of-Rome

The Ante-Nicene Fathers: The Writings of the Fathers down to A.D.325 (1995) Peabody (Mass.): Hendrickson

Maritano, Mario, "Basileiad", in: Brill Encyclopedia of Early Christianity Online, General Editor David G. Hunter, Paul J.J. van Geest, Bert Jan Lietaert Peerbolte. Consulted online on 20 May 2023 http://dx.doi.org/10.1163/2589-7993_EECO_SIM_00000395

Kraft, Heinrich, Early Christian Thinkers: An Intro to Clement of Alexandria and Origen (1964) New York: Association Pr.

Pedrozo, José M. "The Brothers of Jesus and his Mother's Virginity." *The Thomist: A Speculative Quarterly Review* 63, no. 1 (1999): 83-104. https://doi.org/10.1353/tho.1999.0044.

Who Was Mary Magdalene? Bible Questions Answered p. 172 Watchtower Bible and Tract Society of Pennsylvania

Britannica, T. Editors of Encyclopedia (Invalid Date). St. Mary Magdalene. Encyclopedia Britannica. https://www.britannica.com/biography/Saint-Mary-Magdalene

F.F. Bruce, "Christianity Under Claudius," Bulletin of the John Rylands Library 44 (March 1962): 309-326.

Clugnet, Léon. "St. Catherine of Alexandria." The Catholic Encyclopedia. Vol. 3. New York: Robert Appleton Company, 1908. 6 Jun. 2023 <http://www.newadvent.org/cathen/03445a.htm>.

Britannica, T. Editors of Encyclopedia St. Barbara. Encyclopedia Britannica. https://www.britannica.com/biography/Saint-Barbara

Mark Galli (1990) Persecution in the Early Church: A Gallery of the Persecuting Emperors https://christianhistoryinstitute.org/magazine/article/persecution-in-early-church-gallery

"Nero Persecutes the Christians, 64 A.D." EyeWitness to History, www.eyewitnesstohistory.com (2000).

Mark Wilson (May 4, 2023) Alternative Facts: Domitian's Persecution of Christians,

https://www.biblicalarchaeology.org/daily/biblical-topics/post-biblical-period/domitian-persecution-of-christians/

The Works of Josephus, translated by William Whiston, Hendrickson Publishers, 1987

Keresztes, P. (1968). Marcus Aurelius a Persecutor? *Harvard Theological Review, 61*(3), 321-341. doi:10.1017/S0017816000029230

The Acts of the Christian Martyrs, texts and translation by Herbert Musurillo. (c) Oxford University Press, 1972

Paul Johnson (1928) A History of Christianity. New York: Atheneum

Constantine the Great—A Champion of Christianity? (1998) Watchtower Bible and Tract Society of Pennsylvania

Carroll, Warren (1987), The Building of Christendom, Front Royal VA: Christendom College Press, retrieved July 24, 2023

Knox, J. S. (2016, August 23). The Monastic Movement: Origins & Purposes. *World History Encyclopedia*. Retrieved from https://www.worldhistory.org/article/930/the-monastic-movement-origins--purposes/

5 Ways Christianity Spread Through Ancient Rome, Becky Little. HISTORY. A&E Television Networks. Accessed September 8, 2023 https://www.history.com/news/5-ways-christianity-spread-through-ancient-rome

Fletcher, R.A. The barbarian conversion: from paganism to Christianity (1999) Berkeley, Calif.: University of California Press

Dietz, Maribel (2005). Wandering Monks, Virgins, and Pilgrims: Ascetic Travel in the Mediterranean World, A.D. 300-800. *Pennsylvania State University Press.*

Dr. Allen Farber, "Early Christian art," in *Smarthistory*, August 8, 2015, accessed September 26, 2023, https://smarthistory.org/early-christian-art/.

Dr. Allen Farber, "Santa Pudenziana," in *Smarthistory*, August 16, 2023, accessed September 26, 2023, https://smarthistory.org/santa-pudenziana/.

Jason David BeDuhn, Truth in Translation. University Press of America 2003.

Disney, Anthony. R. *A History of Portugal and the Portuguese Empire.* 2007.

Ellul, Max. *The Sword and the Green Cross: The Saga of the Knights of Saint Lazarus from the Crusades to the 21ˢᵗ Century.* 2011.

Madden, Thomas. *Crusades: The Illustrated History.* 2002.

Murray, Alan. *The Crusades: An Encyclopedia.* 2008.

Riley-Smith, Jonathan. *The Knights Hospitaller: In the Levant, c. 1070-1309.* 2012.

Turnbull, Stephen. *The Ottoman Empire: 1326-1699.* 2003.

Barber, M. C. (1984). "The Social Context of the Templars." *Transactions of the Royal Historical Society, 34,* 27–46. https://doi.org/10.2307/3679124

Blanchet, M. (2021). "Chapter 5: The Patriarchs and the Union of the Churches." In *A Companion to the Patriarchate of Constantinople.* Leiden, The Netherlands: Brill. doi: https://doi.org/10.1163/9789004424470_006.

Brand, C. M. (1962). "The Byzantines and Saladin, 1185-1192: Opponents of the Third Crusade." *Speculum, 37*(2), 167–181. https://doi.org/10.2307/2849946.

Coureas, N. (2013). "The Conquest of Cyprus during the Third Crusade According to Greek Chronicles from Cyprus." *The Medieval Chronicle, 8*, 193–204. https://www.jstor.org/stable/48577683.

Faith, J. (2011). *The Knights Templar in Somerset.* History Press.

Ferris, E. (1902). "The Financial Relations of the Knights Templars to the English Crown." *The American Historical Review, 8*(1), 1–17. https://doi.org/10.2307/1832571.

Field, S. L. (2016). "Torture and Confession in the Templar Interrogations at Caen, 28-29 October 1307." *Speculum, 91*(2), 297–327. http://www.jstor.org/stable/43883958.

Forey, A. (2004). "The Siege of Lisbon and the Second Crusade. Portuguese Studies, 20, 1–13." http://www.jstor.org/stable/41105214.

Frankopan, P. (2012). *The First Crusade: The Call from the East.* Belknap Press of Harvard University Press. Retrieved January 31, 2022.

Gilmour-Bryson, A. (1996). "Sodomy and the Knights Templar." *Journal of the History of Sexuality, 7*(2), 151–183. http://www.jstor.org/stable/3704138.

Hill, P. (2018). *The Knights Templar at War, 1120–1312.* Pen & Sword Military.

Humphreys, R. S. (1977). *From Saladin to the Mongols: The Ayyubids of Damascus, 1193-1260.* SUNY Press.

Julien Théry. (2013). "A Heresy of State: Philip the Fair, the Trial of the 'Perfidious Templars,' and the Pontificalization of the French Monarchy." *Journal of Medieval Religious Cultures, 39*(2), 117–148. https://doi.org/10.5325/jmedirelicult.39.2.0117.

Lotan, S. (2015). "The Teutonic Knights and their Attitude about Muslims: Saracens in the Latin Kingdom of Jerusalem and in the Baltic Region." *Fear and Loathing in the North: Jews and Muslims in Medieval Scandinavia and the Baltic Region*, 313-328.

Lourie, E. (1975). "The Will of Alfonso I, 'El Batallador,' King of Aragon and Navarre: A Reassessment." *Speculum, 50* (4), 635–651. https://doi.org/10.2307/2855471.

Martin, S. (2011). *The Knights Templar.* Oldcastle Books.

Murphy, P. (2012). "The Vatican Secret Archive: A History." *Seanchas Ardmhacha: Journal of the Armagh Diocesan Historical Society*, 24 (1), 240–249. http://www.jstor.org/stable/43869514

Napier, G. (2011). *The Rise and Fall of the Knights Templar.* History Press.

Nicholson, H. J. (2011). *The Knights Templar on Trial: The Trial of the Templars in the British Isles, 1308-11.* History Press.

Nowell, C. E. (1947). "The Old Man of the Mountain." *Speculum, 22*(4), 497–519. https://doi.org/10.2307/2853134

Perkins, C. (1909). "The Trial of the Knights Templars in England." *The English Historical Review,* 24 (95), 432–447. http://www.jstor.org/stable/550361

Powell, J. M. (2007). "Church and Crusade: Frederick II and Louis IX." *The Catholic Historical Review,* 93 (2), vi–264. http://www.jstor.org/stable/25166835.

Somerville, R. (1974). The Council of Clermont (1095), and Latin Christian Society." *Archivum Historiae Pontificiae,* 12, 55–90. http://www.jstor.org/stable/23563638.

Valente, J. (1998). "The New Frontier: The Role of the Knights Templar in the Establishment of Portugal as an Independent Kingdom." *Mediterranean Studies, 7,* 49–65. http://www.jstor.org/stable/41166860.

Welsh, W. E. (2016). "Crusader Catastrophe: The Battle of La Forbie." *Medieval Warfare, 6*(5), 26–33. https://www.jstor.org/stable/48578609

Willoughby, J. (2012). "A Templar Chronicle of the Third Crusade: Origin and Transmission." *Medium Ævum, 81*(1), 126–134. https://doi.org/10.2307/43632903

Napier, G. (2011). The Rise and Fall of the Knights Templar. History Press. Chapter 4.

Gilmour-Bryson, A. (1996). "Sodomy and the Knights Templar." Journal of the History of Sexuality, 7 (2), 151–183.

Murphy, P. (2012). "The Vatican Secret Archive: A History." Seanchas Ardmhacha: Journal of the Armagh Diocesan Historical Society, 24 (1), 240–249.

Printed in Great Britain
by Amazon